Sexual Assault

Sexual Assault

The Victims, the Perpetrators, and the Criminal Justice System

Second Edition

Edited by

Frances P. Reddington

and

Betsy Wright Kreisel

CAROLINA ACADEMIC PRESS

Durham, North Carolina

Library of Congress Cataloging-in-Publication Data

Sexual assault : the victims, the perpetrators, and the criminal justice system /
[edited by] Frances P. Reddington and Betsy Wright Kreisel. -- 2nd ed.
    p. cm.
Includes bibliographical references and index.
ISBN 978-1-59460-577-2 (alk. paper)
1. Sex crimes--United States. 2. Rape--United States. 3. Rape victims--
United States. 4. Sex offenders--United States. 5. Criminal justice, Administration of--United States. I. Reddington, Frances P. II. Kreisel, Betsy Wright,
1970- III. Title.

HV6561.S475 2009
364.15'320973--dc22

                                    2009012394

CAROLINA ACADEMIC PRESS
700 Kent Street
Durham, North Carolina 27701
Telephone (919) 489-7486
Fax (919) 493-5668
www.cap-press.com

Printed in the United States of America

To the memory of my parents—
Francis and Pauline. FPR

To my best friend and husband, Lyle;
my wonderful scholar athlete, Jarrett;
my intelligent precious princess, Emma;
and my smart sweet Cole-Bear.
Your support and love make everything possible. BWK

Contents

Part II
The Victims

Part III
The Often Unacknowledged Victims

Part IV
The Offenders

Part V
The Criminal Justice System

Part VI
Public Fear and the Legislative Response

Preface

All it takes is to listen to the news and hear the recent stories of sexual abuse to know that sexual assault is an issue that raises many questions and concerns in the American public. We are all familiar with the cases that make headline news, but, in the world of sexual assault, the high profile cases are the rarest, and the daily business of those sex crimes that come to the attention of the criminal justice system are usually left to be done outside of much of the general public's notice.

This book attempts to fill a gap in our academic literature regarding rape, sexual assault, and in specific, the response of the criminal justice system to sex crimes. However, as the criminal justice system does not exist outside of our society, we felt it imperative to broaden the scope of the reader as well, and to include information designed to educate about the widely misunderstood crime of rape. That is why we included information about rape myths, the history of rape reform and an examination of sexual assault definitions.

Before we begin discussion of an overview of the reader we would like to make a couple of observations. First, the words rape and sexual assault are used almost interchangeably by the authors in the following chapters. That is how it is in our society as well. 'Rape' is still a crime in several states, though other states have changed the language in their criminal codes to something broader, such as 'sexual assault' or 'sexual battery'.

Secondly, most victims of sex crimes are women, and many authors chose to use the feminine pronoun in their articles when referring to victims, and the masculine pronoun when referring to offenders. Again, this was done to reflect the statistical findings that most known sex offenders are men. However, we believe that it was imperative to address the issue of male rape victims in this reader. There are several chapters, which will be discussed below, which address male victimization. Thus, we are not overlooking either male rape victims or female offenders, we are making sure that we represent a statistical reality.

And finally, we wanted to address the issue of the terms 'victims' and 'survivors'. As you will no doubt note, they are used interchangeably as well throughout and within the various chapters. We did not ask the authors to follow any guidelines in their word selection, though some addressed the issue in their writings. The reason we did this, is because this work is designed to bring the reader into the criminal justice arena. In that arena, police, prosecutors and other employees of the criminal justice system, deal with victims of crime and those who victimize others. Victimology, and the study of crime victims, is a relatively new academic component of criminal justice. We did not think it would be right to change the system phraseology. Yet, those same employees of the criminal justice system deal with the survivors of a sexual assault as well. Though some of the literature suggests that survival is a state of recovery to be achieved, we do subscribe to the belief that if you live through a sexual assault—you are a survivor.

The following discusses the various elements of this text. Disbursed throughout the book are special features that emphasize and support the reality of the factual discussions.

Part I

The Crime

In part one, the reader is acquainted with the crime of rape and sexual assault. The first chapter, *An Overview of Sexual Assault and Sexual Assault Myths*, presents a look at the definitions, contradictions and statistics regarding sexual assault. The incidence and prevalence of rape are examined, and are followed with a discussion of the problems associated with an examination of rape statistics. The chapter also includes a brief history of sexual victimization, which sets the stage for much that follows in the reader. The chapter concludes with a comprehensive look at rape myths.

The second chapter *Sexual Assault Definitions* provides a general definition of rape, and offers a discussion of the parameters associated with trying to define rape. The chapter also narrows to a thorough discussion of stranger rape, intimate (date) rape, spousal rape, and group and gang rape. The third chapter *Two Crimes for the Price of One* examines the timely issue of the use of drugs as a facilitator in sexual assaults.

Part II

The Victims

In part two, the reader becomes acquainted with rape victimology. Chapter Four, *Victim Response to Sexual Assault* is a thorough examination of the variety of responses and coping mechanisms that survivors often experience. In addition, the chapter discusses recovery from sexual assault, seeking help and crisis intervention. Chapter Five, *The Ripple Effect: Secondary Sexual Assault Survivors*, presents an overview of the others who are impacted by a sexual assault: partners, family, and friends of the survivor. Chapter Six, *Sexual Abuse of Males*, examines male rape victims and discusses the research which suggests that male victimology can be alike, and yet quite different from female victimology. The differing circumstances of male rape are also presented.

Part III

The Often Unacknowledged Victims

In part III, the reader is brought deeper into sexual assault victimology and those victim groups where we tend to see even greater underreporting are examined. Chapter Seven, *Sexual Abuse of Men in Prison*, examines the prevalence of inmate-on-inmate rape in institutions housing males. While presenting the statistics available, this chapter also includes narrative accounts from actual victims. Chapter Eight, *A Violation of Trust and Professional Ethics: Sexual Abuse of Women Prisoners by Correctional Staff*, examines the issues of female inmates who are victimized by institutional employees. Chapter Nine presents an overview of *Child Sexual Abuse*. Chapter Ten presents a moving account of one survivor's journey from victimization as a child to resolution in *Reading Incest: Interpreting Signs of Victimization and Family Dysfunction in One Survivor's Account*. Chapter Eleven, *Critical Needs for Effective Criminal Justice and Public Health Responses in Preventing Elderly Sexual Abuse*, presents an overview of sexual abuse of the elderly as well as some policy recommendations in dealing with this issue.

Part IV

The Offenders

Part four offers a comprehensive discussion of sex crime offenders. Chapter Twelve, *Sex Offenders and Child Molesters*, offers a thorough discussion of many aspects of those who rape. The chapter begins with a discussion of human behavior and motivation. The chapter continues with a discussion of sex offender typologies—the attempt to classify sex offenders into different groups based on their motivations, choice of victims and actions during the attack. This chapter also discusses classifications of child molesters. Chapter Thirteen, *Juvenile Sex Offenders*, discusses the delicate issue of youth that commit sex offenses against others including the extent of the problem, how juvenile sex offenders compare to other juvenile offenders and sexting, a new class of juvenile sex offenders. Chapter Fourteen, *Sex Offender Treatment, What Works, Who Works and New Innovative Approaches*, presents an overview of various treatment methods currently used with sex offenders.

Part V

The Criminal Justice System

Part five overviews the various components of the criminal justice system as they address the issues of sexual assault. Chapter Fifteen presents *A Brief History of Rape Law and Rape Law Reform in the United States.* This chapters offer a discussion of the roots of American rape law and the major changes in rape law that were initiated in the 1970s. This discussion will lead the reader into the chapters regarding police investigation, prosecutorial duties, and correctional treatment. Chapter Sixteen addresses issues regarding *The Police and Victims of Sexual Assault.* Chapter Seventeen examines why rape has historically been the most under prosecuted crime in *Prosecution of Sex Crimes.*

Part VI

Public Fear and Legislative Response

Part six addresses the legislative response to sexual assault. With public sentiment suggesting that the criminal justice system was failing in rehabilitating or incapacitating sex offenders, the legislature stepped in and created new laws that would address this issue. Chapter Eighteen, *Sex Offenders, The Social Narrative and Public Policy Implications,* discusses the rational and effectiveness of recent public policy concerning sex offenders. Chapter Nineteen, *Sex Offender Laws: Some Legislative Responses,* presents an examination of the creation of registration, notification, sexual predator and chemical castration laws, to name a few. This chapter also addresses concerns expressed regarding the constitutionality of these laws.

Acknowledgments

Many people did a lot of work to make this book happen. We must start with acknowledging the contributions of the authors. The collection of authors in this book is, in a word, diverse. Our contributors include academicians, university students from Master's to Ph.D. level, practitioners in the field, and survivors of sexual assault. We did this because we believe that the collective voice needed to be heard. We especially wanted to give graduate students who have studied sexual assault a chance to speak to other students through this work. The common theme of all our contributors is that they believed that this work was important and that it needed to be done. They devoted their time, talent and energies to make this happen. The result is a reader that is exhaustive in its study of the topic of sexual assault. There are a wide variety of voices to be heard here—from survivors to those who work in the field every day, to those who study the field. The collective product is truly a reflection of their dedication.

We would like to acknowledge Carolina Academic Press for their support, and specifically Beth Hall, who kept us on task and offered us her support. From day one, Beth and Carolina Academic Press believed this was a work that needed to be done.

We would like to thank the University of Central Missouri for the support we receive regarding scholarly endeavors. We also thank Cynthia Adams, our graduate assistant, whose assistance on this project proved invaluable in the first edition.

And finally, we need to recognize the survivors of sexual assault and the people who work every day in any one of numerous capacities to seek justice, healing and hope for sexual assault survivors. We only hope that this work serves to enlighten about sexual assault and the people that it has touched. In addition, we hope this text promotes future research and encourages others to work and/or volunteer in the victimology arena.

Part I
The Crime

Chapter 1

An Overview of Sexual Assault and Sexual Assault Myths

Tammy Garland

Upon the release of *The Accused* (1988), once again, the New Bedford Case that rocked a small town community during the early 1980s was brought to the forefront of public attention. This reconceptualized version of the rape of a young Portuguese woman, Cheryl Araujo, portrayed the heinous crime in a very different light than the original media coverage. The movie depicted the victim, played by Jodi Foster, as just that, a victim. However, the movie failed to illustrate the backlash created by the trial and the incessant media scrutiny. In contrast to the storybook ending in which the victim is vindicated, the initial news coverage of the trial generated a media frenzy leading the Portuguese community to eventually vilify the victim for her own victimization and in essence treat the perpetrators as if they were heroes (Chancer 1998).

The significance of this case is paramount due to its nature and attitudes toward sexual assault. Even though the victim was without a doubt raped in a public place, surrounded by witnesses, and brutalized mercilessly, the victim was still blamed for her own assault. "Victim blaming" in rape cases is a common phenomenon especially in cases in which the accuser has a questionable background. For instance, Henry Wigmore (1942) in the highly respected *Evidence in Trials at Common Law* asserted that "no judge should ever let a sex offense charge go to jury unless the female complainant's social history and mental makeup have been examined and testified by a qualified physician" (Cuklanz 1996, 737). Thus, rather than trying the perpetrator in a court of law, the character of the victim goes on trial. This thought process of victim blaming is a throw-back to the historical and mythological misperceptions of sexual assault. Hence, this chapter will focus on the development and belief of rape myths. Prior to addressing these issues, this chapter must first define what constitutes sexual assault and its prevalence in society.

What Is Sexual Assault?

The literature has demonstrated that methodological problems exist in defining the term, sexual assault. Typically, sexual assault has been used to characterize the word, rape, in a less offensive and unthreatening manner. The term ignores other forms of sexual victimization such as child sexual abuse and sexual harassment, and in addition fails to recognize attempted rape and threat. For the purposes of this chapter, sexual assault will be used interchangeably to define the phenomenon of rape, attempted rape, rape by threat of force, and coercion. In addition, the historical and mythical misperceptions regarding rape will concentrate mainly on the plight of women in society; however, since rape is not limited to women alone, the chapter will also look at non-traditional myths regarding rape including male sexual assaults and interspecies victimization.

The word rape stems from the Latin word rapere, which is defined as "to take by force." Even though this word in itself seems to clearly establish a foundation for rape, historically, the legal definitions of rape has been limited in scope. Under English Common Law, rape was defined as penetration of the vagina by the penis where ejaculation had taken place (Clark 1987, 8—cited in Belknap 2001). In addition, common law held that rape only occurs when a man engages "in intercourse with a woman not his wife; by force or threat of force; against her will and without her consent" (Estrich 1987, 8—cited in Belknap 2001). Although these aforementioned definitions have been expanded to incorporate other factors into the meaning of rape, many of the definitions used today still reflect this archaic ideology. Some states refuse to expand the definition of rape to crimes against males. For instance, rape other than vaginal sexual intercourse in North Carolina is not considered a crime; therefore, the North Carolina State Law on sexual assault does not apply to men (North Carolina State Law § 14-27.2). Moreover, many federal government agencies still define rape as penile—vaginal intercourse. The Uniform Crime Reports define forcible rape as "the carnal knowledge of a female, forcibly and against her will" (Federal Bureau of Investigation 1997, 395). Under this limited classification of sexual assault at both the state and federal levels, males are excluded from obtaining justice against their perpetrator under the law. In an attempt to remedy this problem, the National Crime Victimization Survey expanded the definition of rape as "forced sexual intercourse in which the victim may be either male or female and the offender may be of a different or the same sex as the victim" (BJS 1997, 31). However, this definition fails to take into consideration a number of other factors involved in rape such as sodomy, oral intercourse, attempted rape, threat of rape, and coercion. Even though, a number of governmental agencies have expanded their definition of rape (see Table 1), their definitions still remain limited in scope.

Table 1. Summary of Definitional Elements of Rape and Other Sex Offenses as Used in U.S. Department of Justice Statistical Series

Statistical Series	Age	Sex	Victims Includes Forcible Attempts?	Rape?	Other Sexual Assault?
NCVS	Excludes under 12	Both	Yes	Yes	Yes, attacks involving unwanted sexual contact.
UCR	All	Females only for rape	Yes	Yes	Limited to arrests only. Includes statutory rape and offenses against chastity common decency, and morals.
NIBRS	All	Both	Yes	Yes	Yes, includes sodomy, fondling, incest, statutory rape, and sexual assault with an object.
NPRP	No victim data	No victim data	Yes	Yes	No
NJRP	No victim data	No victim data	Yes	Yes	No
SISCF	Limited to offense	No victim data	Yes	Yes	Yes, includes forcible sodomy, against children statutory rape, and lewd acts with children.
NCRP	Limited to offenses against children	No victim data	Yes	Yes	Yes, includes forcible sodomy, statutory rape, and lewd acts with children.
SHR	All	Both	Yes, but excludes murder	Yes	Yes, includes statutory rape, attempted sodomy, and incest.

Bureau of Justice Statistics. 1997. Sex offenses and offenders: An analysis of data on rape and sexual assault. Washington, D.C.: U.S. Dept. of Justice, 33.

Even in the academic literature, the majority of the literature focuses solely on the sexual victimization of women. Thus, this work will attempt to address the changing perceptions and definitions of rape within our society.

Sexual Assault Statistics

With the women's movement of the early 1970s, rape became a major concern in both the United States and the world. By 1989, the Worldwatch Institute had declared that violence against women was the most common crime worldwide (Lonsway and Fitzgerald 1994; Wolf 1991). Estimates vary on the number of women who will be sexually victimized every year. The World Health Organization (2000) approximates that between 12 and 25 percent of women around the world have been victims of sexual assault. Since obtaining data on rape is difficult to determine, this section will focus on prevalence and incidence rates in the United States.

Incidence and Prevalence among Sexual Assault Victims

Incidence rates are based on measurements collected annually to determine changes in victimization from year to year. UCR and NCVS statistics measure incidence rates (Belknap 2001). According to the Bureau of Justice Statistics (1997), an estimated 260,300 persons, ages 12 or older, reported attempted or completed rapes and approximately 95,000 additional cases were threatened or completed sexual assaults other than rape in 1995. Out of a total of 335,300 victimizations reported in the United States, only 32 percent were reported to law enforcement officials (BJS 1997). Based on the data, the number of rates reported in 1995 significantly decreased from 1993. Between 1993 and 1995, the number of sexual assaults reported decreased from 1 in 435 to 1 in 625. Of these victims, the statistical analysis revealed that those facing the highest risk of sexual victimization are females who are young, unmarried, lower-income, unemployed, and living in a large city (Karmen 2001). As evidenced, rapes/sexual assaults were found to be highest among residents age 16–19, low income residents, and urban residents (BJS 1997). Females are more likely to be victims of sexual assault than men; an estimated 91 percent of the victims of rape/sexual assault were female (BJS 1997). Although reports often argue that minorities, in particular black females, appear to be at a higher risk of rape than their female counterparts (Amir 1971; Russell 1984), BJS (1995) reported that no significant differences in victimization were found based on race of the victim. This inconsistency may be attributable to Russell's analysis (1984) which found that black females are more at risk of stranger rape, while white females were more at risk of acquaintance rapes (Belknap 2001). Even though the data has some discrepancies, the characteristics of those sexually assaulted seldom change.

In contrast to incidence rates, prevalence rates measure the victimization or chance of becoming victimized over a persons' lifetime. Estimations of sexual violence against the female population within the United States range anywhere from 12 to 50 percent (see Edward and Macleod 1999). The UCR indicated that 1 in 4 women may become a victim of rape during her lifetime (FBI 1997). Consistent with this assessment, Koss and Cook (1998) estimated that 1 in 4 college-aged women might have experienced an attempted or completed rape since the age of 14 years old. Moreover, Kilpatrick, Edmunds, and Seymour (1992) asserted that approximately 1.3 forcible rapes occur every minute in this country and that 12.1 million women will be raped during their lifetime (Edward and Macleod 1999). Further data collected using the National Violence Against Women Survey indicated that approximately 18 percent of women and 3 percent of men experienced sexual victimization (Tjaden and Thoennes 1998)—1 in 6 women and 1 in 33 men (Belknap 2001).

Offender Characteristics

What kind of a person commits a rape? Most of the research conducted on rape focuses on the victim; however, there is some research that examines the characteristics of the offender. The literature has consistently found that most rapists tend to be young, white males. As noted by BJS (1997), 99 in 100 rapists are male, 6 in 10 rapists are white, and the average age of a rapist is in their early twenties. Even though statistics have shown that white men are more likely to rape than black males, black men still remain overrepresented in rape cases. This phenomenon is attributable to the fact that black males are more likely to be prosecuted by the criminal justice system and that rapes by white males are typically not reported since the majority of these offenders are known to the victim (Belknap 2001).

Since we know who rapes, we must question why men rape. Nicholas Groth (1979) concluded in his analysis of 500 convicted rapists that men rape for three reasons: power, anger, and sadism. Groth determined that 55 percent of rapes were those of power characterized by a need to possess and control the victim. Although Groth's study allows for insight into the reasons for sexual assault, they do not clearly explain the reasons for rape since the majority of rapists are never convicted (Belknap 2001). Approximately half of those arrested for rape are never convicted (BJS 1997). Interestingly, as social class increases, the likelihood for conviction decreases. "When professional people are accused in the United States, their numbers drop precipitously when the rape charge gets to the prosecutor's office, while the other occupational groups remain about the same (Bartol 1999, 280). In summation, what we know is that most offenders are never reported or caught. Moreover, if those who are caught do not fit the "myth" of a rapist, they are often released.

Problems with Rape Statistics

Although these statistics are extraordinary estimations of the number of sexual victimizations occurring, criminologists must realize that survey figures only represent reported crimes (Allison and Kollenbroich-Shea 2001). As previous research has noted, the majority of rapes/sexual assaults go underreported. Simply put, rape is the most underreported crime in the United States (Allison and Kollenbroich-Shea 2001; Lonsway and Fitzgerald 1994; Ullman 1997).

The problem with determining accurate sexual assault rates is multi-faceted due to the nature of the crime. Until 1973, statistics on sexual victimization were not even collected; however, with the creation of the National Crime Victimization Survey[1] and the Uniform Crime Reports, data has become obtainable allowing for estimations of sexual assault to be retrieved. The problem remains that most people fail to admit to sexual assault, and when they do, they fall short of reporting it to the police. This can be attributed to the dehumanizing effect that rape has on its victims. Most victims have no desire to tell anyone of their victimization including researchers and law enforcement officials; therefore, sexual victimization rates are inordinately underrepresented (Belknap 2001; Karmen 2001).

Another explanation for the invalidation of sexual assault statistics is due to the definition of the crime. The majority of the definitions of rape/sexual assault, as noted above, have historically been vague in their description as to what constitutes this particular type of crime. Not only have many of the definitions failed to acknowledge men as victims, oral and anal intercourse, the sex of the offender, and many other mitigating factors, the definition of rape has been construed as one of force. The problem with this conceptualization of rape constructs an image of victims who have been brutally beaten by a minority stranger. This perception of rape by society has been coined "real" rapes, thus anything other than this has not historically been considered rape by the

---

1. In actuality, the National Crime Victimization Survey was not created until 1992 when it replaced the National Crime Survey. The survey was redesigned in an attempt to ask questions regarding rape in a more forthright manner. After the survey was redesigned, the number of estimated rapes jumped 157 percent (Kindermann and Lynch 1997 cited in Karmen 2001).

criminal justice system. Society has failed to acknowledge that victims of rape are more likely to be sexually assaulted by someone they know than by a stranger. Even the Bureau of Justice Statistics (1997) noted that, "three out of four rape/sexual assault victimizations involved offenders with whom the victim had a prior relationship as a family member, intimate, or acquaintance" (p. 4). However, since neither society nor the criminal justice system has defined rapes under these guidelines, many victims fail to realize that they have even been raped (Belknap 2001; Schwartz and Leggett 1999; Sudderth 1998). For instance, Sudderth (1998) found younger women who were raped by men to be the least likely to define the assaults as rape (Belknap 2001). When rape victims do realize that they have been sexually violated, they are often too embarrassed or afraid that they will not be believed by their friends, their family, and even the community, thus creating a situation that will never be reported.

The History of Sexual Victimization

The fear and shame experienced by rape victims stems from a long cultural and legal precedent that has enabled men to subjugate women without any concern for retribution. Even though the women's movement of the late 1960s/early 1970s helped to change the laws so women could receive equal protection under the legal system, women continue to be indoctrinated with beliefs that keep them fearful of rape. Women remain afraid of being assaulted in the streets; therefore, many do not dare to venture out at night or "to leave their well-guarded fortresses" (Eigenberg 2001, 1). "They learn that their vulnerability restricts their options: where and how they live, and where and when they work and go out" (Belknap 2001, 228). Ironically, as this chapter will address in depth in the myth section, women should not be afraid of those lurking in the streets but those whom they view every day. Women are far more likely to be victimized by men they know than by a stranger; however, through socialization, those in control of women's behaviors, fathers, husbands, brothers, etc., reiterate this myth to maintain dominance over their "weaker" counterparts. Even though women today have more power than ever before to resist the terror that maintains their seemingly powerless position, centuries of subjugation through violence is a difficult phenomenon to overcome.

The Law and Rape

Prior to second wave feminism, the criminal justice system approached rape cases with disregard. Since the American judicial system was based upon that of English Common Law, many of the ideas that prevailed in the old country were incorporated into the new world. As noted by Maschke (1997), most state laws only recognized a rape if the man forced a woman to have sex under the threat of injury, when she had resisted strenuously, and when there was outside corroboration (Van Wormer and Bartollas 2000). Not only were these criterion necessary but proving the "honorable nature" of the victim was also needed to obtain a rape conviction. "The belief that a woman's sexual past is relevant to her complaint of rape reflects, as does the resistance requirement, the law's punitive celebration of female chastity and its unwillingness to protect women who lack its version of virtue" (Estrich 1987, 48). Thus, a woman whose chastity was in question was often forced to prove that she was a legitimate victim of rape. This tradition of discounting rape was neither endemic to the United States nor the time period.

Throughout history, the rape of women has not only been overlooked but has in essence been encouraged by the patriarchal order. Brownmiller (1975) found that the earliest form of mating relationships was characterized by a man raping his intended "bride" to stake his claim. As man evolved, women began to be viewed as property. This newfound perception of women gave men a means to "protect" his chattel under the law against anyone who would dare taint his possession. For instance, under the system of *lex talionis* (an eye for an eye), men were permitted to rape the assailant's wife if his daughter had been raped (Brownmiller 1975). In addition, a rapist could be put to death for the rape of a virgin; however, this means of protection did not apply to married women. If a married woman was raped, she was considered blameworthy and was to be executed along with her attacker unless her husband intervened on her behalf (Karmen 2001).

Throughout the middle-ages, men used rape as a means of obtaining economic power. By raping the daughter of a wealthy man, the aggressor would ensure his position within the family. This caused considerable problems within the social structure since "a common person might bring perpetual disgrace upon a woman of nobility and good family by a single act of defilement and take her to wife to the disgrace of her family" (Brownmiller 1975, 27). As time evolved, only the rape of a woman from nobility carried any form of punishment. Forcing a peasant woman or others not deemed propertied (matrons, nuns, widows, concubines, and prostitutes) rarely received any punishment since loss of wealth was not in question. Even if punishment would have been sought by a victim of non-noble status, the nobleman would not take responsibility but instead blame the crime on his men (Brownmiller 1975). Noblemen were protected from any action for their transgressions and given free reign to victimize as desired. This same approach carried over into the home where rape was justifiable since wives were merely property, and their sole purpose was to please their "master."

Slavery and Rape

Sexual victimization during the United States during the 16th and 17th centuries was common practice. During this period, African-American women were vulnerable to sexual assault due to the implementation of slavery within society. Unlike their white female counterparts, who were protected from sexual victimization by any man other than their husband, female slaves had no such rights (Brownmiller 1975). Slaves were forbidden to marry; therefore, the rape of black women was not sanctioned by the law. In contrast to "white rapes" no reparations could be obtained for the defilement of a female slave. Since the female slave belonged entirely to her white master, she had no legal right to refuse his advances (Brownmiller 1975) even though many states had laws against sexual encounters between the differing races. However, these laws were not applied to white men but only white females to ensure they were not "mixing." Thus, it was acceptable for white men to sleep with black women; however, the rape of female slaves was not limited to that of the master. Often, female slaves were also raped by their black brothers (Van Wormer and Bartollas 2000). Rape among female slaves was not punishable but encouraged since a union might produce another "piece of property," a child.

War and Rape

The taking of women at will evolved from the same lines as the long held belief that women were simply the spoils of war; they, too, were to be conquered. History is laden with references of the capture and defilement of women dating back to Antiquity with stories such as *The Iliad* and the rape of the Sabine Women. This trend persisted throughout history. Rape has been used as a weapon of both terror and revenge in which one final blow could be dealt to the enemy. Even though Article 120 of the American Uniform Code of Military Justice has declared that rape during times of war is to be punishable by death or imprisonment, rape continues to be a common occurrence during wartime (Brownmiller 1975). Recently, the world has watched as the conflicts in Rwanda and the former Yugoslavia have resulted in an outright war against women.

War provides men with the perfect psychologic backdrop to give vent to their contempt for women. The very maleness of the military— the brute power of weaponry exclusive to their hands, the spiritual bonding of men at arms, the manly discipline of orders given and orders obeyed, the simple logic of the hierarchal command—confirms for men what they long suspect, that women are peripheral, irrelevant to the world that counts, passive spectators to the action in the center ring (Brownmiller 1975, 32).

Thus, the shear nature of war allows men to transform themselves into a power in which the enemy, women, are at their mercy.

Rape Myths

Rape is pervasive within our society cutting though all cultural, racial, and class lines (Grana 2002). Although the ubiquitous nature of rape has been acknowledged within the last thirty years, many acts of sexual aggression are still not considered rape. This stems from the historical treatment of this traditionally ignored phenomenon. The problem in addressing rape is due to "conventional sex-role socialization in a gender-stratified society, and traditional sex-role attitudes that serve as the basis for stereotypic beliefs about sexual aggression— "rape myths" (Schwendinger and Schwendinger 1974 cited in Orcutt and Figaro 1988). Simply put, the patriarchal order has socialized women to believe that sexual acts not deemed inappropriate by the traditional, stringent definition of rape does not equate to sexual victimization.

The term, "rape myths," was initially defined by Burt (1980) as "prejudicial, stereotyped, or false beliefs about rape, rape victims, and rapists" (p. 217). Although this definition established a foundation for others to base their work, this definition is limited due to its failure to clearly establish what is meant by the term "myth." In an attempt to rectify the problems in defining rape myths, Lonsway and Fitzgerald (1994) combined the perspectives of various fields to define rape myths as "attitudes and beliefs that are generally false but are widely and persistently held, and that serve to deny and justify male sexual aggression against women" (p. 134). This definition applies to the traditional myths regarding rape; however, when non-traditional myths are taken into consideration, this definition of rape myths also remains limited in scope. Thus, Lonsway and Fitzgerald's definition must be expanded and made generalizeable to include "all sexual aggression against any living creature."

Since Burt's (1980) research on rape myths, a plethora of research has emerged. The diversity of this enormous literature base covers areas ranging from the rape myth acceptance (RMA) (see Lonsway and Fitzgerald 1994, for a review of the literature) to the link between rape myths and religiosity (Freymeyer 1997). Thus, the question must be asked, "What do we know about rape myths?" Even though the majority of the rape myth literature is contradictory, we do know certain things. The one consistent finding in the majority of the research has determined that men are more likely to adhere to rape myths than are women. Other demographic relationships that have been measured in the RMA literature are race/ethnicity, age, and educational/occupational variables have produced incongruous results as have many of the non-demographic variables associated with RMA: responsibility, adversarial sexual beliefs, sex roles, attitudes toward rape, self-esteem, violence acceptance, conviction of rapists, and exposure to sexual and/or violent media (see Lonsway and Fitzgerald 1994). For instance, several studies have noted significant relationships between RMA and sexually aggressive behaviors (Field 1978; Koss, Leonard, Beezley and Oros 1985; Malamuth, et al. 1991; Muehlenhard and Linton 1987; Murphy, et al. 1986; Reilly, et al. 1992) while others have not found such relationships (Epps, Haworth and Swaffer 1993; Forbes and Adams-Curtis 2001; Greendlinger and Byrne 1987; Overholser and Beck 1986). Inconsistencies in the rape myth literature have been attributed to differing instruments used to measure rape myth acceptance.

Even though the literature is often contradictory in its conclusions on rape myths, we must realize that "many Americans indeed believe rape myths," (Burt 1980, 229) and "these views about rape are strongly connected to other, deeply held attitudes such as sex-role stereotyping, distrust of the opposite sex, and acceptance of interpersonal violence" (Orcutt and Faison 1988, 590). The real problem in these societal beliefs about rape is in the fact that they have no basis in reality but produce damaging biases towards the victims of sexual assault (Edward and Macleod 1999). This is especially problematic when the acceptance of rape myths carries over into the criminal justice system. As documented by the historical evidence, the criminal justice system has been less than supportive of rape victims due to their acceptance of rape myths. Police, prosecutors, and jurors often treat the victims as criminals leading them to conclude that there is no basis for their claims.

These stereotypical attitudes held by members of society and the criminal justice system has created an atmosphere in which women are the targets of their own victimization. Therefore, in order to understand these labels, we will look at many of the traditional myths surrounding rape. Since there are a vast number of myths that affect the way rape is perceived, this chapter will look at the most popular myths regarding the rape of women. Many of these myths will be linked to one another; therefore, the history and perceptions of why they exist may be linked to the same tradition. In addition to looking at the traditional myths that have affected women throughout history, the chapter will also address some of the non-traditional myths that apply to rape today. These myths are based on the same principles as those that have been used to target and discriminate against women.

Traditional Rape Myths

The Majority of Rape Claims Are False

The assumption that the majority of rape claims are false is one of the most widely accepted rape myths held within our society. Proponents of this rape myth often argue that women engage in such behavior for two major reasons: guilt and/or vengeance. Proponents of rape myths have construed rape as simply a woman's attempt to redefine an intimate situation in which she feels guilty about after the fact. This myth can be traced back to the idea that women are to remain chaste until marriage; therefore, any sexual transgressions that occur prior to marriage are deemed inappropriate. In theory, any self-respecting woman would want to deny her indiscretion. Advocates of this myth maintain that by crying rape, blame is deflected from the victim (Freymeyer 1997), and the reputation of the female remains intact in most cultures. However, this myth contradicts the reality of rape since any woman who brought forth a claim of rape lost her credibility and value as a prospective wife (Belknap 2001). Thus, a woman would not attempt to regain her innocence through revealing her indiscretions.

In addition to the belief that women cry rape because of guilt, antagonists have argued that women will often cry rape in an attempt to seek vengeance against an individual for not reciprocating her advances. This notion originated and became extremely prevalent in ancient Antiquity; however, the most notable version of this account lies in the Biblical story of Joseph. Joseph, a Hebrew slave of Potiphar, is tempted by Potiphar's wife to engage in sexual acts. Upon her order, the legend holds that the honorable man fled to avoid sinning but was accused by the vengeful woman of rape. Even though Joseph was "innocent" of this accusation, he was thrown in jail until divine intervention won his freedom. According to Brownmiller (1975), the moral of this story "is that a woman scorned can get a good man into a hell of a lot of trouble by crying rape" (p. 22).

This invalidation of women's testimony has occurred throughout history and has remained prevalent even in the last century. As late as the 1960s, legal journals went as far to argue that rape victims were untrustworthy. A monograph in the Columbia Law Review addressed the untrustworthiness of women by reasoning that

> false accusations of sex crimes in general, and rape in particular, are generally believed to be much more frequent than untrue charges of other crimes. A woman may accuse an innocent man of raping her because she is mentally sick or given to delusions; or because, having consented to intercourse, she is ashamed of herself and bitter at her partner; or because she is pregnant, and prefers a false explanation to the true one; or simply because she hates the man whom she accuses. Since stories of rape are frequently lies or fantasies ... such a story, in itself, should not be enough to convict a man of the crime. (Corroborating Charges of Rape 1967, 1138 cited in Cuklanz 1996).

In an attempt to remedy any false accusations of rape, many state laws required corroboration if rape cases were to go to trial.

Even though it has been established that rapes are severely underreported, this myth has been perpetuated by criminal justice agencies "confirmation" that women lie about rape. In 1991, the FBI using UCR data suggested that 8 percent of forcible rape complaints were "unfounded" (Lonsway and Fitzgerald 1994, 135). By painting the picture that rapes are more likely to be unfounded than other felonies, law enforcement statistics have reinforced this myth. Ironically, Bourque (1989) found that these unfounded cases were simply a measure of the percentage of cases that were not successfully brought to trial due to reasons such as sending victim reports to the wrong police jurisdiction, failure of victims to appear in court, and inadequately gathered evidence by both police and medical personnel (cited in Cuklanz 1996). In essence, data collected by law enforcement agencies have only established bias in dealing with rape cases since those deemed unfounded were caused by their own error rather than any wrongdoing of the victim.

Rape Only Happens to "Bad" Women

The belief that we live in a "just world" where bad things happen to bad people and good things happen to good people remains prevalent within our society (Lerner 1980). Hence, there is often a need for society to believe that people get what they deserve, karma. Simply put, victims warrant their own fate. This ideology has led the population to believe that the only women who are victims of rape are those whom society has deemed deviant. Thus, women and girls who fail to adhere to "society's unwritten rules" are blamed when they are raped (Belknap 2001, 215).

Traditionally, there have been two types of women within society, the Madonna or the whore. The Madonna/Whore Duality arises from Judeo-Christian theology where women were viewed as either the traditional wife and/or mother, or characterized as lustful creatures who often prompted men to lose control leading to unseemly behavior (Feinman 1994). This custom of placing women and girls into these mutually exclusive categories has led society to categorize women who do not fit the model of "the Madonna" to be viewed as promiscuous, thus deserving of rape. Women who dress provocatively, have prior sexual experience, drink alcohol, or engage in activities at inappropriate places and/or times are labeled as deviant even though their actions have no connection with the true motivation for rape: power. Nevertheless, the just world approach of blaming the victim values all of these insignificant factors as reasons for rape. According to Lonsway and Fitzgerald (1994), "The belief that only certain types of women are raped functions to obscure and deny the personal vulnerability of all women by suggesting that only 'other' women are raped" (p. 136). This rationalization enables society to believe that only certain types of people will be victimized while those who adhere to the rules of society remain protected from rape (Belknap 2001).

Perceiving victims as "other" not only allows society to place the blame on "bad girls," but it also labels individuals who do not fall into the category of white, middle-class as "other," therefore labeling socially marginal or minority groups deviant. DeFour (1990) argues that women of color are never portrayed as the "good girl," but are depicted as highly sexual, exotic, and/or hot-blooded. For instance, research has indicated that harsher sentences have been handed down when the victim is white than when the victim is black (White, Strube, and Fisher 1998). The reasons behind these discrepancies in sentencing are linked to vestiges of imperialism, colonialism, and slavery. These colonialistic attitudes equate women of color with those who are considered "bad." Thus, their race becomes another means for simply blaming the victim.

The Majority of Rapes Are Committed by a Stranger

From childhood, girls are taught to be weary of strangers. This fear of the unknown does not subside in adulthood but instead is reaffirmed by the myth that women are in constant danger of being raped. Women are inundated with stories and images from childhood (i.e. Little Red Riding Hood) that lead them to believe that out there in the bushes lurks a black man waiting to prey upon them. The idea that African-American men were looking to rape white women originated in the south during the Reconstruction Era. In response, our legal system took hold of the idea and began to incorporate harsher sentences based on this belief. Even though this myth has been proven invalid time and time using statistical evidence, much of the population still maintains that stranger rape, especially those committed by African-Americans, is widespread throughout the nation.

In reality, rape rarely occurs in this manner. Contrary to the popular myth, the majority of rapes are perpetrated by someone the victim knows: family, friends, ex-lovers, and other acquaintances. As noted in the literature, increasing evidence has determined that there is a high incidence of data and marital rape in which the perpetrator was the same race as the victim (Cuklanz 1996). For instance, the Bureau of Justice Statistics (1997) found that 2 in 3 rapes were committed by an acquaintance and 9 in 10 rapes by a family member. Ironically, victims of sexual assault are less likely to report rapes when they have been victimized by someone they know. The nature of this myth creates problems for the victim since many individuals do not consider date, marital, and acquaintance rape as "real rape" (Estrich 1987). Thus, the victims experience all of the negative effects of rape but rarely are able to seek justice.

Rape Is a Black-on-White Crime

This myth stems from the same stereotypical ideology that has perpetuated the belief that all rapists are black even though research has indicated that white males are more likely to be perpetrators of this violent crime. This narrow focus on the rape of white women by black men originated during slavery and continues to prevail throughout society. Despite the literature which has evinced that the majority of rapes occur among victims and perpetrators of the same race, the myth that rape is a black-on-white crime remains imbedded within our culture (Koss and Harvey 1991; White, Strube, and Fisher 1998; Wriggins 1983). This mentality not only "unfairly targets black men as rapists but obscures the significance of the rape of black women" (White, Strube, and Fisher 1998). In addition, Wriggins (1983) maintains that this stereotype also denies the sexual victimizations of white women since the majority of these crimes are perpetrated by white men. Thus, both black and white women are denied vindication within our society.

Women Secretly Wish to Be Raped

This myth stems from the belief that women find satisfaction in being forced to engage in sexual behavior. Hence, proponents of this myth believe that women fantasize about being raped (Allison and Kollenbroich-Shea 2000). Historically our legal system has fortified this myth by creating an image of the female "victim" as lustful. One summation in the Yale Law Journal found that "[A] woman's need for sexual satisfaction may lead to unconscious desire for forceful penetration, the coercion serving neatly to avoid the guilt feeling which might arise after willing participation" (Estrich 1987, 39). This perception not only exists within our criminal justice system but is reified by the media. In the popular film, *Gone with the Wind*, the rape of Scarlet O'Hara by her husband, Rhett Butler, reinforces the idea that women want to be raped. With this assault, the heroine wakes to a new and improved attitude after her "night of passion." Ironically, this portrayal of rape is tame compared to current-day scenes of sexual encounters in which movie goers are immersed. For instance, the movie, *Sliver*, has an unsuspecting Sharon Stone walking though a door only to be thrown against a wall by William Baldwin. Even though the act is construed as "rough sex," the true nature of the scene is that of forced sexual intercourse. These depictions reinforce the traditional belief that women are passive and men are aggressive allowing the myth that women need to be "taken" to remain alive.

When a Woman Says "No" to Sex, She Really Means "Yes"

The widely held myth that "no" means "yes" can be traced back to the aforementioned myth in which women want to be raped. Women are not supposed to be sexual—any contact delineating from the traditional roles assigned to them are viewed as abnormal; therefore, women will protest in an attempt to stay true to that stereotype. As many of the other myths regarding rape, the "no means yes" myth had been reinforced by the legal system. An article in the Stanford Law Review (1966) asserted:

> Although a woman may desire sexual intercourse, it is customary for her to say, "no, no, no" (although meaning "yes, yes, yes") and to expect the male to be the aggressor ... It is always difficult in rape cases to determine whether the female really meant "no" ... The problem of determining what the female "really meant" is compounded when, in fact, the female had no clearly determined attitude—that is, her attitude was one of ambivalence (Estrich 1987, 38).

In essence, the myth holds that in order to fit the assigned role as a passive participant and not be labeled as deviant, women say "no" and allow their male counterparts to be seen as the aggressor.

Rapists Are Mentally Ill

The myth that rapists are mentally ill has prevailed in our society. The typical rapist has been portrayed as mentally insane, crazy, or psychotic. However, the psychoanalytic response to sexual offenders has failed to prove that rapists are any more likely to be mentally ill than non-rapists (Belknap 2001). Rapists do not adhere to the stereotype which society has created. Rapists are typically considered the "average Joe" who fits into any group within our society—students, professionals, and of course, even family members.

Non-Traditional Rape Myths

Men Cannot Be Victims of Rape

The myth that men cannot be victims of rape stems from the traditional idea that women are passive and men are aggressive, thus, women are always the victims and men are always the perpetrators. Admittedly, this is partially true. Men are almost always the perpetrators of sexual assault; however, our society fails to realize that men may also be the victims as well. Male rape first came to the public's attention during the 1970s when men began to publicly acknowledge they had been sexually assaulted while incarcerated. The rape of men in prison was seen as an anomaly that took place due to fact that this "closed society" was without women. What society has failed to realize is that rape is prison is not about sex nor is male-on-male rape about homosexuality. Male sexual assault is perpetrated for the same reason as female sexual assault, an attempt to gain power over another. Although it has long been recognized that men are raped in prison (see Brownmiller 1975), most individuals, especially men, do not believe that rape happens in the real world. Even more shocking is that our criminal justice system has ignored this trend until recently. This is due to the taboo nature of the crime. Reports have indicated that nearly 8 percent of all reported rapes were male victimizations. In addition, rape crisis center records indicated that approximately 1 of every 10 callers were males (Karmen 2001).

Male victims are subject to the same kind of disbelief in which women have been subjected for centuries. Like women, they too are blamed for their own "indiscretions." However, men face a new problem, being labeled homosexual.

Men are disparaged for not being "real men" since they were unable to thwart their attackers (Karmen 2001). Thus, in order to prevent this stereotyping from occurring, most men, as do most women, fail to report their victimization.

Rape Is Strictly Limited to Interactions between Humans

Although many would find this myth to be harmless within our society, one must realize that this myth helps to perpetuate the same mentality as those myths applied to female sexual assault. The idea that animals are forced into intercourse does not typically register in the human mind as sexual assault or rape. However, if one looks at sexism and speciesism, there is a solid like between the two ideologies. According to Piers Beirne (1997), "interspecies sexual assault is the product of a masculinity that sees women, animals, and nature as objects that can be controlled, manipulated, and exploited" (p. 327). We fail to realize that when women are verbally degraded, they are described in animalistic references: bitches, cows, chicks, beavers, pussies, etc. This derogatory language allows the aggressor to dehumanize his "prey" and establish women as "less than" (Bierne 1997).

Today, the system attempts to protect women from sexual victimization; however, few laws exist within our society to protect animals. There are no federal laws to prosecute the sexual victimization of animals and only 27 of 50 states have any statutes that protect against bestiality (see Posner and Silbaugh 1996 cited in Bierne 1997). In addition, when the majority of cases in which interspecies sexual assault occurs, the perpetrator is only charged with a misdemeanor. Even though animals suffer great pain often resulting in death due to human-animal sexual relations, the law fails to seek retribution in any real form. Thus, the tradition of victimization continues within our society.

Conclusion

The acceptance of rape myths within our society is based on the history of the subjugation of women. Traditionally, women were discredited when they brought their victimization to the attention of the criminal justice system. Not only did the system fail to define sexual victimization, they established laws which ensured that sexual offenders would remain unpunished. By establishing criterion such as corroboration, resistance, and no prior relationship with the offender, the legal system maintained the status quo. It was not until the late 1960s/early 1970s that the criminal justice system began to approach rape cases without automatically condemning the victim. For instance, in 1976, Nebraska became the first state to criminalize marital rape (Eigenberg 2001).

Even though laws have been established to protect victims of sexual assault from being victimized twice (the initial assault and the assault by the criminal justice system), police officers, prosecutors, judges, and even members of the jury still look to the victim to prove her/her own victimization. This is attributed to the fact that rape myths are still widely accepted within our society. Although a plethora of research has shed light on many of these myths, as noted, society cannot seem to rid itself of these traditionally held beliefs. This creates an environment in which rape victims are afraid to come forward for fear of being humiliated by the legal system.

In order to rid society of the misperceptions of rape created by those who wish to maintain the patriarchal order, the criminal justice system must seek new methods in approaching sexual assault cases. First and foremost, law enforcement officials must be reeducated in their response to rape. Rather than approaching the case from the perspective that the victim must prove their own victimization, police must approach sexual assault cases as they approach other felonious crimes. In addition, departments must ensure that "evidence" collected during the investigation gets catalogued and appropriately stored for use if the crime goes to trial. Second, police officers, prosecutors, and judges must be educated about the realities of sexual assault (Belknap 2001). Although date, marital, and acquaintance rapes make up the vast majority of sexual assaults against women, prosecutors still hold on to the myth of the "stranger" rape. Since acquaintance rapes are typically in private and seldom leave "tale-tale signs" of brutalization, prosecutors will often fail to try a case in court. Thus, rapists are often released before they ever go to trial. Finally, the public must also be educated and sensitized to the reality of sexual assault. These individuals are the ones serving on juries and ensuring that justice is obtained. By ensuring that all those involved in the trial process in a sexual assault case are informed, society will be able to eliminate the traditional rape myths that have prevailed throughout history. Thus, this will bring society one step closer to eliminating the need to control and dominate another being.

References

Allison, J. and I. Kollenbroich-Shea. "Sexual Assault." In *Women, Crime, and Criminal Justice*, eds. C. Renzetti and L. Goodstein, 154–175. Los Angeles, CA: Roxbury, 2001.

Amir, M. *Patterns in Forcible Rape*. Chicago: University of Chicago Press, 1971.

Bartol, C. *Criminal Behavior: A Psychosocial Approach.* New Jersey: Prentice Hall, 1999.

Belknap, J. *The Invisible Woman,* 2nd ed. Boulder, CO: Wadsworth, 2001.

Bierne, P. "Rethinking Bestiality: Towards a Concept of Interspecies Sexual Assault." *Theoretical Criminology 1,* (1997): 317–340.

Brownmiller, S. *Against Our Will: Men, Women, and Rape.* New York: Bantham, 1975.

Bureau of Justice Statistics. *Sex offenses and Offenders: An Analysis of Date Rape and Sexual Assault.* Washington, D.C.: U.S. Department of Justice, 1997.

Burt, M.R. "Cultural Myths and Supports for Rape." *Personality and Social Psychology 38,* (1980): 217–230.

Chancer, L. S. "Gender, Class, and Race in Three High Profile Crimes: The Cases of New Bedford, Central Park, and Bensonhurst." In *Crime Control and Women,* ed. S. L. Miller, 72–94. Thousand Oaks, CA: Sage Publications, 1998.

Clark, A. *Women's Silence, Men's Violence: Sexual Assault in England, 1770–1845.* London: Pandora Press, 1987.

Cuklanz, L.M. *Rape On Trial: How the Mass Media Construct Legal Reform and Social Change.* Philadelphia: University of Pennsylvania Press, 1996.

DeFour, D.C. "The Interface of Racism and Sexism on College Campuses." In *Ivory Power: Sexual Harassment on Campus,* ed. M. A. Paludi. Albany, NY: State University Press of New York, 1990.

Edward, K.E. and M. D. Macleod. "The Reality and Myth of Rape: Implications for the Criminal Justice System." *Expert Evidence 7,* (1999): 37–58.

Eigenberg, H.M. *Woman Battering in The United States: Till Death Do Us Part.* Prospect Heights, IL: Waveland Press, 2001.

Epps, K.J., R. Haworth, and T. Swaffer. "Attitudes Toward Women and Rape Among Male Adolescents Convicted of Sexual Versus Nonsexual Crimes." *Journal of Psychology 127,* (1993): 501–506.

Estrich, S. *Real Rape.* Cambridge, MA: Harvard University Press, 1987.

Federal Bureau of Investigation. *Uniform Crime Reports.* Washington, DC: Department of Justice, 1997.

Feinman. *Women in the Criminal Justice System.* Westport, CT: Praeger, 1994.

Field, H.S. "Attitudes Toward Rape: A Comparative Analysis of Police, Rapists, Crisis Counselors, and Citizens." *Journal of Personality and Social Psychology 36,* (1978): 156–179.

Forbes, G.B. and L. E. Adams-Curtis. "Experiences With Sexual Coercion in College Males and Females: Role of Family Conflict, Sexist Attitudes, Acceptance of Rape Myths, Self-Esteem, and the Big-Five Personality Factors." *Journal of Interpersonal Violence 16,* (2001): 865–889.

Freymeyer, R. H. "Rape Myths and Religiosity." *Sociological Spectrum 17*, (1997): 473–491.

Grana, S. J. *Women and (In)Justice: The criminal and Civil Effects of the Common Law on Women's Lives*. Boston, MA: Allyn and Bacon, 2002.

Greendlinger, V. and D. Byrne. "Coercive Sexual Fantasies of College Men as Predictors of Self-Reported Likelihood To Rape and Overt Sexual Aggression." *Journal of Sex Research 23*, (1987): 1–11.

Groth, N.A. *Men Who Rape: The Psychology of the Offender*. New York: Plenum Press, 1979.

Karmen, A. *Crime Victims: An Introduction to Victimology*. Belmont, CA: Wadsworth, 2001.

Kilpatrick, D.G., C. N. Edmunds, and A. Seymour. *Rape in America: A Report to the Nation*. Arlington, VA: National Victim Center, 1992.

Koss, M. and S. Cook. "Facing the Facts: Data and Acquaintance Rape are Significant Problems for Women." In *Issues in Intimate Violence,* ed. R. Bergen, 147–156. Thousand Oaks, CA: Sage, 1998.

Koss, M.P. and M. R. Harvey. *The Rape Victim: Clinical and Community Interventions* (2nd ed.). Newbury Park, CA: Sage, 1991.

Koss, M. P., K. E. Leonard, D. A. Beezley, and C. J. Oros. "Nonstranger Sexual Aggression: A Discriminant Analysis of the Psychological Characteristics of Undetected Offenders." *Sex Roles 12*, (1985): 981–992.

Lerner, M.J. *The Belief in a Just World. A Fundamental Delusion*. New York: Plenum, 1980.

Lonsway, K.A. and L. F. Fitzgerald. "Rape Myths: In Review." *Psychology of Women Quarterly* 18, (1994): 133–164.

Malamuth, N.M., R. J. Sockloskie, M. P. Joss, and J. S. Tanaka. "Characteristics of Aggressor Against Women: Testing a Model Using a National Sample of College Students." *Journal of Consultating and Clinical Psychology* 59 (1991): 670–681.

Maschke, K. (ed.). *The Legal Response to Violence Against Women*. New York: Garland Publishing, 1997.

Miller, S. L. (ed.). *Crime Control and Women: Feminist Implications of Criminal Justice Policy*. Thousand Oaks, CA: Sage Publications, 1998.

Muehlenhard, C.L. and M. A. Linton. "Date Rape and Sexual Aggression in Dating Situations: Incidence and Risk Factors." *Journal of Counseling Psychology 34*, (1987): 186–196.

Murphy, W.D., E. M. Coleman, and M. R. Hayes. "Factors Related to Coercive Sexual Behavior in a Nonclinical Sample of Males." *Violence and Victims* 1, (1986): 255–278.

North Carolina State Law § 14-27.2

Orcutt, J.D. and R. Faison. "Sex-Role Attitude Change and Reporting of Rape Victimization, 1973–1985." *The Sociological Quarterly* 29, (1988): 589–604.

Overholser, J.C. and S. Beck. "Multimethod Assessment of Rapists, Child Molesters, and Three Control Groups on Behavioral and Psychological Measures." *Journal of Consulting and Clinical Psychology* 56, (1986): 682–687.

Posner, R.A. and K. B. Silbaugh. *A Guide to America's Sex Laws*. Chicago: University of Chicago Press, 1996.

Reilly, M.E., B. Lott, D. Caldwell, and L. DeLuca. "Tolerance for Sexual Harassment Related to Self-Reported Sexual Victimization." *Gender and Society* 6, (1992): 122–138.

Renzetti, C.M. and L. Goodstein. *Women, Crime, and Criminal Justice: Original Feminist Readings*. Los Angeles, CA: Roxbury, 2001.

Russell, D.E.H. *Sexual Exploitation: Rape, Child Sexual Abuse, and Workplace Harassment*. Beverly Hills, CA: Sage, 1984.

Schwartz, M.D. and M. S. Leggett. "Bad Dates or Emotional Trauma? The Aftermath of Campus Sexual Assault." *Violence Against Women* 5, (1999): 251–271.

Sudderth, L.K. " 'It'll Come Right Back at Me': The Interactional Context of Discussing Rape With Others." *Violence Against Women* 4, (1998): 559–571.

Ullman, S. "Review and Critique of Empirical Studies of Rape Avoidance." *Criminal Justice Behavior* 24, (1997): 177–204.

Tjaden, P. and N. Thoennes. *Stalking in America: Findings from the National Violence Against Women Survey*. Washington, D.C.: National Institute of Justice, 1998.

Van Wormer, K.S. and C. Bartollas, eds. *Women and the Criminal Justice System*. Needham Heights, MA: Allyn and Bacon, 2000.

White, A.M., M. J. Strube, and S. Fisher. "A Black Feminist Model of Rape Myth Acceptance: Implications for Research and Antirape Advocacy in Black Communities." *Psychology of Women Quarterly* 22, (1998): 157–175.

Wolf, N. *The Beauty Myth*. New York: William Morrow, 1991.

World Health Organization. "Violence Against Women," 2000. http://www.who.int/inf-fs/en/fact239.html.

Wriggins, J. "Rape, Racism, and the Law." *Harvard Women's Law Journal* 6, (1983): 103–41.

Special Feature

Letter to the Editor: Silence is Damaging

Does it disturb anyone to know that only one in 20 sex offenses in our civilized nation is reported to law enforcement? ... and the main reason many victims don't come forward is fear of hostility, retaliation, or that they won't be believed?

Numerous sex crime victims, most of whom have never reported the offense, watch silently as sex crime cases gain public attention—and wonder how they might have been treated if they had reported. Our cultural response to sexual violence leaves victims in the harshest predicament. They must choose between speaking out—which carries the risk of being blamed and harassed, and remaining silent—which carries the risk of isolation.

The silence of victims is damaging to the entire community. Unreported sexual violence allows offenders to remain undetected and victimize others ... you, me, our children.

Sexual violence awareness means increasing public awareness of how this human rights and public health issue impacts victims, families and communities. It means asking ourselves and our communities how we can work together to eliminate sexual violence and respond to survivors in a way that enables them to heal and regain control of their lives.

The myth of the "false report" of sex crimes must be replaced by this fact: It is underreporting, not false reporting, that presents the greatest risk to our children and our communities. It is silence that prevents social change.

Kim Vansell

Daily Star Journal, Warrensburg, MO; Thursday, October 18, 2007; p 4.

Chapter 2

Sexual Assault Definitions

Robert Hanser

A General Definition of Female Rape

As implied, this section addresses the issue of sexual assault definitions. However, the reader should understand that the term "sexual assault" is used as a blanket term that refers to a number of sexually related forms of victimization. This term includes all types of sexual offenses that involve touching or penetration of an intimate part of a person's body without consent (LeBeau and Mozayani 2001). Thus, sexual assault includes rape, forced sodomy, forced oral copulation, and any form of undesired sexually related touching (LeBeau and Mozayani 2001). However, society tends to refer to such forms of crime as simply rape. Further, many legal sources continue to use the term rape, particularly in specialized situations such as date rape and/or marital rape. Thus, this discussion will use the term rape most frequently to describe definitions of specific categories of sexual assault.

Also, it should be pointed out that the terms "victim" and "survivor" are used interchangeably throughout this discussion. The particular selection of terms was made, in each case, according to what seemed most appropriate to the particular context in which the issue of rape was being addressed. Likewise, it is important to note that this chapter will focus on definitions of rape that involve female victims. It is fully understood and acknowledged that victims of rape may be male as well as female. But the issue of male victims will not be covered due to the fact that the majority of victims (survivors) are female. Rape of male victims, whether by male or female perpetrators, is covered in other sections of this reader and is so specialized as to not be integral to the broad nature of this chapter. Further, child sexual assault/molestation will not be specifically covered (outside of statutory rape which is not an identical phenomenon) because this is an entire issue unto itself. Though the dynamics have similarities, there are significant distinctions from adult rape. With these points in mind, it is important to provide a rudimentary definition of the rape phenomenon as a baseline for the more in-depth definitions of rape that follow.

For purposes of this chapter, rape is the act of forced penetration of any bodily orifice (vaginally, anally, or orally), or forced cunnilingus or felatio, involving violation of the survivor's body and psychological well being. The assault is accomplished by the use of force, the threat of force, or without force when the survivor is unable to physically or mentally give their consent. Rape is an experience of violation, degradation, and humiliation that has serious negative impact on the survivor. The survivor's reactions can, and often do, vary according to the person, the event, and a number of other multiple variables. Further, the survivor's perception of the experience is affected by many factors such as prior socialization, reactions from people that are told about the incident, and the results of criminal justice agencies. It is important to realize that there are numerous types and definitions of rape. It should be understood that there are personal, social, political, and clinical implications that affect the rape phenomenon. Because of this, it is important to not only examine the physical and psychological well-being of the survivor, but to examine the larger societal constructs attributed to the rape phenomenon as well.

General Rape

Numerous Ways to Define Rape

One main point of this chapter is to illustrate the numerous definitions of rape. These definitions are more varied than may be generally acknowledged. Further, Bourque (1989) notes that this diversity has important ramifications for how rape is reported, prevented, treated, and even researched. In fact, definitions of rape can vary with the defining person's social standing, education, perceptions of, and attitudes towards violence and sexuality (Bourque 1989).

Definitions of rape also vary greatly from state to state, and in many states the term "sexual assault" has replaced the term of rape in their criminal statutes (Bartol 1999). The U.S. Department of Justice defines rape as the "unlawful sexual intercourse with a female, by force or without legal or factual consent" (U. S. Department of Justice, 1988). But other jurisdictions vary widely in their definitions of rape often disagreeing with the Department of Justice's definition. Such disagreement has hampered the effective classification and study of rape offenses (Bartol, 1999).

Bartol (1999) points out that in defining rape, prosecutors require exacting and stringent evidence before even considering an incident as probable rape. From survey data, it has been found that prosecutors often look for four minimal criteria for filling out a complaint for forcible rape: (1) evidence of penetration; (2) a lack of victim consent; (3) threat of force; and (4) and usually the victim must be female (Bartol 1999; Chappell 1977). More contemporary prosecutors may differ on some of these points, particularly with respect to the victim being female, depending on jurisdiction and the crime alleged. However, these differences, combined with the differences among state legislatures, law enforcement agencies, and researchers, demonstrate a need for a clear and distinct definition of rape.

The act of rape should be viewed as but one of many violent and sexual behaviors that humans may engage in. This is because the tendency to separate rape from other human behavior has had two unfortunate consequences (Bourque 1989). First, it has allowed members of society to ignore the wide variety of behaviors that technically meet the definition of rape (Bourque 1989). Second, it ignores the fact that rape only differs in the degree of severity from other violent interactions (Bourque 1989). If we are to lower our tolerance for rape and develop consistent sanctions for dealing with perpetrators, we must understand the wide range of behaviors that rape encompasses.

Sadly enough, many people continue to view "real" rape as some unforeseen attack by some stranger in an isolated area (Bourque 1989). Such a limited definition, allows most people to distance themselves from the reality of rape. This limited definition can also minimize the trauma for survivors of various types of rape. The irony is that this denial of the actual occurrence of rape works not only in the minds of people who are not involved with a rape incident, but also works to mitigate the perceptions of perpetrators, and even those of the victims as well. Thus, some perpetrators may genuinely not perceive their actions as rape. More disturbing is that many victims often do not, themselves, realize that they have been raped (Brownmiller 1975; Buchwald, Fletcher, and Roth 1993).

One useful theory for explaining perceptions of rape is attribution theory (Bourque 1989). In the case of sexual assault, it is assumed that both the perpetrator and survivor of the incident, as well as other observers such as family, friends, and police will evaluate the situation to determine if a rape occurred. It is also assumed that conclusions reached will affect future behavior, future feelings that the victim will have about themselves, and future judgments of other similar situations. Bourque (1989) states that if the woman concludes that a rape did occur and that she was responsible for it, this theory predicts that her behavior will change in ways that are likely to prevent future rapes. It is also assumed that she will feel that other women who are raped under similar circumstances are similarly responsible for assaults made upon them (Bourque 1989). What is alarming about this is that some women may in fact blame themselves for rape to the point that the perpetrator's behavior is normalized or excused.

Conversely, if she concludes that she was not responsible for the rape, her behavior may be less likely to change and her judgments of other rapes will tend to absolve women of responsibility (Bourque 1989). While it is preferred that a victim does not blame themselves for a rape that has been committed against them, it is hoped that victims will see themselves as survivors capable of affecting the outcome of future rape for themselves and others. This of course does happen with many rape survivors. But the example demonstrates that some women may learn a state of helplessness that places them at a greater likelihood for repeat victimization. Thus, the manner in which blame, guilt, and responsibility is attributed is important because when people decide that a rape has occurred, their perception of the rape often considers issues of victim and offender self-responsibility in making this determination. In other words, most observers of rape at least topically consider if the victim and offender acted responsibly or negligently. Many people may consider the possibility that the victim deliberately placed themselves in the precarious position that led to the rape (Bourque 1989). This is despite the fact that it is the perpetrator who is guilty of the rape, not the survivor.

Outlooks such as those previously described often revolve around the particular locus of control that an observer might possess (Rotter 1966). Locus of control differentiates between beliefs about internal and external control events. Locus of control has often been used to describe "states" and "traits." In other words, it can refer to an individual's perception of his or her ability to control events in a single instance, or it can be used to describe the person's general personality profile (Bourque 1989). This concept is important to rape perceptions and definitions because evidence exists that locus of control varies with sex-role attitudes and that it influences both people's perceptions of rape and the victims' sense of self-responsibility (Bourque, 1989). Women who score high on internal control also score high on nontraditional feminism, thus viewing women to be more capable of aggressive behaviors. On the other hand, women scoring high on the external control measure tend to accept socially defined, normative roles of passivity for women. This has also been found to correlate with attitudes on how rape is perceived by some women (Bourque 1989; Krulewitz and Payne 1978).

This has obvious implications for how women may develop self-definitions of rape. Naturally then, this would equally affect rates of reporting rape. Further, men likewise form attributions toward women in rape situations based on an internal/external locus of control schema (Bourque 1989; Rotter 1966). Men, who tend to score higher than women on internal loci of control, tend to hold women as partially or even entirely responsible for the rape acts committed against them. Those scoring lower on internal loci of control may blame environmental factors as well as the perpetrator. Thus, attributions that people make toward the rapist and the survivor affect how they will define rape (Bourque 1989).

Another similar theory that explains how people develop perceptions, and by proxy definitions of rape is the "just world hypothesis" (Bartol 1999; Lerner 1980).This is the simplistic belief that a person gets what they deserve in life. Often people who subscribe to this viewpoint claim that poor life choices and/or deliberately counterproductive decisions serve to place the victim in a position where the consequence is a natural and foreseeable product. This theory contends that victims of misfortune or crime deserve their fate (Bartol 1999). Naturally, those people who subscribe to this theory hold this to be true for survivors of rape as well. According to Bartol (1999), these people will use any number of rationalizations to explain their viewpoints (i.e. she should not be at a bar alone, she should have worn a bra, she should not dance with someone she just met, etc ...) and, as will later be seen, are touted so widely that some of the rationalizations have become rape myths believed by a number of people in society.

In addition to individual perceptions, much of the process of defining rape is likewise dependent on cultural and social factors (Sanday 1981). Naturally, these factors affect individual perceptions, including those held by perpetrators and survivors of rape. Even local community views on rape may greatly affect the likelihood of reporting, the likelihood of apprehension for the offender, and the treatment of the victim (Bourque 1989; Sanday 1981). Therefore, Bourque (1989) contends that community surveys provide the best information about what most community members think about rape. With respect to social indicators, social status and life-style of the persons involved in rape can all have important effects on the perceptions and definitions of rape. Particularly, age, sex, income, education, and religion have been found to affect perceptions of rape (Williams and Holmes 1981).

This is important, because many researchers contend that rape is not about sex, but is about the perpetrator's need to express and exert power (Buchwald, Fletcher, Roth 1993; Steinem 1993). This is often coupled with the idea that our culture in general, and men in particular, hold women as lower status citizens when compared to men (Buchwald, Fletcher, Roth 1993; Dworkin 1993). Such attitudes are often what lead many researchers to conclude that rape has more to do with a desire to express power and domination than to gratify sexual urges (Brownmiller 1975; Groth 1979; Steinem 1993). These attitudes toward women, and the attitudes that women hold about themselves, are held to be products of socialization stemming from both the family and the broader society. But it is society that generates numerous messages that bombard the family with perceptions that dictate the place of women and their role with the rape experience.

One frequently cited medium that affects rape perceptions and definitions comes in the form of erotica and pornography (Steinem 1993). In fact, Steinem states bluntly that "pornography is not about sex, it's about an imbalance of power that allows and even requires sex to be used as some form of aggression" (1993, 31). Perceptions and informal definitions of rape for many people may be greatly affected by visual media, with pornography being a foremost contributor to the confusing manner by which sex and violence are intertwined in much of American culture. The contention is that sex is confused with violence and aggression in all forms of popular culture. The idea that aggression is a normal part of male sexuality, and that passivity is a normal part of female sexuality, are part of the male-dominant culture (Steinem, 1993). Because of the deep-seated differential social value placed upon men and women, and because the issue of power and dominance is interwoven into this differential social value, it becomes clear that untangling sex from aggression would be a very difficult task indeed (Steinem 1993). This point is important, because it is the underlying dynamic that affects the perceptions of men and women toward rape, and by the same token, affects any formal or informal definitions of rape.

But it should also be made clear that social and cultural messages affecting definitions of rape are not limited to direct media processes like pornography. Rather, the linguistics in the general media can affect our definitions of rape as well. Benedict (1993) contends that in the media, the English language itself is a language of rape. Through vocabulary and profiles on television, women are portrayed as sexual or childlike temptresses (Benedict 1993). Such portrayals perpetuate the idea that women are legitimate sexual prey. The scenarios presented in movies often portray rape as an act of unintended pleasure, or of comedy, rather than violence (Benedict 1993). Benedict (1993) even maintains that newspapers and newscasts use words that describe the victim in terms of their beauty; these news media likewise describe the incident so that it diminishes the criminality of the act committed. The language chosen by journalists and news reporters can make rape seem either sexy or not so traumatic (Benedict 1993).

These are all significant observations, because such depictions serve to normalize the occurrence of rape and serve to desensitize the public to its effects.

This failure to accurately report the damage to the victim likewise allows viewers to ignore the stark reality of rape. And of course, the news media, just like individuals in the general population, can itself be responsible for inaccurate attributions made by the reporter who makes the scene. This process tends to reinforce many of the informal social norms and mores that maintain a tolerance of rape. Thus, those seeking to change the manner by which rape is addressed would claim that definitions of rape are biased due to personal perceptions and social factors that affect those perceptions. To ignore this is to ignore the very groundwork upon which all definitions of rape are based.

Rape by Criminal Law v. Civil Law

As has been previously mentioned, creating definitions of rape can be somewhat elusive when one is asked to concretely operationalize the term. From the discussion of perceptions and their effects on definitions, it can be seen that there is likely to be a diversity of viewpoints. More to the point, this seems to have translated into a number of methods by which rape is defined. For example, rape has varying criminal definitions among the fifty states, though most state definitions of rape have their earliest origins in the English common law. Thus this section will provide a general examination of early common law explanations of rape definitions and statutes to provide backdrop knowledge of the earliest definitions of rape. Further, rape has differing definitions based on the type of law being utilized; criminal law vis-à-vis civil law definitions. Lastly, this section will present a variety of criminal law definitions and will conclude with a civil law definition of rape. The diverging origin (crime against the people v. crime against the individual) from which these two forms of law operate provide the background in determining exactly how a rape is processed.

Analyzing statutes as sources of law requires a brief look at common law, which is mainly law that has emanated from long traditions and customs, or from various decisions throughout passed down case law. This is in direct contrast to codified laws that are passed by state legislatures or other governing and law making bodies. According to Reid (1992), the term "common law" generally refers to England's ancient laws that developed from judicial decisions which were decided on a case-by-case basis. The decisions from these cases were passed down to lower courts or were used by other courts and became "precedent" or "case law" upon which future cases were decided (Reid 1992). Early American case law developed from this English tradition which were based on English customs and norms (common law). As American case law developed, it was codified and is now what we know as statutory criminal law.

Under common law, rape was defined as the unlawful carnal knowledge of a female without her consent. For centuries this definition was interpreted to exclude a husband's forced sexual intercourse with his wife (Reid 1992). The carnal knowledge component of the definition referred to sexual intercourse and was strictly limited to acts of penile penetration of the vagina (Reid 1992). Common law rape applied only to female victims and forcing a male to engage in sex was not considered a rape (Reid 1992). Lastly, the issue of consent was a paramount yet difficult component to prove. Proving a lack of consent became a burden that the rape survivor's defense would have to bear.

Similarly, Paquin (1995) defines common law rape as an act of sexual intercourse by a man with a woman, who is not his wife, by force and against her will. Again, the consent issue is particularly problematic; but in situations where the woman is not able to consent, intercourse was generally held to be against her will (Paquin 1995). Situations where the woman could not consent would include those where she is incompetent, drugged, or underage (often referred to as statutory rape and defined later in this section). Paquin (1995) also adds that consent is the primary issue of fact that a court must agree upon. This is especially true in cases where the perpetrator and victim may know each other as cohorts, friends, or even romantic partners who are not married (Paquin 1995). The consent issue then was of critical importance in early rape history and, as will be discovered throughout this discussion of rape definitions, has continued to be the pivotal point in defining an act as rape.

According to Paquin (1995), many feminist scholars claim that the common law intent against rape was to protect her "virtue" or chastity rather than her freedom to choose sexual partners. This is because in centuries past, women were considered to be the property of their fathers or husbands. In several ways, it is the victim's character that is at issue as much as the actions of the rapist under the common law system.

As stated previously, the distinctions between common law and criminal law mostly have to do with the codification of the law. However, MacDonald (1995) provides a clear definition of criminal rape. As one can tell, this definition sounds very familiar to the earlier common law definition. MacDonald (1995) defines rape under criminal law "as the unlawful sexual intercourse with a female without her consent, or when consent is obtained by threats of violence; by deception, for example, by impersonating the woman's husband; or by the administration of intoxicating substances. Women of unsound mind may be incapable of giving legal consent. Penetration of the vagina need not be complete, the slightest penetration is sufficient, and ejaculation need not occur" (p. 4). As can be seen, the issue of consent is the primary concern in determining if a rape has occurred. Factors that mitigate or aggravate the likelihood of truly informed consent likewise become material in defining the occurrence of rape. Thus, consent has historically remained the major snafu in most all instances of rape between adults.

Two other categories of rape that are commonly employed in criminal statutes include statutory rape and rape by fraud. Statutory rape, defined by MacDonald (1995) is unlawful sexual intercourse with a willing female child under the age of consent. At present, the age of consent in American jurisdictions ranges from eleven to seventeen years (MacDonald 1995). In analyzing statutory rape provisions, MacDonald (1995) contends that the age should not be so young that little protection is provided for a child, nor so late that a man can be held for statutory rape when the "victim" is fully capable of informed consent and readily acquiesced to a proposal or even invited a sexual relationship. Boumil, Friedman, and Taylor (1992) explain that unlike other types of rape, statutory rape usually refers to consensual sexual activity, including intercourse between a male and a girl who is under a certain prescribed age that is necessary for legal consent. If the girl is under the statutory age of consent, and even if she willingly participated, the male engaging in sexual activity with her is guilty of statutory rape (Boumil, Friedman, and Taylor 1992). It is also not considered a defense if the man was not aware of the victim's age (Boumil, Friedman, and Taylor 1992). This is of course a controversial concept among many people affected by rape.

The term "statutory" in statutory rape means that the law will call the act rape regardless of whether or not the victim was willing because that victim is considered legally incapable of giving true consent due their diminished ability to fully understand the consequences of their decisions (Boumil, Friedman, and Taylor 1992). This is of course held to be a product of their youth (Boumil, Friedman, and Taylor 1992). Every state has a law that sets a minimum age at which this consent can be given. The minimum age of consent is not necessarily the point of reaching adulthood (i.e. eighteen) and can be much younger than eighteen, depending on the particular state and the particular circumstances (Boumil, Friedman, and Taylor 1992; MacDonald, 1995). The main purpose of these laws is to protect underage children rather than to morally restrict sex from a given population group (Boumil, Friedman, and Taylor 1992; MacDonald 1995). Thus the intent of statutory rape laws is to deter those who would take advantage of a potential victim's youth. All of these laws, regardless of the state in which they are enacted, share the common holding that it does not matter if the victim was willing (Boumil, Friedman, and Taylor 1992). If the child is below the state's minimum age of consent, then it is statutory rape. Further, if the victim was both below the minimum age and not willing, the crime is not only statutory rape, but can likewise be classified as child molestation or child sexual abuse (Boumil, Friedman, and Taylor 1992).

The category of rape by fraud occurs when the perpetrator employs actual, deliberate misrepresentation or concealment to gain access to sexual activity with the victim. Essentially, rape by fraud is having sexual relations with a consenting adult female, but the consent is given under fraudulent conditions (Bartol 1999). Examples of this type of rape might be where the man presents himself as some other identity (such as in the dark impersonating the husband or boyfriend of the victim). Other types of rape by fraud include when the court finds such to exist after examining the nature of a contract or from the relationship of the parties involved. An example of this might be where the man, through acts of deception, tricks the victim into thinking they have been legally married and the two consummate their new marriage, only for the victim to later find that the marriage was a hoax. Another example is when a psychotherapist or a clergy member has sexual intercourse with a patient under the guise of providing treatment or spiritual guidance. Rape by fraud can also occur among women who typically are not considered worthy of such legal protections, though such fraudulent forms of sexual manipulation can and do occur. For example, consider a female prostitute who has sex with a male customer who upon completion of the act, does not pay as agreed. This in fact, can consist of a legal definition for rape by fraud in areas where prostitution is legal or at least decriminalized. Because it is often consensual (even though the causes for consent were given under false pretenses), rape by fraud is very difficult to prove in many cases. Despite this, it is important to remember that this is not "informed consent" in the true sense of the word, and regardless of the woman's position in society, this type of manipulation is considered rape nonetheless because true consent is in fact lacking.

Rape in the Civil Law Context

According to Paquin (1995), rape is not only a crime, but it is also a personal injury against the victim. In addition to criminal systems of recourse, victims may pursue civil systems of redress to obtain financial compensation for the damages they have suffered. There are two primary benefits for rape victims who decide to pursue redress under civil law (Paquin 1995). First, the victim needs a much lower standard of proof than in criminal courts. The standard of proof needed for a civil case is a simple preponderance of the evidence. Thus, at least hypothetically, a case that did not meet the criminal law definition could still meet the level of proof for the civil law definition for liability (Paquin 1995). Second, damages incurred will be compensated directly to the victim. This is because the act of violence is a personal injury to the plaintiff (in this case, the victim of the rape) and as such, liability is strictly maintained from the perpetrator to the victim as a personal injury (Paquin 1999). Thus, civil law tends to "desexualize" the rape and instead treats the act as any form of deliberate personal injury inflicted by a liable party. The result is that the victim has increased odds of obtaining redress under this definition due to lower evidentiary standards when compared to criminal charges of rape.

Stranger Rape—A Stereotypical Definition

For the purposes of this discussion, stranger rape is defined as nonconsensual, or forced sex, on a person who does not know their attacker. According to Boumil (1992), this type of rape is what people usually think of when they think of rape. Most people envision a rapist as an unknown man who ambushes his victim at night armed with some type of weapon that they use to force compliance from their victim (Boumil 1992). The victim is caught by surprise and may or may not resist the attack, depending upon how terrified she is and whether she perceives that it may save her from further attack and/or injury (Boumil 1992). This type of stranger rape can occur in any place where a potential victim can be found, including the victim's home, car, or anywhere outside (Boumil 1992).

This is the stereotypical rape that common law definitions originally recognized. As such, most people have no problems defining this type of rape and empathy for victims of this type of rape is usually readily extended. Because this definition of rape is so well accepted and so straightforward in nature, there is little need for extensive discussion in explaining its definition. The actual rate of frequency of stranger rape as compared to other types of rape has varied depending on the researchers (Bartol 1999; Parrot and Bechhofer 1991; Wiehe and Richards 1995). It must be made clear that the point of this discussion is not to provide exact rates of occurrence for each type of rape, but is to instead demonstrate the various methods for defining rape.

The occurrence of stranger rape, in this society, is more widely accepted than acquaintance rape. This acceptance that stranger rape receives does not limit the shame attached to rape or the trauma felt by the survivor. However, stranger rape is usually seen as "real rape". The purpose of this discussion is not to devalue and belittle the experience of stranger rape. Rather, it should be made clear that other forms of rape do indeed exist. It is the hope that survivors of all types of rape will encounter understanding and awareness and that people close to survivors of rape will recognize the possible differences in the experience of stranger and acquaintance rape. With this is mind, we now move forward to another category of rape that is perhaps less well understood by the general public.

Intimate (Date) Rape

Acquaintance rape is treated with ambivalence by society and the legal system partly because it is difficult to identify situations that clearly constitute acquaintance rape. Therefore, a basic and pragmatic definition of the term must be provided. This definition is borrowed from Parrot and Bechhofer (1991) who describe acquaintance rape as nonconsensual sex between adults who know each other. The word acquaintance is sometimes used to describe a person that is known but who is not close to the person. The word can also be used to describe any person who is known to the victim, this would include any and everyone who is not a stranger (Parrot and Bechhofer 1991). Date rape is a narrower term referring to nonconsensual sex between people who are dating or on a date. Although the two terms "acquaintance rape" and "date rape" are used interchangeably, they do not have the same meaning (Parrot and Bechhofer 1991). Date rape is only one form of acquaintance rape (Parrot and Bechhofer 1991).

In distinguishing between types of rape, one should understand that rape definitions held by individuals in this culture may be broad and inclusive or narrow and restrictive (Parrot and Bechhofer 1991). People whose definitions are at the inclusive extreme believe that all coerced sex is rape, whether the coercion used is physical, psychological, or economic (Parrot and Bechhofer 1991). Those whose definitions lie at the restrictive extreme believe that there is no such thing as rape, or if there is any, it will fit the classic perception of typical stranger rape. According to Parrot and Bechhofer (1991), most people's definition of rape falls somewhere between these two extremes. This includes some acts of coerced sex but also excludes many on the basis of belief in rape myths. People have in their heads an idea of a "real" rape (Boumil 1992). Usually their idea is much narrower than the legal definition and excludes many types of rape that happen more frequently than the classic rape (Parrot and Bechhofer 1991).

The classic "real" rape for many people, is a rape similar to that earlier described as stranger rape. The rapist is commonly thought to be a stranger, attack at night, use a weapon, and the victim resists but is overpowered. But a high number of rapes do not actually fit these criteria (Parrot and Bechhofer 1991). Thus the classic rape scenario does not leave room for acquaintance rape or date rape. In most date or acquaintance rapes and most group rapes, as will be discussed later, no weapon is used. Further, the victim often has engaged in some type of voluntary communication with the perpetrator, which can be as brief as a few leisure conversations to fully intimate discussions among dating or married couples. The problem here is in determining exactly when the voluntary interaction between the two ended and the coercion and/or force began (Parrot and Bechhofer 1991). Since many people have a difficult time explaining these disparities between their definition of rape and the actual circumstances that surround a rape, they create mechanisms that help to justify their ability to disqualify a rape incident from their idea of real rape (Parrot and Bechhofer 1991). These rationalizations are called rape myths (Parrot and Bechhofer 1991).

These common rape myths, as described by Burt (1991), warrant a bit of attention because they serve to "explain away" the significance of acquaintance rape. One myth that is sometimes utilized is that nothing in fact happened (Burt 1991). This myth is based on the notion that a large number of women falsely accuse men of rape to fulfill other ulterior agendas. A second commonly used myth is that no actual harm was done to the victim (Burt 1991; Sanday 1990; Wiehe and Richards 1995). Sexual intercourse is admitted, but the coercion and harm inflicted is denied (Burt 1991). Beliefs that rape is "just sex" fall within this category as well (Burt 1991; Sanday 1990). Further, remarks like "relax and enjoy it" or "at least you were not a virgin" reflect this belief (Burt 1991). Another common myth is the notion that the survivor really wanted the sexual incident to take place (Burt 1991). Essentially, this myth would contend that the woman invited the rape through victim precipitated behavior or that she enjoyed it (Burt, 1991). An example of this exists among fraternities that claim that women who get drunk at their functions do so because they actually desire to have sex with the fraternity members (Burt 1991; Sanday 1990).

Wiehe and Richards (1995) likewise point toward the effects of rape myths, particularly with respect to acquaintance rape. Among these myths is the idea that the victim is responsible for the rape (Wiehe and Richards 1995). Attributions to how the victim was dressed, if she drank alcohol, etc. fall within this line of thinking. What is interesting is that the victim may actually blame themselves for drinking or choosing certain attire, and thus may begin to feel responsible for the rape itself, just as was earlier presented in the discussion of attribution theory (Bourque, 1989; Wiehe and Richards 1995). Yet another myth discussed by Wiehe and Richards (1995) is that women say "no" but really mean "yes." Thinking along this line contends that the woman wants to have sex but has to go through some charade so that it does not appear as if she is promiscuous. Men are aggressive and women are passive, according to this myth, in their sexual encounters (Wiehe and Richards 1995). Thus, women must say no by this gender-based stereotype. One last myth that is commonly purported is that once men are sexually aroused, sex is inevitable (Wiehe and Richards 1995). Essentially, this contends that men have no control over their behavior once their arousal state reaches a certain point. This is of course preposterous and simply serves as an excuse to justify rape.

Rape myths allow rapists to rape without fear of retribution. These myths teach women to blame themselves for their own victimization (Bourque 1989; Burt 1991; Wiehe and Richards 1995). These myths also transform an acquaintance rape into a simple sex act between two people who knew each other, and thus makes it as if there were no rape at all (Burt 1991; Wiehe and Richards 1995). What is more, these myths completely deny the possibility that someone can be raped by someone they know (Burt 1991; Wiehe and Richards 1995). Further, rape myths serve to keep the victim quiet. This is especially true with acquaintance rape where the woman's credibility is at stake, again calling into question any claims of a lack of consent. This is compounded by the fact that lack of consent is perceived to have been less likely if she previously knew her attacker. Thus rape myths, while negatively affecting public perceptions in all types of rape, are especially damaging in acquaintance rape situations.

With stranger rape, it is presumed that as long as the woman resisted, and did not conduct herself in a provocative fashion, then she is not necessarily to blame. But with acquaintance rape, there is a need to explain what may seem perplexing (Bartol 1999; Burt 1991; Wiehe and Richards 1995). The easiest solution is to blame the victim, as this provides some basis for overcoming the need to resolve questions of consent (Burt 1991; Wiehe and Richards 1995). Thus acquaintance rape is about rape and the question of consent. Acquaintance rape does not, and often is not, about force during the act but nonetheless is an act of exploitation rather than sex between two people who know each other. The exploitation comes in the form of robbing the person of the power to give or deny consent to the initiator of the sexual encounter. It is at this point, whether through force, coercion, or sense of obligation, that true consent is questionable and the issue of possible rape arises. In acquaintance rape situations, this is the most difficult area to clearly prove and creates a "grey zone" for those trying to determine if rape in fact exists.

Acquaintance rape is a fairly new notion that has received mixed public support. But the laws are changing as well as social attitudes. Rape myths provide resistance to these positive changes and also reflect cultural attitudes toward the rights of women, the self-control of men, and societal connections attributed to sex, violence, and exploitation (Bourque 1989; Burt 1991; Wiehe and Richards 1995). Acquaintance rape subjects the victim to all of the traumatic experiences encountered in stranger rape. In fact, it could easily be argued that the trauma is greater because the victim must often times face their perpetrator on future occasions. Likewise, in acquaintance rape there is the betrayal of trust between the two who had previously known each other. This is especially true in loving relationships where care and mutual respect are thought to be the basis of the union. It is with this in mind that we now move to our next category of acquaintance rape ... marital rape, which presumes that more personal as opposed to casual knowledge exists between the victim and perpetrator.

Spousal Rape

Wiehe and Richards (1995) define marital rape as any sexual activity by a legal spouse that is performed or caused to be performed without the consent of the other spouse. These activities, as with acquaintance rape, include fondling, oral sex, anal sex, intercourse, or any other unwanted sexual activity. Husband is defined as the male spouse who is legally bound to his wife in marriage (Wiehe and Richards 1995). Wife is defined as the female spouse who is legally bound to her husband in marriage (Wiehe and Richards 1995). Marriage is defined as the legal union of a man and a woman (Wiehe and Richards 1995). With these definitions in mind, it is necessary to at least briefly discuss the history of rape in western civilization to understand why marital rape has traditionally been excluded. With this understanding it will become clearer why marital rape is a necessary category deserving attention of its own.

The basis of the legal history of the marital rape exemption is found in early English common law (Paquin 1995; Reid 1992; Wiehe and Richards 1995). According to this legal framework, the point when the wife consented to marriage expressly implied that she consented to all activities associated with marriage and that therefore there can be no rape in marriage. From the moment of marriage forward, the wife had "given herself" to her husband and could not refuse him sex throughout the term of the marriage (Wiehe and Richards 1995). Another point to understand with rape in general, and with marital rape specifically, is that women were considered chattel of their fathers or their husbands (Brownmiller 1975; Paquin 1995; Wiehe and Richards 1995). Thus traditional rape was viewed as a crime against the economic concerns of the father, if the woman was unmarried, or the economic concerns of the husband, if the woman was the man's wife. Since this economic logic for rape was the framework of the definition, and since the wife was the husband's property, the husband was not thought to be able to rape his own property. Even if this was imaginable, if it is his property, then it was thought that the husband has the right to utilize his property in any manner that seems fitting. After all, it was his to own, have, and hold.

But social concern, social awareness, and societal demand for action have resulted in important changes in the marital rape exemption in laws within the United States. In 1977, Oregon became the first state to repeal the marital rape exemption (Pagelow 1992; Wiehe and Richards 1995). Since then, many states have examined their laws to assess the marital rape exemption (Pagelow 1992; Wiehe and Richards 1995. Currently, all states hold that a husband can be held guilty of raping his wife.

The lack of public awareness of marital rape can be attributed to the secrecy that surrounds the problem (Finkelhor and Yllo 1995). This secrecy is maintained by most parties familiar with the situation, such as the victim, the rapist, and even extended family members who wish to protect the rapist or who believe that marriage problems should be handled between the two involved (Finkelhor and Yllo 1995). In this case, the marital rapist is nothing less than a marital abuser since in fact rape is an assault (Finkelhor and Yllo 1995). These abusers may keep the victim quiet through intimidation, threats, emotional blackmail, and even manipulative forms of "turning the tables," so to speak, making it seem as if the incident(s) were somehow the victim's fault. In discussing these similarities between standard marital violence and marital rape, Finkelhor and Yllo (1995) have created some distinctions with marital rape. Two of these categories, the battering marital rapist and the force-only marital rapist will be presented to demonstrate the differences in force and rationales presented to explain that use of force.

The battering marital rape is a phenomenon in which marital rape victims experience all the typical trauma from abuse, assault, entrapment, and terror as part of being a battered wife (Finkelhor and Yllo 1995). In these types of marital rape occurrences, the sexual violence is just one aspect of the general abuse that the victim must suffer. Thus, just as other researchers contend, rape in this case is more an assault to exploit, humiliate, and degrade, rather than to just gratify sexual needs. The force-only marital rape, according to Finkelhor and Yllo (1995), is when marital rape also occurs in relationships where rape is mainly the only type of violence utilized. In these cases, the amount of force used is usually the minimum amount necessary for the rapist to accomplish their goal (Finkelhor and Yllo 1995). Though these assaults are just as humiliating and create a sense of powerlessness, the use of other types of force in these cases is limited to just enough to accomplish the sex act.

What is important with respect to the rape act is to understand that in both instances the rape is a humiliating, terrorizing, and degrading experience. This act, whether with excessive or minimal force, employs force and lacks consent. Thus, it is an attack upon the person in either case. Further, the fact that both are married tends to minimize the consent issue in the eyes of much of the public, particularly when minimal force is employed. This rationale allows people to then describe such a scenario as little more than a typical "disagreement" about sex in the marriage. However, this is not the case and the completion of the rape simply provides an avenue for the male rapist to demonstrate his power over his spousal victim. Lastly, it should be noted that the traumatic effects of marital rape are the same for the victim as they are in any other rape situation, showing all the more that rape is an assault, and therefore, an act of violence.

The solution to the problem of marital rape starts with breaking the silence that is attributed to rape. It is commonly accepted that reported rapes represent only a small segment of those that actually occur (Wiehe and Richards 1995). Many wives do not seriously consider their right to say no to sexual advances to apply to their marital relationship. It is important to understand that consent is paramount regardless of the relationship, and that consent must be fully informed. This understanding is the key to preventing marital rape. This right to decline sexual activity is nothing less than an indicator of gender equality within the relationship (Wiehe and Richards 1995). Therefore, it is imperative that social perceptions of marital rape entail both a broader understanding of rape definitions and an increased concern for gender equality in and outside of the marital relationship (Wiehe and Richards 1995). Such factors are necessary precursors if wives are to truly be elevated to an equal status with their husbands.

Group Rape and Gang Rape:
Rape Defined by Number of Perpetrators

Brownmiller (1975) defines group rape as any situation in which two or more men sexually assault one female victim. In many cases, victims of rape have suffered at the hands of two or more assailants (Brownmiller 1975; MacDonald 1995; Schwartz and DeKeseredy 1997). This definition may seem objectionable since some researchers (MacDonald 1995) make a distinction between pair rape and group rape. For the purposes of this chapter, such a distinction will be avoided since the dynamics of both types of rape are essentially the same. With both types, there is a sought after advantage through sheer numbers. The increased numerical odds of multiple assailants acting in methodical unison is proof of brutal intention and the desire to humiliate the victim beyond the act of general rape through a process of mass assault (Brownmiller 1975). The act of group rape forges an alliance among the perpetrators against the victim (Brownmiller 1975). This sense of alliance is seen among group rape perpetrators of both male (such as in prisons) and female victims. For female rape however, the group rape is much more common in the broader society and creates a sense of group anonymity among men. This anonymity exists whether the rape occurs among a group by chance such as at a nightclub, or is the product of a group acting with deliberation such as a violent youth gang.

MacDonald (1995) discusses group rape that occurs among men by chance, giving scenarios that have been commonly experienced by victims. An example might be a young woman at a drinking party who remains after the other women have left. The woman may find that the men take advantage of the situation encouraging and even coercing her to drink while "gently" convincing the woman to have sex with one or even all of them (MacDonald 1995). Though the exact point in which consent can be truly given may vary, the amount of "coercion" and the deliberation to drug the victim can result in nothing less than overt sexual assault.

Further, group rape can often be perpetrated against a victim that is already involved or associated with the group. MacDonald (1995) describes one such pattern among group rapists in which a man who has had prior sexual relations with a woman may deliberately place her in a social situation to get raped. The supposed "boyfriend" will invite the woman to a party and upon arriving, the woman may notice that no other women are present. If concern is expressed, the men will explain that other women are on the way. After some drinking and idle conversation, the woman is forcibly raped by all present except her supposed boyfriend. The other men go through the motions of threatening the boyfriend with some sort of weapon to prevent intervention on behalf of the victim, who often has no idea that that her boyfriend was part of the scheme to begin with. This example clearly demonstrates the level of duplicity that may go into group schemes to commit an act of rape (MacDonald 1995). Through the use of previously discussed rape myths, the use of group thought and rationalizations, the group may find justifications for such an action that only serves as further cement in the sense of alliance held among these perpetrators. Such rationalizations often exist as group subcultural norms that encourage and reward such actions.

To expound on this sense of alliance, is should be noted that group rapes can and often do occur with perpetrators who share an initial bond that leads to their acting together in a sexual assault. While this is widely recognized as a behavior among gang members, there are other socially accepted and supported groups that, perhaps unbeknownst to the supportive public, also have a propensity toward rape (Boumil, Friedman, and Taylor 1993; MacDonald 1995; O'Sullivan 1993; Sanday 1990; Schwartz and DeKeseredy 1997). One type of group, the college fraternity, has developed a notorious reputation for engaging in acts that demean women, including sexual assault (Martin and Hummer 1995; O'Sullivan 1993; Sanday 1990). Some researchers demonstrate that group think and notions of in-group superiority, coupled with group reinforcement of masculine behavior are the base elements that encourage group rape among fraternity members (Boumil, Friedman, and Taylor 1993; MacDonald 1995; O'Sullivan 1993; Sanday 1990; Schwartz and DeKeseredy 1997).

According to Martin and Hummer (1995), valued members of fraternities subscribe to narrow conceptions of masculinity that stress competition, athleticism, dominance, winning, conflict, materialism, ability to drink, and sexual prowess with women. Beyond the basic belief-systems inherent to many fraternities, there are some specific practices that fraternities utilize in their method of committing rape. Two are highly relevant and are hallmarks of fraternity rape; the excessive and manipulative use of alcohol, and the commodification of women (LeBeau and Mozayani 2001; Martin and Hummer 1995; Sanday 1990; Schwartz and DeKeseredy 1997). Both of these components need some illustration.

The use of alcohol by fraternity men is considered part of the group's social norm (Martin and Hummer 1995; Schwartz and DeKeseredy 1997). The use of alcohol to obtain sex from women is a common practice that is used to overcome reluctance among female victims (Martin and Hummer 1995; Sanday 1990). Several researchers have found, through firsthand interviews that alcohol is a major tool used to gain sexual mastery over women (Adams and Abarbanel 1988; Ehrhart and Sandler 1985; Martin and Hummer 1995; Sanday 1990; Schwartz and DeKeseredy 1997). In fraternity gang rape scenarios, many fraternity members make a point to target women who are especially vulnerable to alcohol or who have a drinking problem (LeBeau and Mozayani 2001; Sanday 1990; Schwartz and DeKeseredy 1997). Further, in many fraternity subcultures, such strategies for sex are not considered grounds for a lack of consent and therefore are not seen as rape (Martin and Hummer 1995; Sanday 1990). In fact, many fraternities contend that women who drink with fraternities actually desire such sexual activity but do not wish to be viewed as promiscuous, using the drunken incident as a cover to their deep seated desire to have sex with multiple partners (Sanday 1990).

The commodification of women refers to the practice of knowingly and intentionally using women as bait for new members, as servers of fraternity member's needs, and as sexual prey (Martin and Hummer 1995). Through the use of women as bait, the fraternity entices new members by "showing off" women friendly to the fraternity. The message is clear; join the fraternity and we can provide you access to beautiful women (Martin and Hummer 1995). Using women to serve the fraternity usually comes in the form of the "little sister" program, where such women are expected to attend and hostess fraternity parties and to stay around the fraternity house to make it more appealing (Martin and Hummer 1995). Fraternity men are referred to as "big brothers" and assist "little sisters" with such functions as the sorority rush, but the very names big brother and little sister serve to denote the status and rank of each of these persons within the fraternity/sorority power structure (Martin and Hummer 1995). This is important because it reinforces the masculine sub-cultural norms of many fraternities (Martin and Hummer 1995).

Lastly, little sisters are utilized as a sexual tool (Martin and Hummer 1995; Sanday 1990). Many of these women do not belong to sororities and thus have no peer support to refrain from sex if they should decide, for whatever reason, that they do not wish to engage in sex with a fraternity member (Martin and Hummer 1995; Sanday 1990). The access to women that the little sister system provides and absence of support to refuse sexual advances place these women in a particularly vulnerable position during potential sexual encounters with fraternity men (Martin and Hummer 1995; Sanday 1990).

Thus, fraternity norms and practices can heavily influence members to view the sexual coercion of women as a sport, contest, or a game (Martin and Hummer 1995). Further, some fraternity values serve to reinforce specific practices. Values that include a narrow definition of masculinity, an emphasis on competition, athleticism, dominance, and winning, coupled with the emphasis on sexual prowess with women, can reinforce the likelihood of rape among little sisters or other women desiring affiliation with the fraternity. The use of alcohol to commit rape is likewise reinforced by these value systems (Martin and Hummer 1995; Schwartz and DeKeseredy 1997; Sanday 1990). Given all of these coalescing variables, it should not be surprising that group rape is a potentially common occurrence among some fraternities (Martin and Hummer 1995; Sanday 1990).

Another group that is likely to be implicated in group rape is a sports team (Schwartz and DeKeseredy 1997). When looking at the wider question of rapes and sexual assaults of all types, various researchers agree on the basic notion that there is a social problem with male athletes sexually victimizing women (Schwartz and DeKeseredy 1997). Many of the same factors that affect fraternities are important with athletes as well (MacDonald 1995; Schwartz and DeKeseredy 1997). Much of the heightened propensity toward rape among athletic groups is centered on values of hypermasculinity that devalue men who are weak, equating them with being women (Schwartz and DeKeseredy 1997). In this case, women are essentially spurned and toughness is idealized as the prime concern for being a winner. The use of degrading language describing women, whether from coaches or among athletes in the locker rooms, are thought to create an environment that is charged with rape overtones (Schwartz and DeKeseredy 1997).

The effects of this sub-cultural climate are clearly illustrated by MacDonald (1995) in his description of the Spur Posse, a group of high school athletes in Lakewood, California who attracted national attention in 1991. This group consisted of eight members who were arrested for the rape of at least seven girls, ages ten to sixteen (Kimmel 1993; MacDonald 1995). The members of this group scored a point each time they had sex with a different girl. The top scorer had 66 points (MacDonald 1995). Some girls complained that they agreed to have sex with one member of the posse and were then intimidated into having sex with other members of the group (MacDonald 1995). What is interesting is that some of the parents of these boys defended their acts by blaming the victims. There were even reports that some posse members were congratulated when they returned to their classes (MacDonald 1995).

This example is interesting because it demonstrates how group rape among athletes is directly equated to a point scoring athletic event. This shows how subcultural norms among some athletic groups can pervade the sexual realm as well, construing sex as an "event" based on aggressive competition to win. This of course dehumanizes the victim of such conquest. What is even more tragic is that public support for athletes can then be translated as tacit approval for rape by athletes. This disturbing possibility shows how some group subcultural norms may be nothing more than extreme microcosms of values that are also held, albeit to a less grand scale, by the broader society as a whole.

It is also interesting to note that most incidents of group rape occur at the college level (Schwartz and Keseredy 1997). Thus, the vision of group rape being one committed by unsophisticated gangsters in the urban jungle is overly simplistic and serves to ignore a significant source of danger for many victims. Further, incidents are also known to occur among professional athletes (see *Victoria C. v. The Cincinnati Bengals*, a case involving the group rape of a female by numerous members of this professional football team) and other fraternal organizations such as the U. S. Navy (i.e. Tailhook Scandal involving college educated officers who are expected to demonstrate leadership qualities), demonstrating the prevalence of group rape among men belonging to organizations that emphasize athletic achievement, winning, and competition (Buchwald, Fletcher, and Roth 1993; Kimmel 1993; Schwartz and DeKeseredy 1997). Thus, group rape among athletes is a phenomenon that seems to occur throughout the spectrum of age and education levels, leaving room to speculate that it is perhaps the climate of athletic organizations that can encourage such activity.

The last type of rape to be discussed within this category is the phenomenon of gang rape. MacDonald (1995) points out that informal rituals of adolescent gangs are somewhat similar to puberty rites in primitive societies. In many primitive societies, puberty rites may require the male youth to commit rape to prove his manhood (MacDonald 1995). This idea of gender identification through rape has been cited in various public incidents of gang rape. "Gang bangs" or "trains" are a part of the social life of street gangs and serve as initiation rites and confirmation of loyalty and bonding to the gang (Chancer 1994; MacDonald 1995; Ullman 1999). The attack and gang rape of a young female jogger in New York City's Central Park in April 1989 is discussed by Chancer (1994) and demonstrates the manner in which such gangs may execute such rapes. It is important to note that gang rapes have been found to be characterized by fewer weapons, more night attacks, less victim resistance, and more severe sexual assault outcomes when compared with rapes committed by individuals (Ullman 1999). The distinction between gang rape and group rape may in fact be a bit blurred, but the term gang rape is typically reserved for rapes committed by street gangs who are criminally oriented rather than formal or professional groups who are typically created for purposes outside of the criminal enterprise.

Rape Defined as a War Crime

Rape as a war crime has been well documented throughout history (Allen 1996; Brownmiller 1975; Kadic 1995; Schwendinger and Schwendinger 1983). Some researchers have likened rape during warfare as an economic or political policy, reflecting the general value held of women during warfare (Allen 1996; Brownmiller 1975; Kadic 1995; Schwendinger and Schwendinger 1983). The rape of women is not only a sexual act, but is again an act that is designed to demoralize, humiliate, and degrade its victim and those who care about the victim (Brownmiller 1975; Schwendinger and Schwendinger 1983). Rape when used in war becomes an instrument for terrorizing a conquered population, dominating a racial group, defiling an enemy, and seeking vengeance (Schwendinger and Schwendinger 1983).

Recorded accounts have exposed systematic rape by soldiers throughout history. Brownmiller (1975) provides an excellent historical overview of rape throughout ancient and modern warfare up until the 1970's. Within the work of a number of authors there are numerous written accounts and verbal narratives on rape during any number of wars (Allen 1996; Kadic 1995; Schwendinger and Schwendinger 1983). These reports tell of women who have been humiliated, raped, and murdered in front of their families and communities by invading armies (Allen 1996; Kadic 1995; Schwendinger and Schwendinger 1983).

With rape during warfare, the distinction is the manner in which the act is committed. For instance, when committed in public, there is an obvious motive of fear that is implicated. When done in seclusion, the multiple rapes by numerous soldiers demonstrate a savagery that injures the victim much more tragically than a given incident where a woman has sex with multiple sex partners. This is important, because the manner in which the act is committed exceeds the level of injury and force necessary for these male assaulters to simply gratify their sexual urges. Instead, the act is again designed to accomplish violent purposes of intimidation and humiliation (Allen 1996; Brownmiller 1975).

One of the most atrocious acts of warfare consists of the systematic raping of enemy women known as genocidal rape. Allen (1996) refers to incidents in Bosnia-Herzegovina and Croatia in describing these acts as a military policy of rape for the purpose of genocide. One manner in which this is executed is when Serb forces enter a Bosnian-Herzegovinian or Croatian village, take several women from their homes, rape them in public view, and then depart (Allen 1996; Kadic 1995). Another method of conducting genocidal rape that has been experienced during this war is when Bosnian-Herzegovinian and Croatian women held in Serb concentration camps are chosen at random to be raped, often as a prelude to ultimate death (Allen 1996; Kadic 1995). Yet another manner by which this gruesome act is perpetrated is through the use of rape/death camps (Allen 1996; Kadic 1995). Within these camps, the Serbs raped enemy women systematically for extended periods of time (Allen 1996; Kadic 1995). Such rapes were either part of torture preceding death or part of torture leading to forced pregnancy. Pregnant victims were then raped consistently until their pregnancies had advanced beyond the possibility of a safe abortion and were then released (Allen 1996). Thus, either through death of the victim or the forced pregnancy of a Serb child, the Serbian goal of genocide was perpetrated (Allen 1996). This Serbian war policy considers the child to be Serb and thus an accomplishment toward the genocidal goals of the Serbs (Allen 1996).

One must understand that the ultimate goal of this systematic rape was not sexual in nature, at least not exclusively. The underlying dynamic that motivated these rapes was one of violence and aggression to the enemy. Such violence was a methodical and systematically executed attempt to ultimately displace Serbian enemies. The fact that sexual gratification is included was of course valued by the perpetrators, but the long-term goal of this ghastly form of mass rape was to ultimately exterminate certain races of people. This then demonstrates how genocidal rape is in essence an assault against an entire people.

As was stated earlier in this discussion, rape is one of many acts of violence that humans may engage in. As such, the main distinguishing factor comes in the means of the severity of physical and psychological damage done to the victim (Bourque 1989). In the case of genocidal rape, the ulterior intention is to inflict physical and psychological damage to the specific victim, and to that victim's entire ethnic group. The sexual gratification, while instrumental in partly explaining the rape act, cannot explain such acts of genocidal rape in full. The level of violence and forethought go well beyond that necessary to meet sexual gratification needs. This point is important as it demonstrates the truly violent nature of the rape act itself, rather than emphasizing the sexualized nature of this crime as many rape myths tend to do. Recognition of rape as a form of assault is thus the first step in recognizing the crime against the victim and the actual criminal behavior of the perpetrator.

Conclusion

Sexual assault is a more contemporary term for the crime of rape. Social definitions of rape have been shown to be historically limited and narrow. Public understanding of rape has been affected by a variety of perceptions that demonstrate various biases affected by individual and group social beliefs. The tendency to explain incidents of rape that do not fall within such narrow definitions have become manifest through the form of rape myths. These myths are perpetuated throughout society and fail to acknowledge the varied forms of rape that exist. Further, these myths and their accompanying narrow definitions of rape serve to trivialize the experiences of those who have survived such traumatic and tragic injuries.

Lastly, it is through the clarification of the numerous definitions and distinctions of rape that a true understanding of the blanket term "sexual assault" will occur. This very term serves to denote the assaultive, and thus violent and aggressive nature of rape; being of course, coupled with a sexual component. But it is important for the public to understand that rape is not about simple sexual gratification, but is about the desire to dominate, exploit, and humiliate another person. Failure to acknowledge this is a failure to acknowledge the damage to the survivor that occurs during such trauma inducing experiences. Failure to acknowledge this is nothing less than a failure to acknowledge the victim.

References

Adams, A., and G. Abarbanel. *Sexual Assault on Campus: What Colleges Can Do*. Santa Monica, CA: Rape Treatment Center, 1988.

Allen, B. *Rape Warfare: The Hidden Genocide in Bosnia-Herzegovina and Croatia.*
Minneapolis, MN: University of Minnesota Press, 1996.

Bartol, C. R. *Criminal Behavior: Psychosocial Approach* (5th ed.). Upper Saddle River, NJ: Prentice Hall, 1999.

Benedict, H. "The Language of Rape." In *Transforming a Rape Culture*, eds. E. Buchwald, P. R. Fletcher, and M. Roth. Minneapolis, MN: Milkweed Editions, 1993.

Boumil, M. M., J. Friedman, and B. E. Taylor. *Date Rape: What it is, What it Isn't, What it Does to You, What You Can D About It.* Deerfield Beach, FL: Health Communications, Inc, 1992.

Bourque, L. B. *Defining Rape.* Duke University Press, 1989.

Brownmiller, S. *Against Our Will: Men, Women and Rape.* New York: Simon and Schuster, 1975.

Buchwald, E., P. R. Fletcher, and M. Roth. *Transforming a Rape Culture.* Minneapolis, MN: Milkweed Editions, 1993.

Burt, M. R. "Rape Myths and Acquaintance Rape." *In Acquaintance Rape: The Hidden Crime*, eds. A. Parrot and L. Bechhofer. New York: Wiley-Interscience Publication, 1991.

Chancer, L. "Gender, Class and Race in Three High Profile Crimes: The Cases of New Bedford, Central Park, and Bensonhurst." *Journal of Crime and Justice 17* no. 2 (1994): 167–187.

Chappell, D. *Forcible Rape: A National Survey of the Response by Police (LEAA).* Washington, DC: USPGO, 1977.

Dworkin, A. "I Want a Twenty-Four-Hour Truce During Which There is No Rape." In *Transforming a Rape Culture*, eds. E. Buchwald, P. R. Fletcher, and M. Roth. Minneapolis, MN: Milkweed Editions, 1993.

Ehrhart, J., and B. Sandler. *Campus Gang Rape: Party Games?* Washington, DC: Association of American Colleges, 1985.

Finkelhor, D., and K. Yllo. "Types of Marital Rape." In *Rape and Society: Readings On the Problem of Sexual Assault*, eds. P. Searles and R. J. Berger. Boulder, CO: Westview Press, Inc, 1995.

Groth, A. N. *Men Who Rape: The Psychology of the Offender.* New York: Plenum Press, 1979.

Kadic, Nina. "Dispatch from Bosnia-Herzegovina: A Seventeen-Year-Old Survivor Testifies to Systematic Rape." In *Rape and Society: Readings on the Problems of Sexual Assault*, eds. P. Searles and R. J. Berger. Boulder, CO: Westview Press, Inc, 1995.

Kimmel, M. S. "Clarence, William, Iron Mike, Tailhook, Senator Packwood, Spur Posse, Magic.... and Us." In *Transforming a Rape Culture*, eds. E.

Buchwald, P. R. Fletcher, and M. Roth. Minneapolis, MN: Milkweed Editions, 1993.

Krulewitz, J. E., and E. J. Payne. "Attributions About Rape: Effects of Rapist Force, Observer Sex and Sex Role Attitudes." *Journal of Applied Social Psychology 8*, (1978): 291–305.

LeBeau, M. A., and A. Mozayani. *Drug Facilitated Sexual Assault: A Forensic Handbook*. New York: Academic Press, 2001.

Lerner, M. J. *The Belief in a Just World: A Fundamental Delusion*. New York: Plenum Press, 1980.

MacDonald. *Rape: Controversial Issues*. Springfield, IL: Charles C. Thomas Publisher, 1995.

Martin, P. Y., and R. A. Hummer. "Fraternities and Rape on Campus." In *Rape and Society: Readings on the Problem of Sexual Assault*, eds. P. Searles and R. J. Berger. Boulder, CO: Westview Press, Inc, 1995.

O'Sullivan, C. "Fraternities and the Rape Culture." In *Transforming a Rape Culture*, eds. E. Buchwald, P. R. Fletcher, and M. Roth. Minneapolis, MN: Milkweed Editions, 1993.

Pagelow, M. D. Adult Victims of Domestic Violence: Battered Women. *Journal of Interpersonal Violence 7*, (1992): 87–120.

Paquin, G. W. "The Legal Aspects of Acquaintance Rape." *In Intimate Betrayal: Understanding and Responding to the Trauma of Acquaintance Rape*, eds. V. R. Wiehe, and A. L. Richards. Thousand Oaks, CA: SAGE Publications, 1995.

Parrot, A. and L. Bechhofer. *Acquaintance Rape: The Hidden Crime*. New York: Wiley-Interscience Publication, 1991.

Reid, S. T. *Criminal Law* (2nd ed.). New York: MacMillan Publishing Company, 1992.

Rotter, J. B. "Generalized Expectancies for Internal and External Control of Reinforcement." *Psychological Monographs: General and Applied, 80* no 1, 1966.

Sanday, P. R. "The Socio-Cultural Context of Rape: A Cross-Cultural Study." *Journal of Social Issues 37*, (1981): 5–27.

Sanday, P. R. *Fraternity Gang Rape: Sex, Brotherhood, and Privilege on Campus*. New York: New York University Press, 1990.

Schwartz, M. D., and W. S. DeKeseredy. *Sexual Assault on the College Campus: The Role of Male Peer Support*. Thousand Oaks, CA: SAGE Publications, 1997.

Schwendinger, J. R., and H. Schwendinger. *Rape and Inequality*. Beverly Hills, CA: SAGE Publications, Inc, 1983.

Searles P. and R. J. Berger. *Rape and Society: Readings on the Problem of Sexual Assault*. Boulder, CO: Westview Press, Inc, 1995.

Steinem, G. "Erotica vs. Pornography." In *Transforming a Rape Culture*, eds. E. Buchwald, P. R. Fletcher, and M. Roth. Minneapolis, MN: Milkweed Editions, 1993.

Ullman, S. E. "A Comparison of Gang and Individual Rape Incidents." *Violence and Victims 14* no 2, (1999): 123–133.

U.S. Department of Justice. *Report to the Nation on Crime and Justice: The Data* (2nd ed.). Washington, DC: USGPO, 1988.

Victoria C. v. The Cincinnati Bengals, Inc., et al., Order No. C92-658 (Feb. 24, 1993).

Wiehe, V. R., and A. L. Richards. *Intimate Betrayal: Understanding and Responding to the Trauma of Acquaintance Rape*. Thousand Oaks, CA: SAGE Publications, 1995.

Williams, J. E., and K. A. Holmes. *The Second Assault: Rape and Public Attitudes*. Westport, CT: Greenwood Press, 1981.

Chapter 3

Two Crimes for the Price of One: A Comprehensive Overview of Drug-Facilitated Sexual Assault

Elizabeth Quinn DeValve

Introduction

It has been estimated that about 20 million women living in the United States have been raped in their lifetimes (Kilpatrick, Resnick, Ruggiero, Conoscenti, and McCauley 2007). Kilpatrick et al. reported that about 18 million women were forcibly raped, 3 million were raped with the facilitation of drugs (drug-facilitated sexual assault), and an additional 3 million were raped after self-induced intoxication (or incapacitated rape). Kilpatrick et al. found that in 2006 approximately 1 million women were forcibly raped, 200,000 were victims of drug-facilitated sexual assault, and 300,000 were victims of incapacitated rape. Negrusz, Juhascik, and Gaensslen (2005) determined that 64 out of 100,000 women are raped annually. As of July 1, 2007 there were approximately 153 million females living in the United States (www.census.gov, visited October 8, 2008). This translates to approximately 97,000 women who are raped every year. Though these two estimates are vastly different (1 million versus 97,000) there is sufficient evidence to support the notion that not only is rape a rampant crime, but that substances are not an uncommon factor in the facilitation of rape. This is a relationship worthy of continued and intensive investigation. This chapter will provide the reader with a thorough examination of drug-facilitated sexual assaults (DFSA), including a discussion of the definition of DFSA, estimates of the incidence of this offense, offender characteristics, reactions of victims to DFSA, types of substances commonly associated with DFSA, effects of the substances used to perpetrate DFSA, alterations to the drugs to prevent misuse, and challenges for medical and criminal justice personnel working on the front lines with victims of DFSA.

Definition of Drug-Facilitated Sexual Assault (DFSA)

It would be remiss to begin an examination of drug-facilitated sexual assault without providing a definition for this phenomenon. Probably the most recognized definition, in part due to media attention on the issue, states that drug-facilitated sexual assault occurs when an assailant covertly gives a person a substance for the purpose of impairing the victim's cognitive and/or motor skills rendering them vulnerable to a sexual assault (Negrusz, Juhascik, and Gaensslen 2005). For purposes of discussion, we will call this definition DFSA1. Benyon, McVeigh, McVeigh, Leavey and Bellis (2008) indicate that the common scenario by which one could create a potential victim begins with the surreptitious placement of a date-rape drug into a consumer's drink, thereby rendering that person mentally and/or physically incapable of warding off an assault. Benyon et al. (2008) call this act "drink spiking". Those persons incapacitated as the result of a substance typically do not remember what they did or what happened to them for an extended period of time, but when they do regain "consciousness" they *feel* that something has happened to them or they see evidence that something happened, such as blood in the panties, waking up naked, being sore in the vagina and/or rectum (Abarbanel 2001). The following block quotes describe DFSA1 and common recollections of victims of this crime.

> I went to college on an athletic scholarship. Our team was ranked one of the top three in the country. At my school, the male athletes and the female athletes spent a lot of time together. We were close friends. One night, after studying, one of the star male athletes invited me to a party at his apartment. When I arrived, no one else was there yet. He offered me a glass of wine. The next thing I remember is waking up eight hours later on the floor of this guy's living room. I was on my back, completely naked. Next to me was a used condom. My clothes were rolled up in a ball across the room. I had been raped. Guys were asleep in the other room. They would have had to walk over me to get into their bedroom. They either saw what happened, or maybe they participated (Abarbanel 2001, p. 20).

We sat down at the table and had a drink. I remember the waitress looking at me funny when I tried to order my dinner, as if my speech was impaired. I woke up the next morning in my own bed and I had no idea what had happened after I ordered my dinner, nor how I got home—even though my car was in the driveway and I had driven it to dinner that evening. It felt like I had had sex, but I didn't remember it (personal communication with victim of DFSA, summer of 1998).

Illustrative in these scenarios are feelings of confusion and helplessness—common reactions to rape in general, but also particularly manifest in DFSA (Abarbanel 2001). Additionally, there are other common elements of a DFSA: quick onset of drug side effects, substantial loss of bodily control, lack of memory or very vague memory of events after ingesting the drug,

Numerous researchers support broadening the definition of drug-facilitated sexual assault, to include both surreptitious drugging of a victim *and* incidents in which voluntary consumption of alcohol or drugs results in an altered state in which someone is assaulted. Kilpatrick et al. (2007) define two types of sexual assault where substances are involved in drug-facilitated sexual assault, one, in which the victim is given a drug surreptitiously for the purpose of assault, and two, incapacitated rape, where the victim self-intoxicates and is assaulted while in the altered state. For the sake of discussion, we will label incapacitated rape DFSA2. Alternatively, Abarbanel (2001) references three types of drug-facilitated sexual assaults: 1) involuntary ingestion—in which the victim is drugged unknowingly (DFSA1), 2) mixture of voluntary and involuntary substance ingestion—in which the victim self-intoxicates but is also given a substance of which she is unaware (also known as DFSA3), and 3) voluntary ingestion—in which the victim self-intoxicates and is rendered vulnerable to the assault (Kilpatrick et al.'s incapacitated rape). Negrusz, Juhascik, and Gaensslen (2005) state that regardless of the manner in which DFSA is accomplished individuals who become intoxicated are at greater risk for sexual assault (see also, Kahn, Jackson, Kully, Badger and Halvorsen 2003; Kaysen, Neighbors, Martell, Fossos, and Larimer 2006; Martin and Bachman 1999). Because of the link between alcohol/drugs and sexual assault a broader definition of DFSA will be examined in this chapter as all types of DFSA are considered harmful and in need of serious investigation for the purposes of detection and prevention.

Estimates of DFSA in the United States

The true incidence of rape is unknown. That rape is one of the least reported crimes was confirmed by Kilpatrick et al. (2007) when they found that only 16% of victims reported their rape to a law enforcement agency. In instances of DFSA 1 two crimes are actually being committed—the act of drugging the victim and the act of rape (LeBeau and Mozayani 2001). Furthermore, the victim may never know who committed either act. Because of the anesthetic effect of the drug, the victim may not know if the person who raped her was a date, acquaintance, intimate partner or stranger (Abarbanel 2001). In light of this information it seems logical that victims of drug-facilitated and incapacitated rape were even less likely to report the incidents to the authorities than victims of forcible rape alone (Kilpatrick et al 2007). Common reasons for choosing not to report rape (any type) include: guilt, fear of not being believed, fear of retaliation, police response, uncertainty about whether the incident was a crime and/or if there was enough evidence to support a claim of rape, unable to finger a perpetrator, and not wanting others to know (Abarbanel 2001; Kilpatrick et al. 2007; Tjaden and Thoennes 2006). These reasons are exacerbated when the victim has been raped while mentally and physically incapacitated due to the ingestion of a substance that inhibits motor and cognitive abilities. Offenders do not have to worry about a victim yelling for help or putting up a fight and this makes the act much easier to perpetrate (Abarbanel 2001).

Abarbanel (2001) purports that as of 2001 there hadn't been any systematic examinations of the incidence of DFSA. One additional finding of particular interest was that the Uniform Crime Reports didn't include drug-facilitated sexual assaults in their statistics—they relied solely on reports of forcible rape in which there was the acknowledged use or threat of force toward the victim. Because victims of DFSA are often unable to recall the sexual assault in its entirety or at all they cannot confirm force or the threat of force. The author suggests that in the case of incapacitated rapes, the public may not be as sympathetic to the victim as her self-intoxication may aggravate her level of responsibility for the assault. The lack of research estimating the incidence of DFSA was somewhat corrected in 2005 and later in 2008 by Negrusz, Juhascik, and Gaensslen (2005) and Benyon et al. (2008).

Benyon et al. (2008) set out to examine the prevalence of drug-facilitated sexual assaults as reported in the research literature across disciplines. They concluded that approximately 2% of all alleged DFSA incidents were in fact verifiably DFSAs. Nevertheless, their research highlighted an important point—that alcohol and other drugs (including those drugs known as the "date-rape" drugs) may not stay in the body for a long period of time. Because one of the effects of some of these drugs is amnesia, it may be impossible to really garner a true estimate of DFSAs because of the confusion of the victim and the time element associated with identifying drugs within the system.

Negrusz, Juhascik, and Gaensslen (2005) conducted a study analyzing specimens from subjects undergoing a forensic physical exam in response to a rape/sexual assault at four clinics across the United States. They ran analyses for illegal, prescription, and over-the-counter drugs and found that 61.9% of participants (out of n=144) had substances in their systems. They found that approximately 35.4% of participants who visited the clinics for the forensic exams qualified as DFSA potentials and that 4.9% of the participants had the traditional "date rape drugs" found in their systems. The larger percentage (35.4%) includes both the DFSA1 and DFSA2 definitions (covertly administered drugs and incapacitated rapes).

Garriott and Mozayani (2001) report that in a 1999 publication, Dr. El-Sohly revealed the results of a three-year study on drugs found in urine samples of rape victims who believed they had been drugged and who subsequently underwent forensic medical exams in hospitals. Dr. ElSohly's studied revealed that more than 20 substances were identified in the urine samples of these rape victims. In only 37% were no drugs or alcohol found, meaning that in 63% of the cases there was evidence of some substance in the victims' systems.

Finally, in their study on rape attribution and blame Girard and Senn (2008) found that 3% of the men in their sample acknowledged using drugs or alcohol to induce a woman into having sex and 7% of the women in their sample reported being given drugs and/or alcohol by men for the purpose of having sex with them.

Offender Characteristics: How and Why Do They Do It?

Welner (2001) conducted a study that examined the cases of 34 convicted perpetrators of DFSA. It was found that DFSAs initiated and/or took place in personal residences, businesses, medical establishments, and social settings. Welner (2001) suggests that although the offenders studied varied widely in age, occupation, social circle, and ultimate venue for perpetration, there were four common elements to their offenses: 1) they had access to the drugs necessary to sedate their victims; 2) they had secure settings in which they could conduct the assault uninterrupted; 3) they had the opportunity to commit the crimes by getting their victims alone and/or by exercising some level of control over them; and 4) they recognized that the event was in fact a crime and they attempted to "persuade" the victim (through obfuscation or pleading) to not report the offense, so they might thus avoid a criminal charge. Welner (2001) states that DFSA perpetrators also have well-honed sets of social skills which is one thing they count on when engaging in the perpetration of their crimes. Additionally, they rarely showed remorse after the event, even when confronted by overwhelming evidence of their guilt. They continued to deny to law enforcement and the victim that the act was not consensual. In fact, a common element of DFSA is the lack of physical force, such as beatings and/or use of weapons, used to get the victims into a submissive position. Welner (2001) suggests that despite the low number of subjects in his study, he believes that there is strong evidence supporting the notion that DFSA perpetrators have a high likelihood of reoffending. In regard to why these offenders commit these acts, it was suggested that self-gratification was the cause. They had a lack of regard for other human beings and perceived them as means to ends. DFSA perpetrators were not characterized by an overwhelming amount of lust or fantasies ... their offenses were not about sexual compulsions, but rather more reflective of self-absorption or narcissism.

Effects of Drug-Facilitated Sexual Assault on the Victims

Victims of sexual assault can experience great emotional and physical trauma in the aftermath of the crime. Depression, shame, guilt, anger, and lack of interest in activities that were once important to the victim are common reactions to a sexual assault (Karmen 2007). Representations of physical harm can include bruising, lacerations, permanent physical disabilities (such as the inability to bear children), and the acquisition of sexually transmitted diseases, including HIV. Numerous victims have reported that they feel "dead" and/or that a part of them is changed forever after the rape (Abarbanel 2001). One effect that victims of drug-facilitated sexual assault experience that victims of other types of sexual assault may not is something Abarbanel (2001) calls "mind rape", which is essentially the robbing of the cognitive awareness of the crime and the ability to retrieve memories of the crime afterwards. Though this may seem odd, that DFSA victims would suffer from this lack of memory surrounding the incident, the loss of this cognitive tool inhibits the ability of the DFSA victim to heal as they don't have the ability to talk about components of the rape and to move through them by careful examination with a therapist, clergy person, support group, or support person. The inability to recall information about the incident often prolongs the helplessness they feel as a victim of a "double crime" (Abarbanel 2001).

Substances Used in the Facilitation of Rape/Sexual Assault

An Old Game with a New Twist

Beynon et al. (2008) suggest that the utilization of drugs and/or alcohol to commit a criminal act is rather common and dates well back to the 1800s when persons were drugged with "Mickey Finn specials" in order to facilitate robberies of patrons by bartenders. Similarly, Emmett and Nice (2006) purport that drug-facilitated sexual assault is an old game. The substances that are used in the facilitation have evolved in more recent years; whereas alcohol was the "typical" substance to be used to ply someone into "giving consent" for a long time, now more potent drugs are being used, often in concert with alcohol. Abarbanel (2001) purports that though drugs have been used in the past to make a person vulnerable to victimization (in particular robbery), there was a dramatic change in the 1990s, at which time greater numbers of victims reported being drugged and subsequently raped. Drugs that are well-known in the media as "date rape drugs" include Rohypnol®, GHB, and Ketamine, but these are by no means the only drugs utilized for the facilitation of sexual assault/rape. All substances associated with DFSA typically manifest themselves in at least one of the following three ways: 1) they render the victim unconscious, 2) they impair the victim's memory, or 3) they limit the victim's ability to make decisions (Negrusz, Juhascik, and Gaensslen 2005). This section of the chapter will provide an overview of drugs coined as "date rape drugs" in addition to other substances that are known to be used for drug-facilitated sexual assaults.

Date Rape Drugs

There are three drugs that are commonly known as the "date rape drugs": Rohypnol, Gamma-Hydroxybutrate (GHB), and Ketamine. Rohypnol® and GHB tend to garner the greatest amount of attention, but Ketamine has also been attributed the label of date rape drug. Each of these three drugs will be discussed separately in the following paragraphs.

Rohypnol®

Flunitrazepam, the clinical name of Rohypnol®, is a sedative belonging to the benzodiazepine family, along with Valium and Librium (Emmett and Nice 2006; Robertson and Raymon 2001). Flunitrazepam, similar to other benzodiazepines, was manufactured in the 1970s as an anesthetic and anxiety reducer. Rohypnol® is said to be "ten times more potent" than other sedatives (Emmett and Nice 2006 p. 228). According to Emmett and Nice (2006) it is manufactured in the Europe and is prescribed on the short-term for insomnia. Rohypnol® produces anterograde amnesia when administered at the right dose. Anterograde amnesia results in the individual failing to remember what occurred for a period of time, which could mean that when used in a DFSA the victim may not be able to identify the perpetrator or describe the actual crime that occurred. Nesgrusz (2003) found that a single 2 mg dose of flunitrazepam remains detectable in the urine for up to five days, and its highest concentration was between six-24 hours after ingestion. Additionally, it was found that it was still detectable in hair at one month. Robertson and Raymon (2001) stated that Rohypnol® has never been approved for use by the FDA. The pill comes in either green or white and has a blue core. The word "ROCHE" is imprinted on the pill along with a number 1 or 2, indicating the dosage amount of that particular pill and is commonly called a "roofie". The drug takes effect within approximately 30 minutes and can last up to eight hours, with a peak at two hours (Emmett and Nice 2006). Persons under the influence of flunitrazepam may experience "symptoms of intoxication, sedation, loss of inhibitions, loss of motor control, dizziness and confusion" (Emmett and Nice 2006, p. 231). Side effects also include a dramatically impaired memory or no memory at all of a period of time post-ingestion.

In both the United States of America and the United Kingdom, Rohypnol® has found a following in the dance club scene as it is often used to ease the symptoms of stimulants such as cocaine or ecstasy (Emmett and Nice 2006). It has also been reported to be sold as an aid to facilitate one in perpetrating nonconsensual sex (Emmett and Nice 2006). Dealers typically procure their supplies from persons to whom the drug has been prescribed legally. Additionally, a number of Internet sites provide the drug for sale as well (Emmett and Nice 2006). Robertson and Raymon (2001) reported that the evidence suggests that Rohypnol® is not used as widely as the media might imply. In one study, Rohypnol® was found in urine samples of six out of 1033 alleged rape victims and that alcohol, marijuana and other benzodiazepines were found to a substantially greater degree (Robertson and Raymon 2001). The same authors stated that flunitrazepam has been found more often in the urine samples of DUI drivers and appears to be used more for its "intoxicating effects" than for DFSA (p. 100). A study by Dr. Mahmoud ElSohly found that over a three-year period Rohypnol® was found in only 0.3% of alleged rape victims who underwent forensic medical exam in emergency rooms (Garriott and Mozayani 2001).

In 1998, the manufacturer of Rohypnol® added a blue dye to the tablet which dissolves in a potential victim's beverage, thus warning her that her drink has been altered (Pope and Shoudice 2001; Robertson and Raymon 2001). Additionally, a white scum or cloudy appearance forms in drinks as well, further warning the potential drinker that someone has tampered with the beverage (Emmett and Nice 2006). Emmett and Nice (2006) state, however, that counterfeit versions of the drug do not have these safety features.

GHB

Gamma-hydroxybutrate (GHB) (marketed as Xyrem®) was developed in the 1960s to be used "as an anesthetic and hypnotic agent" (Ferrera, Frison, Tedeschi, and LeBeau 2001, p. 107). Whereas GHB use is no longer allowed in Europe, the United States continues to utilize this drug to treat narcolepsy and cataplexy (Emmett and Nice 2006; Ferrera et al. 2001). When used to facilitate a sexual assault GHB use results in a decrease in inhibitions and may produce euphoria, an increase in one's libido, and relaxation at lower doses and unconsciousness and subsequent amnesia with higher doses (Emmett and Nice 2006). Ferrera et al. (2001) suggest that a bystander might think the person under the influence of GHB is simply drunk from alcohol. Additionally, because one may experience amnesia as a result of taking this drug, this would render that individual virtually unable to identify her rapist and/or determine if a rape had occurred in the first place.

GHB circulates throughout the body very quickly, remaining in the urine for a mere 12 hours and in the blood for eight hours (Ferrera et al. 2001; Pope and Shouldice 2001). Another complicating factor with this drug is that it is a naturally occurring drug in the human body, thus as time goes by it is often impossible to distinguish "foreign" GHB from "native" GHB (Ferrera et al. 2001). The effects of GHB intake can be seen in 10–15 minutes after ingestion, but may wear off within 3–4 hours—a somewhat shorter time span than Rohypnol®. There are still a number of forensic labs that do not have the tools needed to detect GHB in the urine or blood, so even if a specimen is collected within the short window in which it is detectable the lab used to evaluate the specimen must have the test needed to discover it. In a study by Dr. ElSohly (previously referred to) GHB was found in 3% of forensic medical exams following alleged sexual assaults over a three-year period (Garriott and Mozayani 2001).

GHB is almost exclusively found in liquid form and resembles water (Emmett and Nice 2006). It is sometimes called "liquid ecstasy" or "liquid X". Other nicknames, more related to DFSA, include "Easy Lay" and "Scoop Her". Ferrera et al. (2001) purport that it is fairly easy to create GHB and there are several recipes for the drug scattered across the Internet. Similar to Rohypnol®, GHB is very popular in the club scene both in the UK and the US, thus many people take it voluntarily to experience a pleasant state of euphoria, relaxation, sensuality, and placidity (Ferrera et al. 2001). Dissimilar to Rohypnol® the manufacturers of GHB have not added any safety measures for unknowing victims to detect the drug in their drinks. However, Emmett and Nice (2006) suggest that there are some companies who have created kits by which people can detect GHB in their drinks on their own.

Ketamine

Ketamine hydrochloride (Ketamine) was developed in the early 1960s and is used primarily as an anesthetic for both humans and animals (Emmett and Nice 2006). It is found in many forms including powder, liquid, tablet, capsule and crystal. The effects of Ketamine include a "cocaine-like euphoria" which increases the blood pressure and pulse and may also include amnesia—a characteristic attractive to perpetrators of DFSA (Emmett and Nice 2006). One side effect different from Rohypnol® and GHB is that humans sometimes experience hallucinations after taking Ketamine. In regular medical practice, children are the most likely of human subjects to take the drug as the hallucinogenic effects are not as prevalent in that population (Emmett and Nice 2006).

Ketamine is commonly snorted when taken voluntarily. It can be taken orally via tablet or capsule or smoked with tobacco or marijuana. It can also be injected, but this is the least likely method by which voluntary users ingest the drug. It may take up to 20 minutes for the effects to be felt and it lasts between three to four hours. Common nicknames for Ketamine include "Special K", "Vitamin K", Kit-Kat, ket, jet, super acid, and cat valium.

The United States Congress implemented the *Drug Induced Rape Prevention and Punishment Act* (1996) in an effort to increase penalties for the use of drugs to facilitate sexual assault (Benyon et al. 2008). In particular, drug traffickers in flunitrazepam were to receive a 20 year prison sentence and those in possession of the drug (namely buyers) could receive up to a 3 year prison sentence (Benyon et al. 2008).

Alcohol

The most commonly used substance to assist perpetrators with conducting a sexual assault is alcohol (Girard and Senn 2008). Benyon et al. (2008) found that alcohol was far and above the most frequently detected substance in the bodily systems of sexual assault victims and the implication is that it is still the most widely used "date rape drug". Dr. ElSohly's study (referred to previously) found that alcohol was detected in 40% of urine samples of rape victims—by far the most representative substance associated with sexual assault (as seen in Garriott and Mozayani 2001). Ullman, Karabatsos, and Koss (1999) suggest that alcohol is involved in approximately 33–66% of rape cases. The authors further suggest that alcohol can be used in three different ways to increase the likelihood of a sexual assaulted influenced by alcohol—1) the offender may become more aggressive due to decreased inhibitions, 2) victim use of alcohol may lead to less forceful resistance efforts, and 3) victim alcohol use may occur in settings where there is a higher risk of an attack. In fact, the authors found that victims may have been more vulnerable targets to motivated offenders simply because of their inebriated states and perceived reduction in their ability to ward off an attack (Ullman, Karabatsos, and Koss 1999; see also, Kaysen et al. 2006; Ullman 2003). Garriott and Mozayani (2001) state that alcohol is often found in the bodily systems of *both* victims and perpetrators. In addition, Martin and Bachman (1999) found that the ingestion of alcohol by the perpetrator of a rape increased the likelihood of injury suffered by the victim. They posited that this may be due to a decrease in inhibitions of the perpetrator and/or the inability of an inebriated victim to fight back. In an examination of characteristics of rape victims presenting in emergency rooms it was found that victims who had used alcohol or drugs in a social setting were more prone to sexual violence by just-met acquaintances and that perhaps the ability of the victim to detect the potential for harm and/or respond to threatening behavior becomes compromised (Logan, Cole, and Capillo 2007). Kaysen et al. (2006) found that those who typically drank more were more likely to be a rape victim than those who drank less. Additionally, those who experienced an incapacitated rape (DFSA2) were more likely to increase their drinking after the incident as well.

Alcohol, as the primary substance involved in the DFSA, would be most associated with the DFSA2 definition of drug-facilitated sexual assault as the rape victims are most likely to ingest this substance voluntarily (Garriott and Mozayani 2001). The fact that alcohol is consumed voluntarily contributes to feelings of guilt and/or righteous blame for a DFSA survivor and leads to fewer numbers of reports to law enforcement (Cameron and Strizke 2003; Girard and Senn 2008; Kahn et al. 2003). Additionally, Kahn et al. (2003) suggest that alcohol use by the victim may contribute to the lack of identification of the incident as a sexual assault because victims blame themselves for not being able to adequately resist. The following block quotes provide examples of the state of mind of the victims who do not label their incidents as rape:

> He took me to his bedroom and I layed down because I was tired but then he got on top of me and started kissing me … Then he started going a little further, and before I knew it he was taking my clothes off. I remember thinking that I didn't really didn't want to continue, but

I couldn't really do anything to stop him. I was so drunk it just seemed pointless to argue, or to put up any fight ... (Kahn et al. 2003, 240–241). We were drunk. I didn't have control over myself and I didn't have the cognitive ability to say NO. I can't remember everything, but I know we had sex and if I were sober it would not have happened. I just could not control myself at all (Kahn et al. 2003, 241).

The effects of alcohol include decreased inhibitions, impaired perceptions, and possibly amnesia and/or loss of consciousness (meaning the victim may have no memory of the event and/or the perpetrators and is easy to physically manipulate due to decreased motor functioning). Alcohol is also the most common substance to which other drugs used to facilitate sexual assaults can be added.

It is gratifying to know that in one study (Girard and Senn 2008) participants attributed a high degree of blame to perpetrators who surreptitiously gave drugs to female victims or plied them with an overabundance of alcohol for the purpose of committing a sexual assault. However, it was confirmed that individuals who voluntarily ingested illicit drugs themselves or got themselves drunk were still held highly responsible for being raped.

Additional Drugs Associated with DFSA

Other drugs that have the potential to be used as date rape drugs and/or have been proven to be used as date rape drugs include Phencyclidine (PCP), Ecstasy, Opioids (including, but not limited to: morphine, codeine, and temazepam) and prescription and over-the-counter medications.

PCP is related to Ketamine and is well known for its ability to impair individual's speech, thought processes, attention and memory. These characteristics make it attractive as a date rape drug as the victim likely will not remember the perpetrator and/or the event, may be physically challenged and thus unable to resist, and finally may not be able to assess danger and be able to ward off an attack because of the altered state (Raymon and Robertson 2001). However, PCP may also induce psychosis which would make a potential victim an unattractive prospect for a sexual assault because of the unpredictability of the person's behavior (Negrusz, Juhascik, and Gaensslen 2005). Negrusz, Juhascik, and Gaensslen (2005) analyzed 144 cases to assess for a number of different drugs that could be used in a DFSA. They initially found one case positive for PCP in their sample of 144 rape victims, but upon a secondary test the confirmation was negative. It was stated that another drug was also found in the system which could have interfered with the detection of PCP.

Ecstasy was created by Merck in 1912 and was used for its psychotherapeutic effects (Pope and Shouldice 2001). It creates a feeling of euphoria and contributes to a decrease in inhibitions. The effects of Ecstasy begin approximately 30–60 minutes after ingestion with peak effects between 1–5 hours and symptoms maintaining up to eight hours (Pope and Shouldice 2001). Negrusz, Juhascik, and Gaensslen (2005) did not find any cases of Ecstasy in their sample of 144 rape victims. They posited that because it is a stimulant it may not necessarily be a good option for a date rape drug; however, they did note that because Ecstasy could compromise a person's sense of reality, this may make the individual an easier target for sexual assault.

Jufer and Jenkins (2001) indicate that opioids can produce sedation and muscle relaxation, two elements essential to successful DFSA. In addition, they state that there are studies that support the notion that opioids may also affect one's memory. Because opioids decrease the pain sensation, resistance may be less likely when under the influence of this group of drugs. Jufer and Jenkins (2001) confirm that opioids have been used to facilitate sexual assault. Negrusz, Juhascik, and Gaensslen (2005) found 14 cases of confirmed opiates in the specimens of rape victims in their study. None of the participants admitted to voluntarily ingesting any drug in the opioid family which suggests that these drugs may have been used to facilitate sexual assault.

Jones and Singer (2001) state that prescription and over-the-counter medications can have one of a number of properties believed to be attractive to perpetrators of DFSA. Prescription and over-the-counter medications can produce sedation and amnesia as side effects, may be odorless and tasteless, may dissolve easily in alcohol and are easily absorbed into the system in relatively short periods of time (between 10–30 minutes) which make them ideal choices for DFSA. Negrusz, Juhascik, and Gaensslen (2005) found that approximately 28% of the subjects in their study tested positive for prescription or over-the-counter medications. Whether or not this contributed to the sexual assault was not clear. Moore and Valverde (2000) point out that in the mid 1990s a rapist offending in the Toronto area used Halcion® to drug his hundreds of victims and that in the current dialogue this would not have been classified as a "date-rape drug".

Whether taken purposely or given to a victim surreptitiously it is clear that because of the potential for sedation and possible memory impairment possible from taking these groups of drugs that they should be included in the discussion of date rape drugs. The overview provided in this section detailing the potential for abuse of substances other than the three drugs coined "date rape drugs" illustrates the need for society to broaden its definition of date rape drugs and provide both education to the public about the potential for harm from all substances and also increase the ability of labs to detect drugs that may be used for the purposes of sexual assault.

Additionally, Benyon et al. (2008) suggest that public health campaigns that focus solely on warning individuals of the possibility of a drug being dropped into a drink and thus making the individual vulnerable to a sexual assault are perhaps dangerously misleading. Whereas the authors recognize the importance of these public health campaigns, they suggest that it is even more important to inform the public of the dangers of voluntary alcohol and/or drug consumption as the research supports the notion that more people are victims of DFSA through voluntary consumption versus surreptitious consumption. Similarly, Moore and Valverde (2000) submit that we should be wary of "believing the hype" surrounding certain drugs acquiring the label of "date rape drug", particularly because of the lack of empirical evidence suggesting that this group of drugs is significantly more likely to be used in drug-facilitated sexual assaults.

Challenges to Medical Personnel, Investigators and Prosecution

Probably one of the biggest challenges to medical personnel in the detection of DFSA is the inability to detect all substances that can be used to facilitate sexual assault. Numerous studies found that when forensic rape kits are submitted for analysis the person submitting the test must be certain that the lab to which the kit is sent has the capability to test for the drugs that are considered likely for each individual case (Archambault, Porrata, and Sturman 2001). Because of the lack of memory experienced by many victims of DFSA, they may not be able to assist medical personnel in narrowing down the potential list of substances that could have been used to incapacitate the victim.

Some of the challenges for criminal justice agents when both investigating and attempting to prosecute DFSA cases include: potential for non-reporting or limited cooperation for fear of getting in trouble for voluntary illicit drug use, the lack of memory of the victim, and the lack of empathy for victims of DFSA by society members when voluntary substance use may have led to the inability to anticipate or prevent the rape. Negrusz, Juhascik, and Gaensslen (2005) stated that victims may perceive a large obstacle to reporting a DFSA to law enforcement if they were using illegal drugs at or around the time of the assault. Victims may be asked to supply a urine sample so it can be tested for date rape drugs, but they may fear being charged with a drug crime if the illegal drug they were using is also tested for and shows up on the urine analysis. Abarbanel (2001) stated that a victim may not be able to report the crime to police because of the lack of a clear memory of the event … she may believe that she doesn't have sufficient evidence of an assault to justify a police report. Additionally, if the victim voluntarily drank alcohol there may be feelings of shame or guilt that will prevent them from reporting an offense because they may feel partially responsible. A study by Wiley found that if a victim couldn't remember the event it negatively affected the outcome of the case (presumably that the defendant was not convicted because the jury questioned the veracity of the victim's testimony) (as seen in Negrusz, Juhascik, and Gaensslen 2005). Furthermore, LeBeau and Mozayani (2001) stated that victims of DFSA have limited abilities to assist in trials against their offender(s) because of the lack of memory. When victims are the main witnesses used by the prosecution victims of DFSA are at a severe disadvantage in court. Finally, attributions of blame tend to land on the victim when she is intoxicated (Cameron and Stritzke 2003; Marx, Van Wie, and Gross 1996). If a victim was inebriated at the time of the assault some people believe she made herself "fair game" by not staying alert and aware of her surroundings (Marx, Van Wie, and Gross 1996). Lack of memory, trepidation about reporting the crime, and the lack of public (and specifically jury) support add complicating elements to a crime that is already difficult to prove in the first place. This leaves victims of DFSA in the dark … perhaps without the ability to gain some closure on the event.

Archambault, Porrata and Sturman (2001) suggest that criminal justice personnel need to be particularly attentive and nonjudgmental when working with victims of DFSA. They purport that the victim may not "seem" as if she is troubled by the offense, but she may be dealing with two important realities: 1) that she likely doesn't know exactly what happened to her, and 2) that she still may be under the influence of the drug administered to facilitate the sexual assault in the first place. It is important for people talking with the victim (dispatchers, police officers, rape crisis counselors) to recognize that she may still be under the influence of the drug and it may affect the way she behaves. Additionally, it was suggested that victims be informed that they will not be prosecuted for their own illegal drug use and that officers be aware that in DFSA physical force and/or the threat of force is unlikely to have happened.

Kerlin, Riviera, and Paterson (2001) suggest that in order for DFSA cases to be more successfully investigated and prosecuted in the future there needs to be focused efforts at educating law enforcement and prosecutors, as to how to investigate and prosecute a DFSA case, and the community as to the characteristics of a DFSA and the types of drugs that can be used so that they do not prejudge the victim due to a lack of understanding about the unique issues involved in a DFSA.

Conclusion

If you take only one thing with you after reading this chapter it should be this: drug-facilitated sexual assault is larger than the stereotypical scenario proposed by the media in which a woman is slipped one of three potential date rape drugs into her drink and is subsequently raped. DFSA is a serious crime or set of crimes that may not comport to any specific example. If we are short-sided in our understanding of DFSA we could aid in the revictimization of its victims.

References

Abarbanel, G. (2001). The Victim. In *Drug-Facilitated Sexual Assault: A Forensic Handbook*, by M.A. LeBeau and A. Mozayani (Eds.), pp. 1–38. San Diego, CA: Academic Press.

Archambault, J., Porrata, T., and Sturman, P. (2001). Investigating DFSA cases. In *Drug-Facilitated Sexual Assault: A Forensic Handbook*, by M.A. LeBeau and A. Mozayani (Eds.), pp. 253–272. San Diego, CA: Academic Press.

Benyon, C.M., McVeigh, C, McVeigh, J., Leavey, C., and Bellis, M.A. (2008). The Involvement of Drugs and Alcohol in Drug-Facilitated Sexual Assault. *Trauma, Violence, and Abuse, 9* (3), 178–188.

Cameron, C.A. and Stritzke, W.G.K. (2003). Alcohol and Acquaintance Rape in Australia: Testing the Presupposition Model of Attributions About Responsibility and Blame. *Journal of Applied Social Psychology, 33*(5), 985–1008.

Emmett, D. and Nice, G. (2006). *Understanding Street Drugs: A Handbook of Substance Misuse for Parents, Teachers, and Other Professionals* (2nd ed.). London: Jessica Kingsley Publishers.

Ferrera, S.D., Frison, G., Tedeschi, L., and LeBeau, M. (2001). Gamma-Hydroxybutyrate (GHB) and related products. In *Drug-Facilitated Sexual Assault: A Forensic Handbook*, by M.A. LeBeau and A. Mozayani (Eds.), pp. 107–126. San Diego, CA: Academic Press.

Garriott, J.C. and Mozayani, A. (2001). Ethanol. In *Drug-facilitated Sexual Assault: A Forensic Handbook*, by M.A. LeBeau and A. Mozayani (Eds.), pp. 73–88. San Diego, CA: Academic Press.

Girard, A.L. and Senn, C.Y. (2008). The Role of the New "Date Rape Drugs" in Attributions About Date Rape. *Journal of Interpersonal Violence, 23*(1), 3–20.

Jones, G. and Singer, P. (2001). Miscellaneous Prescription and Over-The-Counter Medications. In *Drug-Facilitated Sexual Assault: A Forensic Handbook*, by M.A. LeBeau and A. Mozayani (Eds.), pp. 173–196. San Diego, CA: Academic Press.

Jufer, R.A. and Jenkins, A.J. (2001). Opioids. In *Drug-Facilitated Sexual Assault: A Forensic Handbook*, by M.A. LeBeau and A. Mozayani (Eds.), pp. 149–172. San Diego, CA: Academic Press.

Kahn, A.S., Jackson, J., Kully, C., Badger, K., and Halvorsen, J. (2003). Calling it Rape: Differences in Experiences of Women Who Do or Do Not Label Their Sexual Assault as Rape. *Psychology of Women Quarterly, 27*, 233–242.

Karmen, A. (2007). Crime Victims: An Introduction to Victimology. Cengage Publishing.

Kaysen, D., Neighbors, C., Martell, J., Fossos, N, and Larimer, M.E. (2006). Incapacitated Rape and Alcohol Use: A Prospective Analysis. Addictive *Behaviors, 31*, 1820–1832.

Kerlin, K., Riveira, D.M., and Paterson, S.J. (2001). In *Drug-Facilitated Sexual Assault: A Forensic Handbook*, by M.A. LeBeau and A. Mozayani (Eds.), pp. 273–300. San Diego, CA: Academic Press.

Kilpatrick, D.G., Resnick, H.S., Ruggiero, K.J., Conoscenti, L.M., & McCauley, J. (2007). *Drug-facilitated, Incapacitated, and Forcible Rape: A National Study.* Charleston, SC: Medical University of South Carolina.

LeBeau M. and Mozayani, A. (2001). Collection of evidence from DFSA. In *Drug-Facilitated Sexual Assault: A Forensic Handbook*, by M.A. LeBeau and A. Mozayani (Eds.), pp. 197–210. San Diego, CA: Academic Press.

Logan, T.K., Cole, J., and Capillo, A. (2007). Differential Characteristics of Intimate Partner, Acquaintance and Stranger Rape Survivors Examined by a Sexual Assault Nurse Examiner (SANE). *Journal of Interpersonal Violence, 27*(8), 1066–1076.

Martin, S.E. and Bachman, R. (1998). The Contribution of Alcohol to the Likelihood of Completion and Severity of Injury in Rape Incidents. *Violence Against Women, 4*(6), 694–712.

Marx, B.P., Van Wie, V., and Gross, A.M. (1996). Date Rape Risk Factors: A Review and Methodological Critique of the Literature. *Aggression and Violent Behavior, 1*(1), 27–45.

Moore, D. and Valverde, M. (2000). Maidens at risk: 'date rape drugs' and the formation of Hybrid Risk Knowledges. *Economy and Society, 29*(4), 514–531.

Negrusz, A., Juhascik, M., & Gaensslen, R.E. (2005). Estimate of the Incidence of Drug-Facilitated Sexual Assault in the U.S. Chicago, IL: Department of Biopharmaceutical Sciences, College of Pharmacy, University of Illinois at Chicago.

Pope, E. and Shouldice, M. (2001). Drugs and Sexual Assault: A review. *Trauma, Violence, and Abuse, 2*(1), 51–55.

Raymon, L. and Robertson, M. (2001). Hallucinogens. In *Drug-Facilitated Sexual Assault: A Forensic Handbook*, by M.A. LeBeau and A. Mozayani (Eds.), pp. 127–148. San Diego, CA: Academic Press.

Robertson, M. and Raymon, L. (2001). Rohypnol® and other benzodiazepines. In *Drug-Facilitated Sexual Assault: A Forensic Handbook*, by M.A. LeBeau and A. Mozayani (Eds.), pp. 89–106. San Diego, CA: Academic Press.

Tjaden, P & Thoennes, N. (2006). Extent, Nature, and Consequences of Rape Victimization: Findings from the National Violence Against Women Survey. Special Report. Washington, D.C.: National Institute of Justice and the Centers for Disease Control and Prevention.

Ullman, S.E. (2003). A Critical Review of Field Studies on the Link of Alcohol and Adult Sexual Assault in Women. *Aggression and Violent Behavior, 8*, 471–483.

Ullman, S.E., Karabatsos, G., and Koss, M.P. (1999). Alcohol and Sexual Assault in a National Sample of College Women. *Journal of Interpersonal Violence, 14*(6), 603–625.

Welner, M. (2001). The Perpetrators and Their *Modus Operandi*. In *Drug-Facilitated Sexual Assault: A Forensic Handbook*, by M.A. LeBeau and A. Mozayani (Eds.), pp. 39–72. San Diego, CA: Academic Press.

Part I: The Crime

Suggested Questions, Activities and Videos

Discussion Questions:

1. Discuss one rape myth in particular that you think people may believe, and what might result from believing that false information.
2. Provide some solutions for debunking public belief in rape myths?
3. Summarize the various types of DFSA.

Suggested Activities:

- Find a sex crime case that was covered in the local media. Have the class discuss the case in terms of rape myths. (My use was a local case entitled: *Teen Accused of Raping Elderly Woman*).
- Ask the class if they can give any examples of a rape myth presented as fact. Send them out for a week, hunting for such examples in life or in the popular and news media.
- Have students draft a letter to the editor of a local paper explaining the dangers to the public regarding the belief in one of the rape myths.
- Create an information program or brochure regarding drug facilitated sexual assault that could be delivered to targeted groups on campus or in the community.
- Look into the various programs and information your campus or community provides regarding sexual assault. Bring that information back into the class for discussion and sharing. Is there any vital information that the community is missing?

Suggested Videos:

- Date Rape: A Violation of Trust: Cambridge Educational
- Nonconsensual Sexuality: Films for the Humanities and Sciences
- It's Not About Sex: Educational VideoCenter

Part II

The Victims

In the Words of a Rape Survivor

"One thing I always think about being a victim, now a survivor, I live a life sentence. Once I was a victim the first time I was stripped of my freedom. I haven't gotten that back in my fifty years. **Freedom**. They walk the streets and I live a life sentence. I'll live it to the day I die—I can't shake it."

"When both rapes happened, I learned the impact of **fear**—there was a knife in the first one and the second was physically violent so … I'm always worrying 'what if'… so I try to avoid it at all costs."

"**Knowledge**—the more I would try to learn and read, the more I learned about rape. I would pick up bits and pieces. I would learn I was normal. Knowledge is the one thing that saved me."

"When a rape is reported, someone has to step in who can be **strong** for that person, because that person's not strong."

"You're kind of like a **leper**, too, if you've been raped."

KC
50 years of age
Survivor of 2 rapes—one at 14, one in her thirties

Chapter 4

Victim Response to Sexual Assault

Diane M. Daane

Introduction

How a victim responds to a sexual assault depends on many different factors. The reaction will be affected by her age, life situation, personality, the circumstances of the rape, the response from those with whom she comes in contact immediately after the assault, the response of her family and friends, the response of the criminal justice system, and her own attitudes about rape. Many survivors have adopted society's traditional attitudes about rape, including many of the myths. If she believes in these myths, she may have greater difficulty understanding and integrating the rape into her life experiences.

Males and females can be sexual assault victims. Since the majority of known rape victims are female, and the majority of research involves female victims, the victim in this paper will be referred to by pronouns normally used to indicate a female. This is not intended to either deny the existence of male survivors or to trivialize the trauma experienced by male rape victims. However, information specific to male survivors is included. Limited research indicates that the responses of male victims of sexual violence are similar to the responses of female victims (Frazier 1993). The perpetrator will also be referred to as male for the same reasons.

Coping Behaviors at the Time of the Assault

Victim response before and during the actual attack also varies. Burgess and Holmstrom (1976) identified basic coping strategies used by sexual assault victims before the attack. The first strategy is cognitive assessment, which is where the victim copes with the threatened sexual assault by assessing the situation and determining possible alternatives. This may include looking for a means of escape or a plan to fight back, but most often it involves planning to remain calm so that the attacker does not panic and injure or kill the victim in response to her actions. The second coping strategy used by sexual assault victims before the attack involves verbal tactics, such as stalling for time or trying to talk their way out of the assault. Many victims try to reason with their attackers attempting to change their minds. Some victims try to gain sympathy from their assailant by telling him that they are pregnant or sick. Other victims use flattery, joking, sarcasm, and verbal aggression to prevent the attack. Another verbal strategy is to tell the rapist that someone is coming soon, or that the victim's brother, father, or boyfriend will find him and kill or hurt him. The majority of coping behaviors are verbal. The last coping strategy used before the attack identified by Burgess and Holmstrom is physical action. Physical action includes both physical resistance as well as running away.

There has been much debate over physical resistance by rape victims. Common law rape required victims to resist with all of their strength throughout the assault. Modern law has made significant changes in rape law, but many states still require some resistance by the victim as a measure of force used by the perpetrator. Many rape victims do not fight back physically because they fear that it will escalate the violence and result in greater injury to them. Ullman (1998) found that the type of resistance used by the victim matches the type of force used by the assailant. Physical resistance is more likely to be used by victims who are threatened with weapons or where the offender uses physical force initially. Gidycz, Van Wynsberghe, and Edwards (2008) suggest that offender aggression, as well as a victim's prior intent to use physical resistance if assaulted, predict the use of physical resistance strategies in response to an assault. The use of verbal resistance may be predicted by perpetrator aggression and whether the victim has had any previous sexual victimization (Gidycz et al.).

Research indicates that women who physically fight back in response to the perpetrator's physical attack may experience less severe sexual abuse without suffering any greater injury than women who do not physically resist (Ullman 1998). Offender violence during and after the attack is related to the initial force used by the perpetrator rather than the resistance by the victim. Victim resistance in response to verbal or physical attacks may not lead to increased offender violence after the rape (Ullman).

While there may be an emphasis on physical resistance, research has consistently indicated that rape completion is less likely with almost any form of resistance (Tark and Kleck 2004). However, when looking at reducing the probability of injury rather than at rape completion, Bachman, Saltzman, Thompson, and Carmody (2002) found that non-physical forms of resistance were more effective than either no resistance or physical resistance. It is important to remember that a victim who survives sexual assault responded appropriately. No amount of second-guessing can replicate the circumstances of the assault.

Many rape victims experience tonic immobility during their contact with their attacker (Galliano, Noble, Travis, and Puechl (1993). Tonic immobility "is an unlearned state of profound motor inhibition typically elicited by a high-fear situation that involves threat and/or restraint." (Galliano et al. p.110). Responses during tonic immobility include a catatonic-like posture, cessation of vocalization, tremors, periods of eye closure, a decrease in heart-rate, and an increase in body temperature and respiration. Gidycz, Van Wynsberghe, and Edwards (2008) found that immobility during an assault was predicted by experiences of childhood sexual victimization or other previous sexual victimization. Tonic immobility has rarely been studied in humans, but has been linked to the immobility response experienced by many victims during a rape (Galliano et al.).

Earlier research referred to a similar response known as traumatic psychological infantilism (Symonds 1976). Psychological infantilism is induced by terror and results in helplessness that makes the victim appear friendly and cooperative. The victim experiencing psychological infantilism, also known as frozen fright response, will submit to the attacker in order to avoid being killed. Unfortunately, the victim's partner, family, friends, the police, hospital staff, crisis interveners, and even the victim may misinterpret this response. The survivor who misunderstands her own response during the rape itself may blame herself for her victimization and have a more difficult time recovering from the experience.

Some victims feel anger as well as fright, but normally if there is any hope for survival, fright will override anger and the victim will engage in submitting behavior (Symonds 1976). Anger may be shown through active or passive resistance. When anger is repressed we see passive resistance patterns that appear in the form of crying, slowness to obey commands, and the appearance that they are unable to understand exactly what is demanded of them. Passive patterns of resistance also include verbal attempts to make the rapist feel guilty or to appeal to his conscience in order to coerce him to cease the attack (Symonds).

Active patterns of resistance attempt to produce in the attacker a fear of being hurt or apprehended. Since active, physical aggression has traditionally been socially disapproved for women, the rape victim's active patterns of resistance may also be verbal, though this may vary with the age of the victim (Symonds 1976). The victim's response at the time of the rape may have a substantial impact upon her ability to cope with the experience and her ultimate ability to recover from the incident.

Burgess and Holmstrom (1976) also identify coping strategies used by sexual assault victims during the attack. One coping strategy is the cognitive strategy where a victim focuses on something else during the attack. This helps victims to avoid the reality of the event and to focus on their own survival. This coping strategy helps them to remain calm and to prevent provoking additional violence. Many victims will concentrate on memorizing details, such as the assailant's face or general appearance; others concentrate on advice they have been given on how to cope with such an occurrence. Compliance is often used to survive the attack and to get through it.

Coping strategies during the attack also include verbal strategies and physical action similar to the strategies used before the attack, such as screaming for help, talking to the attacker to try and calm him, threatening him, running away, and struggling with the attacker. Victims who struggle often struggle up to the point of penetration, and then realize that it is hopeless, so they stop struggling to avoid any further injury (Burgess and Holmstrom 1976).

Not all coping behavior is voluntary (Burgess and Holmstrom 1976). Victims report physiological responses such as choking, gagging, nausea, vomiting, pain, urination, hyperventilating, and losing consciousness. It is interesting that some rape prevention theorists and self-defense enthusiasts advocate responses such as urinating, defecating, and vomiting if attacked by a rapist. It is the rare victim who can engage in these behaviors at will, especially under such adverse circumstances.

Victims of drug-facilitated rape are incapacitated by the drug and unable to sense danger or employ coping strategies (Fitzgerald and Riley 2000). They are disabled and overpowered by an invisible drug (usually Rohypnol or GHB) slipped into their drink that renders them unconscious. Some victims of drug-facilitated rape remember brief, intermittent periods of awakening during their assault. They were aware of their surroundings, but were unable to move or speak before they passed out again.

Response after the Assault

Coping behavior is also important immediately after the attack. The victim must seek safety by escaping from the rapist, freeing herself from where she has been left, or securing her location. Generally she also tells others of her need for help or safety. When victims of drug-facilitated rape regain consciousness, sometimes hours later and in a different location, some are unsure if they have been sexually assaulted, while others find signs of their rape, such as being undressed, semen stains on their bodies, and/or physical trauma (Fitzgerald and Riley 2000). The victims were not only unconscious during their assault, but Rohypnol causes amnesia for the time period when the drug is in effect. Many drug-facilitated rape victims do not seek assistance because they are still impaired by the drug even after they regain consciousness and they are unable to recall exactly what happened.

There is a lack of consensus in the literature regarding the precise nature of the victim's reaction to a rape experience. The more recent literature often ignores the issue completely. However, there is agreement on some issues to victim response to rape. There is agreement that rape is a highly traumatic crisis causing disruption for the victim physically, behaviorally, emotionally, and interpersonally. There is also agreement that the victim's immediate reaction to rape is indicative of extreme disruption, and that long-term effects of the assault are fairly significant (Gilmartin-Zena 1985). This is generally true for all victims, regardless of ethnicity (Arellano, Kuhn, and Chavez 1997).

Rape-Related Posttraumatic Stress Disorder

Rape is a horrible, unspeakable event in the lives of victims. Most survivors suffer from distress symptoms and psychological harm from the trauma of rape. Very little attention was given to rape and the impact of rape on the victims before the women's movement of the 1970s. It was at this time that it was first recognized that women in civilian life suffer from post-traumatic problems. Many did not view post-traumatic stress, in general, as a credible problem. It was not until 1980 that the American Psychiatric Association included Post-traumatic Stress Disorder (PTSD) in the official manual of mental disorders (Post-traumatic Stress 2001).

PTSD involves the development of specific symptoms after an event that threatened death or serious bodily injury, or threat to one's physical integrity (American Psychiatric Association 2000). To meet the diagnostic criteria, the victim's response to the assault must involve intense fear, helplessness, or horror. The symptoms must include persistent re-experiencing of the assault, persistent avoidance of reminders of the rape, numbing of general responsiveness, and persistent symptoms of increased arousal. These symptoms must be present for more than one month and they must cause significant distress or impairment in social, occupational, or other important areas of the victim's life. PTSD is one of the most common effects of sexual assault; in fact, sexual assault has a higher prevalence of PTSD than other types of traumatic events (Kilpatrick, Amstadter, Resnick, and Ruggiero 2007; Gilboa-Schechtman &

Foa 2001). Since rape involves the intentional actions of another human being rather than a natural disaster or other less personal trauma, the trauma may be especially severe or long lasting.

Under the diagnostic criteria, re-experiencing the assault can take several different forms. The survivor may have repeated thoughts of the assault, or distressing dreams that are related to her victimization. Occasionally, a victim has flashbacks and behaves as though she is experiencing the attack at the moment. These flashbacks are often associated with some cue related to the incident, anniversaries of the rape, or criminal justice proceedings. Cues related to the rape are things that trigger a reminder of assault. A rape victim who is attacked by a man wearing a dark blue shirt may recall or re-experience the rape whenever she sees a man in a dark blue shirt. Cues are often visual, but can be associated with any sense, such as a scent or sound. Perhaps the attacker was wearing cologne or she heard a train whistle in the distance. Now every time the victim smells that cologne or hears a train whistle, she recalls or relives the attack.

Survivors who experience PTSD also avoid thoughts, feelings, or conversations about the rape, and avoid activities, situations, or people who cause her to recall her attack. For example, a victim who is assaulted while leaving the library may avoid the library, or a victim who is raped while on a date may stop dating. She will avoid situations where cues that will trigger recollection of the event are present.

Shortly after the rape, victims often experience psychic numbing, where their responses to the outside world are reduced. They may no longer wish to participate in activities that they enjoyed before their sexual assault, and may feel emotions less intensely than before the assault. Emotions related to sexuality, intimacy, and closeness are the most common areas for rape victims to experience a diminished capacity. Many victims also feel a sense of detachment from other people, and the feeling of a shortened lifespan. They may feel that their family and friends just don't, or can't, understand. They may not see any future for themselves.

Sexual assault survivors with PTSD are more anxious than before the assault. They may have nightmares, irritability, outbursts of anger, difficulty concentrating, or trouble sleeping. They may be unable to complete tasks, be extremely cautious, or be startled easily.

Recent research has examined the connection between characteristics of the assault, victim history, and victim response to the assault and the development and severity of PTSD. Ullman, Filipas, Townsend, and Starzynski (2007) found that the characteristics of the assault such as offender violence, assault severity, and victim-offender relationship did not significantly affect PTSD symptom severity. However, they did find that a history of traumatic events and childhood sexual abuse contributed to sexual assault victims' PTSD symptom severity. Other research indicates that childhood sexual abuse is related to higher rates of adult victimization which affects the level of PTSD symptoms (Nishith, Mechanic, & Resick 2001).

Researchers have also found that tonic immobility may influence the development of PTSD and the severity of the symptoms (Bovin, Jager-Hyman, Gold, Marx, and Sloan 2008). Many factors have been associated with developing PTSD after sexual assault. Masho and Gasmelseed (2007) found a relatively higher risk of PTSD among women who were assaulted for the first time as minors and that "not being married, having less education, perceived poor/fair health status, and perceived threat during the assault were important predictors" (p. 270).

Attribution

Self-Blame

Who a victim blames for her sexual assault is referred to as attribution. Many victims blame themselves for the rape. Self-blame includes behavioral self-blame, which is based on the victims' belief that their behavior in some way brought about their rape. They believe that if they had done something differently, they would not have been assaulted. Perhaps they should not have slept with the window open, worn a short skirt, or accepted a date with someone they did not know very well. They may believe that if they fought the attacker, or fought harder, they would not have been sexually assaulted. Self-blame also includes characterological self-blame. With characterological self-blame, the victim believes that she was victimized because of her character. Self-blame is reinforced by society's myths about rape. It is not unusual for the police, hospital personnel, the victim's family and friends, coworkers, and the public to blame the victim. Research indicates that victims who experience a negative reaction when they disclose their victimization to others are more likely to blame themselves for the incident (Ullman 1996; Ullman, Townsend, Filipas, and Starzynski 2007). Disapproving attitudes of those with whom the victims confide contribute to the victims' feelings of self-blame, especially if they already believe in the myths.

Certain types of victims are more likely to engage in self-blaming following a sexual assault. Society tends to be more supportive of victims of stranger rape who lead conservative lifestyles. There also tends to be more support and less blame for sexual assault victims who experience high levels of additional violence during the attack. Less blame by society often results in less self-blame. Victims of acquaintance rape generally receive more societal blame and are more likely to blame themselves than victims of stranger rape (Katz and Burr 1988 as cited in Arata 1999). Victims of drug-facilitated rape often have feelings of guilt or self-blame because they were drinking when they were drugged (Fitzgerald and Riley 2000). A history of child sexual assault or incest is also associated with greater self-blame after rape (Frazier 1991).

Galliano, Noble, Travis, and Puechl (1993) found that victims who were immobile during their assault held significantly stronger beliefs that greater resistance on their part would have stopped the rape and would also have decreased disbelief by others that they were raped. Survivors' immobility at the time of their victimization may lead to greater self-blame as well as less supportive responses by those to whom they disclosed their rape. The responses of others often have a dramatic impact on the survivors' feelings of self-blame, adjustment, and recovery.

Self-blame also leads to devaluation of self (Morrow and Sorrel 1989). Incest and sexual assault victims often see themselves as cheap or sexually devalued. Reaction of others after victim disclosure has a significant impact on self-blame and devaluating one-self for sexual abuse and assault victims. For childhood incest victims, response to disclosure by the mother and the perpetrator have a dramatic impact on the survivors' perception of self (Morrow and Sorrel). Victims blame themselves less when their mother is supportive and the perpetrator accepts responsibility for the abuse.

Some theorists believe that a victim's feelings of guilt and self-blame are in fact defense mechanisms that help them to cope with the rape (Evans 1978). If the victim believes that the rape was her fault, especially if she is experiencing behavioral self-blame, then she believes that by changing her behavior, she can prevent this from ever happening to her again. The thought of experiencing another sexual assault is generally intolerable for a rape victim. By believing that they can prevent a future assault, they are able to restore some sense of control and reduce their feelings of vulnerability.

Recent studies dispute the theory that behavioral self-blame is helpful for a sexual assault survivor, and in fact, indicate that self-blame may be detrimental. Frazier (2000) found that behavioral self-blame is not associated with the belief that future rapes can be prevented or are less likely by changing behavior. Frazier further found that a victim's perception about whether she could have prevented her assault is unrelated to the opinion that future assaults can be controlled or prevented. Miller, Markman, and Handley (2007) found that self-blame is detrimental to women following sexual assault and contributes to vulnerability to revictimization, thus increasing revictimization risk.

Many experts believe that guilt and self-blame by the victim prevent recognition of the trauma they have experienced and that it interferes with her ability to cope with crisis. Frazer (2000) recommends that sexual assault survivors distinguish between the responsibility for being raped and control over the future. Victims should be encouraged to decrease vulnerability without blaming themselves for past incidents. Whether self-blame is behavioral or characterological, it is associated with greater stress immediately after the rape, increased symptoms, and poorer long-term recovery.

Both behavioral, sometimes referred to as situational, and characterological self-blame are common in sexual assault survivors. Both types of self-blame are associated with greater distress both immediately after the rape and over time. Both are also generally associated with greater use of self-destructive coping strategies, increased symptom levels, and higher rates of Posttraumatic Stress Disorder (Arata 1999; Ullman et al. 2006), though some research indicates that characterological, but not behavioral self-blame is associated with psychological distress (Breitenbecher 2006). Survivors who blame the assault on their own character, or on society tend to feel that sexual assaults in the future are likely and less controllable (Frazier 2000).

Victims who blame themselves for the rape are often perceived by others as less adjusted and as more responsible for the rape, which can compound how they already feel about themselves and can negatively affect recovery (Thornton, et al. 1988).

External Blame

When a sexual assault survivor attributes her victimization to external factors, such as society, it is referred to as external attribution. Research indicates that rape victims blame external factors the most for their rape, followed by behavioral self-blame, then characterological self-blame (Frazier, 2000). While most treatment programs for rape victims encourage blaming external factors for the assault, external blame is not always conducive to recovery. Blaming external factors often leads a victim to believe that bad things happen and that there is nothing that can be done to prevent it. Higher levels of hostility are often found in survivors who blame society. External attribution is also associated with high levels of anxiety and depression. Both behavioral self-blame and blaming society are strongly associated with depressive symptoms (Frazier).

Coping Strategies after the Assault

Coping strategies used by sexual assault survivors often have a significant impact on their ultimate recovery. Research has tried to identify which coping strategies are the most effective in aiding victim recovery. Some coping strategies are actually associated with greater symptom levels in the survivor and a longer recovery period. The type of coping strategy used and its effectiveness are influenced by many factors. Several coping behaviors have been identified, but we still know very little about the coping process used by sexual assault victims.

Minimization

One coping strategy involves minimizing the seriousness of the assault and downplaying the violence and horrifying aspects of it (Burgess and Holmstrom 1979, Adaptive). Victims using this method of coping are less likely to seek help or support from others because they want to reduce the focus on the assault and act as though the incident was not as traumatizing as it was. The research is mixed on the effectiveness of minimization as a coping strategy.

Neville and Pugh (1997) believe that there may be a greater tendency for African American women to minimize their assault because they believe that their inner strength to survive economic, racial, and gender oppression will get them through the aftermath of their assault. Staying strong and minimizing their trauma may be an adaptive coping strategy, but it places added stress on the survivor who must cope with their assault without assistance.

Cognitive Coping

Some victims cope by trying to make sense of the assault and explaining why it happened and why it happened to them (Arata 1999). Many victims will dwell on the incident going over every detail or reliving the event over and over. Cognitive coping that involves attributing blame is sometimes referred to as a cognitive appraisal rather than cognitive coping.

Avoidance

Other survivors try to forget about the rape. They try not to think about the assault and avoid any cues that would remind them about it. These survivors often sleep excessively or stay very busy. Avoidance is associated with greater levels of psychological distress and with social adjustment problems (Frazier and Burnett 1994). Avoidance is more likely to be used by sexual assault survivors who experienced negative reactions from others when they disclosed information about their assault, and those who blame themselves. (Arata 1999;

Littleton and Breitkopf 2006). There may also be greater use of avoidant coping by rape victims who are also survivors of childhood sexual abuse (Arata).

Religious Coping

A survivor's religious views may help them to make sense of and find meaning in a traumatic event, and may provide them with a social support network that can help to alleviate self-blame. Frazier, Tashiro, Berman, Steger, and Long (2004) found that sexual assault survivors who relied on their religious faith to cope also reported more positive life changes.

Nervous/Anxious Coping

Being irritable, nervous and anxious is another coping mechanism. Survivors who engage in nervous/anxious coping are more likely to experience greater feelings of fear and negative mood states (Burr and Katz 1987 as cited in Frazier and Burnett 1994). They often experience more physical symptoms. Victims who have also experienced childhood sexual abuse are more likely to cope using nervous/anxious methods than victims who do not have a history of sexual abuse (Arata 1999).

Withdrawal

Some victims withdraw and stay at home with very little social contact. Withdrawal is associated with greater symptom levels, including fear, depression, and sexual dissatisfaction. Research indicates that fewer sexual assault survivors choose withdrawal as a means of coping with their attacks than other coping mechanisms (Frazier and Burnett 1994). Victims who experience behavioral self-blame may be more likely to withdraw, which may be associated with greater distress (Frazier, Mortenson, and Steward 2005).

Taking Precautions

Taking precautions is one of the most common coping strategies used by rape survivors. This includes locking doors, not opening the door to a stranger, putting bars on the windows and moving to a safer location. Making lifestyle changes such as quitting drinking or being careful about where they go is also a form of taking precaution. While taking precaution is reported to be helpful by many survivors and is associated with lower symptom levels, it is not the most effective coping strategy as associated with recovery (Frazier and Burnett 1994).

Expressive Strategies

Other survivors cry or express their feelings openly to trusted family members, friends, and counselors. Expressive coping is significantly associated with fewer trauma symptoms (Arata 1999) , and is commonly mentioned by rape victims as helpful in their recovery process (Frazier and Burnett 1994). Expressive coping is also more likely to facilitate social support, which is identified by rape victims as very helpful and is clearly identified with better adjustment (Frazier and Burnett). Frazier et al. (2004) found that social support was related to reporting positive life change soon after the assault. Social support is particularly important for rape victims because it helps to alleviate self-blame and because society in general may not be supportive due to the rape myths. It is important to recognize that social support is helpful for all sexual assault survivors, not just the survivors who choose to talk about the incident.

A survivor who chooses to talk about their assault within the first few days is most likely to tell her boyfriend, mother, female friends, or sister. Victims rate the sexual assault nurse examiners and their sisters as the most supportive (Frazier and Burnett 1994). Frazier and Burnett found husbands and male relatives to be the least frequently confided in by survivors, but other males were confided in as often as females, with males being rated as supportive, but less supportive than women.

Stress Reduction Techniques

Meditation, listening to music, long hot baths, drawing, and other stress reduction techniques are associated with fewer symptoms and better adjustment than staying at home and withdrawing (Frazier and Burnett 1994).

Self-Destructive Strategies

Some victims turned to self-destructive behaviors such as drug and alcohol abuse, smoking, and/or excessive eating. These coping behaviors are associated with longer recovery and more psychological symptoms such as depression, fear, and anxiety. Alcohol as a coping strategy may increase the likelihood of engaging in risky sexual behavior. Victims who report an increase in sexual activity after their assault also report an increase in alcohol consumption (Deliramich and Gray 2006). Sturza and Campbell (2005) found that 43% of their sample of rape victims were using prescription medications, most through a prescription, but some were self-medicating. They suggest that rape victims could be at higher risk for use of prescription drugs than women who have not been sexually assaulted, which would fit into the self-destructive category if they are doing so without a doctor's prescription.

Sexual assault is also associated with suicide attempts by survivors, especially those who were subjected to oral and genital rape (Bridgeland, Duane, and Stewart 2001). Self-blame and guilt about the assault are also related to greater frequency of suicide attempts. Research on men who have been sexually assaulted reveals that they tend to have higher levels of depression than non-assaulted males and are also more likely to develop a dependence on alcohol after the assault (Larimer, Lydum, Anderson, and Turner 1999).

Age may be a factor related to the use of self-destructive strategies. Unwanted sexual activity during childhood or adolescence is associated with several psychological symptoms as well as with self-destructive behaviors such as suicide ideation, self-mutilation, binging or purging, increased voluntary sexual activity, and unsafe sexual practices (Morrow and Sorrel 1989). Saunders (1999) found increased substance abuse among child rape victims even into adulthood, and speculated that it may be a way of coping with abuse-related memories or the symptoms associated with depression and Posttraumatic Stress Disorder. Research comparing sexually active adolescent boys and girls who were forced into sexual activity found girls' responses included fighting, increased sexual activity, suicidal intent, and repeat pregnancies. Boys' responses included suicidal intent, increased sexual activity, and laxative abuse (Shrier, Pierce, Emans, and DuRant 1998). Type, severity, and duration of abuse are predictors of low self-esteem, depression, and negative behavior in incest victims (Morrow and Sorrel). Negative behaviors included self-destructive coping behaviors such as attempted suicide, self-mutilation, drug and alcohol use, and promiscuity.

Finding Positive Meaning

Finding positive meaning is another strategy that sexual assault survivors use to cope with their situation. Finding positive meaning includes appreciating life, being more assertive, reevaluating goals, strengthening relationships, being more cautious, taking better care of one's self, and growing spiritually in response to the rape. Finding positive meaning does not mean that the victims see their rape as a positive thing, only that they can continue to see the world in a positive light despite their assault. Individuals who are able to find positive meaning in tragic events are more likely to cope more successfully (Frazier 2000).

While feelings of guilt and many of the coping strategies used by sexual assault victims are not part of the diagnostic criteria for Posttraumatic Stress

Disorder, they are associated with it, particularly in cases where rape is the traumatic event. Coping strategies and symptoms associated with Posttraumatic Stress Disorder are self-destructive and impulsive behavior, social withdrawal, hostility, and feeling constantly threatened.

Child Sexual Abuse or Prior Sexual Assault and Coping

Sexual abuse as a child or prior sexual assaults play a major role in the survivor's coping strategies and ultimate recovery from a recent sexual assault (Arata 1999). Adult rape victims with a history of child sexual abuse generally have higher initial levels of distress and longer recovery times. Survivors with a history of sexual abuse are more likely to blame the assault on their character and to use negative coping strategies, such as avoidance, withdrawal, and self-destructive behaviors. They have higher symptom levels and longer recovery. Repeat victims who believe that they were victimized because of some character trait were more likely to adopt self-destructive coping behaviors, whereas, those who believed that external factors were to blame for their assault were more likely to use expressive coping and had fewer symptoms (Arata).

The long range effects of child sexual abuse include diverse coping methods, lasting emotional problems, high risk behaviors, and suicide (Bridgeland, Duane, and Stewart 2001). Sexual abuse during childhood dramatically increases the risk for development of future psychological problems, adult depression, and Posttraumatic Stress Disorder (Saunders 1999).

Recovery from Sexual Assault

Several theorists labeled and identified stages or phases of recovery for rape survivors. These phases were originally identified as the acute phase and the long-term process by Burgess and Holmstrom (1974) in their classic article identifying Rape Trauma Syndrome. Some theorists divide recovery into three stages while others divide recovery into six or seven stages. This chapter will discuss only the commonalities of the literature on phases of recovery; it will not detail each author's interpretation. What is important to understand is that there is an acute and long-term recovery process as a result of an attempted or a completed sexual assault, and that the process lasts for months or years after the rape.

Acute/Impact Phase

The first phase of recovery is the Acute/Impact Phase that occurs during the period immediately following the rape. It may last for several days. During the initial phase the victim is generally experiencing an overwhelming sense of shock and is unable to believe what she has just gone through. She often has the feeling of total helplessness and powerlessness (Burgess and Holmstrom 1974). No one is ever prepared to experience such a traumatic event. The victim is also experiencing gross anxiety, feelings of total loss of control, confusion and a sense of unreality. She feels very vulnerable. Victims of drug-facilitated rape often suffer a more extreme sense of powerlessness due to their unconscious state during the attack and their lack of ability to recall what happened (Fitzgerald and Riley 2000). Guilt and shame are also fairly universal feelings immediately after a sexual assault. The experience itself will often bring on exhaustion, but she may not be able to sleep due to muscle tension or edginess.

One of the primary victim responses at this phase is extreme fear, sometimes bordering on panic. Many victims report that they believed that they would be killed. Their entire sense of safety has been shattered. Victims also fear retaliation by the rapist and that no one will believe them. Anger is not a primary emotion at this stage. Anger typically surfaces at later stages in the recovery process. When victims do feel anger, it is often aimed at themselves in a form of self-blame for putting themselves in a position to be raped or for not offering more resistance. Their anger may be repressed and be experienced as guilt or shame. Women traditionally have been expected to be passive and express less aggression, which often leads to anger being transformed into culturally supported self-blame (Notman and Nadelson 1976). While little research has been conducted on male survivors of sexual assault, studies that have been done find that males report similar responses as females, with one exception. Anger is a more common response to rape by male victims. Frazier (1993) found that males exhibit more depression and hostility than female victims, concluding that her results were consistent with the clinical data that males are more likely to react with anger.

Immediately after the assault, the victim is also faced with concerns about sexually transmitted diseases, the gynecological examination, and pregnancy as a result of the rape. If she plans to prosecute her attacker, she also has to undergo evidence collection for the rape kit and interviews while trying to understand the criminal justice process. She will endure many trying moments at a time when she is likely to be both physically and emotionally exhausted. Rape victims who do not report physical injury often experience soreness and bruising after the assault and often suffer from other symptoms such as nausea, stomach pains, loss of appetite, vaginal discharge, and an itchy, burning sensation upon urination. Survivors forced to perform oral sex may suffer oral irritation and throat infections, while victims of anal penetration often experience rectal bleeding and/or pain (Posttraumatic Stress 2001).

Outward Adjustment Phase

During the next phase of recovery through which a sexual assault survivor passes, she appears to have adjusted to the event. This phase is often referred to as the Outward Adjustment Phase, and may last for weeks or months (Posttraumatic Stress 2001). In reality, the victim rarely has adjusted well at all. She feels pressure from society to return to her previous lifestyle and appears to have adjusted. Returning to the normal routine as soon as possible denies the impact of the highly personal and violent nature of rape. The sexual assault victim is generally in psychological denial, with little insight into her situation. She tends to approach life very superficially and mechanically.

The victim continues to feel the same emotions that she felt immediately after the rape; however, these feelings generally will be less intense. In addition, victims often feel alienation, isolation, and depression. They may also experience nightmares, sleeplessness, flashbacks, and anxiety caused by some small cue that reminds them of the rape (Posttraumatic Stress 2001). These cues may be such things as being alone, darkness, a male whose appearance is similar to her attacker, or the make of a car in which the assault occurred. Many victims begin to avoid situations where those cues might be present. This aspect of the aftermath of sexual assault may be different for victims of drug-facilitated rape. Because they cannot remember what happened, they have to cope with a gap in their memory. "They experience the horror, powerlessness, and humiliation of not knowing what was done to them. They can only imagine what happened." (Fitzgerald and Riley 2000, p. 12).

The rape victim may also experience physical symptoms such as headaches, stomach or gastrointestinal problems, dizziness, unintentional weight loss, difficulty in breathing, and sexual dysfunction. Emotional responses include moodiness, decreased concentration, crying spells, tension, sadness, decreased self-confidence and self-esteem, and feelings of being out of control (Gilmartin 1985). She may also feel embarrassment and humiliation. She may want revenge, even though many victims blame themselves.

Depression Phase

The next phase, or Depression Phase, for the sexual assault victim includes the same responses, but with some adjustment. She may suffer from obsessive memories, low self-esteem, and fear that she will not be able to bring her life back into control (Posttraumatic Stress 2001). It is at this time that the survivor tends to make lifestyle changes. She may move, change jobs, change phone numbers, refuse to go out alone or at night, and change patterns of work, studying or socializing. These are also often referred to as behavioral changes. It is at this time that victims begin to experience some interpersonal problems. She will often begin to experience difficulty in relationships with her husband or boyfriend, parents, children, employer, and/or friends. This phase may last for days or months.

Integration and Resolution Phase

Eventually the survivor reaches the phase where she feels anger, the Integration and Resolution Phase (Posttraumatic Stress 2001). Generally she has shifted the blame and anger from herself to the rapist. Her anger may also be directed toward the police, prosecutor, society, her counselor, or males in general. She is generally still anxious and depressed, and often lacks trust in men. She frequently wants someone to suffer for what has happened to her. However, the anger is rarely expressed in aggressive behavior. This phase may last months to years.

The victim who can successfully integrate the rape into her life experiences will also experience some sense of resolution (Forman 1980). She will finally be able to put the experience behind her, and will even be able to discuss it without intense feelings.

While several phases may be identifiable, it does not necessarily mean that each rape victim experiences each phase in sequence, or that each phase is experienced only once. It is common for a rape victim to have setbacks when she experiences another trauma, and especially when she again becomes involved in the criminal justice processing of her rape case. It is not unusual for a victim to experience extreme trauma during the trial.

Early theorists believed that most rape victims were able to accomplish resolution in a fairly short period of time. Unfortunately, recovery takes a substantial period of time, and for some victims, resolution where she returns to pre-rape levels of functioning never occurs. Kilpatrick, Resick, and Veronen (1981) found that victims continue to suffer from the effects of sexual assault for at least one year after the rape. Many problems experienced post rape are significant, but the primary problems are typically rape-related fear and anxiety. Kilpatrick, et al. further found that the bulk of improvement by rape victims occurs in the first three months following the rape. They found no significant difference in functioning between the three-month, six-month, and one-year time periods.

A sexual assault survivor's response to victimization and recovery depends on numerous factors, including age, life situation, prior abuse, and circumstances of the assault. It is suggested that life stage is a significant factor in adjusting to trauma. According to Notman and Nadelson (1976), younger victims, single victims, divorced or separated victims, and middle-aged victims experience more serious concern over their independence after a sexual assault. Research by Zweig, Crockett, Sayer, and Vicary (1999) suggests that greater levels of violence have more negative impact on sexual assault survivors' psychological and psychosocial adjustment.

Life situation may create a complex set of factors affecting the survivor's response. Homeless women often suffer a pattern of abuse beginning in their childhood. When a homeless woman is sexually assaulted, there is a strong possibility that it is not the first time she has been abused or suffered from sexual violence (Stermac and Paradis 2000). In addition, research shows that homeless women are more likely than housed women to be raped by a stranger, in a public place, and with greater levels of violence, all of which may impact her response to victimization and her recovery.

Seeking Help

Although sexual assault survivors generally experience many psychological problems as a result of their victimization, a majority of them do not seek mental health services. Sexual assault survivors are more likely to be seen by their primary care physician than they are by mental health professionals (Koss, Koss, and Woodruff 1991). Survivors often see themselves as being in poorer health than non-victims, and many report somatic symptoms that are commonly recognized as stress-related. Victims are more likely to see their doctor for the somatic symptoms of the stress of the assault than for injuries sustained during the rape. In addition to the perception of poorer health and the manifestation of stress in physical symptoms, sexual assault survivors may believe that there is less stigma involved in seeing a medical doctor than in seeing a mental health professional.

Kimerling and Calhoun (1994) found that victims continued to have psychological symptoms throughout the year after their assault without seeking psychological services at any greater frequency than non-victims, but they did have an increased utilization of medical services. Their data also showed some evidence that sexual assault victims experience psychological distress as an illness and that victims often report symptoms such as pounding heartbeats, headaches, nausea, and unintentional weight changes, which are symptoms of depression and anxiety. It is also possible that rape victims report more somatic symptoms because psychological stress can result in weakening the immune system (Kiecolt-Glaser and Glaser1992 as cited in Kimerling and Calhoun).

Support from friends and family members plays a major role in helping sexual assault survivors cope with the emotional distress and the somatic symptoms caused by the attack. A survivor who is supported by friends and family is more likely to see herself as healthy. Kimmerling and Calhoun (1994) found that "The victim's social network immediately after the assault seems particularly important. If the victim initially perceives positive social support, there is less evidence of increased medical service utilization 1 year post-assault" (p. 338).

There are several factors that affect a survivor's likelihood of visiting mental health professionals. Research indicates that older age, being married, alcohol dependence, PTSD, depression, and sexual orientation were all associated with greater odds of seeking mental health care (Ullman and Brecklin 2003; Starzynski, Ullman, Townsend, Long, and Long 2007). In addition, mental health service seeking was associated with more education, being Caucasian, greater social support, and having medical insurance (Ullman and Brecklin 2002). Sometimes victims are simply unaware that services are available.

Race may play a significant role in a sexual assault survivor's decision to seek mental health counseling, or even to disclose a rape to mental health professionals (Starzynski et al. 2007). One study indicates that African American women cited inner strength as a factor in their decision not to seek any help after their assault (Neville and Pugh 1997), while other studies indicate that minority women receive more negative social reactions when they disclose sexual assault (Ullman and Filipas 2001).

Crisis Intervention

"Crisis intervention is obviously a humane effort to reduce the severity of a victim's crisis, to help the victim win as much mastery over the crisis experience as possible." (Understanding and Responding 2001, p. 2). Crisis intervention immediately after any type of sexual assault is critical to the victim's adjustment and recovery. Effective crisis intervention helps the victim get through the immediate crisis and helps her avoid severe adjustment problems and even psychological disorder as a result of the rape (Burgess and Holmstrom 1973). How a victim copes with rape depends for the most part on her experiences immediately following the rape. The short-term goal of crisis intervention is to help the victim cope with her immediate trauma and to restore her sense of security and control over her life (Woods 2000). The long-term goal is to provide the support necessary for the survivor to return to pre-rape levels of functioning.

Anyone who comes in contact with a victim immediately after her assault should be prepared to do crisis intervention. Victim advocates are not the only crisis interveners. A police officer is often the first person to respond to a victim, and therefore must be prepared to do intervention, in addition to assessing medical needs, collecting evidence, gathering information, notifying personnel that need to respond, and securing the crime scene. Interveners also include emergency medical personnel, investigators, hospital staff, chaplains, college counselors, and in many cases, volunteers. Friends are often the first person a victim calls, and must serve as crisis interveners. In a study of college freshmen, one third of the respondents reported that someone had disclosed a date/acquaintance rape experience to them, leading the authors to conclude that education about the aftermath of rape and helpful reactions to disclosures would be beneficial, particularly in a college environment (Dunn, Vail-Smith, and Knight 1999).

The circumstances and personality of the victim of each sexual assault vary. How the crisis intervener handles the situation will also vary according to the circumstances and the victim's needs. How the intervener approaches the victim will set the stage for any interaction the victim has with the crisis intervener (Woods 2000). The intervener should be calm, pleasant, and supportive. An intervener who is nervous, agitated, or shocked with the situation will not be helpful to the victim. The intervener must be able to put the victim at ease. The first thing that the crisis intervener needs to do is to introduce herself, using her title, and stating why she is present (Woods, 2000). Sitting down to talk to the victim so that the victim and intervener are at the same level and can make eye contact can help to put the victim at ease with the intervener. It is important for the victim to understand that the crisis intervener is there to help her through the difficult period, and at times to be her advocate.

Believing the victim and being supportive is critical to effective crisis intervention (Dunn, et al. 1999). The intervener must learn to be patient with silence and allow the victim to share her experiences at a pace that is comfortable for her. The intervener should never be critical of the victim, no matter what the intervener personally believes. The intervener should not touch or hug the victim without asking the victim if she is comfortable with physical contact.

In rape cases, it is especially important for first responders to be prepared for any type of emotional reaction. Victims of sexual assault are deeply traumatized by the intensely personal nature of their assault, and by the fear that they will be killed or seriously injured during the attack. They may be crying uncontrollably, or present themselves in a very calm and subdued manner. Interveners must be nonjudgmental and supportive when faced with any type of reaction by the victim.

A rape victim's behavior may not be what people expect and may be misinterpreted. Crisis interveners and law enforcement officers must be careful not to misinterpret a victim's calm demeanor as evidence of a false report. Burgess and Holmstrom (1973) identified two different styles of behavior common among rape victims during the period immediately after the incident. This research is supported by Ruch, Gartrell, Ramelli, and Coyne (1991). One style is the expressed style where feelings of fear, anger, or anxiety are expressed verbally or shown through such behavior as crying, shaking, smiling, restlessness, and tenseness. Victims with the controlled style mask their feelings and appear calm, composed, and subdued.

Both behavioral styles are common. It is not unusual for one victim to have both responses during the course of one interview. While both responses are common and to be expected, Forman (1980) notes that the behavioral style most frequently displayed in metropolitan emergency rooms is the controlled style. The normal emotional style of the victim influences what behavioral style the victim of sexual assault will assume during the initial phase. Other factors such as exhaustion, the attitude of those in attendance, and her normal verbal style are also factors influencing her behavioral style.

If the intervener is called before the victim decides whether or not to report the rape to the police, the intervener must help the victim understand the issues involved and provide sufficient information to the victim so that she can make that decision. It is imperative that the intervener does not make that decision. The rape victim generally feels powerless, helpless, and a total loss of control (Understanding and Responding 2001). Survivors who perceive greater control over their recovery process have less severe PTSD symptoms (Ullman et al. 2007). Allowing the victim to make the decision to report the crime will help the victim restore her sense of control. It is essential that the victim feel a sense of control return to her life as quickly as possible. The intervener faced with an emotionally devastated individual may think that they are making it easier for the victim by making this decision for her, but in reality, this prolongs her recovery process. Obviously if the victim is in immediate need of medical attention, the intervener cannot delay medical treatment.

Whether the victim chooses to report the rape to the police or not, she will need medical attention. She has suffered a physical trauma and should be examined for injury. If the intervener meets with the victim prior to her seeking medical treatment, the intervener must let the victim know how important it is to receive medical treatment, and encourage her to get medical attention, even if she thinks that she has not been injured (Woods 2000). The victim must not only consider treatment for injuries sustained in the assault, but also pregnancy and sexually transmitted diseases. Victims who seek medical attention tend to have a quicker emotional recovery than victims who do not seek treatment. Seeking medical attention helps the victim to recognize that she has undergone a serious physical trauma. The support she receives from medical personnel also serves as crisis intervention and helps her recovery process as well.

Many communities have specialized emergency medical technicians to respond to rape victims and to transport them to a hospital or medical center that also specializes in caring for sexual assault victims. If the victim's injuries are not life threatening or serious, she should be given the option to request such special assistance. These medical personnel are specially trained to treat not only the physical injuries of the victim, but also to attend to her emotional needs caused by the trauma. Perhaps one of the most important aspects of this specialized treatment is that most communities allow medical personnel to volunteer for the training and assignment, suggesting a commitment to help victims of sexual assault.

Victims' Basic Needs during Crisis Intervention

One of the first responsibilities of the intervener is to assess the needs of the victim. The three major needs of any crime victim are: the need to feel safe, the need to express their emotions, and the need for information about what will happen next (Woods 2000).

Victims' need to feel safe. One of the primary emotions felt by a rape victim is fear. The principal need for any rape victim, therefore, is the need to feel safe. Sexual assault survivors often feel vulnerable, fearful, and helpless (Understanding and Responding 2001). She typically experiences a sense of total loss of control. It is important to reassure the victim that she is safe now. The crisis intervener's mannerisms, tone of voice, and posture may do as much, or more, to reassure her as the words used. Using a sympathetic tone of voice, natural eye contact, and assuming the same level as the victim, rather than standing over her, can help a victim to feel safer (Woods 2000). A non-judgmental attitude and concerned approach is critical to good crisis intervention with a sexual assault victim.

Since a sexual assault survivor generally feels out of control, asking the survivor simple questions will allow her to make decisions and assert herself to regain some sense of control. Asking her how she would like to be addressed is an example. She may prefer to be called by her first name, or she may want to be addressed more formally. Offering to call friends or family not only can help her to regain control, but it may help her general sense of safety. Asking if the victim needs anything is helpful, but if she wants to prosecute the assault, she should not eat or drink anything if there was forced oral sex. She also should not use the bathroom or bathe. Small things concerning the victim's comfort, such as being cold, uncomfortable, or feeling exposed can have a significant impact on her feelings of safety and should be considered by the intervener (Understanding and Responding 2001). It is also helpful to keep the media away from the victim, or to help her respond to the media if she wishes to talk with them.

Many times the victim will express unrealistic or irrational concerns. The intervener can help to alleviate those concerns by discussing them with the victim and explaining why they may be unrealistic or irrational. This must be done in a supportive and non-condescending manner. The victim must feel free to express any feelings to the intervener without worrying about the intervener being judgmental (Understanding and Responding 2001). Anyone who has undergone a severe emotional and physical crisis like rape can be expected to have many concerns, some of which may be more realistic than others.

Fear and anxiety will continue to be the most predominate emotions for the victim to handle even months after the rape. No amount of support, crisis intervention, or counseling will completely eliminate her fear during the initial period after the assault. However, some amount of safety can be experienced if the proper emotional support is offered.

The victim's need to express their emotions. Victims need to allow their emotions to show and to be accepted by nonjudgmental listeners. Crisis interveners should be prepared to help a sexual assault survivor cope with her feelings. Typical emotional responses include fear, disbelief, self-blame, anger, shame, and sadness (Woods 2000). Emotional distress may be expressed in what the intervener sees as unusual ways. Victims may be calm, crying, or laughing, as found by Burgess and Holmstrom (1973) and Ruch, et al. (1991).

It is important for interveners to allow the victim to express their emotions in their own way. People are often uncomfortable when others show their emotions and sometimes tell them that their emotions are not legitimate or that they should not express them. This generally is not meant to be callous; it simply reflects discomfort with the expression of emotions. For example, someone might tell a victim not to cry, that everything will be all right. The truth is that it is beneficial for the victim to cry if that is how she is expressing her feelings, and everything is not going to be all right for quite some time. The victim who feels that her emotions are being discounted may withdraw, which may negatively impact her recovery. Crisis interveners should also be aware of a victim's body language, such as her posture, facial expressions, tone of voice, gestures, eye contact, and general appearance (Wood 2000). Reading a victim's body language helps the intervener to understand the victim's feelings and improves the ability to respond to her needs. The intervener must not force the victim to discuss or deal with her emotions before she is ready. A sense of trust must be developed between the intervener and the victim before any meaningful communication can begin.

While victims do not want to think that what has happened to them is common, it is helpful for them to know that their response to the traumatic event is not abnormal. "While most reactions are normal, most people have not experienced such intense feelings, so they think they are "going crazy." Survivors should be reassured that while the crisis has thrown their lives into chaos, they are not, as a consequence, crazy" (Understanding and Responding 2001, p. 7).

Since sexual assault victims often blame themselves for their assault, it is important for the crisis intervener to counter that self-blame (Woods 2000). Victims need to hear that they did not do anything wrong and that their assault was not their fault. It is also helpful for the victim to understand that self-blame is not uncommon for sexual assault survivors, but the responsibility for her victimization lies with her rapist, not with her. Helping the victim to understand that rape is a violent crime using sex as a means of power and violence may alleviate some of the survivor's feelings of guilt and self-blame.

An important technique in helping victims overcome feelings of guilt and self-blame is to explore the coping behavior that they used before and during the attack. They need to understand that their rapist used terrorization which, with most violent crime, leads to immediate compliance of the victim (Symonds 1976). Since many victims respond to the attack with frozen fright response, which appears to be cooperative behavior, they need to recognize that it is merely a means of reacting in order to preserve their life (Symonds). Perhaps survivors who understand that their immobility was a reflexive response commonly experienced in high-fear situations will have better chances for adjustment and recovery.

Victims may respond to the sexual assault with a variety of coping behaviors. Helping the victim comprehend her coping behavior when faced with a traumatic event is an essential step in crisis intervention (Burgess and Holmstrom 1976). Listening to the sexual assault survivor tell their story of the rape, the intervener can identify coping behavior and help the victim understand her behavior. This support lets the victim know that her behavior helped her to survive and can help alleviate guilt and self-blame and enhance their recovery process. The intervener should remember that survivors who blame themselves tend to suffer from more symptoms and have a lengthier recovery process and, therefore, should encourage the victim to seek counseling soon after the event (Frazier 2000).

Victims need to tell their story after a crime (Woods 2000). Ventilation refers to the process of victims telling their story over and over again. "The repetitive process is a way of putting the pieces together and cognitively organizing the event so that it can be integrated into the survivor's life" (Understanding and Responding 2001, p.5). This process takes place over a period of time. Crisis interveners should not force a victim to repeatedly tell their story, but should allow them to tell it if they choose to do so. It is normal for the victim's story to start very narrowly and become more complete over time (Understanding and Responding 2001). Interveners must allow victims a sense of permission to express their feelings and validation that those feelings are normal.

Victim's need for information. The rape victim will need information about what to do immediately after the rape as well as information about long-term issues. She will need information about medical and counseling services, the rights of victims, and the emotional and psychological consequences of rape. If she chooses to prosecute, she will also need information about what will be expected of her and what she can expect from the criminal justice system. Helping a victim to understand what to expect in the aftermath of the rape may relieve some of her anxiety (Woods 2000; Hensley 2002).

If the victim chooses to report the rape to the police, she should be advised not to wash, change clothes, or freshen-up in any way before going to the hospital. Bathing can wash away evidence that can help her to prosecute her case. Her appearance may also provide evidence that could be helpful for prosecution. Most victims feel dirty and want to bathe and change clothes before going anywhere. It is important for them to understand the importance of preserving evidence. Even if she does not wish to prosecute at this time, she may change her mind at a later date.

The victim should not be left alone in the emergency room. She will feel safer with someone with her, and she needs information about what is coming next. The crisis intervener can make the victim's hospital experience less traumatic by advising them what to expect and allowing her to regain some control over the procedures. Many times a rape victim with no life-threatening injuries will have a fairly long wait in a hospital emergency room before she is treated. It will help her if she knows that the hospital staff is taking her injuries seriously, but that those with life-threatening or serious injuries will be given priority. She may also need help completing forms and dealing with questions prior to her examination.

The crisis intervener can make her visit to the hospital less stressful by explaining to her what to expect and why the questions and procedures are important (Woods 2000; Hensley 2002). For example, she will be asked about her health, menstrual cycle, sexual practices, and details of her sexual assault. This information is important to diagnose and treat her appropriately. Her physical appearance and emotional state will be recorded for treatment and prosecution purposes.

A physical examination, including a pelvic exam, is generally performed on a sexual assault victim to evaluate injury and to collect evidence. It is critical that a rape victim be aware that these examinations will be performed before they begin. The victim often feels re-victimized by the process, but if she is informed about the process and the importance of it, she may find it easier to cope with the exam. Allowing the victim to indicate when she is ready to proceed with the examination helps her to reestablish some control in her life. This is where a crisis intervener may need to act as an advocate for the victim, making sure that the medical personnel know how important it is for the victim to have a sense of control.

It is also of utmost importance that the victim be examined in private. Privacy recognizes the trauma that the victim has already experienced as well as allowing her to regain some sense of control over the situation. If the medical staff does not automatically provide the victim with a private examining room, explain the medical process to her, and treat her with respect and empathy, the crisis intervener must be an advocate for the victim. Traditionally, medical staff did not see a rape victim as a legitimate consumer of medical services because her injuries often did not appear to be significant. Today, many hospitals and trauma centers have specially trained Sexual Assault Nurse Examiners (SANE) to handle rape cases in an area of the hospital that is private and removed from the emergency room. Research indicates that SANE programs are effective at providing medical care and emotional support to survivors as well as effectively collecting evidence for prosecution (Campbell, Patterson, and Lichty 2005).

The sexual assault survivor should also be made aware that she will be asked to give blood samples for toxicology and serology testing to look for evidence of alcohol, drugs, and disease. If the victim has used any substance to try to cope with her assault, the hospital staff should be made aware of that fact. This may also help the victim's credibility if her sobriety at the time of the assault is an issue raised by the defense. The intervener helping a drug-facilitated rape victim should inform her that urine testing is necessary to detect traces of rape drugs in her system (Fitzgerald and Riley 2000). Since most jurisdictions use rape kits that do not routinely include obtaining a urine specimen, the drug-facilitated rape victim may have to request it.

Some of the more difficult parts of evidence collection, other than the pelvic exam, are head and pubic combings to collect hairs that may have been left by the rapist, head and pubic hair plucking, and using a Woods Lamp on the victims thighs and genital area to search for dried semen. The Woods Lamp will cause semen to fluoresce so that it can be swabbed and collected as evidence. Hair must be plucked to establish that the loose hairs found are not the victims. Fingernail scraping is less embarrassing, but also not a pleasant part of the procedure. Photographs of the victim may be taken to document injuries. If the victim is aware that these things will be done and why they are being done, she has a much better sense of control over the situation and is less likely to feel re-victimized. The victim should be made aware that she could request these photographs to be taken by a female police officer rather than a male.

In addition to treatment for immediate injuries and collecting evidence, the medical exam must also address issues of unwanted pregnancies and sexually transmitted diseases. The physician will discuss the victim's present birth control method and menstrual cycle with her, consider her present health, and determine what course of action to take. If she is given "the morning after pill," she should be advised of the side effects of the drug, including nausea and abdominal pains (Burgess and Holmstrom 1976). Since the crisis intervener may not have medical training, it would be more appropriate to act as an advocate asking the medical personnel to explain side effects to the victim. Routine treatment of rape victims usually includes antibiotics for the prevention of sexually transmitted diseases. The victim should be advised that six-week follow-up testing is advisable for both pregnancy and sexually transmitted diseases. The victim may also need assistance obtaining items after the exam, such as a glass of water, a warm washcloth, or fresh clothing. While it is not a good idea to go into too much detail on what to expect later in a criminal prosecution, the victim should be made aware of some of the general procedures and what will happen next. It may be helpful for her to know that she is likely to have more interviews with the police, that she may be asked to identify her attacker from a series of photographs, and that she may also have interviews with the prosecutor if her attacker is apprehended. The names and phone numbers of victim advocates with law enforcement agencies and the prosecutor's, as well as their role in helping the victim through the criminal justice process can help relieve some of the victim's anxieties about the system.

She may also need to prepare for how her friends, family, neighbors, and coworkers will react to her assault. Because a victim's mate, family, and friends may react to the rape based on their own beliefs in the myths about rape, the victim may choose not to tell them about the assault. Victims typically are selective in who they tell about their rape, often telling one person and asking them to tell others. Most victims tell persons whom they expect to be supportive (Frazier 1991; Frazier and Burnett 1994). Since support from others is important to the victim's adjustment and recovery, crisis interveners should assist the victim in determining who she can expect to be supportive and to whom she should not disclose her victimization (Burgess and Holmstrom 1979).

Since feeling safe is critical to a victim's adjustment and recovery, before the intervener leaves, she should make sure the victim's basic needs are cared for. If she wants friends and family present, they should be called. If she is in the hospital emergency room, transportation home, or wherever she wants to go, should be arranged. She should have adequate clothing if she is not at home. Many hospitals have a clothing closet for rape victims since there clothing is usually kept for evidence collection. The victim should be asked if she has any special concerns or needs (Woods 2000).

Crisis interveners should counsel victims that lapses of concentration, memory losses, depression, and physical complaints are normal reactions for sexual assault survivors and encourage them to seek counseling (Woods 2000; Hensley 2002). The crisis intervener should refer the victim to local agencies and programs that offer support and counseling services for sexual assault survivors. Ideally, the crisis intervener will follow-up with the victim through telephone calls 24 to 48 hours after the assault to check on her adjustment and to see if further assistance is necessary.

Conclusion

Sexual assault is a violent and traumatic event in the life of a victim. How the victim responds depends on a variety of factors, including the circumstances of the assault, the response of those to whom she discloses her rape, and her life situation. Coping strategies used before and during the assault may have a dramatic impact on her adjustment, recovery, and coping methods after the assault. Many victims suffer from Posttraumatic Stress Disorder, which may be complicated by feelings of self-blame.

Recovery from sexual assault is a long process that may take years. Some victims never integrate the rape into their lives and return to pre-rape levels of functioning. During the recovery process the victim will experience physical, psychological, behavioral, and social changes. A victim's chances of full recovery are greater if the victim has effective crisis intervention and a good support system.

References

American Psychiatric Association. (2000). Diagnostic and Statistical Manual of Mental Disorders(4th ed. TR). Washington, DC: Author.

Arata, C. M. (1999). Coping with Rape. *Journal of Interpersonal Violence,* *14,* 62–79.

Arellano, C. M., Kuhn, J. A., and Chavez, E. L. (1997). Psychosocial Correlates of Sexual Assault Among Mexican American and White Non-Hispanic Adolescent Females. *Hispanic Journal of Behavioral Sciences, 19,* 446–460.

Bachman, R., Saltzman, L. E., Thompson, M. P. and Carmody, D. C. (2002). Disentangling the Effects of Self-Protective Behaviors on the Risk of Injury in Assaults Against Women. *Journal of Quantitative Criminology, 18(2),* 135–157.

Bovin, M., Jager-Hyman, S., Gold, S., Marx, B., and Sloan, D. (2008). Tonic Immobility Mediates the Influence of Peritraumatic Fear and Perceived Inescapability on Posttraumatic Stress Symptom Severity Among Sexual Assault Survivors. *Journal of Traumatic Stress, 21*(4), 402–409.

Breitenbecher, K. H. (2006). The Relationships Among Self-Blame, Psychological Distress, and Sexual Victimization. [Abstract] *Journal of Interpersonal Violence, 21*(5), 97. Retrieved September 24, 2008, from Criminal Justice Periodicals database.

Bridgeland, W. M., Duane, E.A., and Stewart, C. S. (2001). Victimization and Attempted Suicide Among College Students. *College Student Journal, 35,* 63–77.

Burgess, A. W., and Holmstrom, L. L. (1973). The Rape Victim in the Emergency Ward. *American Journal of Nursing, 73,* 1740–1745.

Burgess, A. W., and Holmstrom, L. L. (1974). Rape Trauma Syndrome. *American Journal of Psychiatry, 131,* 981–986.

Burgess, A. W., and Holmstrom, L. L. (1976). Coping behavior of the rape victim. *American Journal of Psychiatry, 133,* 413–418.

Burgess, A. W., and Holmstrom, L. L. (1979). Adaptive Strategies and Recovery from Rape. *American Journal of Psychiatry, 136,* 1278–1282.

Burgess, A. W., and Holmstrom, L. L. (1979). Rape: Disclosure to Parental Family Members. *Women and Health, 4,* 255–268.

Campbell, R., Patterson, D., and Lichty, L. (2005). The Effectiveness of Sexual Assault Nurse Examiner (SANE) Programs: A Review of Psychological, Medical, Legal, and Community Outcomes. [Abstract] *Trauma, Violence and Abuse, 6*(4), 313–329. Retrieved September 20, 2008, from Academic Search Premier.

Davis, R., & Brickman, E. (1996). Supportive and Unsupportive Aspects of the Behavior of Others Toward Victims of Sexual and Nonsexual Assault. *Journal of Interpersonal Violence, 11*(2), 250–262.

Deliramich, A. N. and Gray, M. J. (2008). Changes in Women's Sexual Behavior Following Sexual Assault. *Behavior Modification, 32*(5), 611–621.

Dunn, P. C., Vail-Smith, K., and Knight, S. K. (1999). What Date/Acquaintance Rape Victims Tell Others: A Study of College Student Recipients of Disclosure. *Journal of American College Health, 47*, 213–220.

Evans, H. I. (1978). Psychotherapy for the Rape Victim: Some Treatment Models. *Hospital and Community Psychiatry, 29*, 309–312.

Fitzgerald, N. and Riley, K. J. (2000, April). Drug-Facilitated Rape: Looking for the Missing Pieces. *National Institute of Justice Journal*, 9–15.

Forman, B. (1980). Psychotherapy with Rape Victims. *Psychotherapy: Theory, Research, and Practice, 17*, 304–311.

Frazer, P. A. (1991). Self-Blame as a Mediator of Postrape Depressive Symptoms. *Journal of Social and Clinical Psychology, 10*, 47–57.

Frazer, P. A. (1993). A comparative Study Of Male and Female Rape Victims Seen at a Hospital-Based Rape Crisis Program. *Journal of Interpersonal Violence, 8*, 64–76.

Frazier, P. A. (2000). The Role of Attributions and Perceived Control in Recovery from Rape. *Journal of Personal and Interpersonal Loss, 5*, 203–226.

Frazier, P. A. and Burnett, J. W. (1994). Immediate Coping Strategies among Rape Victims. *Journal of Counseling and Development, 72*, 633–640.

Frazier, P., Mortensen, H., and Steward, J. (2005). Coping Strategies as Mediators of the Relations Among Perceived Control and Distress in Sexual Assault Survivors. *Journal of Counseling Psychology, 52*(3), 267–278.

Frazier, P., Tashiro, T., Berman, M., Steger, M., and Long, J. (2004). Correlates of Levels and Patterns of Positive Life Changes Following Sexual Assault. *Journal of Consulting and Clinical Psychology, 72*(1), 19–30.

Galliano, G., Noble, L. M., Travis, L.A., and Puechl, C. (1993). Victim Reactions During Rape/Sexual Assault. *Journal of Interpersonal Violence, 8*, 109–114.

Gidycz, C. A., Van Wynsberghe, A., and Edwards, K. M. (2008). Prediction of Women's Utilization of Resistance Strategies in a Sexual Assault Situation. [Abstract] *Journal of Interpersonal Violence, 23*(5), 571. Retrieved September 20, 2008, from Criminal Justice Periodicals database.

Gilboa-Schechtman, E. and Foa, E. B. (2001). Patterns of Recovery from Trauma: The Use of Intraindividual Analysis. *Journal of Abnormal Psychology, 110*, 392–400.

Gilmartin-Zena, P. (1985). Rape Impact: Immediately and Two Months Later. *Deviant Behavior, 6*, 347–361.

Hensley, L. (2002). Drug-Facilitated Sexual Assault on Campus: Challenges and Interventions. *Journal of College Counseling, 5*(2), 175–181.

Kilpatrick, D., Amstadter, A., Resnick, H., and Ruggiero, K. (2007). Rape-Related PTSD: Issues and Interventions. *Psychiatric Times, 24*(7), 50–58.

Kilpatrick, D. G., Resick, P. A., and Veronen, L. J. (1981). Effects of a Rape Experience: A Longitudinal Study. *Journal of Social Issues, 37*, 105–122.

Kimerling, R. and Calhoun, K. S. (1994). Somatic Symptoms, Social Support, and Treatment Seeking Among Sexual Assault Victims. *Journal of Consulting and Clinical Psychology, 62*, 333–340.

Koss, M. P., Koss, P. G., and Woodward, W. J. (1991). Relation of Criminal Victimization to Health Perceptions Among Women Medical Patients. *Journal of Consulting and Clinical Psychology, 58*, 147–152.

Larimer, M. E., Lydum, A. R., Anderson, B. K., and Turner, A. P. (1999). Male and Female Recipients of Unwanted Sexual Contact in a College Student Sample: Prevalence Rates, Alcohol Use, and Depression Symptoms. *Sex Roles: A Journal of Research, 40*, 295–308.

Littleton, H., and Breitkopf, C. (2006). Coping with the Experience of Rape. *Psychology of Women Quarterly, 30*(1), 106–116.

Masho, S., and Ahmed, G. (2007). Age at Sexual Assault and Posttraumatic Stress Disorder Among Women: Prevalence, Correlates, and Implications for Prevention. *Journal of Women's Health, 16*(2), 262–271.

Miller, A. K., Markman, K. D., and Handley, I. M. (2007). Self-Blame Among Sexual Assault Victims Prospectively Predicts Revictimization: A Perceived Sociolegal Context Model of Risk. *Basic and Applied Social Psychology, 29(2)*, 129–136.

Morrow, K. B., and Sorrel, G. T. (1989). Factors Affecting Self-Esteem, Depression, and Negative Behaviors in Sexually Abused Female Adolescents. *Journal of Marriage and the Family, 51*, 677–686.

Neville, H. A. and Pugh, A. O. (1997). General and Culture-Specific Factors Influencing African American Women's Reporting Patterns and Perceived Social Support Following Sexual Assault. *Violence Against Women, 3*, 361–381.

Nishith, P., Mechanic, M. B., and Resick, P. A. (2000). Prior Interpersonal Trauma: The Contribution to Current PTSD Symptoms in Female Rape Victims. *Journal of Abnormal Psychology, 109*, 20–25.

Notman, M., & Nadelson, C.C. (1976). The Rape Victim: Psychodynamic Considerations. *American Journal of Psychiatry*, 133(4), 408–413.

Posttraumatic Stress Disorder, Rape trauma Syndrome, and Battery. (April 19, 2001). In Student Material: Victim Empowerment: Bridging the Systems Mental Health and Victim Service Providers (chap. 3).Retrieved July 18, 2002 from http://www.ojp.usdoj.gov/ovc/publications/infores/student/welcome.html.

Ruch, L. O., Gartrell, J. W., Ramelli, A., and Coyne, B. J. (1991). The Clinical Trauma Assessment: Evaluating Sexual Assault Victims in the Emergency Room. *Psychological Assessment, 3,* 405–411.

Saunders, B. E. (1999). Prevalence, Case Characteristics, and Long-Term Psychological Correlates of Child Rape Among Women: A National Survey. *Child Maltreatment, 4,* 187–200.

Shrier, L. A., Pierce, J. D., Emans, S. J., and DuRant, R. H. (1998). Gender Differences in Risk Behaviors Associated With Forced or Pressured Sex. *Archives of Pediatrics and Adolescent Medicine, 152,* 57–63.

Starzynski, L., Ullman, S., Townsend, S., Long, L., and Long, S. (2007). What Factors Predict Women's Disclosure of Sexual Assault to Mental Health Professionals? *Journal of Community Psychology, 35*(5), 619–638.

Stermac, L. and Paradis, E. K. (2000, Fall–Winter). Homeless Women and Victimization: Abuse and Mental Health History Among Homeless Rape Survivors. *Resources for Feminist Research,* 65–81.

Sturza, M., and Campbell, R. (2005). An Exploratory Study of Rape Survivors' Prescription Drug Use as a Means of Coping with Sexual Assault. *Psychology of Women Quarterly, 29*(4), 353–363.

Symonds, M. (1976). The Rape Victim: Psychological Patterns of Response. *The American Journal of Psychoanalysis, 36,* 27–34.

Tark, J., and Kleck, G. (2004). Resisting Crime: The Effects of Victim Action on the Outcomes of Crimes. *Criminology, 42(4),* 861–909.

Thornton, B., Ryckman, R., Kirchner, G., Jacobs, J., Kaczor, L., and Kuehnel, R. (1988).

Reaction to Self-Attributed Victim Responsibility: A Comparative Analysis of Rape Crisis Counselors and Lay Observers. *Journal of Applied Social Psychology, 18,* 409–422.

Ullman, S. E. (1998). Does Offender Violence Escalate When Rape Victims Fight Back? *Journal of Interpersonal Violence, 13,* 179–193.

Ullman, S., and Brecklin, L. (2003). Sexual Assault History and Health-Related Outcomes in a National Sample of Women. *Psychology of Women Quarterly, 27*(1), 46–57.

Ullman, S.E., and Filipas, H.H. (2001). Correlates of Formal and Informal Support Seeking in Sexual Assault Victims. *Journal of Interpersonal Violence, 16,* 1028–1047.

Ullman, S., Filipas, H., Townsend, S., and Starzynski, L. (2006). The Role of Victim-Offender Relationship in Women's Sexual Assault Experiences. *Journal of Interpersonal Violence, 21(6),* 798–819.

Ullman, S., Filipas, H., Townsend, S., and Starzynski, L. (2007). Psychosocial Correlates of PTSD Symptom Severity in Sexual Assault Survivors.
Journal of Traumatic Stress, 20(5), 821–831.

Ullman, S., Townsend, S., Filipas, H., and Starzynski, L. (2007). Structural
Models of the Relations of Assault Severity, Social Support, Avoidance
Coping, Self-Blame, and PTSD Among Sexual Assault Survivors. *Psy-
chology of Women Quarterly, 31*(1), 23–37.

Understanding and responding to the trauma of victimization. (April 19, 2001).
In Student Material: Victim Empowerment: Bridging the Systems Mental
Health and Victim Service Providers (chap. 2). Retrieved July 18, 2002 from
http://www.ojp.usdoj.gov/ovc/publications/infores/student/welcome.html.

Woods, T. O. (2000). First Response to Victims of Crime. Washington, DC:
U. S. Department of Justice: Office for Victims of Crime.

Zweig, J. M., Crockett, L. J., Sayer, A., and Vicary, J. R. (1999). A Longitudinal Examination of the Consequences of Sexual Victimization for Rural
Young Adult Women. *The Journal of Sex Research, 36*, 396–409.

Chapter 5

The Ripple Effect: Secondary Sexual Assault Survivors

Diane M. Daane

Introduction

The family, partner, and friends of a sexual assault victim commonly experience emotional trauma as a result of the victimization of their loved one. Mental health professionals, victims' advocates, and volunteer crisis line workers suffer from secondary posttraumatic stress as well. The effect of sexual assault on the victim's personal or professional network has long been overlooked in the literature, in victim services agencies, and by the general public. Recognizing the impact of sexual assault on the people who care about sexual assault victims, and addressing their needs, not only helps them through the crisis, but also helps them to provide a better support network for the victim.

"Victimization has a ripple effect, spreading the damage in waves out from victims to all those with whom they have intimate contact." (Remer and Ferguson 1995, p. 407). Secondary posttraumatic stress is a natural response to learning about a traumatizing event experienced by a partner, friend, or family member, or the stress resulting from helping a traumatized crime victim (National Victim Assistance Academy 2002, chap. 6.1). Those who are affected by the sexual assault of the primary victim are secondary victims. The trauma suffered by secondary victims with a close relationship to the victim is similar to the trauma suffered by the primary victim (Schneider 2001). This includes feelings of powerlessness, guilt, vulnerability, and anger. In addition, they sometimes feel a sense of failure and self-blame for not protecting their loved one from harm (Schneider).

Close family and friends are considered to be secondary victims because they did not directly experience the sexual assault. It is a common misperception that the feelings experienced by secondary victims are less intense than those experienced by the primary victim (Remer and Ferguson 1995). While there is no empirical data comparing levels of loss or suffering between primary and secondary rape victims, there is significant data and anecdotal evidence of significant trauma experienced by secondary victims. Little attention has been paid to the trauma experienced by secondary victims; what research has been done often examines the affect that secondary victims' responses have on the primary sexual assault victim, rather than concentrating on the impact of the assault on those close to the victim.

How a secondary victim responds to the sexual assault of a partner, family member, or friend depends on many different factors. Attitudes held before the rape, circumstances of the assault, and the closeness of the relationship held with the primary victim are critical issues in how a secondary victim responds to the sexual assault. Their own recovery and their ability to support the victim are also linked to these dynamics. While primary victims focus on their own healing first, secondary victims must provide support for the primary victim, then tend to their own healing process and the healing process for the relationship. While there is often a formal or informal support network for the primary victim, there is rarely any support network for the secondary victim.

Healing and Stages of Recovery

Several theorists have identified stages or phases of recovery for primary rape victims. Burgess and Holmstrom (1974) originally identified these phases as the acute phase and the long-term process. Very little research has been done on the phases of recovery for secondary victims, but limited study suggests that secondary victims heal in a very similar manner to primary victims. The process may last for months or years after the rape.

Trauma Awareness Phase

Secondary victims cope with rape and pass through stages of recovery in much the same way as the primary victim. One critical difference in the primary and secondary victims' experience is trauma awareness. The secondary victim is dependent upon the primary victim to provide information about the assault (Remer and Ferguson 1995). The primary victim sometimes has to experience some healing before she is able to discuss the rape, leaving the secondary victim in a position of crisis over the assault without knowing the facts about what occurred. It often takes days, weeks, or months before the primary victim is able to discuss the details of the assault with those closest to her. Some primary victims never arrive at this point and carry their trauma alone for life. Trauma awareness is generally an ongoing process because the primary victim may only reveal small bits and pieces of information about the assault at a time.

Crisis and Disorientation Phase

Once the secondary victim is aware of the trauma, a period of crisis and disorientation is generally experienced (Remer and Ferguson 1995). They will experience many of the same responses as the primary victim. This period of disorientation may include anger, sadness, self-blame, feelings of powerlessness, and disruption to routine activities. They may also suffer from rape-related Posttraumatic Stress Disorder (PTSD). Secondary PTSD involves the transfer of trauma symptoms from those who are primary trauma victims to those who have close and extended contact with them (Motta, Kefer, Hertz, and Hafeez 1999). The American Psychiatric Association's (2000) diagnostic criteria for PTSD includes learning about unexpected serious harm or threat of death or injury experienced by a family member or someone with whom there is a close relationship. PTSD involves the development of specific symptoms after learning about the violence. To meet the diagnostic criteria, the secondary victim's response to learning of the assault must involve intense fear, helplessness, or horror. In addition, they must persistently reexperience the assault, avoid reminders of the rape, and repeatedly experience symptoms of increased arousal, such as difficulty sleeping, irritability, difficulty concentrating, or hypervigilance. These symptoms must be present for more than one month and they must cause significant distress or impairment in social, occupational, or other important areas of the secondary victim's life.

During the crisis and disorientation phase, attribution for the crime often manifests itself in self-blame, which is also similar to the response of primary victims. While primary victims blame themselves by believing that their behavior at the time of the assault caused their assault, or that they were attacked because of their character (Arata 1999), secondary victims often feel that it was their responsibility to protect the victim, and that they failed (Cwik 1996). This is especially true for husbands, boyfriends, fathers, and brothers, who may be seen by society as having the role of protector.

Outward Adjustment Phase

Like primary victims, secondary sexual assault victims use coping strategies to come to terms with the situation and to try to recover from the trauma

(Remer and Ferguson 1995). These coping mechanisms often result in a period of apparent outward adjustment. During this phase, it appears that the lives of the primary and secondary victims have returned to a fairly normal routine. Others may actually believe that everything has returned to normal. However, in reality, there may be little healing that has taken place.

The secondary victim's role is often seen as providing support for the primary victim without legitimately needing help or support of his or her own. This results in the secondary victim receiving very little support. They often feel pressured to act like nothing happened and to return to normal. This pressure from society to return to their previous lifestyle often makes it appear that the primary and secondary sexual assault victims have adjusted. Unfortunately, returning to the normal routine too soon may promote psychological denial, and may cause the primary and secondary victims to approach life very superficially and mechanically, with little insight into the situation.

There is also an outward adjustment phase for the relationship between primary and secondary victims. During this phase, previously established role patterns will prevail in these relationships (Remer and Ferguson 1995). The primary victim's relationship with her partner, family members, and friends appears to be the same as it has always been, even if they are just going through the motions out of routine or desire to return to a previously comfortable, or less stressful, situation.

Reorganization Phase

Further healing by either the primary victim or the secondary victim will require a reevaluation and adjustment of the relationship. This phase, called the Reorganization Phase, will occur on both the personal and relationship levels (Remer and Ferguson 1995). During this phase, the primary victim tends to make lifestyle changes. These lifestyle changes often affect the secondary victim, particularly a partner, who is also going through a reorganization phase. The primary victim may want to move, change jobs, change phone numbers, or refuse to go out alone or at night. She may also change patterns of work, studying, or socializing. It is at this time that primary victims begin to experience more interpersonal problems, such as difficulty in relationships with their partner, parents, children, employer, and/or friends. During this phase, the relationship between the primary and secondary victim will evolve into new roles and new patterns of interaction will develop. These new roles and patterns may, or may not, be positive and healthy. Victims typically find themselves going through this phase several times. The trauma of rape is considerable, requiring significant healing that often takes place a little bit at a time.

Integration and Resolution Phase

Eventually the primary and secondary survivors reach the Integration and Resolution Phase, where they integrate the rape into life experiences and feel some sense of resolution (Forman 1980; Posttraumatic Stress 2001). Integration and resolution, in a sense, is no different for the secondary victim than for the primary one (Remer and Ferguson 1995). Early theorists believed that most rape victims were able to accomplish resolution and integration in a fairly short period of time. However, recovery takes a substantial amount of time, and for some primary and secondary victims, return to pre-rape levels of functioning never occurs.

While several phases may be identifiable, it does not necessarily mean that each victim experiences each phase in sequence, or that each phase is experienced only once. It is common for sexual assault victims to have setbacks, particularly as they are processed through the criminal justice system. The secondary victim's recovery is related to the primary victim's healing, and therefore, when the primary victim suffers a setback, the secondary victim also experiences it as well.

Partner Response

The research on partner reaction to the sexual assault of their mate is very limited, and often does not show males in a positive light. The published scholarship on partner reaction to rape focuses on males whose female partner is the primary victim, not female partners in either heterosexual or lesbian relationships. The literature also focuses greater attention on how the partner can help the primary victim rather than on what the partner experiences as a secondary victim.

Sexual assault victims often choose not to tell others about their assault because they are concerned about the reaction that they will receive. They generally choose whom they will tell based on the response they expect to receive from them. Persons whom the victim expects to be the most supportive and helpful are those most likely to be told of the assault (Frazier 1991; Frazier and Burnett 1994). This person is most commonly her husband, boyfriend, or lover (Feldman-Summers and Ashworth 1981).

Since males are most commonly the partners of sexual assault victims, it is relevant to look at male attitudes toward rape and rape victims. Research shows that males hold more negative attitudes toward rape victims (White, Robinson, and Sharon 1999). Young males often have the most negative attitudes toward rape victims and hold greater belief in the rape myths. "Men believed that a 'good girl' was less likely to be raped, and that if a woman was raped, she should blame herself because of her behaviors." (White et al. p. 993).

Some literature suggests that men are socialized to devalue women and to consider women as less moral and worthy of respect than men (Earl 1985). The objectification of women in the entertainment, advertisement, and pornography industries devalues women and encourages negative beliefs towards women. These negative beliefs perpetuate the myths that rape victims are to blame for their victimization. "Many of these unstated beliefs or cultural experiences come to the surface in behaviors that are hostile to the victim of rape" (Earl p. 262).

Partner response and potential for secondary trauma, as well as possible support for the primary victim, depends on the partner's attitude about rape in general. Partners who believe in the myths about rape are generally less supportive of the primary victim and suffer a significantly different type of loss. One crucial element in the male mate's response to rape is whether he sees the rape as sex or violence. Primary victims generally see the sexual assault as violence, but their husbands or boyfriends may not be able to clearly distinguish between sex and violence (Cwik 1996). It is not unusual for a male partner to react to the sexual aspects of the crime rather than to the violent nature of the victimization (Silverman 1978). This is most likely to happen when the partner believes that nice women don't get raped or that if she really didn't want it to happen, she could have stopped it. This further results in anger, because they believe that the rape was somehow their mate's fault. These feelings of anger and resentment are often expressed indirectly rather than directly, in the form of doubting the truthfulness of the victim's story, suggesting that she was not as careful as she should have been, or that she enjoyed the sexual assault (Silverman).

Another cultural myth is that a woman is the property of her father, boyfriend or spouse. If women are possessions to be admired by others, then a woman who has had sex, even forced sex, is devalued and tainted, decreasing the male's property interest in her (Earl 1985). Male mates may feel personally wronged by the rape because their exclusive right to their woman has been violated (Cwik 1996; Silverman 1978). While it is difficult to believe that many men have such opinions, it happens often enough that the concept cannot be ignored. Fortunately, the status of women has progressed sufficiently that rape is considered to be a violent personal crime, rather than a property crime against the proprietary rights of the male, as was true in ancient Rome and continues on in other cultures.

Another important issue in the reaction that male mates have to the rape of their partner is self-blame. Men who see themselves as the protector in the relationship often feel that they should have been there to protect their partner (Cwik 1996). These men often believe that the rape is their fault. They may feel guilty and believe that their masculinity has been challenged by their failure to protect their partner (Notman and Nadelson 1976). These feelings of guilt often lead to a desire for revenge or over protectiveness, neither of which is helpful toward healing or the relationship.

Feelings of powerlessness and loss of control are common reactions to rape for both primary and secondary victims. Revenge is often used as a means for the partner of a primary sexual assault victim to regain control. The partner's desire for revenge to regain control may lead to physical violence toward the perpetrator of the sexual assault (Cwik 1996), but more commonly these feelings remain at the fantasy level rather than leading to violence (Notman and Nadelson 1976). This desire for revenge by the secondary victim often puts the primary victim in the position of trying to comfort her partner, rather than focusing on her own well-being. It may also cause stress in the relationship because he may not be able to understand why she does not want to get back at her attacker. The secondary victim's wish for revenge may also make it difficult for him to understand the primary victim's reluctance to prosecute.

Feelings of responsibility for the assault because he did not protect her often lead to an effort to protect his partner at all times. After awhile, this may lead to resentment by the secondary victim that he has to spend so much time and effort protecting his partner (Cwik 1996). It also limits the primary victim's freedom, which may deny her the ability to regain control as soon as possible, and cause her to feel that her partner blames her for the rape or distrusts her or her judgment. This over-protectiveness may also cause stress in the relationship because both partners feel frustrated, out of control, and restricted by the other.

Belief in the rape myths and secondary trauma may make it extremely difficult for the male significant other to respond to the rape of his wife/girlfriend in an empathetic and supportive manner. Crisis Centers rarely provide adequate, if any, information to secondary victims, making it very difficult for even the most supportive partner to know what to expect or how to be supportive in this situation. Male socialization may also be a factor causing difficulty. "Since traditional male gender role socialization does not prepare a man to be emotionally expressive, the male significant other's ability to express his feelings about the rape and provide the needed emotional support is limited" (Cwik 1996, p. 102). Partners, even those with the best intentions, are often unaware that their attitudes and actions are not supportive or are detrimental to the primary victim's recovery.

While the research often focuses on the male partner's negative responses to rape, it is important to recognize that the partner is a legitimate secondary victim and that many males respond with genuine sympathy and support for the primary victim. Partners rarely receive the support they need to get through the crisis. Few sexual assault crisis agencies have counselors who work with the secondary victim at the time of initial disclosure or through the recovery process. The partner's feelings of crisis and the disruption in his life are overlooked both in the literature and in life, despite the fact that they are likely to be the primary victim's most important and constant source of support.

Research indicates that partner or spouse support is the most important support that a primary sexual assault victim can receive (Denkers 1999). Support from someone with whom the primary victim feels safe, secure, and close can most effectively support her after the assault. In fact, some research shows that primary victims not only need support from their partner the most, it also indicates that partners do, in fact, give the most support. Denkers (1999) found that primary victims received more support from their partners than they actually needed, and that only 6% of victims received less support from their mate than they needed. Denkers further found receiving sufficient support from their partner appeared to safeguard the primary victim's well-being.

Family Response

Family members respond to the rape of one its members with shock, anger, and feelings of powerlessness and loss of control. They feel many of the same things that the primary victim feels. Family members also experience post-traumatic stress and go through phases of recovery. Their attitudes about rape before the incident will be a critical factor in their response to the assault. Attitudes that reflect societal myths about rape will make their reaction more challenging for the primary victim to cope with, and make everyone's recovery more difficult.

Family response to the rape of a family member can be very diverse, depending on a variety of factors. The family's ability to function and act as a support system prior to the assault will have a significant impact on the family's reaction to the rape and on their ability to cope with the situation. After a rape, family dynamics may change, interrupting routines and disrupting patterns of coping with everyday stresses. Family roles and attitudes must be adjusted in order to cope with the trauma of rape and to begin the healing process (Erickson 1989). The age, developmental stage, and maturity of the primary victim will also affect the family's response and ability to cope with the rape (Mitchell 1991).

Feelings of powerlessness and loss of control often lead to a loss of any sense of security and the desire for revenge on the part of family members in much the same way it does for partners. This wish for revenge is much more common among fathers and brothers of the primary victim than among other family members (Cwik 1996; Silverman 1978). Generally this desire for revenge does not lead to physical confrontation with the perpetrator; the response is limited to detailed descriptions of what the father or brother would do if they ever caught the rapist (Erickson 1989).

Like the primary victim's mate, family members often feel guilty for not protecting the victim. Mothers often face the realization that they could not protect their child the way they had hoped to do. This may lead to a sense of failure as a parent and a loss of identity as a mother (Mitchell 1991) and doubt about her maternal competence (Schneider 2001). Mothers are often seen as the rock in the family; they are the person who holds everything together during the tough times. The sexual assault of one of her children may cause significant grief, a sense of loss, and frustration at not being able to fix it. Her distress over the rape may be the first time the primary victim and other family members see their mother as vulnerable; they now have to face their mother as a human being with limits and shortcomings (Mitchell).

Family members' feelings of guilt often result in patronization and over-protection of the primary victim (Silverman 1978). Families may move to a "safer" location or insist that someone goes with the primary victim everywhere she goes. The primary victim may be treated as if she is fragile and incompetent (Mitchell 1991). These attempts may serve to reinforce the victim's already existing feelings of helplessness and prevent her from using her own coping mechanisms (Mio and Foster 1991). The primary victim may lose any remaining sense of independence and self-confidence. Over-protection also makes it more difficult for the primary victim to regain control of her own life, which is one of the most important steps for her recovery.

Distraction is another coping mechanism often used by families (Silverman 1978). Distraction is where family members attempt to keep the primary victim busy, hoping that she will forget about the rape. This may make the primary victim feel that her family is trivializing the seriousness of her experience and trauma. She may be denied the opportunity to progress through the phases of recovery and to have genuine support. Family members may also try to keep the primary victim busy because they are uncomfortable with the fact that she was raped. They may not know what to say or do, so they overcompensate by keeping her busy and avoiding the topic.

Other family members may feel shame and humiliation because of the primary victim's rape. They may try to keep the incident a secret to prevent others from knowing about their failures or shame (Silverman 1978). Secondary victims may also want to keep the incident a secret because discussing it is too painful. Whatever the reason, treating the rape as a secret reinforces the primary victim's feelings of shame, guilt, and humiliation, and prevents her from validating her own perceptions (Mize, Bentley, Helms, Ledbetter, and Neblet 1995). It also denies her the support of her family. This refusal to discuss their feelings and fears also becomes destructive to the relationships in the family (Feinauer 1982). The family that refuses to deal openly with the situation will destroy any sense of family security and trust. When this loss of family support occurs, the trauma of the assault is worsened.

Children

Children in the family pose special problems for a family coping with rape. "Being part of a family system, children are affected by the changing boundaries that occur after the incident of rape." (Mio and Foster 1991 p. 147). Families often feel the need to protect children from the distressing news that their mother or older sister was raped, especially when the family views the rape as sexual rather than violent. Children are likely to know something is wrong. They may not know or understand what has happened, but they are aware that something has changed the family dynamics. If they are excluded from family discussions, it is likely to have a significant negative impact on the children and prevent the child from being part of the healing process. Even minimal awareness of traumatic events can have a mild to profound effect on a child (Mio and Foster). The parents and older family members may be so involved in their own trauma that they do not notice the child's feelings of exclusion and inability to deal with the changing boundaries within the family.

We still know very little about children's responses to traumatic events and the factors that make some children more vulnerable to developing posttraumatic stress reaction than others. However, research does indicate that the child's degree of exposure to the traumatic event seems to be a critical variable (Udwin 1993). Children's posttraumatic stress is also directly related to the parents' reaction to the event. The more posttraumatic stress experienced by the parent, the greater the posttraumatic stress experienced by the child (Udwin). Children of emotionally distressed mothers have been found to demonstrate higher levels of anxiety and depression than other children (Newberger, Gremy, Waternaux, and Newberger 1993). The level of adjustment in the parent is a significant factor in a child's experience of trauma and ability to adjust (Leibowitz, Mendelsohn, and Michelson 1999). Research suggests that trauma in childhood may impact many aspects of the child's developmental process. The extent to which a child is able to resolve trauma is influenced by the manner in which other members of the family deal with it. The parents' inability to provide emotional support for the child is also an important factor in the child's posttraumatic stress.

The literature consistently suggests that children should be made aware of the traumatic event and involved in the healing process. However, it is not necessary for the child to be given all of the details of the incident, nor is it necessary for the child to be involved in all family discussions of the rape. Including children in the recovery process helps the child integrate the trauma of rape into the family system and learn how to cope with trauma in life.

Response of Friends

Friends are often the first people to whom a primary victim discloses her sexual assault, and as such, often provide invaluable social support (Mize, et al. 1995). Despite the fact that friends are often the first to know of a sexual assault, little is known about the disclosure or about the impact of the disclosure. Family therapists often work with the families of rape victims, but outside college campuses, there are few, if any, programs or groups designed to help people deal with a sexual assault disclosure by a friend. Even college campuses offer very little for secondary sexual assault victims.

The friends who are told about a rape by the primary victim are often friends with whom there is some degree of social intimacy or trust already existing in the relationship (Dunn, Vail-Smith, and Knight 1999). Friends' responses are generally supportive of the primary victim. These responses include offering comfort to the victim by listening, offering reassurance, believing the victim, and offering to go with the victim if she chooses to report the sexual assault to the police. Friends also offer advice to the primary victim. Advice generally includes the suggestion that the primary victim seek medical treatment and testing for sexually transmitted diseases, report the incident to the police, and speak with a professional counselor (Dunn et al).

Not all responses by friends of primary sexual assault victims are positive or supportive of the victim. Less than constructive responses from friends were similar to the negative responses by partners and family members. These responses include doubting the victim's story, blaming the victim, and seeking revenge on the perpetrator (Dunn, Vail-Smith, and Knight 1999). Friends, like family members and partners, who respond to disclosure in a counterproductive manner often do so because they are surprised and don't know what to do or say.

Dakof and Taylor (1990) found that friends, acquaintances, and co-workers are more likely to withdraw from the victim than are family members.

Friends who are uncomfortable with what to say or how to act around the victim sometimes physically avoid the victim and decrease their communication with her. While Dakof and Taylor worked with victims of cancer, their work is applicable to sexual assault victims. The strain that victimization puts on a relationship varies with the nature of the relationship. Withdrawal leads to a lack of social support, which can worsen the trauma experienced by a primary sexual assault victim (Mitchell 1991) and lead to poorer functioning and negative changes in the relationship (Ahrens and Campbell 2000). Negative responses by family members are more likely to be overprotectiveness and hovering, while friends are more likely to withdraw. Dakof and Taylor report that primary victims find avoidance of social contact by friends to be the most unhelpful action exhibited by friends. Emotional support is the most helpful support from either friends or family.

Ahrens and Campbell (2000) found that most friends to whom the primary victim disclosed their sexual assault felt positive about the experience of helping their friend. They often felt needed and that the survivor was appreciative of the support provided. Many of these secondary victims reported that their friendship grew closer (Ahrens and Campbell). They also found few incidents of friends avoiding the primary victim or of friendships ending. Friends who reported a positive experience also exhibited more empathy, greater understanding of the life-threatening nature and devastating impact of sexual assault. They were also less likely to blame the primary victim for the assault.

Not all secondary victims in the study by Ahrens and Campbell (2000) reported a positive experience helping a friend through the trauma of sexual assault. Those who described their experience as neutral and having no positive or negative changes in the friendship also reported greater feelings of confusion, distress, and ineffectiveness in their help. Those who reported a negative experience indicated stronger feelings of ineffectiveness, more emotional distress, and did not feel good about the relationship. These friends also reported negative behavioral changes in the friendship.

The literature suggests that men may react more negatively to rape victims than women (Davis and Brickman 1996). "Compared with women, men blamed the survivor more, were less empathetic, more confused, felt more ineffective, experienced fewer positive and more negative changes in the friendship" (Ahrens and Campbell 2000, p. 966). Despite the fact that Ahrens and Campbell found men significantly less supportive than women, unsupportive behavior by male friends is fairly rare.

Secondary victims who are friends of the primary victim also report experiencing trauma as a result of the disclosure (Dunn, Vail-Smith, and Knight 1999). The level of trauma in secondary victims is related to the closeness of the relationship to the primary victim. Close friends report more trauma than casual friends and acquaintances. Type of assault, level of violence, personal assault history, length of friendship, and gender influence the level of secondary trauma and long-term consequences (Ahrens and Campbell 2000). Ahrens and Campbell further found that friends of rape survivors might be less traumatized than family members. Friends are likely to experience strong feelings of anger and revenge, but are less likely to feel depression and shame than family members and partners.

Support for Secondary Victims

Most crime victims do not report the crime to the police; they usually seek help from family and friends (Kaukinen 2002). Since sexual assault victims are more likely to ask for help from family and friends than from the police or the criminal justice system, there needs to be a means of providing support to these informal help sources. Secondary victims need to be given the skills, resources, and information they need to appropriately support the primary victim and to cope with their own stress (Kaukinen, 2002). Positive social response from secondary victims can be a significant factor in reducing PTSD symptoms for the primary victim (Ullman, Filipas, Townsend, and Starzynski 2007; Ullman, Townsend, Filipas, and Starzynski 2007; Ullman, Filipas, Townsend, and Starzynski 2006). While friends feel positive about the support that they can provide for a primary sexual assault survivor, they still need support and guidance during the process (Ahrens and Campbell 2000).

Early intervention is critical to prevent psychological and psychosomatic problems resulting from the sexual assault for both the primary and secondary sexual assault victim. Intervention should include education about rape and its aftermath. This education should include the myths and facts about rape, the coping strategies used by rape victims during and after the attack, the phases of healing that the primary and secondary victims are likely to experience, the possibility of suffering from Posttraumatic Stress Disorder, the best ways to support the primary victim, how to support other secondary victims, and where to go for help (Mio and Foster 1991; Washburn 2003). Helping secondary victims understand that the primary victim has suffered a life-threatening experience helps them to understand the primary victim's reactions and helps them to focus less on the sexual aspects of the crime (Silverman 1978). Educating secondary victims allows them to better understand what the primary victim is experiencing and helps them to anticipate some of the reactions and phases the primary victim will experience (Feinauer and Hippolite 1987).

Education also gives the secondary victim the confidence and skills to help the primary victim and to feel good about his or her role as a help provider. Secondary victims can learn how to allow a victim to express their feelings openly and freely and to provide the emotional support that can help the primary victim recover more quickly. The more prepared the secondary victim is to handle a rape disclosure, the better he or she will handle the situation. Less secondary trauma will also result when the secondary victim is prepared to handle the situation and feel positive about how it was handled.

In addition to education, support services should be made available to secondary sexual assault victims. Like the primary victim, the secondary victims must begin a process of healing to deal with the effects of the trauma. Secondary victims may need to adjust to their own roles, attitudes, and behaviors before they can heal. Relationships that have the ability to shift roles, such as the caregiver role, are more likely to have resolution than relationships that are less flexible (Cwik 1996). Without learning about victim response to rape and without adequate support, it is very difficult for secondary victims to heal.

Support services provided for secondary victims need to include friends as well as family (Mitchell 1991). Dunn et al. (1999) suggest that there is a need to alert both male and female college students about the possibility that they may be the recipients of rape-related disclosures, and that education about the aftermath of rape may help the secondary victim provide support for the primary victim and handle their own stress from the disclosure. Dunn, Vail-Smith, and Knight also recommend support services for friends and family who accompany a primary sexual assault victim to a health service provider.

Victim Advocate and Counselor Trauma

Secondary victimization is not limited to partners, family, and friends of the primary victim. Victim service providers such as sexual assault counselors, police officers, and crisis line volunteers are prime candidates for vicarious trauma (Campbell and Wasco 2005). "Their acute and chronic exposure to the trauma, grief, and other reactions that are common to many crime victims can have a cumulative, and often devastating, effect on their view of the world and, sometimes, on their choice of careers." (National Victim Assistance Academy 2002 chap.6.2, p. 2). The personal and devastating nature of sexual victimization may intensify the vicarious trauma experienced by counselors and advocates working with sexual violence survivors. Victim advocates, trauma counselors, and others who come into regular contact with sexual assault victims may experience physical problems, anger, fear, sadness, anxiety, sleeping disorders, and increased need for social support.

Long-term exposure to the trauma experienced by sexual assault victims may affect the counselor's beliefs about the world, safety, and the trustworthiness of people (McCann and Pearlman 1990). The research indicates that the number of traumatized clients in a therapist's caseload may be related to secondary traumatic stress (Arvay 2001). While Baird and Jenkins (2003) indicate that counselors seeing more clients report less vicarious trauma, Schauben and Frazier (1995) report that counselors who have a large percentage of patients who are sexual violence survivors report more disrupted beliefs about themselves and others, more posttraumatic stress-related symptoms, and more vicarious trauma than counselors who see fewer sexual assault victims. Schauben and Frazier further found that the beliefs most likely to be altered by counselors working with sexual assault survivors are beliefs involving the goodness or trustworthiness of other people.

Victim advocates, counselors, healthcare workers, and police officers who work with sexual assault victims may also feel anger based on their dealings with others while advocating for or trying to help the primary victim. Wasco and Campbell (2002) interviewed experienced rape victim advocates and found that they experienced anger in response to encounters with perpetrators as well as with some individuals associated with the health care and criminal justice systems. They further found that many of these secondary victims were able to turn their anger into personal growth and an increased commitment to primary victims.

Many persons who work with sexual assault victims have learned to proactively take care of themselves to offset the negative impact of working with people experiencing trauma and crisis. Research indicates that victim advocates use a variety of techniques to deal with the stress; some talk about their work with others, some turn to their spiritual life, and others actively engage in social and recreational activities (Wasco, Campbell and Clark 2002). Taking care of oneself is important for sexual assault advocates because it helps them to stay healthy and keep a positive outlook as well as allowing them to better help the primary victim.

Conclusion

Anyone who is exposed to the trauma experienced by a sexual assault victim may experience secondary victimization. Family, friends, first responders, and sexual assault counselors are all at risk for suffering secondary trauma through their efforts to help a rape victim. The closeness of the relationship and the duration of the contact with the primary victim are factors in developing this secondary trauma. Other factors that have an impact on the development of secondary victimization are the attitudes held before the assault, the circumstances of the assault, and the availability of a support network.

Secondary victims often experience the same healing process and stages of recovery as the primary victim. One major difference in recovery is that the secondary victim is dependent upon the primary victim for information about the assault. This may be a lengthy process since the primary victim often has to experience some healing before they are able to share the details of their attack.

Partner response to a sexual assault is often not conducive to healing for the victim. Male partners who believe in the myths about rape may blame the victim for their rape or see the attack as a sexual encounter rather than as an act of violence. Partners often blame themselves for the sexual assault; they believe that it was their job to protect the victim, and that they failed in their responsibility. Partners may seek revenge on the perpetrator, often placing the victim in a position of calming her husband or boyfriend rather than focusing on her own recovery. Despite negative responses by males who believe in the myths about rape, many partners are supportive and help the sexual assault victim heal and become a sexual assault survivor.

Family members of sexual assault victims also experience secondary post-traumatic stress. Family members often become overprotective of the victim, depriving her of support and the opportunity to regain control over her own life. Family members may also try to distract the victim in the mistaken belief that keeping the victim busy and not allowing her to think about the assault will help her recovery. This also denies her support. Some families feel shame and humiliation at the rape of a family member and may try to keep the assault a secret. The family may feel that they are protecting the victim by keeping things quiet, but in reality they may be reinforcing the victim's feelings of guilt, shame and self-blame.

Friends are generally supportive of sexual assault victims, offering them reassurance, support, and advice. Friends often offer to accompany the victim to the police station or to the hospital. However, not all responses from friends are positive. Friends may doubt the victim's story, seek revenge, or withdraw from the victim because of their own discomfort with the situation. Friends are often less traumatized than family members or partners because there may be less closeness in the relationship.

Secondary sexual assault victims rarely receive the support and intervention that will help them heal and become secondary sexual assault survivors. Lack of knowledge of the truth about sexual assault and the recovery process may make secondary victimization more difficult to handle. Lack of knowledge may also impair their ability to be supportive and helpful to the primary victim's healing process. Lack of support for secondary victims generally impedes their own healing and recovery process.

In addition to partners, family, and friends of primary sexual assault victims, service providers for victims also suffer from the trauma of secondary victimization. Factors related to secondary trauma for counselors, volunteers, and first responders include the number of trauma victims they encounter and the support they receive. Many victim service providers are able to counter their trauma by feeling positive about the help and support they offer primary victims.

Secondary victimization is a fairly new concept in the literature as well as in victim services organizations. Additional research needs to be done to further explore the causes and consequences of secondary trauma on partners, family, friends, and service providers. Educational and support services for secondary sexual assault victims need to be implemented in law enforcement agencies, victim service groups, hospitals, and mental health care providers. Recognizing the plight of secondary sexual assault survivors is the first step in efforts to improve services for them.

References

Ahrens, C. E., Cambell, R. (2000). Assisting Rape Victims as They Recover From Rape: The Impact on Friends. *Journal of Interpersonal Violence, 15*, 959–986.

American Psychiatric Association. (2000). Diagnostic and Statistical Manual of Mental Disorders (4th ed. TR). Washington, DC: Author.

Arata, C. M. (1999). Coping with Rape. *Journal of Interpersonal Violence, 14*, 62–79.

Arvay, M. J. (2001). Secondary Trauma Stress Among Trauma Counselors: What Does the Research Say? *International Journal for the Advancement of Counseling, 23*, 283–293.

Baird, S. and Jenkins, S. R. (2003). Vicarious Traumatization, Secondary Traumatic Stress, and Burnout in Sexual Assault and Domestic Violence Agency Staff. *Violence and Victims, 18*, 71–86.

Burgess, A. W., and Holmstrom, L. L. (1974). Rape Trauma Syndrome. *American Journal of Psychiatry, 131*, 981–986.

Campbell, R. and Wasco, S. M. (2005). Understanding Rape and Sexual Assault; 20 Years of Progress and Future Directions. *Journal of Interpersonal Violence, 20*(1), 127–131.

Cwik, M. S. (1996). The Many Effects of Rape: The Victim, Her Family, and Suggestions for Family Therapy. *Family Therapy, 23*, 95–115.

Dakof, G. A., and Taylor, S. E. (1990). Victims' Perceptions of Social Support: What is Helpful from Whom? *Journal of Personality and Social Psychology, 58*, 80–89.

Davis, R. C., Brickman, E., and Baker, T. (1991). Supportive and Unsupportive Responses of Others to Rape Victims: Effects of Concurrent Victim Adjustment. *American Journal of Community Policing, 19*, 443–451.

Denkers, A. (1999). Factors Affecting Support After Criminal Victimization: Needed and Received Support from the Partner, The Social Network, and Distant Support Providers. *The Journal of Social Psychology, 139*, 191–201.

Dunn, P.C., Vail-Smith, K., and Knight, S.M. (1999). What Date/Acquaintance Rape Victims Tell Others: A Study of College Student Recipients of Disclosure. *Journal of American College Health, 47*, 213–219.

Earl, W. (1985) Rape as a Variable In Marital Therapy: Context And Treatment. *Family Therapy, XII*, 259–272.

Erickson, C. A. (1989). Rape and the Family. In Figley, C. R. (Ed.), Treating Stress in Families (pp. 257–289). New York: Brunner/Mazel.

Feinauer, L. L. (1982). Rape: A Family Crisis. *The American Journal of Family Therapy, 10*, 35–39.

Feinauer, L. L. and Hippolite, D. L. (1987). Once a Princess, Always a Princess: A Strategy for Therapy with Families of Rape Victims. *Contemporary Family Therapy, 9*, 252–262.

Feldman-Summers, S., and Ashworth, C. (1981). Factors Related to Intentions to Report Rape. *Journal of Social Issues, 37*, 53–70.

Frazer, P. A. (1991). Self-Blame as a Mediator of Postrape Depressive Symptoms. *Journal of Social and Clinical Psychology, 10*, 47–57.

Frazier, P. A. and Burnett, J. W. (1994). Immediate Coping Strategies Among Rape Victims. *Journal of Counseling and Development, 72*, 633–640.

Kaukinen, C. (2002). The Help-Seeking Decisions of Violent Crime Victims. *Journal of Interpersonal Violence, 17*, 432–456.

Leibowitz, S., Mendelsohn, M., and Michelson, C. (1999). Child Rape: Extending the Therapeutic Intervention to Include the Mother-Child Dyad. *South African Journal of Psychology, 29*, 103–109.

McCann, I. L., and Pearlman, L. A. (1990). Vicarious Traumatization: A Framework for Understanding the Psychological Effects of Working with Victims. *Journal of Traumatic Stress, 3*, 131–149.

Mio, J. S. and Foster, J.D. (1991). The Effects of Rape Upon Victims and Families: Implications for a Comprehensive Family Therapy. *The American Journal of Family Therapy, 19*, 147–159.

Mitchell, M. E. (1991). A Family Approach and Network Implications of Therapy for Victims of Violence as Applied in a Case of Rape. *Journal of Family Psychotherapy, 2,* 1–13.

Mize, L. K., Bentley, B., Helms, S., Ledbetter, J. and Neblett, K. (1995). Surviving Voices: Incest Survivors' Narratives of Their Process of Disclosure. *Journal of Family Psychotherapy, 4,* 43–59.

Motta, R. W., Kefer, J. M., Hertz, M. D., and Hafeez, S. (1999). Initial Evaluation of the Secondary Trauma Questionnaire. *Psychological Reports, 85,* 997–1002.

National Victim Assistance Academy (2002, June). Mental Health Needs: Trauma and Assessment Intervention. In National Victim Assistance Academy Textbook (chap. 6.1) Retrieved May 25, 2003, from http://www.ojp.usdoj.gov/ovc/assist/nvaa2002/chapter6_1.html#1.

National Victim Assistance Academy (2002, June). Mental Health Needs: Stress Management. In National Victim Assistance Academy Textbook (chap. 6.2) Retrieved May 25, 2003, from http://www.ojp.usdoj.gov/ovc/assist/nvaa2002/chapter6_2.html#1.

Newberger, C. M. , Gremy, I. M., Waternaux, C. M., and Newberger, E. H. (1993). Mothers of Sexually Abused Children: Trauma and Repair in Longitudinal Perspective. *American Journal of Orthopsychiatry, 63,* 92–102.

Notman, M. T. and Nadelson, C. C. (1976). The Rape Victim: Psychodynamic Considerations. *American Journal of Psychiatry, 133,* 408–413.

Posttraumatic Stress Disorder, Rape trauma Syndrome, and Battery. (April 19, 2001). In Student Material: Victim Empowerment: Bridging the Systems Mental Health and Victim Service Providers (chap. 3). Retrieved July 18, 2002 from http://www.ojp.usdoj.gov/ovc/publications/infores/student/welcome.html.

Remer, R. and Ferguson, R.A. (1995). Becoming a Secondary Survivor of Sexual Assault. *Journal of Counseling and Development, 73,* 407–412.

Schauben, L. J., and Frazier, P.A. (1995) Vicarious Trauma: The Effects on Female Counselors of Working with Sexual Assault Survivors. *Psychology of Women Quarterly, 19,* 49–64.

Schneider, H. J. (2001). Victimological Developments in the World During the Past Three Decades: A Study of Comparative Victimology. *International Journal of Offender Therapy and Comparative Criminology, 45,* 539–555.

Silverman, D. C. (1978). Sharing the Crisis of Rape: Counseling the Mates and Families of Victims. *American Journal of Orthopsychiatry, 48,* 166–173.

Udwin, O. (1993). Children's Reactions to Traumatic Events. *Journal of Child Psychology and Psychiatry, 34,* 115–127.

Ullman, S., Filipas, H., Townsend, S., and Starzynski, L. (2006). The Role of Victim-Offender Relationship in Women's Sexual Assault Experiences. *Journal of Interpersonal Violence, 21*(6), 798–819.

Ullman, S., Filipas, H., Townsend, S., and Starzynski, L. (2007). Psychosocial Correlates of PTSD Symptom Severity in Sexual Assault Survivors. *Journal of Traumatic Stress, 20*(5), 821–831.

Ullman, S., Townsend, S., Filipas, H., and Starzynski, L. (2007). Structural Models of the Relations of Assault Severity, Social Support, Avoidance Coping, Self-Blame, and PTSD Among Sexual Assault Survivors. *Psychology of Women Quarterly, 31*(1), 23–37.

Wasco, S., and Campbell, R. (2002). Emotional Reactions of Rape Victim Advocates: A Multiple Case Study of Anger and Fear. *Psychology of Women Quarterly, 26*(2), 120–130.

Wasco, S., Campbell, R., and Clark, M. (2002). A Multiple Case Study of Rape Victim Advocates' Self-Care Routines: The Influence of Organizational Context. *American Journal of Community Psychology, 30*(5), 731–760.

Washburn, P. (2003). Why me? Addressing The Spiritual and Emotional Trauma of Sexual Assault. *Topics in Emergency Medicine, 25*(3), 236–241.

White, B. H., Robinson, K., and Sharon, E. (1999). Attitudes Toward Rape Victims: Effect of Gender and Professional Status. *Journal of Interpersonal Violence, 14*, 989–996.

Chapter 6

Sexual Abuse of Males

Elycia Daniel

Traditionally, when one thinks of rape, they think of a female as the victim. However, the face of the rape victim is ever changing to that of a male victim. While societal concern has focused on the female victims of rape, and the vast majority of literature on rape refers to the female victim, there has been some interest in male rape victims. Kaufman, et al. (1980), notes that male rape was believed to occur in one of three circumstances: an aberration of prison life, a form of vicarious rape against women and as a violent outgrowth of the homosexual culture. He also suggests that many people assume that the male victims of sexual assault are usually children and the prey of child molesters.

Sexual assault is the most rapidly growing violent crime in America (Dupre, Hampton, Morrison, and Meeks 1993). It is estimated that fewer than 50% of rapes are reported each year and male victims represent only 5% of these reported sexual assaults (American Academy of Pediatrics 1994). According to the U.S. Department of Justice Statistics, 1999, only 25,000 men are victims of rape or attempted rape compared to over 343,000 female rapes or attempted rapes. Rape crisis centers have reported that 10 to 20% of rape victims were men (Forman 1982; Kaufman, et al. 1980).

In a survey done by Sorenson (1987) of Los Angeles citizens, of 1480 men interviewed, 7.2% reported that as adults they had been pressured or forced to have sexual contact. They also further reported that the incidence rate rose to 16% for white, college educated men ages 18 to 39 years old. Most of the cases were by female acquaintances, usually by verbal pressure.

Not only are fewer male rapes reported, but, the legal consequences for the rapes appear to be different as well. A study conducted by Hill (2000) found that homosexual males accused of sexually assaulting non-homosexual males were more often found guilty than heterosexual males who assault heterosexual females or homosexual males accused of assaulting homosexual males. In contrast, New York and North Carolina are two states in which the rape of a male is a lesser charge than rape of a female. An area for further research may be into the analysis of rape criminal codes across the country.

Just as in female rape cases, according to Groth and Burgess (1980) male rape appears to be underreported because of the stigma associated with it. Before reviewing literature on the specifics of male rape, it is important to review the literature on the reasons that males do not report the rape. Smith, Pine, and Hawley (1988) suggested that male subjects viewed the episode in sexual terms and failed to grasp the violence component of the rape. The do report however, that male victims have greater difficulty in dealing with their traumatic experience than do females. Males seldom reveal their experiences to others because they are ashamed of what happened to them and don't expect others to understand the level of trauma they have experienced. They fear being stigmatized if they reveal what happened to them. Groth and Burgess (1980) found that the male victim may be bewildered by his physiological response during the sexual assault and, therefore, may be discouraged from reporting the assault for fear associated with his sexuality; he may have a fear of being viewed as a homosexual.

A study of social cognitions about adult male victims of female sexual assault viewed the male victim more likely to be judged as having initiated or encouraged the sex acts. Laurent (1993) reported that the male masculinity has already been challenged once by the attack, and the male victim, when reporting the incident, may feel that authorities will challenge it again. Similarly, Groth and Burgess (1980) stated three reasons that male victims gave for not reporting rape: 1) feelings that he should have been able to defend himself against sexual assault, 2) fear that his sexuality will become suspect, and 3) distress associated with recalling and describing the incident.

The next component of male rape to look at is the attackers. We will look at both methods used and reasons for the attack. Women are taught to be careful of their behavior, be mindful of their surroundings and always travel in groups at night. However, when it comes to men, our society doesn't seem to require them to take such extreme measures. Groth and Burgess (1980) stated that men are assaulted where they live, work, travel and relax. They appear to be at greater risk in solitary activities, such as hitchhiking. In their study, 38% of the victims were hitchhiking and 36% were engaged in an out-of-doors activity, such as swimming at a beach or hiking in the woods. Finkelor and Russell (1984) reported that 84% of those who rape males are male and a vast majority of them are heterosexual. A study by Frazier (1993) that designed to compare information about male and female rape victims found that male victims were more likely to have been raped by more than one assailant, by a Caucasian assailant and were more likely to have been physically harmed. The style of attack of the offenders seemed to vary. Groth and Burgess (1980) stated that the offenders show three major methods: entrapment, intimidation and/or physical force. In a study conducted of convicted rapists, Groth and Burgess (1980) reported that in some cases, the gender of the victim didn't seem to be of primary importance to the rapist, in other cases the intended targets were males.

There are five possible categories for the victims and their attackers: female attacker/male victim, male heterosexual attacker/male heterosexual victim, male heterosexual attacker/male homosexual victim, male homosexual attacker/male heterosexual victim, and male homosexual attacker/male homosexual victim. As we look at male victims responses to rape and the motives and methods of the attackers, these distinctions often become important. An area for further research would be to examine the extent of these five attacker victim relationships.

Like female rape, male rape is more often about domination than sex. In those cases where the intended targets were in fact males, the rapist's assaults were attempts to deal with unresolved and conflict-ridden aspects of their lives. Similarly, Kaufman, et al. (1980), reported that the male victims of sexual assault seemed in general to be unaffiliated with the homosexual community. In accordance with other studies, they did find that sexual assaults of males appeared to be an expression of anger, power and dominance over another. In a study conducted with 930 gay men, Hickson, Davies, Hunt and Weatherburn (1994), 27.6% reported they had been subject to nonconsensual sex at some point in their lives; 3% involved female assailants. One-third reported that they had been forced into activity, usually anal intercourse, by men with whom they had previously had or were currently having sexual activity. The results did not support the assertion that male rape is usually committed by men identified as heterosexuals, primarily as an expression of power and control.

In terms of the sexual acts themselves, Groth and Burgess (1980) found that in slightly more than half of the cases (N=12; 55%) only a single type of sexual activity occurred during the offense, and in fewer than half of the cases (N=10; 45%) several types of sexual acts (oral, anal, and masturbatory) took place. In the majority of the assaults (N=14; 64%) the offender sexually penetrated his victim in some fashion, whereas the offender accepted penetration, by performing fellatio on his victim, only in 7 of their cases (32%). The most common sexual act was sodomy, with oral penetration being the next most frequent act. Comparably in Kaufman, et al. (1980), they reported that all of their males victims (N=14) were sodomized and 9 were forced to commit fellatio.

Much of the research literature suggested that males commonly experience many of the reactions that females experience (Manzano 1998; Isley 1991; Brochman 1991; Mezey and King 1989), such as depression, sexual dysfunction, anger, self-blame, suicidal feelings, guilt, flashbacks and increased sense of vulnerability. According to a study by Struckman-Johnson and Struckman-Johnson (1992), 60% of male survivors believed they were going to be killed during the assault. They also noted that men suffer from some of the same emotional issues as that of women. In a study conducted by Groth and Burgess (1980), 22 convicted rapists reported the impact of rape on male victims was similar to the effect of rape on female victims, disrupting their biological, psychological and social functioning.

According to Frazier (1993), male victims were rated as more depressed and hostile immediately following the rape than were female victims. Groth and Burgess (1980) reported that male victims make it clear that 1) rape is stressful, 2) reporting the assault is difficult, and 3) one's lifestyle becomes disrupted. Struckman-Johnson and Struckman-Johnson (1994) suggested that most men had no or very mild negative reactions to the unwanted female contact. However, there was evidence of moderate to strong negative reactions to the experience of a male-initiated unwanted contact. Brochman (1991) reported that the experience may affect gay and heterosexual men differently. Most rape counselors pointed out that gay men have difficulties in their sexual and emotional relationships with other men, and think that the assault occurred because they are gay, whereas straight men often begin to question their sexual identity and are more disturbed by the sexual aspect of the assault than the violence involved. Struckman-Johnson and Struckman-Johnson (1994) stated that heterosexuals were the most upset by contact initiated by another man, either acquaintance or stranger, and especially if it occurs in a sudden or unexpected manner or involves any kind of physical restraint. The researchers contributed it to their feelings about their own sexual identity and fear of homosexuality. Romano and DeLuca (2001) reported that the effects of sexual abuse was similar in males to that of females and includes depression, self-blame, low self-esteem, anger, anxiety and sexuality problems. Coxell and King (1996) studied coercion in gay relationships in the UK with a sample of 1,480 males and found that problems reported after sexual assault by males include confusion about sexual orientation, sexual problems, posttraumatic stress disorder, problems facing close relationships, mistrust of adult men, suicide and various mood disorders. They further reported that sexual assault by females may leave men less traumatized than sexual assaults by men because they are less likely to involve physical force and because same-sex sexual contact, which heterosexuals may find traumatic itself, is not involved.

Contradictory to many other research findings, in a longitudinal study conducted by Gil-Rivas, Fiorentine, Anglin and Taylor (1997), of 330 participants from 26 outpatient programs, results suggested that sexual abuse among women was associated with higher levels of depression, anxiety, suicidal ideation, suicide attempts, and post-traumatic stress disorder (PTSD), and for men sexual abuse was only associated with anxiety. They further reported no significant association between sexual and physical abuse for men.

In a study of male rape in the UK, Rogers (1997) stated that even though some evidence is being reported that male rape survivors develop posttraumatic stress disorder (PTSD) following the assault, to date there have been no systematic prevalence studies that have found a relationship between PTSD and assault in male survivors of rape.

Calderwood (1987) suggested that most male rape is by other men, and males often sustain more injuries than females. A study conducted by Kaufman (1980) compared 14 male rape victims treated in a county hospital emergency room over a 39-month period with 100 randomly selected female victims treated over the same period. Their findings showed that the males as a group sustained more traumas, were more likely to have been a victim of multiple assaults from multiple assailants, and were likely to have been held captive longer. The males were also more reluctant to reveal initially the genital component of their assault and were more likely to use denial and control their emotions in reaction to the assault.

A study conducted by Mitchell, Hirschman, and Hall (1999) examined the differences concerning the relationship between the sexual orientation of a male victim and attributions of the victim's degree of responsibility, pleasure, and trauma associated with assault. The results showed that victims attributed more responsibility, more pleasure, and fewer traumas to a homosexual victim than a heterosexual one. Male respondents more than females attributed more responsibility and pleasure. Frazier (1993) suggested that male victims were rated as more depressed and hostile immediately following the rape than were female victims.

Another study conducted by Smith, Pine, and Hawley (1988) suggested that compared to other victims-assailant conditions, the male victims of sexual assault were judged more likely to have encouraged or initiated the episode, to have derived more pleasure from it and to have experienced less stress. In terms of pleasure, 47% of male subjects in their particular study rated the sexual episode as pleasurable, compared with only 9% of females.

Treating the male victim has proven to be even tougher. Calderwood (1987) suggested that some of the problems in treating the male rape victim include the reluctance of many men to report sexual assault, lack of facilities for helping men, and lack of knowledge about the phenomenon. Frazier (1993) as well as Groth and Burgess (1980) suggested that one reason male survivors of sexual assault may be less likely to report or seek treatment for their assault is partly because they view rape crisis centers and hotlines as serving only women. According to Kaufman (1980) proper diagnosis and treatment of male rape victims requires a high index of suspicion and sensitivity to the likelihood of major, hidden trauma. Leskela, Dieperink and Kok (2001) suggested that group therapy is an effective modality in treating men who have been sexually assaulted. Due to some of the stigmatization of male rape, these victims need their own facilities devoted to their treatment needs.

Most of the studies of male rape victims indicated that they face serious psychological problems due to being raped. However, due to underreporting by male victims, as well as society's view of the male rape victim, we don't really know enough about the victim to draw conclusions. Much is left to be said about the male rape victim. From the literature that is available, we are able to conclude that most male victims suffer from some of the same psychological problems as female victims. One major component to look into is the sexual orientation of the victim and the offender and how that affects the victim.

It does seem that male rape victims are going through some of the same painful processes that female rape victims go through. Females were and some still are embarrassed about the rape, just as the men are, and feel that it was somehow their fault. Females also had the stigma of rape attached to them, just as males do. Before the passage of Rape Shield Laws, female victims were even more reluctant to report out of fear of being ridiculed or blamed. The court system may want to reassess their laws regarding rape of males.

References

American Academy of Pediatrics. *Committee on Adolescence: Sexual Assault and the Adolescent.* Washington DC: Author, 1994.

Brochman, S. "Silent Victims: Bringing Male Rape Out of the Closet." *The Advocate* 582, (1991): 38–42.

Calderwood, D. "The Male Rape Victim." *Medical Aspects of Human Sexuality* 21 no. 5, (1987): 53–55.

Coxell, A.W., and M. B. King. "Male Victims of Rape and Sexual Abuse." *Sexual and Marital Therapy* 11 no 3, (1996): 297–308.

Dupre, A.R., H. L. Hampton, H. Morrison, and G. R. Meeks. "Sexual Assault." *Obstetrical and Gynecological Survey* 48, (1993): 640–648.

Finkelhor, D. and D. Russell. "Women as Perpetrators." *Child Sexual Abuse: New Theory and Research.* New York Free Press, 1984: 171–187.

Forman, B. D. "Reported Male Rape." *Victimology International Journal 7,* (1982): 235–236.

Frazier, P.A. "A Comparative Study and Female Victims Seen at a Hospital-Based Rape Crisis Program." *Journal of Interpersonal Violence* 8 no. 1, (1993): 64–76.

Gil-Rivas, V., R. Fiorentine, M. D. Anglin, and E. Taylor. "Sexual and Physical Abuse: Do They Compromise Drug Treatment Outcomes?" *Journal of Substance Abuse Treatment* 14 no. 4, (1997): 351–358.

Groth, N., and W. Burgess. "Male Rape: Offenders and Victims." *American Journal of Psychiatry* 137, (1980): 806–810.

Hickson, F. C. I., P. M. Davies, A. J. Hunt, and P. Weatherburn. "Gay Men as Victims of Nonconsensual Sex." *Archives of Sexual Behavior* 23 no. 3, (1994): 281–294.

Hill, J.M. "The Effects of Sexual Orientation in the Courtroom: A Double Standard." *Journal of Homosexuality* 39 no. 2, (2000): 93–111.

Isley, P. "Adult Male Sexual Assault in the Community. A Literature Review and Group Treatment Model." *Rape and Sexual Assault III: A Research Handbook.* New York: Garland Publishing, Inc, 1991.

Kaufman, A., P. Divasto, R. Jackson, P. Voorhees, and J. Christy. "Male Rape Victims: Noninstitutionalized Assault." *American Journal of Psychiatric Association* 137 no. 2, (1980): 221–223.

Laurent, C. "Male Rape." *Nursing Times* 89 no. 6, (1993): 10–16.

Leskela, J., M. Dieperink, and C. J. Kok. "Group Treatment with Sexually Assaulted Male Veterans: A Year in Review." *Group* 25 no. 4, (2001): 303–319.

Manzano, L. J. "Men Raped: Supporting the Male Survivor of Sexual Assault on the College Campus." (1998) http://www.uvm.edu/~vtconn/journals/1998/manzano.html (retrieved July 2003).

Mezey, G., and M. King. "The Effects of Sexual Assault on Men: A Survey of 22 Victims." *Psychological Medicine* 19 no. 1, (1989): 205–209.

Mitchell, D., R. Hirschman, and G. C. N. Hall. "Attributions of Victim Responsibility, Pleasure and Trauma in Male Rape." *Journal of Sex Research* 36 no. 4, (1999): 369–373.

Rogers, P. "Post Traumatic Stress Disorder Following Male Rape." *Journal of Mental Health-UK* 6 no. 1, (1997): 5–9.

Romano, E., and R. V. DeLuca. "Male Sexual Abuse: A Review of Effects, Abuse Characteristics, and Links with Later Psychological Functioning." *Aggression and Violent Behavior* 6 no. 1, (2001): 55–78.

Smith, R., C. J. Pine, and M. Hawley. "Social Cognitions About Adult Male Victims of Female Sexual Assault." *The Journal of Sex Research* 24, (1988): 101–112.

Sorenson, S.B., J. A. Stein, J. M. Siegel, J. M. Golding, and M. A. Burman. "The Prevalence of Adult Sexual Assault: The Los Angeles Epidemicologic Catchment Area Study." *American Journal of Epidemiology* 126, (1987): 1154–1164.

Struckman-Johnson, C., and D. Struckman-Johnson. "Acceptance of Male Rape Myths among College Men and Women." *Sex Roles: A Journal of Research* 27 no. ¾, (1992): 84–100.

Struckman-Johnson, C., and D. Struckman-Johnson. "Men Pressured and Forced Into Sexual Experience." *Archives of Sexual Behavior* 23 no. 1, (1994): 93–114.

U.S. Department of Justice, Bureau of Justice Statistics. *Criminal Victimization in the United States, 1999.* Washington, D. C.: Government Printing Office.

Guidelines for Helping Sexual Assault Victims

- Listen to her and let her reveal information at her own pace.
- Let her express her emotions in her own way.
- Believe her.
- Reassure her that she is safe now.
- Stay with her if she wants you to stay.
- Encourage her to report the assault to the police. Let her have control of the decision.
- Encourage her to seek medical attention. Let her have control of the decision unless there is a medical emergency.
- Allow her to make her own decisions about who to tell.
- Be supportive by using a sympathetic tone of voice, maintaining natural eye contact, using empathetic facial expressions and body language, and keeping a nonjudgmental attitude.
- Offer to get whatever she needs or to make phone calls for her.
- Let her know that her feelings and responses are normal reactions to a traumatic event.
- Tell her that she did nothing wrong and that her victimization was not her fault.
- Let her talk about the assault as often as she wants to talk about it.
- Be patient. Recovery from a sexual assault takes a long time.
- Support her through the stages of recovery.
- Respect her wishes.
- Offer to help her find resources for support, such as a local rape crisis center.
- Offer to accompany her to the hospital, police, station, rape crisis center, or court.
- Offer to be available when she needs to talk.
- Don't physically touch or hug her without asking if she is comfortable with it.

- Don't vent your own shock, anger, and outrage at the assault to her.
- Don't seek revenge against the perpetrator(s).
- Don't try to keep her busy so she won't think about it.
- Don't dwell on the sexual aspects of the assault.
- Don't overprotect her. Allow her to exercise her independence.

Compiled by Diane Daane, Ph.D. in Frances P. Reddington and Betsy Wright Kreisel (eds.). *Sexual Assault: The Victims, the Perpetrators, and the Criminal Justice System* (2004). Carolina Academic Press: Durham, NC.

Special Feature

Guidelines for Taking Care of Yourself: When a Friend or Family Member Discloses a Sexual Assault to You

- Recognize that her assault will have an impact on you, including emotional trauma.
- Accept that the assault was not your fault. The perpetrator is only one responsible.
- Understand that you will also experience stages of recovery.
- Know that it is normal to experience anger, sadness, self-blame, and feelings of powerlessness.
- Realize that while a desire for revenge is a common response, acts of revenge are detrimental to recovery.
- Allow yourself to express your feelings about the assault, and to seek support from formal or informal sources.

Compiled by Diane Daane, Ph.D. in Frances P. Reddington and Betsy Wright Kreisel (eds.). *Sexual Assault: The Victims, the Perpetrators, and the Criminal Justice System* (2004). Carolina Academic Press: Durham, NC.

Part II: The Victims

Suggested Questions, Activities and Videos

Discussion Questions:

1. Define victim blaming.
2. Discuss why many victims of rape do not report the crime.
3. Discuss the Madonna/Whore Duality.
4. Discuss why there are varying definitions of rape.
5. Discuss the attribute theory and its relation to rape.
6. As a supporter of a survivor, why is it important to take care of your own well-being?

Suggested Videos:

- Victim Impact: Listen and Learn: Office of Victims of Crime
- A Rape in a Small Town: The Florence Holloway Story: Films for the Humanities & Sciences
- The News Media's Coverage of Crime and Victimization: Office of Victims of Crime
- Listen to My Story: Communicating with Victims of Crime

Suggested Activities:

- Invite a victim advocate or crisis counselor to speak on victimization.
- Have students locate all the local resources available to sex crimes victims in your area.
- Using the information learned in this text, visualize, write or role-play your response to someone divulging their victimization to you.

Part III

The Often Unacknowledged Victims

Chapter 7

Sexual Abuse of Men in Prisons

Robert D. Hanser & Chad Trulson

Introduction

There currently exists no national level data on the prevalence of inmate-on-inmate rape in prisons (Human Rights Watch 2001).[1] Of the research on prison sexual violence, what is known has been generally divided into two areas. One area focuses on the narrative accounts from actual victims. The second area of research has attempted to construct a picture of the actual incidence of prison rape among male inmates.

Despite what is known, most all attempts at measuring the incidence of prison sexual violence, both qualitative and quantitative, are plagued with problems of discovery, documentation, and the generalizability of findings (Dumond 2000; Lockwood 1994). Indeed, many sexual incidents are simply not discovered, many fail to get documented, and research, whether qualitative or quantitative, is simply limited to the time, institution, and population studied. In the end, the bottom line is that sexual violence among male inmates is largely a hidden event and what is known is likely a small and distorted portion.

---

1. We use prison "rape" interchangeably for inmate "sexual violence" or "sexual assault." This definition does not include the more ambiguous definition of a solicitation, later accompanied only by a physical assault with no sexual intent or overtone. This does not include other sexual related victimization, most notably sexual harassment, gesturing, or propositions. Though not specifically defined as sexual violence, these behaviors are nonetheless important when understanding how event build toward the ultimate rape act itself. Thus, these behaviors will also be discussed to provide the reader with a complete understanding of prison sexual violence.

There are other reasons for the conservative numbers on sexual violence in prisons. One of these is the failure to report by the victims themselves (Robertson 1999; Saum, et al. 1995). Fear of retaliation, embarrassment, humiliation, and the lack of an adequate means of redress are frequently given as explanations for the underreporting of sexual violence among male inmates (Bowker 1980; Eigenberg 1989; Nacci and Kane 1983; Propper 1981; Saum, et al. 1995). Other reasons for underreporting, which seem to be more unique to male victims, also relate to differing social mores and norms within the prison and society at large (Robertson 1999; Saum, et al. 1995). These factors will be explored further through an analysis of the social context in which sexual violence occurs among male inmates. Furthermore, the issue of sexual violence is preceded by many behaviors that pave the way toward victimization of many inmates. These behaviors may include, but are not limited to, intimidation, posturing, gesturing, and various forms of sexual harassment (Robertson 1999). We explore these dynamics in framing the issue of prison sexual violence.

The purpose of this chapter is to first explain the misleading nature of "homosexual rape" as it is applied to male sexual violence in prisons. Second, this chapter examines the notion that there is a higher incidence of sexual violence in prisons than is documented in official statistics. Lastly, this chapter demonstrates the complex nature of sexual violence in prisons and frames sexual violence from a power-based class system perspective. That is, the power dynamics between differing social groups, expressed in the form of sexual violence, domination, and exploitation, emerge as common themes within the prison environment and can help situate the issue of sexual violence in prisons.

Sexual Violence as Power and Social Status: The Misnomer of Homosexual Rape

Violence, in many ways, is an expression of power (Riedel and Welsh 2002). For those lacking the means to obtain desired goods and services, violence or the threat of violence becomes a viable and potentially effective option (Riedel and Welsh 2002). In prisons this is even more so the case given the restricted accesses to various commodities that individuals in the free society would otherwise be able to obtain. Indeed, Gresham Sykes observed over 40 years ago that the "pains of imprisonment," including the deprivation of liberty, goods, services, autonomy, security, and heterosexual relationships become important wares in the prison environment (Sykes 1958). Those able to procure these commodities, or a semblance of them, are frequently those who hold the power within correctional institutions.

Much as in the wider society, sex in prisons is a commodity which is open for trade. Sex is often an expression of power and status in prisons (Bowker 1980), and violence is one way of obtaining this commodity. The sexually violent inmate gains an increase in both status and power, while the victimized and assaulted inmate suffers a corresponding loss in status and prestige (Robertson 1999; Scacco 1975; Tucker 1981). Indeed, one's place in the stratified inmate subculture is partly sex-based with sex roles being grounded in aggression (Dumond 1992; Robertson 1999). Aggressive and dominant forms of inmate roles include that of the "wolf," "pitcher," and the "daddy," with submissive roles often being referred to as "punk" or "fag" (Knowles 1999; Robertson 1999; Sykes 1958).

Perpetrators and Victims: Homosexual Conversion, Homosexual Rape, and Sexual Harassment

When considering male prison rape, violence and the threat of violence allow for the domination and control of the victim, even in such relationships that prison officials may term voluntary or consensual (Davis 1982; Eigenberg 1989). This connection between forced and voluntary "homosexuality" has been illustrated in interviews conducted by Davis (1982) where he found that most "consensual" homosexuals were really heterosexuals who had been forced to engage in sex to avoid harm (Robertson 1999).[2] This process, referred to as being "turned out" or "punked out" effectively redefines the victim's role in the prison as that of a "homosexual." Indeed, once the role as a "homosexual" or "punk" is attached, the victim acquires a clearly defined "jacket". This "jacket", which is prison slang for a role label, becomes a new external identity that is ascribed to the inmate via the prison subculture (Nacci 1978; Smith and Batiuk 1989; Tucker, 1981). Again, in this type of situation the victim is not, in actuality, of homosexual orientation by self-choice. The motivation for engaging in these activities is one of fear from the threat of harm (Davis 1982; Tucker 1981). For instance, one inmate described his situation:

> I had no choice but to submit to being Inmate B's prison wife. Out of fear for life, I submitted to ... sexual activity [our wording] ... and

---

2. See Lockwood (1994) for a competing view of this dynamic of inmate sexual violence.

performing other duties as a woman, such as making his bed (HRW, Interview with M.R.).

Openly homosexual males are not immune from sexual violence either, and in many instances, can be targeted for more intense victimization because of their self-professed sexuality, their outward appearance, and importantly, the ambivalence by prison administrators due to the belief that the alleged victimization is "consensual" because of their sexual orientation. One homosexual inmate remarked:

> Since I've been in prison I have endured more misery than most people could handle ... All open homosexuals are preyed upon and if they don't choose up they get chosen (HRW, Interview with M.R.).

The perpetrator, on the other hand, is typically heterosexual when in mainstream society, but plays the role of aggressor to avoid the role of victim (Smith and Batiuk 1989; Scacco 1975; Weiss and Friar 1974). Within the prison subculture, rapists are considered masculine conquerors of effeminate "punks" (Weiss and Friar 1974). The aggressor is not considered a homosexual, but is simply assuming a "one up" position within the norms of prison life. In fact, "most sexual aggressors in prison are neither homosexual nor bisexual; they are heterosexuals who define sexual aggression as affirmation of heterosexuality even though their victims are of the same sex" (Robertson 1999, 26).

It cannot be overemphasized that the pursuit of power via sexual violence, coupled with the enslavement of weaker prisoners, is an integral feature of imprisonment in prisons throughout the United States (Knowles 1999; Rideau and Wikberg 1992). However, rape in prison should not be perceived as a solely sexual act, but is an act of violence that reflects both politics and power roles (Knowles 1999; Rideau and Wikberg 1992). According to Knowles (1999), "the act of rape in the ultra masculine world of prison constitutes the ultimate humiliation visited upon a male by forcing him to assume the role of a woman" (p. 8). Rideau and Wikberg (1992) further elaborate by noting that sexual assault in prison is not considered "sexual" and not really regarded as "rape" in the same sense that society regards the term. In fact, one of the perverse mores in the world of the prison subculture is that victims of sexual violence are rarely regarded as victims (Knowles 1999). A key element of the prisoners' belief system is that a 'man' cannot be forced to do anything that he does not want to do (Knowles 1999). Thus, a 'real man' cannot be exploited (Knowles 1999). Those unable to meet these rigid demands are consequently not considered 'men', but rather as being weak and unworthy of respect from those who are 'men' (Knowles 1999). Accordingly, their weakness both invites and justifies exploitation (Knowles 1999; Rideau and Wikberg 1992).

For many inmates who have been socialized into this system, sexual arousal has come to be associated with aggression (Knowles 1999). It is interesting to point out that this is no different for any other type of rapist who finds pain infliction and violence to be associated with sexual arousal and gratification (Holmes and Holmes 2002). For the perpetrators of these acts, the degree of satisfaction derived from the sex act is often directly proportional to the degree of force and humiliation inflicted upon the victim (Bartol 1999; Holmes and Holmes 2002; Knowles 1999; Wooden and Parker 1982). In its most extreme form, this sexualized aggression is manifested in outright acts of violence such as rape. But in prison, less severe cases such as sexual intimidation, domination, and manipulation, can lead to the same eventual victimization (Knowles 1999; Wooden and Parker 1982). For example, although not physically coerced, one inmate explains the events that led to his subsequent victimization:

> One inmate would stake a claim to you by becoming your "friend" hanging out with you all the time. In reality, he was saying "don't touch he's mine." It's a gradually [sic] process that you become dependent on this person whether its financial, physical, or emotional. But sooner or later there comes a time when he wants a return in his investment ... you don't want to ruin your "friendship" by saying no ... so you do what he wants, I did, and that's how you get hooked (HRW interview with P.E.).

The above discussion shows how behaviors that are not overt attacks can still coerce victims into a sexual relationship. Similarly, other acts such as the sexual harassment of inmates by other fellow inmates and/or prison staff can likewise be very damaging, despite the fact that no overt assault has taken place (Robertson 1999). The emotional humiliation inflicted by sexually harassing behaviors serves to label and intimidate the victim into ultimate compliance. This is especially true in shaping the behaviors of victims who are engaged in 'voluntary' sexual relationships within the prison (Knowles 1999).

Sexual harassment among male inmates, like prison rape, can be attributed to the conditions of confinement as well as the sub-cultural values that inmates bring with them to prison. These two factors share a common theme: that sexual harassment among male inmates is an act of sexual aggression born from a need to dominate others (Robertson 1999). In need of affirming their masculinity, some inmates turn to a strategy that is readily open to them in the prison environment-victimization of their fellow inmates (Robertson 1999). Western males in general and lower class males in particular, who comprise much of the prison population, equate aggression and domination with masculinity

(Robertson 1999). As the ultimate act of domination, prison rape is thus transformed into a statement of one's masculinity and strength.

> Rape is not primarily motivated by the frustration of sexual needs. It is more the sexual expression of aggressive expression of sexuality.... The rape of male inmates occurs in correctional settings not because it is a substitute for sex with women, but for the same reasons it occurs in the community: to hurt, to humiliate, to dominate, to control, and to degrade (Cotton and Groth 1982, 50).

Within this context, sexually suggestive behaviors among male inmates perform at least two functions. First, predatory heterosexual inmates employ sexually harassing behaviors as a means of feminizing inmates targeted for sexual exploitation (Robertson 1999). Second, sexually suggestive behaviors among male inmates promote an involuntary identity transformation and role assignment within the inmate social world. By succumbing to the pressure to be a "punk" a victim of such suggestive behavior acquires a clearly defined "jacket" as that of a sex slave who can be traded during the remainder of his incarceration (Robertson 1999). Evidence indicates that sexually suggestive behaviors among male inmates are widespread; much more so than actual prison rape (Hensley 2000; Lockwood 1994).

Though most male inmates define themselves as heterosexual, many are still propositioned for sexual activity (Struckman-Johnson and Struckman-Johnson 2000; Robertson 1999). Unless these propositions are forcefully rebutted, propositions can mark the targeted inmate as a homosexual (Lockwood 1994; Robertson 1999). In addition to propositions, other forms of related behavior, such as touching and rubbing potential victims are frequent and serve to test masculine boundaries (Robertson 1999). These forms of sexual harassment are typically not overt enough to be detected by prison staff, nor serious enough to be reported by inmates. However, this form of sexual harassment sets the foundation for the role that selected male inmates will play during the remainder of their prison sentence. Despite this obvious system of conversion from new inmate to recycled punk, prison staff often fail to appropriately intervene in this process of victimization, even if it is known (Weiss and Friar 1974).

Sex for Trade

For the middle and upper-class in the larger society, power is exerted through various mechanisms such as education, money, politics, and law—for the poor, the most immediate means of achieving power are quite frequently physical (Messerschmidt 1999; Tucker 1981). The upper and middle-class condemn this method of achieving equality as it upsets their comfortable status quo (Messerschmidt 1999; Tucker 1981).

In prisons however, with its deprivations and disproportionate populations of lower-class members, there are no proscriptions against violence. Indeed, violence is the most direct means to obtain power over this commodity, and is the tool most often employed. Thus, it is sex that becomes the medium by which social status is determined in prisons and violence becomes the means to obtain it. "Ready to kill or maim rival inmates, the prison rapist monopolizes his selected victim's services, for punks are a commodity always in short supply" (Weiss and Friar 1974, 138). Therefore, sex is a commodity within the prison economy and being a perpetrator equals status and power (Robertson 1999; Tucker 1981).

The masculine identity within prison for male inmates becomes crucially important, for if one is not masculine, one is by proxy considered feminine. There is little middle ground or room for negotiation. "The end result of victimization in a correctional institution is usually sexual aggression and domination as a political act based on a show of force" (Scacco 1975, 3). Thus, sexual aggression is more than an act of sexual gratification as a result of heterosexual deprivation, it is an outward demonstration of his own masculinity (Scacco 1975). Prior sexual and social styles of masculinity are thus adapted and shaped within prisons so that the male inmate does not lose his position of dominance and control. To fail to do so results in the male inmate accepting a subservient role, or in the prison subculture, the role of the woman. In essence, the mindset is that of 'rape or get raped,' those who rape are the "haves" in the prison economy, and those who get raped are the "have nots."

With this in mind, it becomes easy to see why sexual assault goes unreported. Those who are the "haves" do not wish to loose their hold on their precious resource; the punks who serve them. Those who are the "have nots," on the other hand, cannot possibly report their situation without living in constant fear of retaliation. Further, for those who ultimately report their victimization, the result is absolute isolation from the mainstream of prison life and the few amenities that are offered; amenities not available when placed under close institutional protection.

Prison staff also has little incentive to report or prevent sexual assault since the power-base of the current inmate "pecking order" serves to perpetuate a sense of informal institutional structure and order. For these reasons, a veritable "dark figure" of sexually violent crime exists within many prison systems, leaving most institutional sexual assaults largely undetected, or at the very least, unreported. From this point, we now turn our attention to these issues and their impact on reported rates of prison sexual assault.

The Dark Figure of Sexually Violent Crime in Prison

Similar to the often cited dark figure of crime within society at large, researchers have suggested that there is a significant dark figure of sexual violence that occurs within the prisons of America (Dumond 2000; Saum, et al. 1995). By whatever definition, sexual victimization, ranging from harassment to rape has been said to be "one of the most illusive statistics in the criminal justice field" (Struckman-Johnson and Struckman-Johnson 2000, 379).

The most recent research on inmate sexual violence has estimated that more minor forms of sexual victimization (e.g., fondling or failed attempts at intercourse) are most prevalent and hover around 15–20 % in samples of prisoners studied, while actual completed rapes are less frequent, about 1–2 % in samples of inmates (Hensley 2000; HRW 2001; Struckman-Johnson and Struckman-Johnson 2000).[3] Previous research has generally confirmed this finding (Lockwood 1994). Yet despite these most recent figures, identifying, detecting, and documenting sexual victimizations in prisons are difficult at best. Indeed, it is a falsity to talk of prisons and prisoners as if only one kind existed, and research has generally been limited to the study of a few particular institutions within larger prison systems, or several interstate comparisons of the prevalence of sexual violence. At the least, there are significant differences both within and between correctional systems around the country, not to mention conflicting methodologies and definitions utilized in correctional research which serve as further impediments to accurate accounts of sexual violence in prisons (Lockwood 1994; Saum, Surratt, Inciardi, and Bennett 1995). Simply, what we know about sexual violence in prisons is plagued by underreporting, underdiscovery, lack of generalizability, and importantly, inconsistent definitions of what sexual violence actually entails.

There is a great deal of difficulty in determining a distinction between rape and consensual sexual activity. According to Eigenberg (1989), "research has failed to clearly distinguish between consensual homosexual acts and acts of rape" (p. 39). Eigenberg explains that "inmates who participate in homosexual acts

---

3. See Wooden and Parker for estimates of completed rape which are as high as 14% of their samples in a California medium-security prison.

after threats of rape are bona fide rape victims, yet these acts are frequently perceived as homosexual acts rather than acts of rape" (1989, 40). Again, in the end it seems that many acts of sexual violence fail to be uncovered and/or reported, while what is known suffers from definitional issues in determining what even constitutes prison sexual violence.

Coupled with the previous problem, the discrepancy in official statistics occurs because many male inmates who have been victims of sexual violence are too embarrassed to confide in their experience—and this contributes significantly to sexual violence as an underreported event (Davis 1982; Eigenberg 1989; Saum, Surratt, Inciardi, and Bennett 1995; Weiss and Friar 1974). For many male inmates, there is no shame that can equal this loss for it is a perceived loss of manhood which is real in its consequences (Weiss and Friar 1974). Research on the rape of women in society at large has demonstrated that attitudes which stigmatize the victim or imply that the victim is somehow at fault also contribute to underreporting (Eigenberg 1989). This same stigmatization and trauma may be equally true for male inmates (Cotton and Groth 1982). For instance, one male inmate professed that:

> I was put in a cell with a gang member who made me give him oral sex ... I went to see a psychologist who told me that I'd caused that inmate to sexually abuse me ... I can see that I was going through a brake down [sic] mentally. Anyway, I'd made up my mind that I was taking my life.... it is truly impossible to put into words what goes through one's mind when becoming a victim of rape. Being made into a person of no self worth, being remade into what ever the person or gang doing the raping wants you to be (HRW, interview with R.G.).

Despite the embarrassment of reporting, there is also the fear of retaliation for male inmates who report sexual victimization. There is an understood rule against being a "snitch" and going to prison staff, meaning that problems between inmates are to be handled inmate-to-inmate. Violating this norm can have lethal repercussions if the inmate is not protected by the prison administration (Sykes 1958). Yet to gain protection results in being ostracized by other inmates and retaliation is a looming threat during the following months or even years (Weiss and Friar 1974). In short, there is a skeptical attitude toward institutional protection and most "inmates have little faith in the ability of guards to protect them from retaliation should they complain about sexual assaults" (Scacco 1975, 30). Some inmates are essentially told that they have three options outside of snitching, they can "... submit, fight, or go over the fence" (Weiss and Friar 1974, 3).

Related to the previous point, many male inmates simply see no adequate from of redress in which to air their grievance. In these instances, grievance procedures simply pay 'lip service' to airing complaints, failing to truly investigate or resolve inmate concerns. Further, many inmates find that the institutional system simply does not care, does not believe the inmate allegations, and even encourages sexual violence through deliberate indifference. According to Scacco, "the shocking fact is that there is both overt and covert implication of officers in the attacks that take place in penal institutions" (1975, 30). Likewise, Weiss and Friar (1974) comment that prisoners are convinced that prison rape is an integral part of the prison punishment system—in part the belief that rape is sanctioned by prison authorities. They view it as the ultimate method of control and punishment (Eigenberg 2000; Weiss and Friar 1974). In this same way, Tucker (1981) adds that "rape exists and will continue to exist in confinement institutions because it serves the interests of too many powerful elements of jail and prison societies, including the administration" (p.6). Similarly, Knowles (1999) points out that officials use the fear of rape to divert institutional aggression, destroy potential leaders, and to intimidate prisoners into becoming informers (Eigenberg 2000). Knowles observed that these tactics were used by New Mexico prison officials just prior to the New Mexico prison riot (1999). Further, Scacco (1982) states that inmates at the top of the prison power structure benefit sexually, psychologically, and financially, from the punks who are turned out by this male rape process. With both prison administrators and powerful inmates benefiting from this form of violence, incentive to change such a power structure is unlikely to materialize.

Considerations for Sexual Violence among Male Inmates

The decision of the U.S. Supreme Court in *Farmer v. Brennan* (1994) was a landmark precedent for those concerned with the issue of prison rape (Donaldson 1994). The "deliberate indifference" of state prison systems regarding inmate rape denied inmates the minimal means of safety necessary to serve their sentence. "The Court resolutely pronounced that prison rape 'serves no legitimate penological objective' cannot be squared with 'evolving standards of decency' and is simply no part of the penalty" (Donaldson 1994, 2).

This is important as prison rape and sexual exploitation serve no functional purpose within the Constitutional requirements of the criminal justice system. Yet, prisons and their staff, either through negligence or gross criminal violation of their duties, have experienced great difficulty in achieving environments free of sexual violence. Is prison sexual violence among male inmates an elusive culprit that well meaning prison systems are not equipped to handle? Or is it instead the case that sexual violence is a tool that has served the prison system well, through the intimidation, exploitation, control, and domination of those inmates who are the most difficult to control? In either case, it would appear that prison sexual violence is a concern deserving significant attention, particularly when considering potential long-term social costs for such violence.

In fact, Scacco (1982) argues the most serious cost of prison rape to society is that it takes non-violent offenders and turns them into people with a high potential for violence, full of rage and eager to take vengeance on the society which they hold responsible for their utter humiliation and loss of manhood.[4] The value structure of the lower-class subcultures found in prison, regardless of their racial or ethnic background, places extreme emphasis on maintaining and safeguarding the inmate's manhood and his sense of masculinity (Wooden and Parker 1982).

To be sure, there are other considerations coupled to prison sexual violence. Of the many considerations, some of the most notable relate to the threat of sexually transmitted diseases, medical injuries, and continued victimization, in addition to the profound impact of being labeled and stigmatized (Dumond 2000). Other areas worthy of consideration fall outside of inmate-on-inmate victimization and outside the prevue of the current discussion, but rather center on the sexual victimization of inmates by corrections officers, or corrections officers by inmates (see Marquart, Barnhill, and Balshaw-Biddle 2001).

The following discussion addresses the Prison Rape Elimination Act of 2003.

The Prison Rape Elimination Act (PREA) of 2003

On September 4th, 2003, Congress passed Public Law 108-79, a law that is commonly known as the Prison Rape Elimination Act of 2003. The Act's initial paragraphs conclude that insufficient research has been conducted and that insufficient data have been reported on the extent of prison rape. Within these findings, the 108th Congress noted that while specific numbers could not be produced, experts had conservatively estimated that at least 13 % of all inmates in the United States had been sexually assaulted in prison. Over time, it

---

4. Lockwood (1994) does dispute this claim and cites there is little credible evidence that suggest that victims will commit crimes upon release because of their "hate and hostility" towards the public (p. 99).

was estimated that the total number of inmates who had been sexually assaulted in the prior 20 years was somewhere near 1,000,000.

Furthermore, the findings conclude that most prison staff are not adequately trained nor prepared to prevent, report, or treat inmate sexual assaults. As a result, most prison rape goes unreported and results in inadequate treatment for inmate victims of sexual assault. The Act notes the detrimental psychological and physiological effects of sexual assault and suggests that these effects could increases recidivism among those inmates who are eventually released back into the community. The Act states: "prison rape endangers public safety by making brutalized inmates more likely to commit crimes when they are released" adding that "victims of prison rape suffer severe physical and psychological effects that hinder their ability to integrate into the community and maintain stable employment upon their release from prison" (pg. 973). The report by the 108th Congress further notes that these victims are likely to end up homeless and are also likely to be more dangerous than when they were initially placed into prison.

Importantly, the findings of the Prison Rape Elimination Act (PREA) states that the "high incidence of sexual assault within prisons involves actual and potential violations of the United States Constitution" (p. 973). Further, the PREA cites the Supreme Court 's ruling in *Farmer v. Brennan* (1994) which held that deliberate indifference to the substantial risk of sexual assault violates prisoner rights under the Cruel and Unusual Punishments Clause of the Eight Amendment. The PREA takes the issue of prison system accountability one step further by clearly and succinctly providing definition to what constitutes deliberate indifference when addressing prison sexual assault. Specifically, the PREA reads as follows: "states that do not take basic steps to abate prison rape by adopting standards that do not generate significant additional expenditures demonstrate such indifference" (p. 973). This is significant because it clearly indicates that states must fund the prison rape program that they implement. Failure to do so, and to do so to a level that is substantive, constitutes deliberate indifference on the part of the state prison systems. Further narrative from PREA explains that "pursuant to the power of Congress under Section Five of the Fourteenth Amendment, Congress may take action to enforce those rights in States where officials have demonstrated such indifference" (p. 973). This is important because it demonstrates both clarity in defining deliberate indifference and because it shows that Congress intends to enforce the requirements of the act. This essentially serves as a warning to state prison systems.

When articulating the requirements of, and intentions related to, the Prison Rape Elimination Act, Congress notes that its purpose is to:

1. Establish a zero-tolerance standard for the incidence of prison rape in prisons in the United States.
2. Make the prevention of prison rape a top priority in each prison system.
3. Develop and implement national standards for the detection, prevention, reduction, and punishment of prison rape.
4. Increase the available data and information on the incidence of prison rape, consequently improving the management and administration of correctional facilities.
5. Standardize the definitions used for collecting data on the incidence of prison rape.
6. Increase the accountability of prison officials who fail to detect, prevent, reduce, and punish prison rape.
7. Protect the Eight Amendment rights of Federal, State, and local prisoners.
8. Increase the efficiency and effectiveness of Federal expenditures through grant programs such as those dealing with health care; mental health care; disease prevention; crime prevention, investigation, and prosecution; prison construction, maintenance, and operation; race relations; poverty; unemployment; and homelessness.
9. Reduce the costs that prison rape imposes on interstate commerce.

It can be seen from the above list that the PREA intends to develop a baseline of the US prison rape problem and to hold accountable those administrations that do not take this issue seriously.

Perhaps one of the greatest contributions that the PREA provides is its detailed instructions on how prison rape is to be studied. Indeed, the specific guidelines in conducting the sampling process in evaluating prison rape throughout the nation are quite detailed. The act reads as follows:

> The review and analysis under paragraph (1) shall be based on a random sample, or other scientifically appropriate sample, of not less than 10% of all Federal, State, and county prisons, and a representative sample of municipal prisons. The selection shall include at least one prison from each State. The selection of facilities for sampling shall be made at the latest practicable date prior to conducting the surveys and shall not be disclosed to any facility or prison system official prior to the time period studied in the survey. The review and analysis under paragraph (1) shall be based on a random sample, or other scientifically appropriate sample, of not less than 10% of all Federal, State, and county prisons, and a representative sample of municipal prisons (p. 974).

Further, the PREA specifically states that the selection of prisons would in-clude at least one prison from each State. With this in mind, the Bureau was required to use appropriate methods, surveys, and other statistical studies of current and former inmates from a sample of Federal, State, county, and mu-nicipal prisons. Importantly, the PREA maintains that the identity of inmates providing information shall remain anonymous. These requirements demon-strate that the PREA was as much a victory for researchers as it was for advo-cates of humane treatment of inmates. As noted earlier in this chapter, there had been a lack of research on prison rape within the widespread literature. This, in part, has allowed the phenomenon of prison rape to go undetected within formal literature, being all but invisible to the eye of persons not affil-iated with a correctional agency. Thus, the PREA has required that states pro-vide transparency in the reporting of prison rape by allowing researchers to examine this phenomenon in a more rigorous and detailed fashion. Further, the PREA has opened the door to increased funding through grant provisions made through the federal government. This enables states to make genuine good faith efforts to change their operations and staff training regarding prison rape. The specific means by which these changes can be implemented among prison staff are discussed in the section that follows.

Solutions and Conclusions

Some argue that to deal with the problem of prison rape the inmate social structure itself must be changed (Eigenberg 1989; Knowles 1999; Robertson 1999). Ibrahim (1974) argues there are several ways to decrease prison violence. One method suggested is to institute conjugal visits or home furlough release pro-grams (Knowles 1999; Ibrahim 1974). But Lockwood (1980) contends that conjugal visits would not help most sexual aggressors, because very few in-mates are legally married or have common-law wives. Also, Knowles (1999) points out that most offenders would be ineligible for home furlough because they are too violent and would put communities at risk if released. Alternatives such as conjugal visits also do not appear to be a satisfactory solution because the foun-dation of prison rapes has been shown to be grounded in power gratification, rather than sexual gratification (Bowker 1980; Knowles 1999; Robertson 1999; Scacco 1975; Tucker 1981).

One possible remedy to prison sexual violence is to improve the inmate classification process. Knowles (1999) contends that the classification systems should identify potential rapists, or more importantly the potential victims, and separate them. A particularly effective classification system might target what could be called the "irreducible 10%" of our nation's most persistent and chronic violators (Trulson 2002). At the other end, classification systems might also lend more support to those who fit the category of the most "vulnerable 10%" or those inmates with little physical redress to ward off attacks.[5] Indeed, Lockwood's (1994) research suggests that targets of sexual exploitation who revert to "demonstrations of violence," even after being the victim of sexual violence, were almost always only one time victims (p. 99). Thus, their show of violence was a "protective" factor against chronic sexual assaults or other forms of sexual victimization. Further separating the two extremes might produce dividends by isolating the irreducible 10% and protecting the vulnerable 10% to preempt any need for the show of violence in the first place.

Yet while potential remedies such as those just mentioned seem to possess intuitive appeal, it is likely that such procedures would be costly and overly optimistic. This is especially true when considering the burgeoning prison population within the United States. The manipulative inmate will easily find means by which they can circumvent classification schemes. In fact, identification of prison rapists and prison victims has proven difficult simply because of the natural resistance of the inmate population to disclose such activities. Unlike classification systems that can more readily identify problem inmates such as gang members, trying to tag the potential rapist in prison is fraught with ambiguities. At best, prison policies might only be reactive in nature when dealing with sexually predatory inmates especially when compared to other problem populations in the prison setting.

By focusing on these largely topical remedies, the true problem of sub-cultural beliefs held by both staff and inmates will then simply be overlooked. This is precisely where problems with prison rape develop and are maintained, for if sub-cultural definitions of power were different, much of the motivation for prison sexual violence would be eliminated. It is then apparent that the deep-seated belief systems held by the culture of both prison inmates and the prison administration is where the true basis for the etiology of sexual victimization in prison can be found. Rather than focusing on programs designed to alleviate sexual outlets, or programs that attempt to 'outsmart' the efforts of determined inmates, a better approach is likely to entail the eradication of the initial motivation to dominate and exploit others—though this may be easier said than done.

---

5. The "irreducible 10%" is a subjective figure that notes those groups falling outside of the "typical" inmate. Indeed, almost 10% of our nation's prisoners, across all state prison systems, are considered threatening enough to be placed in administrative or punitive segregation. The vulnerable 10% are those in custodies for protection (e.g., protective custody).

Though changes in the inmate subculture may be the most effective process, such changes are difficult given the well established norms held in the prison environment. These norms are based on the crudest and most basic of human motivations for dominance and environmental control. Until these norms are challenged and modified, other attempts at intervention or prevention will provide only band-aid solutions and stop-gap measures to the problem of sexual violence in prisons. It is possible that training programs for staff and inmates, coupled with initiatives that provide positive reinforcement for compliance with new cultural norms, that changes in the subculture might be slowly implemented (Eigenberg 2000). However, change is difficult and this must be recognized as a long term process in which victimizations will undoubtedly be experienced in the short term.

Regardless of the means by which such change is implemented, it is certain that change will be an absolute necessity for any prison system that truly desires to eliminate sexual violence within its confines. Failure to do so will provide continued tacit approval for such sub-cultural norms, regardless of any official form of response. In short, overlooking the needed change in sub-cultural norms will produce nothing but short-sighted and disastrous results. This ironically has the potential of leaving the victim of prison sexual assault worse off than they had been before the intervention had ever been applied.

References

Bartol, C. (1999). *Criminal Behavior: A Psychosocial Approach*. New Jersey: Prentice Hall.

Bowker, L. H. (1980). *Prison Victimization*. New York: Elsevier.

Cotton, D. J. and A. N. Groth. (1982). "Inmate Rape: Prevention and Intervention." *Journal of Prison and Jail Health* 47.

Davis, A. J. (1982). "Sexual Assaults in the Philadelphia Prison System and Sheriff's Vans." In *Male Rape: A Casebook of Sexual Aggressions, ed.* A. M. Scacco, Jr. New York: AMS Press, Inc.

Donaldson, S. (1994). "Rape of Incarcerated Americans: A Preliminary Statistical Look" (7th ed.). Available: http:// www.igc.org/spr/docs/stats, 1994.

Dumond, R. W. (1992). "The Sexual Assault of Male Inmates in Incarcerated Settings." *International Journal of Sociology 20*.

Dumond, R. W. (2000). "Inmate Sexual Assault: The Plague that Persists." *The Prison Journal 80* (4): 407–414.

Eigenberg, H. (1989). "Male Rape: An Empirical Examination of Correctional Officers' Attitudes Toward Rape in Prison." *The Prison Journal 69*: 39–56.

Eigenberg, H. (2000). "Correctional Officers and Their Perceptions of Homosexuality, Rape, and Prostitution in Male Prisons." *The Prison Journal 80(4)*: 415–443.

Farmer v. Brennan, 511 U.S. 825, (1994).

Hensley, C. (2000). "Consensual and Forced Sex in Male Oklahoma Prisons." Paper presented at the annual meeting of the Academy of Criminal Justice Sciences, New Orleans, L.A (March).

Holmes, S. T., and R. M. Holmes. (2002). *Sex Crimes* (2nd ed.). Thousand Oaks, CA: Sage Publications.

Human Rights Watch. (2001). No Escape: Male Rape in U.S. Prisons. http://www.hrw.org/reports/2001/prison/report.html.

Ibrahim, A.I. (1974). "Deviant Sexual Behavior in Men's Prisons." *Journal of Crime and Delinquency, 20*: 38–44.

Knowles, G. J. (1999). "Male Prison Rape: A Search for Causation and Prevention." *Howard Journal of Criminal Justice 38(3)*: 267–283.

Lockwood, D. (1980). *Prison Sexual Violence.* New York: Elsevier.

Lockwood, D. (1994). "Issues in Prison Sexual Violence." In *Prison Violence in America (2nd Edition),* eds. M. Braswell, R. Montgomery and L. Lombardo. Cincinnati: Anderson Publishing Co.

Marquart, J.W., M. Barnhill, and K. Balshaw-Biddle. (2001). "Fatal Attraction: An Analysis of Employee Boundary Violations in a Southern Prison System, 1995–1998." *Justice Quarterly 18* (4): 877–910.

Messerschmidt, J. A. (1999). "Masculinities and Crime." In *Criminological Theory: Past to Present, eds.* F. T. Cullen and R. Agnew. Los Angeles, CA: Roxbury Publishing Company.

Nacci, P. L. (1978). "Sexual Assault in Prisons." *American Journal of Corrections 40*: 30–31.

Nacci, P. L., and T. R. Kane. (1983). "The Incidence of Sex and Sexual Aggression in Federal Prisons." *Federal Probation 7*: 31–36.

Propper, A.M. (1981). *Prison Homosexuality: Myth and Reality.* Lexington, MA: D C Heath.

Rideau, W. and R. Wikberg. (1992). *Life Sentences: Rage and Survival Behind Bars.* New York: Time Books, Random House.

Riedel, M. and W. Welsh. (2002). *Criminal Violence: Patterns, Causes, and Prevention.* Los Angeles, CA: Roxbury Publishing Company.

Robertson, J. E. (1999). "Cruel and Unusual Punishment in United States Prisons: Sexual Harassment Among Male Inmates." *American Criminal Law Review 13(1)*.

Saum, C. A., H. L. Surrat, J. A. Inciardi, and R. E. Bennett. (1995). "Sex in Prison: Exploring the Myths and Realities." *The Prison Journal 75(4)*: 413–430.

Scacco, A. M., Jr. (1975). *Rape in Prison.* Springfield, IL: Charles C. Thomas.

Smith, N. E., and M. E. Batiuk. (1989). "Sexual Victimization and Inmate Social Interaction." *The Prison Journal 69*: 29–38.

Struckman-Johnson, C., and D. Struckman-Johnson. (2000). "Sexual Coercion Rates in Seven Midwestern Prison Facilities for Men." *The Prison Journal 80* (4): 379–390.

Sykes, G. M. (1958). *The Society of Captives.* New Jersey: Princeton University Press.

Trulson, C. (2002). *Judicial Intervention, Desegregation, and Inter-Racial Prisoner Violence: A Case Study of Desegregation in the Texas Prison System.* Unpublished doctoral dissertation, Sam Houston State University.

Tucker, D. (1981). *A Punk's Song: View from the Inside.* Fort Bragg, CA: AMS Press Inc.

Weiss, C. and D. J. Friar. (1974). *Terror in Prisons: Homosexual Rape and Why Society Condones It.* Indianapolis: Bobbs-Merril, Inc.

Wooden, W.S. and J. Parker. (1982). *Men Behind Bars: Sexual Exploitation in Prison.* New York: Plenum Press.

Chapter 8

A Violation of Trust and Professional Ethics: Sexual Abuse of Women Prisoners by Correctional Staff

Zelma Weston Henriques & Delores Jones-Brown

"Sexual violence in prison consists not only in direct victimization, but also in the daily knowledge that it's happening."
> T.J. Parsell, prisoner rape survivor and President of Stop Prisoner Rape, in testimony before the National Prison Rape Commission, 2005.[1]

"That was not part of my sentence, to ... perform oral sex with the officers."
> Tanya Ross, prisoner in New York, November, 1998 as cited by Amnesty International, 1999

"It's not consensual—they have the power, the uniform, the badge."
> Elizabeth Bouchard, prisoner in Massachusetts, November, 1998 as cited by Amnesty International, 1999

Introduction

In 2000, R.W. Dumond noted that the problem of inmate sexual assault had been known and examined for 30 years. Since that time, based primarily on activism, research and educational efforts by various community organizations, government agencies, academic researchers and professional groups, significant

---

1. As cited in Stop Prisoner Rape, 2006.

strides have been made in the methods by which authorities gather data concerning the prevalence and nature of such assaults.

Although inmates are at risk for sexual abuse and assault from both inmates and staff, sexual contact between correctional staff and correctional residents presents special problems of power imbalance, improper personal and professional ethics (for staff members), victimization and trauma (for inmates) and threats to system integrity (for the criminal justice system). While both male and female inmates run the risk of sexual abuse and assault from staff, this chapter focuses on the unique vulnerability of women offenders to sexual advances from those whose job it is to keep them confined.

Background

According to Rafter (1990) the very structure and function of prisons and jails make them conducive to the exploitation of women. She notes:

> The custodial model was a masculine model: derived from men's prisons, it adopted their characteristics—retributive purpose, high security architecture, a male-dominated authority structure, programs that stressed earnings, and harsh discipline ... (p. 21 as cited in Pollock 1997, 42).

Given these characteristics, women became potential sexual victims on several fronts. In contrast to the Tanya Ross quote noted above, under retributive ideology, sexual assaults by staff could be viewed (by the perpetrators) as part of the deserved punishment being meted out by dutiful employees, since women in custodial units were considered the "dregs of the state prison population" (Rafter 1990, 21). Pollock (1997) recounts a 1930s description of women entering a women's prison where fondling by the warden was part of the intake routine. In addition, the orientation speech included a warning that anyone "who do[es] not submit to their superiors will be punished" (p. 43).

Prison literature dating back to 1871 includes references to the sexual exploitation of women by their male overseers (Anonymous 1871). The prevention of such abuse was a main goal of women reformers such as Elizabeth Fry, who advocated for separate correctional institutions for women in the early 1800s (Henriques and Gilbert 2000; Freedan 1974).

Even with the advent of separate facilities, women's prisons continued to be controlled by males. Some women who found themselves in these male-dominated high security structures viewed themselves as tainted and undeserving of decent treatment. Hence, they became prime targets for sexual exploitation by coercion or "consent" (Henriques 2001; Williams 1996).[2] For these women, sexual contact with staff sometimes involved forcible rape. Or, in keeping with the masculine model, they learned that they could "earn" various privileges, favors, or necessities in exchange for sex. In an investigation by Sims (1976), women reported trading sexual favors in order to receive "better treatment," a candy bar, or a Coke. In other accounts, women reported having to engage in various forms of sexual contact with staff in order to receive tampons, sanitary napkins, or other items to meet hygienic and other needs (Bomse 2001). In modern prisons (and jails), sex can be traded for desirable work assignments and better living quarters (Bomse 2001; Pollock 1997). A Human Rights Watch (HRW) Report (1996) notes that male officers "have used their near total authority to provide or deny goods and privileges to female prisoners, to compel them to have sex, or in other cases, to reward them for having done so" (quoted in Bomse 2001, 85).

Many women are vulnerable to sexual exploitation by correctional staff because of the relational nature of women's socialization (Covington 2008; Swift 2008; Gilligan, Brown, and Rogers 1990) and the isolating nature of the correctional setting. That is, some women inmates may enter into sexual relationships with correctional staff members in order to resolve feelings of loneliness (Rafter 1990) and in order to fulfill their need for intimacy. While both the inmate and the staff member may see the relationship between them as consensual, as noted in the opening quote by Elizabeth Bouchard, the imbalance of power between the two makes such relationships inherently coercive and violates canons of professional ethics and institutional rules (or criminal statutes) that prohibit *any* staff-inmate sexual contact (see Amnesty International 1999; Bureau of Justice Statistics (BJS) 2004).

In 2005, speaking for both male and female prisoners, T.J. Parsell, quoted at the beginning of this chapter, notes:

> … It [sexual violence in prison] approaches legitimacy in the sense that it's tolerated. Those who perpetuate these acts … often receive little or no punishment. To that extent alone, corrections officials render these acts acceptable (Stop Prison Rape (SPR) 2006, 3).

In addition, while Richie (1996) notes that many women who end up in the criminal justice system have already acquiesced to a lifetime of male influence, domination and control, hence making them more vulnerable to sexual ex-

---

2. See Williams, 1996 quoting a twenty-two-year-old inmate at Bedford Hills Correctional Facility for women in New York: "In their eyes I was the criminal, so why not go with the officer."

ploitation within male-dominated correctional settings, contemporary reports of sexual misconduct by correctional staff have included incidents where the staff member was female (Reilly 2003).[3] While same-sex abuse of female inmates by staff does occur, according to Amnesty International (1999), in the overwhelming majority of complaints for sexual abuse by female inmates against staff, men are reported as the perpetrators. They attribute this, in part, to the fact that, contrary to international standards, prisons and jails in the US employ men to guard women and, with the exception of a few states, place relatively few restrictions on the duties of male staff. One estimate places the figure for male staff working in female prisons at 70%. As a consequence, much of the touching and viewing of their bodies by staff that women experience as shocking and humiliating is permitted by law (Amnesty International 2007 and 1999).

Defining the Problem

Unlike the common law offense of rape, which could only be perpetrated by a man upon a woman (and only if that man was not her husband), in many jurisdictions, *sexual assault* is the gender-neutral term now used to refer to the sexual violation of both women and men by a perpetrator that is male or female (Henriques and Gilbert 2000). Tuite (1992) defines *criminal sexual assault* as "any genital, anal, or oral penetration, by a part of the accused's body or by an object, using force or without the victim's consent" (quoted in Henriques and Gilbert 2000, 260). While the terms *sexual assault* and *sexual abuse* are sometimes used interchangeably, it has been suggested that the term *assault* more accurately describes a specific incident and *abuse* indicates a pattern of behavior. The term sexual contact, used throughout this chapter, is intended to cover both these types of sex crimes which typically involve physical contact of some sort. But, as used here, the term also addresses incidents of non-contact *sexual harassment*, considered a pattern of sexual abuse. As such, sexual abuse, in the form of harassment, includes solicitations for sex with the promise of reward, and/or the imposition of punishments for failure to comply with requests for sexual favors.

---

3. For example, in 2000, a female corrections officer at the Edna Mahan Correctional Facility for Women, in Hunterdon County, New Jersey was charged with official misconduct and criminal sexual contact for allegedly groping four inmates during the prior three years. She was sentenced to probation following a guilty plea.

Williams (2001, p. 161) identifies demands or requests for sexual exchanges by correctional staff from inmates as "high-level corruption." Similarly, some jurisdictions (New Jersey, for example) by statutory definition, make it a sex crime for persons in prison settings, with supervisory positions over inmates, to engage in sexual contact with such inmates whether consensual or not. In fact, the way the New Jersey law is designed, while in the correctional setting, legally, the inmate cannot give consent. This is also the case under federal law. 18 U.S. C. section 2243(c) makes a sexual act that would have been considered consensual if it occurred outside of a prison, criminal sexual abuse when it occurs inside a prison (Inspector General Report 2005).

Even when not considered a sex crime per se, various forms of sexual behavior between custodial staff and inmates may fall under the rubric of official misconduct. For example, in 2003, a lieutenant and 20-year veteran of the New Jersey Department of Corrections was charged with two counts of second-degree sexual assault and three counts of second-degree official misconduct for allegedly photographing a nude inmate at the women's correctional facility and for having had sexual contact with her, apparently in exchange for money.[4] The lieutenant was also accused of taking nude photographs and having sexual contact with another woman in a community-based corrections program and offering to take nude photos of yet another inmate. Under New Jersey statutes, conviction for this kind of misconduct can result in a 10-year prison sentence (Reilly 2003).

Given the complexity of the situation, the responsibility falls to individual correctional departments (DOCs) to develop standards of conduct that comply with legislative and institutional ethical demands. In 1997, the Federal Bureau of Prisons (BOP) defined staff-on-inmate sexual abuse/assault as:

> Engaging in, or attempting to engage in a sexual act with any inmate or the intentional touching of an inmate's genitalia, anus, groin, breast, inner thigh, or buttocks with the intent to abuse, humiliate, harass, degrade, arouse, or gratify the sexual desire of any person (as cited in AMA 2000, p. 1).

The provision further noted that, "Sexual acts or contacts between an inmate and staff member, even when no objections are raised, are always illegal" (AMA) 2000, p. 1).

Under the Prison Rape Elimination Act of 2003 (PREA), discussed in more detail later in this chapter, the term "rape" is defined as:

---

4. The allegations include the fact that he "sent her money" (Reilly 2003).

... the carnal knowledge, oral sodomy, sexual assault with an object, or sexual fondling of a person, forcibly or against that person's will: or not forcibly or against the person's will, where the victim is incapable of giving consent because of his or her youth or his or her temporary or permanent mental or physical incapacity (BJS 2004, p. 2).

The definition also covers circumstances where the carnal knowledge, etc. is "achieved through the exploitation of the fear or threat of physical violence or bodily injury. The definition assigns the label of rape or sexual assault to three categories of inmate-on-inmate sexual violence and *all* incidents of staff sexual misconduct (BJS 2004). The three categories include 1) completed non-consensual sexual acts; 2) attempted non-consensual sexual acts; and, 3) abusive sexual contacts. However, it seems that these distinctions are virtually irrelevant when an incident involves behavior engaged in by correctional staff.

The BJS report notes that "[A]ll sexual acts involving staff are considered misconduct and are covered under the Act" (BJS 2004, 2). For staff, misconduct includes "*any* behavior *of a sexual nature*" (emphasis added) that is "directed toward" an inmate. The term "staff" is defined to include employees, volunteers, official visitors, and other "agency representatives." The behaviors amounting to staff misconduct include completed acts and attempts, whether threatened or requested. Indecent exposure, invasion of privacy and voyeurism are specifically identified as falling within this realm.

This portion of the legislation is responsive to an Amnesty International (1999) report which had noted: "[M]any women in prisons and jails in the USA are victims of sexual abuse by staff, including sexually offensive language, male staff touching inmates' breasts and genitals when conducting searches; [and] male staff watching inmates while they are naked ..." (at p. 38). Thus, the rape/sexual assault definitions under PREA cover the less overtly violent offenses that did not previously equate to rape.

The Problem of Assessing the Magnitude of the Problem

In 2000, the American Medial Association (AMA) recognized custodial assaults and sexual misconduct by staff against inmates as a potentially significant problem. It also noted that the lack of a national, systematic data collection procedure left the actual extent of such incidents unknown. Even in the absence of concrete numbers, for the AMA, the situation of staff-on-inmate sexual misconduct represented a major health concern for incarcerated women.

The organization issued a report directed at state legislators and medical professionals in correctional facilities. Its intent was to push both towards taking steps to report and prevent such occurrences.

Resolution 404 (1-99) was submitted as part of the Medical Student Section. It encouraged the Board of Trustees to:

1. Urge health care professionals working in prisons to be aware of the growing problem of custodial assault and sexual misconduct, and report it to the proper authorities without requiring the inmate to report it him/herself to alleviate guard retaliation; and,
2. Urge all states to create statutes providing legal protection for inmates against custodial molestation and abuse (Report 2 of the Council on Scientific Affairs (1-00).

Similarly, in 2000, the National Institute of Corrections (NIC) issued a report titled "Sexual Misconduct in Prisons: Law, Remedies, and Incidence ..." which provided information on efforts and changes that prisons had taken to prevent sexual abuse of inmates by staff, since its previous report in 1996. In 2000, it was reported that all but eight states[5] had statutes that prohibited sexual misconduct involving correctional staff and inmates. Among those states having statutes, eight defined such sexual misconduct as a misdemeanor. Twenty-seven of the states defined the offense as a felony. In five states, the conduct could be charged as a felony or misdemeanor depending upon the nature of the behavior and the circumstances under which it occurs. Currently, Amnesty International reports that only one state, Vermont, has no law that prohibits custodial sexual misconduct (Amnesty International 2007).

Prior to enactment of PREA, efforts to assess the extent of custodial sexual abuse of inmates by staff yielded significantly different results. Figures from 1993 had conservatively estimated the number of male and female inmates sexually assaulted behind bars at more than 290,000 (Donaldson 1993; Henriques and Gilbert 2001). For female inmates only, some sources (see Alarid 2000 citing Donaldson 1995) placed the figure significantly lower, at about 5,000. Other sources estimated that one in four women prisoners suffer sexual victimization (Stuckman-Johnson and Stuckman-Johnson 2000 as cited in SPR 2006). Between 1996 and 2000, information from surveys conducted with correctional officials, lawyers, advocacy groups and prisoners incarcerated in prisons in six jurisdictions (California, Georgia, Illinois, Michigan, New York, and The District of Columbia) implied that sexual abuse of women

---

5. Alabama, Kentucky, Minnesota, Montana, Oregon, Utah, Vermont and West Virginia.

is widespread as is retaliation by the accused officer and his or her colleagues (HRW 1996). Evidence of the prevalence of the problem has also been suggested by data showing that approximately half of U.S. State Departments of Correction (DOCs) reported involvement in litigation arising from sexual misconduct (National Institute of Corrections (NIC) 1996; NIC 2000 as cited in AMA 2000).

The Promise and Challenges of PREA

In response to the accumulating evidence, on September 4, 2003, then President George W. Bush signed into law, The Prison Rape Elimination Act of 2003. Also known as Public Law 108-79, highlights of the legislation include:

- A requirement that, each calendar year, BJS carry out a comprehensive review and analysis of the incidence and effects of prison rape
- That the review and analysis be based on a scientifically appropriate sample of not less than 10% of all federal, state and county prisons and a representative sample of local jails.
- That federal, state or local officials and facility administrators are required to participate in a national survey and provide access to inmates in their custody
- The establishment, within the Department of Justice (DOJ), of a Review Panel on Prison Rape
- A requirement that the Attorney General submit a report on the activities of the Review Panel each year
- A process for identifying state and local governments that do not cooperate with the survey; and a notation that the lack of cooperation will affect the ability to utilize federal grants
- The survey will report the facilities with the highest number of incidents and those with the least number of incidents (BJS 2004).

In contrast to many previous forms of data collection on this topic, under PREA, BJS surveys inmates directly through an Audio Computer-Assisted Self Interview (ACASI), whereby inmates use headphones, a touch screen and an interactive computer-assisted questionnaire to report their victimization. The results of the interviews are reported in the National Inmate Survey (NIS) (Beck and Harris 2007). The results of the first such survey were reported in 2007.

The survey recorded approximately 184,000 reports of sexual victimization from state and federal prisoners. For staff sexual misconduct, incidents were reported in two categories: "unwilling activity" and "willing activity." These categories were further subdivided into "excluding touching" and "touching only." The overwhelming majority of incidents in both the willing and unwilling activity categories were reported as "excluding touching." The numbers were 22,700 and 22,600, respectively. The figures for "touching only" were 2,100 and 5,700 with the unwilling touching being more than twice the number that were identified as willing activity. These figures represent national estimates based on weights applied to the totals gleaned from the survey sample. Overall, it was estimated that 60,500 inmates or 4.5% of the nation's inmates experience sexual violence while in custody.

By some previous reports (see Donaldson 1993 for example) these estimates seem particularly low. In testimony to the National Prison Rape Elimination Commission, T.J. Parsell noted that: "… we can't expect a rape victim to report it if [s]he anticipates a lack of responsiveness, a lack of sensitivity or basic protection by those who are charged with [her] care."[6]

Although the ACASI is designed to collect data from inmates in a manner that minimizes their exposure to retaliation by staff, the extent to which inmates continue to feel vulnerable to the possibility and therefore may fail to report or underreport the prevalence and nature of their victimization cannot be known. BJS is considering ways to collect data from inmates who are near release or have been released in order to address these concerns (BJS 2004).

Another potential source of underreporting is related to the fact that the NIS is only required to be administered to 10% of the nations correctional facilities. The 2007 report included responses from 146 locations. According to one BJS report, 8,727 facilities are covered by PREA (2004, 3).

Finally, the NIS figures reported here are not disaggregated by gender. And, while women make up a significantly smaller proportion of the inmate population than their male counterparts, in this chapter we have suggested a number of reasons why women may be more vulnerable to sexual contact while in correctional custody. In their study of sexual coercion reported by women in three Midwestern prisons, Struckman-Johnson and Struckman-Johnson (2002) found that the percent of inmates reporting sexual assaults ranged between 8% and 27%. If these figures are used as estimates, applying them to the number of females in prison in 2000 (when the study was conducted), the figures for the potential number of female inmates (nationally) who have been sexually assaulted, might range from 7,458 (8% of 93,234)[7] to 25,173 (27%), with a substantial number of these assaults having been perpetrated by correctional

---

6. The actual quote uses masculine pronouns.
7. See Sabol, Couture and Harrison 2007.

staff (Struckman-Johnson and Struckman-Johnson 2002 citing Bell et al. 1999, HRW 1996 and Amnesty International 1999).

The critical need to accurately assess and address the problem of women's sexual assault and exploitation by correctional staff (both in public and private facilities) cannot be ignored. While in 2000, the number of women in the state and federal system stood at 93,234, by 2005 it had risen to 107,626; by 2006 to 112,498; and, by 2007 to 114,420 (Beck and Harrison 2007; Sabol, Couture and Harrison 2007; West and Sabol 2008). These figures represent a 22.7% growth over an eight year period. When jail incarcerations are included, the number of women confined in 2000 rises to 163,648 and for 2007 it rises to 214,467 (Beck and Harrison 2007; Sabol, Couture and Harrison 2007; West and Sabol 2008). Hence, although there is uncertainty as to the number of women who actually suffer sexual abuse in prisons and jails, the pool of *potential* victims continues to grow.

The PREA has responded to more than 30 years of investigation and active complaints about the government's failure to address the prison sexual violence issue. Its data collection and reporting requirements are a beginning to developing solutions. Its mere existence creates hope that the integrity of the correctional system can be increased and that female offenders can serve their sentences with dignity and a heightened sense of safety.

References

Alarid, L. F. (2002). "Sexual Assault and Coercion Among Incarcerated Women Prisoners: Excerpts from Prison letters." *The Prison Journal 80*(4) 391–406.

American Medical Association (AMA) (2000). *Report of the Council on Scientific Affairs (1-00): Preventing Assault and Rape of Inmates by Custodial Staff.* Retrieved on line: www.ama-assn.org/ama/pub/article/2036-3592.html.

Amnesty International. (2007). *Abuse of Women in Custody: Sexual Misconduct and Shackling of Pregnant Women.* Stop Violence Against Women (2007). Retrieved from http://www.amnestyusa.org/women/custody/abuseincustody.html.

Amnesty International. (1999). *Not Part of My Sentence: Violation of Human Rights of Women in Custody.* Campaign on the United States. New York.

Anonymous (1871). *An Illustrated History and Description of State Prison Life By One Who has Been There.* Written by a Convict in a Convict's Cell [Prison Life, 1865–1869]. New York: Globe, 1871.

Beck, A. and Harrison, P. (2007). *Sexual Victimization in State and Federal Prisons Reported by Inmates, 2007.* Washington, DC: Bureau of Justice Statistics, U.S. Department of Justice, 2007.

Bell, C., M. Coven, J.P. Cronan, C.A. Garza, J. Guggenmos, L. Storto. Rape and Sexual Misconduct in the Prison System: Analyzing America's Most "Open" Secret. *Yale Law and Policy Review, 18,* 195–223.

Bomse, A. (2001). Prison Abuse: Prisoner-Staff Relations. In *Discretion, Community, and Correctional Ethics,* eds. J. Kleinig and M. Smith. Lanham, MD: Rowman & Littlefield Publishers, Inc.

Bureau of Justice Statistics. (2004). *Data Collections for the Prison Rape Elimination Act of 2003.* Washington, DC: U.S. Department of Justice.

Bureau of Justice Statistics. (2002). *Summary Findings.* BJS Homepage. Retrieved from www.ojp.usdoj.gov.

Bureau of Justice Statistics. (2001). *Demographic Trends in Correctional Population By Gender, 1986–97.* BJS Homepage. Retrieved from www.ojp.usdoj.gov.

Bureau of Justice Statistics. (1995). *National Crime Victimization Survey.* Washington, DC: U. S. Department of Justice.

Bureau of Prisons (BOP). (1997). *Health Services Manual.* December 31.

Covington, S. (2008). The Relational Theory of Women's Psychological Development: Implications for the Criminal Justice System. In *Female Offenders: Critical Perspectives and Effective Interventions,* ed R. Zaplin. Sudbury, MA: Jones and Bartlett.

Donaldson, S. (1995). Rape of Incarcerated Americans: A Preliminary Statistical Look. 7th ed. Fort Bragg, CA: Stop Prisoner Rape ... web cite refer PRISON Journal article Vol. 80 #4 p.413—Dumond—Inmate Sexual Assault article.

Donaldson, S. (1993). *Prisoner Rape Education Program: Overview for Administrators and Staff.* Bandon, VT: The Safer Society Press.

Dumond, R.W. (2000). Inmate Sexual Assault: The Plague that Persists. *The Prison Journal,* 80 (4): 406–414.

Freedan, E.B. (1974). Their Sisters' Keepers: An Historical Perspective on Female Correctional Institutions in the United States, 1870–1900. *Feminist Studies* 22: 77–95.

Gilligan, B. L., L.M. Brown, and A. Rogers. (1990). Psyche Imbedded: A Place for Body, Relationships, and Culture in Personality Theory. In *Studying Persons and Lives,* eds. A. Rabin, R. Zucker, R. Emmons, and S. Frank. New York: Springer.

Henriques, Z. W. (2001). The Path of Least Resistance: Sexual Exploitation of Female Offenders as an Unethical Corollary to Retributive Ideology and Correctional Practice." In *Discretion, Community, and Correctional Ethics,* eds. J. Kleinig and M. Smith. Lanham, MD: Rowman & Littlefield Publishers, Inc.

Henriques, Z. W., and E. Gilbert. (2000). Sexual Abuse and Sexual Assault of Women in Prison. In *It's a Crime: Women and Justice*, 2d ed, ed. R. Muraskin. Saddle River, NJ: Prentice Hall.

Human Rights Watch Women's Rights Project. (1996). *All Too familiar: Sexual Abuse of Women in U.S. State Prisons.* New York: Human Rights Watch.

National Institute of Corrections (NIC) Information Center. (2000). *Sexual Misconduct in Prisons: Law, Remedies, and Incidence.* Longmont, Colorado.

National Institute of Corrections Information Center. (1996). *Sexual Misconduct in prisons: Law, Agency Response, and Prevention.* Longmont, Colorado.

Office of the Inspector General. (2005). Deterring Staff Sexual Abuse of Federal Inmates (April). Retrieved from http://www.usdoj.gov/oig/special/0504/index.html.

Pollock, J. M. (1997). *Prisons: Today and Tomorrow.* Gaithersburg, MD: Aspen Publishers.

Pollock-Byrne, J.M. (1990) *Women, Prison and Crime.* Pacific Grove, CA: Brooks/Cole.

Rafter, N. H. (1990). *Partial Justice: Women, Prisons and Social Control* (2nd ed.). Boston: Northeastern University Press.

Richie, B. (1996). *Compelled to Crime: The Gender Entrapment of Battered Black Women.* New York: Routledge.

Reilly, M. "Ex-Corrections Officer at Hunterdon Women's Prison Indicted on Charge," *The Star Ledger*, May 9, (2003): 45, 47.

Sabol, W., H. (1976). Couture and P. Harrison. *Prisoners in 2006.* Washington, DC: Bureau of Justice Statistics, U.S. Department of Justice.

Sims, P. (1976) Women in Southern Jails. In *The Female Offender*, ed L. Crities. Lexington, MA: D.C. Heath.

Stop Prisoner Rape. (2006). In the Shadows: Sexual Violence in U.S. Detention Facilities. A Shadow Report to the U.N. Committee Against Torture. Los Angeles, CA.

Struckman-Johnson, C. and D. Struckman-Johnson. (2002). Sexual Coercion Reported by Women in Three Midwestern Prisons. *The Journal of Sex Research, 39* (3): 217–227.

Swift, C. (2008). Surviving Violence: Women's Strength Through Connection. In *Female Offenders: Critical Perspectives and Effective Interventions,* ed R. Zaplin. Sudbury, MA: Jones and Bartlett.

Tuite, P. (1992). Ignorance is No Excuse. Chicago: Nelson-Hall.

Wasserman, J. (2003). Prison Rapes 'Routine', *Daily News,* January 28: 72.

West, H. and W. Sabol. (2008). *Prisoners in 2007.* Washington, DC: Bureau of Justice Statistics, U.S. Department of Justice.

Williams, J. (2001). Ideology into Practice/Practice into Ideology: Staff-Offender Relationships in Institutional and Community Corrections in an Era of Retribution. In *Discretion, Community, and Correctional Ethics*, eds. J. Kleinig and M. Smith. Lanham, MD: Rowman & Littlefield Publishers, Inc.

Williams, M. (1996). "Bill Seeks to Protect Inmates from Guards Who Seek Sex." *The New York Times*, April 23: A1, B1.

The authors would like to thank their students, Alibe Hamacker and Nicole Hanson for their assistance in researching the revisions for this chapter.

Chapter 9

Child Sexual Abuse

Angela G. Dunlap

Introduction

Her name is Jessica. During the 13 years of her life, she has been the victim of sexual abuse by her mother, father, and her mother's boyfriend, all of these traumatic incidences occurring before she reached the age of 10. Her mother, an alcoholic and drug-user, neglected and fondled her young daughter and recently died of her own addictions. Jessica's father is serving a ten year sentence in prison for drunken driving and child endangerment. According to Jessica, before her father was convicted, he raped her more than twenty times. Her mother's boyfriend raped Jessica twice—the first time he solicited the assistance of another man to hold her down, and the second time he was alone. Now a young teenager, Jessica should be looking forward to the youthful exuberance associated with high school activities, the prom, getting her first driver's license, but instead, she lives in a group home surrounded by victims close to her own age whose experiences and backgrounds are tragically similar to her own. Jessica's story is not unique—sadly, hers is one of a growing number of cases involving child sexual abuse.

According to the federal Child Abuse Prevention and Treatment Act, child sexual abuse includes the "employment, use, persuasion, inducement, enticement, or coercion of any child to engage in, or assist any other person to engage in, any sexually explicit conduct or simulation of such conduct for the purpose of producing a visual depiction of such conduct" (42 U.S.C.A §5106g). Sexually explicit conduct includes such acts as rape, statutory rape (in cases of caretaker or inter-familial relationships), molestation, prostitution, and incest with children (42 U.S.C.A §5106g). By statutory definition, a child generally refers to all persons who have not yet reached the age of eighteen or who are otherwise not an emancipated minor.

This chapter will examine a broad range of topics related to child sexual abuse. Specifically, this chapter provides an overview of the various types of child sexual abuse acts, statistical data representing the prevalence of sexual abuse, typical signs of abuse, the long term emotional and psychological consequences of child sexual abuse, and the criminal justice system's response to child sexual abuse. The chapter will conclude with a discussion on where victims can turn for help.

Types of Child Sexual Abuse

The National Center on Child Abuse and Neglect identifies child sexual assault as "contacts or interactions between a child and an adult when the child is being used for sexual stimulation of the perpetrator or another person when the perpetrator or another person is in a position of power or control over the victim" (quoted in Newton 2001, n.d.). Generally, the act of child sexual abuse takes place any time that a child is engaged in a sexual act with an adult or is involved in a sexual situation with an adult. Acts of sexual exploitation can include actual physical contact, such as fondling or rape, but it also includes making a child watch sexual acts or pornography, using a child in any aspect of the production of pornography, or an adult exposing his genitals to a child (Newton 2001). The National Crime Victimization Survey, a statistical instrument sponsored by the Department of Justice, Bureau of Justice Statistics, defines sexual assault as a "wide range of victimizations, separate from rape or attempted rape. These crimes include attacks or attempted attacks generally involving (unwanted) sexual contact between victim and offender. Sexual assaults may or may not involve force, such as grabbing or fondling, and may also include verbal threats" (Finkelhor, Hammer, and Sedlak 2008 p.8).

Some common types of child sexual abuse acts and/or exploitation include exhibitionism, fondling a child's genitals, intercourse with a child or other form of penetration of the child's genitals with a part of the body or an object, oral sex with a child, and engaging in sexual intercourse in the child's presence. Other acts include incest with children, coerced masturbation and prostitution, showing X-rated books or movies to a child, or otherwise using a child in a pornographic production of any kind.

How Prevalent Is Child Sexual Abuse?

Quantifying Incidents of Child Sexual Abuse: The Challenges

From a statistical research standpoint, one of the most difficult challenges facing the criminal justice practitioner regarding child sexual abuse is trying to determine the extent to which this kind of abuse happens. The crime of child sexual abuse typically occurs over a period of time and the offender involves someone whom the child trusts. According to Englander (2007), the crime of child sexual abuse is generally underreported because the victims of such abuse, like victims of other types of physical abuse, are too young to report, too ashamed to report, or too reluctant to report a family member (i.e. a stepfather), or perhaps all three. In addition, perpetrators of child sexual abuse use a number of psychological techniques to ensure that their victims do not report the abuse. For instance, perpetrators make the child feel emotionally responsible, and lead the child to believe that he or she will get into trouble by talking to someone about their secret relationship (Moffatt 2003). In extreme but rare cases, perpetrators murder their victims to silence them, but most perpetrators do not kill their victims. Most likely, their tactics include threats to harm the child, the child's pet, the child's parents or siblings, or threats to have the police arrest the child and put him or her in jail as punishment for reporting the abuse (Moffatt 2003).

In addition, many times sexually abused children feel that they will not be believed—a fear that is both real and detrimental. According to Moffatt (2003), children are too young and lack the mental and cognitive development and financial resources necessary to resolve their own case of molestation and abuse. They must initially rely on adults, and too often these adults either do not believe their story or simply do not want to believe them (Moffatt 2003). This is particularly true when the adults to whom the children confide in are the parents. The parents of sexually abused children feel a range of emotions and respond in a variety of ways upon discovering that their child has been sexually abused. They may choose not to believe reports of abuse because such acknowledgement means that they have failed as a parent by not being able to protect the child from the abuser. Also, the parents may choose not to report the abuse at all because they believe that they can protect their child from further abuse and avoid the traumatic experience of making their case public. In other cases of abuse, parents choose not to report in order to protect the perpetrator—particularly when an immediate family member or someone in a position of trust is involved (Moffatt 2003). As Moffatt points out, "pedophiles don't walk around with signs on their shirts identifying themselves as such" (p. 75). Sexual perpetrators are skilled in the art of building a parent's trust, and they may work at that for weeks or months before they begin abusing their targeted victim (Moffatt 2003).

Finally, another reason parents do not report incidents of sexual abuse is that they blame their children for the abuse and therefore have no intention of contacting the local authorities or social services. One such example would be a case where the child finds the abuse pleasurable, not traumatic, particularly in situations where the molestation is not painful. Likewise, if the sexual encounters occur between a father and daughter, the child perceives the abuse as a way to feel closer to the parent. The child's awareness that the encounters constitute abuse transpires either when the behavior is discovered or when he/she reaches puberty and realizes that the relationship is inappropriate. Unfortunately, this realization accompanies feelings of guilt, shame, and, of course, feelings of responsibility. In some instances of this type of child sexual abuse, the mother may be aware of the abuse, but resents the relationship between the father and child, and therefore blames the child instead of the other parent (Moffatt 2003).

But the parents are not alone in their reluctance to report child sexual assault. Public agencies, such as schools, churches, and private businesses fail to report known cases of child sexual assault in order to protect the child from the trauma of public disclosure or to protect the organization's image and reputation. In addition, the threat of lawsuits, with their attending public disclosure, may prevent some organizations from reporting as well as the personal loyalty they feel toward the abuser. A well-known example of such organizational child sexual abuse involves the Catholic Church. According to Moffatt (2003), the allegations of child sexual abuse reached to such a high level in 2002 that the Vatican took notice and then had to take action. For example, a jury in Louisiana awarded $1 million to the family of a child who had been abused by a priest on the basis that the Catholic bishop knew the priest had a problem and still moved him to a different parish where he came into contact with and abused other children (Moffatt 2003). Taking notice of this case, in 2002 the U.S. Conference of Catholic Bishops enacted policies and provisions to address sexual abuse and to protect children by drawing attention to the measures taken by abusive priests to protect their reputation and thus hide their deviancy. Such measures, unfortunately, consist of relocating to a different parish (Moffatt 2003). Since then, though, the nationwide occurrences of child sexual abuse among Catholic priests have spanned to an unprecedented level, and monetary settlements awarded to victims have been in the millions.

Quantifying Incidents of Child Sexual Abuse: The Data

Professionals in the field of social and psychological services generally agree that the available data reporting the number of incidences of child sexual abuse underestimates the actual incidents of abuse, but the reasons for the disparity within the statistical data vary, as noted in the previous section (Finkelhor, Hammer, and Sedlak 2008; Englander 2007; Moffatt 2003; Finkelhor and Jones 2004; Jones and Finkelhor 2001).

Data from the National Incident-Based Reporting System (NIBRS) covering incidents in 2000 and 2001 capture information on more than 418,000 violent crime victims known to law enforcement in twenty-two states. According to the NIBRS, 26% of the victims of violent crime reported to law enforcement agencies in 2000 and 2001 were juveniles—persons under the age of 18. Of this percentage of violent crime victims, juveniles were the victims in 70% of the sexual assault incidences. According to this same data, females account for a majority of the violent crimes known to law enforcement in 2000–2001. For example, 72% of the victims of juvenile sexual assault were female, while 24% consisted of juvenile male victims. On the offender side, an adult was the primary offender against 60% of all juvenile victims of violent crime in general. The NIBRS classifies violent crime as including murder, kidnapping, sexual assault, robbery, aggravated assault, and simple assault. Specifically, adult offenders were more common in juvenile kidnappings (90%), murders (86%), and sexual assaults (63%), but less common in the remaining types of violent crime (Snyder and Sickmund 2006).

Even more telling, the youngest juveniles (those under age six) are more likely than the oldest juveniles (those ages 15–17) to be sexually assaulted by a family member. For example, 56% of the youngest juveniles were assaulted by a family member compared with 19% of oldest juveniles (Snyder and Sickmund 2006). This data is consistent with the victimology characterizing familial relationships in child sexual abuse cases. For example, Douglas et. al. explain that the child typically has a family connection with the offender, and there is often a history of prior abuse or conflict with the offender (2006).

The NIBRS also found 64% of violent crimes with a juvenile victim occurred in a residence, 19% occurred outdoors, 10% in a commercial area, and 6% in a school. Most sexual assaults (81%) occurred in a residence. This data is also consistent with the crime scene indicators reported in child sexual abuse cases. As noted by Douglas, et.al., the crime scene typically involved in child sexual abuse cases is either the victim's or the offender's residence (2006). A 2003 study sponsored by the Office of Juvenile Justice and Delinquency Prevention found that juveniles living in single parent homes were 50% more at risk of violence than those living in two-parent homes. In addition, juveniles living in disadvantaged communities (i.e. high percentages of poverty, unemployment, households receiving public assistance, single-parent homes) were more likely to be the victim of a violent crime (Snyder and Sickmund 2006).

As previously mentioned, offenders take advantage of the contact they have with their victims in various situations when they are in a position of authority or trust (i.e. family, school, church, etc.), but another means of reaching victims occurs through the Internet. In 1999, the Youth Internet Safety Survey collected information about incidents of online victimization via telephone interviews with 1,500 youth ages 10–17 who used the Internet at least once a month for the preceding six months. This survey addressed three main issues regarding inappropriate conduct: sexual solicitations and approaches, unwanted exposure to sexual material, and harassment (Snyder and Sickmund 2006). The survey findings did not reveal a high percentage of inappropriate online sexual solicitations, but perhaps the fewer reported incidences were due to the time period when the information was collected—fewer households had Internet accessible computers in the late nineties versus the number of households today. Perhaps more current research on this problem would yield different results.

Nonetheless, this survey found that approximately 1 in 5 Internet users between the ages of 10 and 17 had received an unwanted sexual solicitation in the past year, but none of the solicitations resulted in actual sexual contact or assault. More specifically, 5% of the surveyed youth reported receiving a solicitation that made them feel very or extremely upset or afraid. A smaller number (3%) received more overt contact and solicitations, asking to meet them somewhere, called them on the telephone, or regularly sent something such as mail, money or gifts. Snyder and Sickmund also noted that females were twice as likely as males to be solicited, as they accounted for 2 out of every 3 youth solicited. Whereas the youngest juveniles represent the highest percentage of sexual assault victims who are abused by a family member, Internet solicitations victimize a higher number of juveniles who are older. For instance, 76% of the youths who were solicited were teenagers ranging in age from 14 to 17 (Snyder and Sickmund 2006).

Signs of Child Abuse

According to the National Center for Missing and Exploited Children, the typical signs of child sexual exploitation include the following:

- Changes in behavior, extreme mood swings, withdrawal, fearfulness, and excessive crying;

- Bed-wetting, nightmares, fear of going to bed, or other sleep disturbances;
- Acting out inappropriate sexual activity or showing an unusual interest in sexual matters;
- A sudden acting out of feelings or aggressive or rebellious behavior;
- Regression to infantile behavior; clinging;
- School or behavioral problems;
- Changes in toilet-training habits;
- A fear of certain places, people, or activities;
- Bruises, rashes, cuts, limping, multiple or poorly explained injuries;
- Pain, itching, bleeding, fluid, or rawness in the private areas.

It should be noted, though, that some of these behaviors could be due to other causes than child sexual abuse, such as a medical condition, family problems, or problems in school (National Center for Missing and Exploited Children 2008; Englander 2007). A child's response to trauma varies according to his or her age. According to Englander (2007), the symptoms exhibited by younger children will likely be different from those exhibited by older child victims. For example, depression and difficulties in school are common symptoms among child sexual abuse victims of all ages. However, anxiety is more common among the preschool group and becomes less common among older children. In addition, nightmares, sexualized behavior, hyperactivity, and regression are common symptoms among the preschool and school-age children, but less common among adolescents. By contrast, adolescent victims of sexual abuse are more likely than younger victims to show signs of low self esteem, to be withdrawn or suicidal, they may engage in self-destructive behavior, run away, and/or get into trouble with the law (Englander 2007).

It should also be noted that, for many reasons, child victims of sexual assault may exhibit many of the above symptoms as a result of the abuse, but still not receive the attention and help they need. According to Douglas, et.al., if child rape and sexual assault occur over a period of time, signs of the abuse such as vaginal or anal scarring may appear on the victim. They also point out, however, that the lack of medical corroboration does not prove that the child was not sexually victimized (2006).

For instance, two sisters, ages fifteen and fourteen, were sexually abused repeatedly by their mother's live-in boyfriend. The abuser forced the girls to take naps and showers with him, and engage in acts of fondling, and forced oral and vaginal sex. In order to coerce the girls into silence, he threatened them with physical violence if they reported the abuse to anyone. This continued for a period of eight to ten years, usually in the abuser's home. Food, clothing, and adequate medical attention were denied to them, even though one of the girls

received severe burns to her palms when she was forced to touch a hot radia-
tor. When neighbors reported suspected child abuse to social services, a social
worker interviewed the two sisters, but they denied the abuse under duress of
the abuser's threats of physical harm. The girls were not allowed to take school
administered physical examinations. One of the girls had her arm twisted by
the abuser when she tried to resist his sexual advances. She was taken to the hospital, and her arm was X-rayed and placed in cast. On a separate occasion, the
abuser threw a milk carton at the other sister, and this injury left a facial scar.
The forensic findings revealed that hospital and child protective records were
reviewed, which indicated that child abuse had been suspected several times.
However, the abuser escaped arrest every time because he provided a plausi-
ble enough explanation that allowed him to avoid criminal charges. When he
was finally charged with child sexual abuse in the case of the two sisters, he
plea-bargained the charges and received five years probation (Douglas, et.al. 2006).

Consequences of Child Sexual Abuse

Whether or not the abuse will have long-term emotional and psychological
effects on the victim depends on a wide variety of factors including, but not
limited to, the age of the child when the abuse began, the duration of the abuse,
whether or not the offender was a family member, and the extent to which the
child received proper medical attention and continued treatment. As Havig
(2008) acknowledges, the very definition of child sexual abuse is subject to ongoing debate, and the lack of consensus surrounding a common definition further confounds the research and our understanding of accurate prevalence and
long-term effects. However, what is not in dispute is the relationship between
child sexual abuse and serious and chronic adult physical and psychological
consequences (Havig 2008). According to documented studies, the adult physical effects of child sexual assault include, but are not limited to, compromised
immune system functioning, sexual, gynecological, and reproductive concerns,
urinary and gastrointestinal problems, heart disease, cancer, liver disease, obesity, headaches, generalized pain, musculoskeletal complaints, and medically
unexplained conditions (Havig 2008).

In addition to the physical effects, the long-term psychological consequences
of child sexual abuse often include posttraumatic stress disorder, depression,
anxiety, suicidal tendencies, interpersonal and relational difficulties, substance
abuse, dissociation, shame, embarrassment, avoidance of care, increase utilization
of health care, cognitive and perceptual disturbances, poor self-esteem, and
eating disorders (Havig 2008). Medical treatment for physical and psycholog-

ical disorders presents a challenge for health care providers because treatment plans are highly individualized and depend on the level of disclosure offered by the victim. Havig (2008) emphasizes the importance for health care providers to understand all of the underlying factors of traumatic stress and the associated implications, which may include individualized triggers, dissociation, somatization, stimulus and conditioned responses, and the ebb and flow of the recovery process (Havig 2008). Havig goes on to explain that the symptoms associated with post traumatic stress disorder, such as trauma reactions and triggers, may be highly individualized and not clearly discernible to an observer without a full disclosure of the victim's background and a complete understanding of the complexities that are related to the trauma. For instance, for the victim of child sexual abuse, the typical process of a medical exam can, in and of itself, be a trigger and re-traumatizing experience. Non-victims of child sexual abuse take the routine steps of a medical exam for granted, but the act of disrobing, lack of privacy, submissive body positioning, being touched, and invasive procedures are not only disturbing to victims, but may prevent them from seeking out care in the first place (Havig 2008).

While the long-term effects for female victims of child sexual abuse tend to be physical, emotional, and psychological, the trend for male victims suggests that their childhood sexual abuse sparks a pattern known as the cycle of abuse that he will carry into adulthood. For instance, what is known about male victims of child sexual abuse is that there is a reasonably high likelihood that they will become adult sexual offenders of children (Connolly and Woollons 2008).

Connolly and Woollons (2008) conducted a study of 125 incarcerated males who comprise three separate offense groups: rapists, child molesters, and non-sexual offenders. These men were asked a series of questions ranging in topic from general information (age, race, education) to family information (parents, parents' education, religion), to their views about children's sexual behaviors, to their own pre-adolescent sexual experiences. The study revealed that 71% of the rapists and 45% of the child molesters had been sexually abused during their childhood versus 28% of the non-sexual offenders. Notably, the rapists and child molesters reported experiencing abuse evenly across three categorical age ranges: less than 10, between 11and 15, and 16 to 18 years. By contrast, 66% of the non-sexual offenders reported that their abuse occurred at an older age. Where gender of the offender was reported by the respondents, the rapist group reported 35% by women versus 30% by men, the child molester group reported 48% men versus 24% women, and the non-sexual group reported 13% men versus 21% women.

Not surprising, and consistent with the notion that the abused becomes the abuser, 84% of the child molester group and 57% of the rapist group reported that during their adolescence up to adulthood, they had abused others, but there was a significant difference in the target victim between each group. For instance, the rapists reported only abusing females of various ages, but the child molesters abused both boys and girls. In fact, the rapists focused most of their abuse toward adult women (75%), while 80% of the child molesters abused children (as one would expect). Another notable difference is that 58% of the rapist group reported abusing strangers, while 53% of the child molesters reported that their victims were family members, thereby indicating that the abuse was much closer to home (Connolly and Woollons 2008).

Significant Court Decisions and Restorative Justice

On a summer afternoon in late July, 1994, Megan Nicole Kanka, seven years old, was riding her bicycle with her friend in the neighborhood of her Hamilton, New Jersey, home. Later that afternoon, while Megan was still out on her bike, Jesse Timmendequas, a neighbor who lived across the street from her, called her over to ask Megan if she wanted to see his puppy. In order to lure her inside his house, he told Megan that the puppy was too young to come outdoors. Once inside the house, Jesse grabbed Megan by the back of her pants and sexually assaulted her, but the child fought back fiercely. During the struggle, Megan fell back and hit her head on a dresser. Timmendequas would later say that he did not want Megan to tell anyone about the assault, so he decided to kill her. He then reached for a belt hanging on the back of a door and used it to strangle Megan to death. In a panic that the blood stains would connect him to her death, he wrapped two plastic bags over her head, placed her body in an old toy box and loaded it into the back of his truck. He later testified that he thought he heard coughing noises coming from inside the box, and believed at first that she may still be alive. Timmendequas then drove to nearby Mercer County Park, where he dumped her body in the weeds. However, before he left, he sexually assaulted her a second time (Moffatt 2003, McGraw n.d.).

This was not the first time that Timmendequas committed child sexual assault. In 1979, he attacked a five-year-old girl who lived across the street from him. Timmendequas lured her into a wooded area and tried to fondle her, but a nearby teenager heard the girl's screams and rescued her. He was arrested the next day, pleaded guilty to a charge of sexual assault, and was sentenced to five years, which was suspended. Then, in 1981, Timmendequas sexually assaulted seven-year-old Leanna Guido in a wooded area behind a local high school. He grabbed her off of her bicycle, and dragged her into the area where he raped and attempted to kill her. He choked her until she lost conscious-ness, and he left her body in the woods thinking she was dead. She survived, however, and he was arrested again, and following his conviction, he was sen-tenced to ten years in prison. Timmendequas, however, was released for good behavior after serving six years of the ten-year sentence (Moffatt 2003).

But it was the violent rape and murder of Megan Kanka that would lead a jury to render the death penalty[1] sentence to Jesse Timmedequas. In addition, this high-profile case served as the basis to establish Megan's Law, the New Jer-sey legislation that requires convicted sex offenders to register in their com-munities. Since it was passed by the legislature in 1994 in New Jersey, President Bill Clinton signed legislation in1996 that directed state legislatures to adopt statutes that would not only require convicted sex offenders to register with their local law enforcement agency after release, but added the component of granting public access to such registries. All fifty states and the District of Co-lumbia have adopted statutes modeled after the federal legislation (Moffatt 2003; Federal Sex Offender Legislation).

Elsewhere in the criminal justice system, notable court decisions have made an impact on child victims and those convicted of child sexual assault. The Sixth Amendment to the U.S. Constitution gives the accused the right to be confronted with the witnesses against him or her. However, the 1990 case, *Mary-land v. Craig*, established an exception to the Sixth Amendment confrontation clause when the Court ruled that it is permissible to cross-examine young vic-tims via closed-circuit television if the face-to-face confrontation would cause them trauma. By allowing the states to record testimony via closed-circuit tel-evision, the Court acknowledged that the traumatizing circumstances in child sexual abuse cases took precedence over the defendant's right of confrontation.

However, that exception has been challenged, and prosecutors are now re-quired to put child victims on the stand to testify face-to-face against the ac-cused. In the 2004 case, *Crawford v. Washington*, the Supreme Court overruled the exception to the Sixth Amendment confrontation clause. In *Crawford*, the Court ruled that out-of-court statements made to police by an unavailable wit-ness violated a criminal defendant's Sixth amendment right to confront wit-nesses. The troubling result of this decision has been that victims of child abuse and child sexual abuse are re-traumatized by having to face the offender in the

---

1. Since the death penalty sentence was handed down to Jesse Timmendequas in 1997, the state of New Jersey has abolished the death penalty. On December 17, 2007, Governor Jon Corzine signed a bill that abolished the death penalty and replaced it with a sentence of life without parole. The Governor commuted the sentences of the eight men on death row to life without parole sentences.

courtroom. In addition, many times the prosecutor's case against a defendant hinges on the testimony of the victim. For example, Jessica (the child sexual abuse victim mentioned at the beginning of this chapter) was required to testify against her abuser face-to-face in court, and her testimony is the reason why the abuser was found guilty and sentenced to a prison term.

Most recently, in June 2008, the U.S. Supreme Court (in a 5–4 decision) struck down a Louisiana law that allowed the execution of those convicted of raping a child. The Court held that the law violated the Constitution's Eighth Amendment ban on cruel and unusual punishment. Defendant Patrick Kennedy was convicted in 2003 of raping his 8-year-old stepdaughter, and received the death penalty. The Louisiana prosecutors who charged Kennedy with child sexual assault argued that the attack caused severe emotional trauma, internal injuries and bleeding, and required extensive surgery. In the majority opinion, Justice Anthony Kennedy wrote that upon a review of the "history of the death penalty for this and other nonhomicide crimes, current state statutes and new enactments ... we conclude there is a national consensus against capital punishment for the crime of child rape" (qtd. in Mears 2008). If Defendant Kennedy had been put to death for the offense of child rape, he would have been the first convicted rapist since 1964 to be executed in a case in which the victim was not killed (Mears, 2008).

Aside from the above mentioned legislation and court decisions, another relatively recent development in the criminal justice system, restorative justice, is now being considered for juvenile offenders convicted of child sex offenses. Restorative justice is an alternative approach that emphasizes restoring the damage caused by crime through healing the victim, the offender, and the community (Siegel and Senna 2008). Unlike the traditional adjudication process of the criminal justice system that relies on punishment, stigma, and disgrace, the restorative approach seeks to repair the harm caused by crime and includes all parties affected by crime, such as the victim, offender, and the community at large (Siegel and Senna 2008). The general objectives of restorative justice as are to reintegrate offenders into their communities, repair the harm suffered by victims, and restore the relationship between victim and offender (Cossins 2008). Of primary importance is to assist the victim and to the extent possible, make the victim whole again. In an effort to repair the relationship between victim and offender, the restorative justice process coordinates victim-offender mediations, where the two parties voluntarily meet face-to-face in a safe and structured environment, and the victim expresses the physical, emotional and financial impact that the crime has had on him or her.

According to Cossins (2008), the rationale for the use of restorative justice for child sex abuse crimes is primarily based on the understood limitations of the trial process to treat victims appropriately and at the same time, secure convictions. Proponents of restorative justice in child sexual abuse cases believe that this method will be a more effective form of justice in two distinct ways: (1) in a symbolic way, restorative justice will provide social censure for the crime, and (2) in a practical sense, restorative justice will reduce recidivism. However, some critics question whether or not restorative justice is an appropriate alternative in child sexual assault cases. As Cossins points out, "it is unclear whether it is possible to achieve the philosophical ideas of restoration when bringing together an offender and a victim in an informal meeting to deal with one person's exploitation of another" (2008, p. 360). Currently, the restorative justice model for child sex offenses has been utilized as an experimental approach to child sexual abuse cases in Australia, the United Kingdom, and New Zealand, but if this approach is further applied and met with a measurable degree of success, the United States may consider adopting a similar model for use in child sexual abuse cases.

Help for Victims

Although the number of child sexual abuse cases is still too high despite the documented decline (as reported in Jones and Finkelhor 2001), there is help available for victims of child sexual abuse and their families. One such organization where victims can seek assistance is through the national Court Appointed Special Advocates (CASA) program. Founded in 1977 by a Seattle judge, this program is designed to use trained community volunteers to speak on behalf of abused and neglected children in court. In 1990, the United States Congress expanded the use of court appointed advocates with the passage of the Victims of Child Abuse Act. Today, this organization has grown to a network of more than 59,000 volunteers that serve 243,000 abused and neglected children through 900+ local program offices nationwide. These court advocates, also known as volunteer guardians ad litem in some jurisdictions, are appointed by judges and act as officers of the court. For more information, visit the national CASA website at http://www.nationalcasa.org.

Another resource where child victims of sexual abuse and their families can seek help is through one of the Children's Advocacy Centers (CAC), funded by amendment to the Victims of Child Abuse Act, and certified through the National Children's Alliance. The CACs play an important role in the response to child sexual abuse and other child maltreatment in the United States. The CACs were created in response to the growing need for child abuse victim advocates to reduce the stress on the victims and their families created by traditional child abuse investigation and prosecution procedures, and to improve the effectiveness of the response. Established in 1986, the CACs were designed to provide a sensitive environment for child abuse interviews, to provide victims and their families with medical and child protection services, and coordinate abuse investigations. As of 2006, the National Children's Alliance had certified more than 600 centers across the United States (Cross, et. al. 2008). For more information about the National Children's Alliance, visit their website at http://www.nca-online.org/, or the national Children's Advocacy Center at http://www.nationalcac.org/.

For more comprehensive information on related programs and services offered by the U.S. Department of Justice, Office of Justice Programs, visit their website at http://www.ojp.usdoj.gov/. From that website, you can access and browse the various child protective service programs offered by the Office for Victims of Crime and the Office of Juvenile Justice and Delinquency Prevention.

References

Child Abuse Prevention and Treatment Act, 42 U.S.C.A. §5106g (1996).

Connolly, M. and Woollons R. (2008). Childhood Sexual Experience and Adult Offending: An Exploratory Comparison of Three Criminal Groups. *Child Abuse Review: 17(2)*, 119–132.

Cossins, A. (2008). Restorative Justice and Child Sex Offences. *British Journal of Criminology: 48(3)*, 359–378.

Crawford v. Washington, 541 U.S. 36 (2004).

Cross, T.P., Jones, L.M., Walsh, W.A., Simone, M., Kolko, D.J., Szczepanski, J., Lippert, T., Davison, K., Cryns, A., Sosnowski, P., Shadoin, A., and Magnuson, S. (2008). Evaluating Children's Advocacy Centers' Response to Child Sexual Abuse. Washington, D.C.: U.S. Department of Justice, Office of Justice Programs, Office of Juvenile Justice and Delinquency Prevention.

Douglas, J.E., Burgess, A.W., Burgess, A. G., and Ressler, R.K. (2006). *Crime Classification Manual: A Standard System for Investigating and Classifying Violent Crimes* (2nd ed.). San Francisco: Jossey-Bass.

Englander, E.K. (2007). *Understanding Violence* (3rd ed.). Mahwah, NJ: Lawrence Erlbaum.

Federal Sex Offender Legislation. U.S. Department of Justice, Office of Justice Programs. Retrieved on October 10, 2008, from http://www.ojp.usdoj.gov/smart/legislation.htm.

Finkelhor, D., Hammer, H. and Sedlak, A.J. (2008). *Sexually Assaulted Children: National Estimates and Characteristics* (NCJ 214383) Washington, D.C.: U.S. Department of Justice.

Finkelhor, D. and Jones, L. (2004). *Explanations for the Decline in Child Sexual Abuse Cases* (NCJ199298). Washington, D.C.: U.S. Department of Justice.

Havig, K. (2008). The Health Care Experiences of Adult Survivors of Child Sexual Abuse. *Trauma, Violence, and Abuse: 9(1)*, 19–33.

Jones, L. and Finkelhor, D. (2001). *The Decline in Child Sexual Abuse Cases* (NCJ 184741). Washington, D.C: U.S. Department of Justice.

Maryland v. Craig, 497 U.S. 836 (1990).

McGraw, S. (n.d.) *Megan Kanka*. Retrieved October 9, 2008, from http://www.trutv.com/library/crime/serial_killers/predators/kanka/1.html

Mears, B. (2008, June 25). *Child Rapists Can't be Executed, Supreme Court rules*. Retrieved October 10, 2008 from http://www.cnn.com/2008/CRIME/06/25/scotus.child.rape/index.html.

Moffatt, G.K. (2003). *Wounded Innocents and Fallen Angels*. Westport, CT: Praeger.

National Center for Missing and Exploited Children. (2008). Signs of sexual abuse in children. Retrieved August 6, 2008, from http://www.ncmec.org/missingkids/servlet/PageServlet?LanguageCountry=en_US&PageId=1485.

Newton, C.J. (2001). Child Abuse: An Overview. Retrieved July 21, 2008, from http://www.casanet.org/library/abuse/overview.htm.

Plummer, C.A. and Eastin, J.A. (2007). System Intervention Problems in Child Sexual Abuse Investigations: The mothers' perspectives. *Journal of Interpersonal Violence: 22(6)*, 775–787.

Siegal, L.J. and Senna, J.J. (2008). *Introduction to Criminal Justice* (11th ed.). Belmont, CA: Thompson Higher Education.

Snyder, H.N. and Sickmund, M. (2006). Juvenile Offenders and Victims: 2006 National Report.

Washington, D.C.: U.S. Department of Justice, Office of Justice Programs, Office of Juvenile Justice and Delinquency Prevention.

Chapter 10

Reading Incest: Interpreting Signs of Victimization and Family Dysfunction in One Survivor's Account

Miriam R. Fuller

My name is Miriam R. Fuller. I have a doctorate in English literature, and am a university professor. I am married with two children. I enjoy theater, music, gourmet cooking, and travel. I have also survived childhood sexual abuse, occurring between the ages of three and seventeen, the perpetrators of which were two male relatives. I am now at a point where, having been through several years of therapy and done extensive reading on the topics of incest and sexual abuse, I am recovered, not only enough to lead a full and satisfying life, but to inform others about my experience, in the hope that doing so will help people who have been in similar circumstances and help those in the criminal justice and counseling systems assist victims of child sexual abuse. My goals in this particular essay are to help dispel some of the prevalent and harmful myths about incest victims and perpetrators by describing the circumstances of my own abuse and my family of origin; to discuss the elements in our culture that reinforce and even enable sexual abuse of children and adults; and to offer my own perspective on what we can do to aid victims of sexual abuse and to stop that abuse from occurring. Since I am trained as a literary critic, this chapter will be in the form of a narrative and a deconstruction and interpretation of that narrative—a presentation and discussion of the signs, as it were, of the abuse I experienced and the family framework that surrounded and informed it.

My father sexually abused me beginning when I was around three years of age. It developed very insidiously out of cuddling, with my father gradually touching me in increasingly inappropriate places. The abuse occurred mainly at night and in my room. It escalated in severity and frequency in my ninth year, after my father's mother died, again occurring mainly at night in my room, though sometimes at the dinner table as well. When I was seventeen my father raped me while we were out of town at an audition. As well as abusing me physically, my father abused me verbally and psychologically, a very common pattern for incest perpetrators. He would discuss his sexual experiences with my mother and other women with me and describe the sort of women who attracted him. Whenever he took me out to eat when I was a teenager, he would announce loudly that I was his daughter and not his date, and then make me take out my driver's license to prove it to the other diners—he did this to one of my older sisters too. My older brother (I am the youngest of four children and my siblings are all considerably older than I) abused me as well, though the abuse was not as severe. It took the form of grabbing me in inappropriate places and exposing himself to me. I blocked out most of my father's abuse for many years until I began getting disturbing flashbacks at the age of twenty-five, and began therapy.

Since I had blocked out most of the abuse consciously, it manifested in various indirect ways and affected me negatively even after I recovered my memories of it. I had frequent nightmares. At the age of three I developed stress-induced asthma. From the ages of nine—when the abuse started escalating—to eleven I had a recurring ear infection that frequently kept me out of school. As a teenager and young adult my relationships were sometimes unhealthy, and I developed a compulsion about checking and re-checking that all the doors and windows were locked at night. I had reproductive surgery and fertility problems. Though the actual sexual abuse stopped over twenty years ago, I am still dealing with its effects. It is not a situation that I would wish on anybody.

It is imperative to realize that child sexual abuse can occur in any family, regardless of income, race, ethnicity, religion, education, occupation, political affiliation, or social class. My parents were middle-class Jews from the East Coast; my father was in business, my mother attended college, both were well-read and culturally sophisticated, and we lived in a fairly affluent suburb on the West Coast. I have met survivors from very diverse backgrounds: one woman was abused by her father, a bank president; another came from a family that ran a crime syndicate; one upper-middle-class woman was abused by her babysitter; another, abused by her uncles, grew up in a poor rural community; one woman , molested by her father, was raised in the inner city by social activists. Child sexual abuse, like cancer, can be found in all walks of life. *There is no "typical" kind of family where sexual abuse occurs.*

Thus, child sexual abuse, like other kinds of domestic violence, can occur in families that look fine to outsiders, and in fact, sexual abuse can occur in families that may be successful and emotionally healthy in other aspects. In fact, abuse is harder to spot in families whose members are very intelligent or well-educated, because the family members often develop very complex and effective mechanisms to disguise, rationalize, or cope with the abuse. Often they will intellectualize the problem to keep their emotional turmoil at bay. When I was 17, shortly after I was raped, I wrote a term paper for a psychology class on the effects of father-daughter incest on the daughter—I had decided that I was going to become a psychologist and treat rape and incest victims. I had blocked out the severest episodes of incest from my memory, and the less severe incidents I had rationalized as "not being abuse." Writing that term paper and deciding to "help" other victims was an extremely complicated coping mechanism that enabled me to deal with my own situation at a safe distance, and also to implicitly "announce" to my family that there was a problem. I would, for example, leave the research books I had checked out lying around the kitchen table for days, all the while thinking that I really ought to put those books in my bedroom, and that I hoped no one thought that I was implying that my father was molesting me. My family thought there was nothing strange about my research topic, but my high school teacher, after having read the paper, kept me after class, and asked me very gently if there was anything going on in my family that I wanted to discuss. I was rather frightened—I remember thinking that I didn't want to get my father in trouble—and replied that everything was fine at home. At that time, since the incest was still occurring, I was not able emotionally to face this trauma on anything but an academic level. However, I was also able to help myself in a way by finding out about the effects of incest and by understanding, at some level, that I was not to blame for what was happening to me. I still feel that researching and writing that paper helped to avoid, unconsciously, some of the most severe aftereffects of the abuse.

As the above incident shows, sexual abuse had not injured my intellectual ability. In fact, many abuse victims do very well in academics, athletics, performing arts, etc. I was actively involved in theatre and music while in high school and college, and I know several survivors who are artists of various kinds. Being a "high achiever" often helps the victim to avoid the trauma of dealing with the reality of the abuse, especially when the abuse is still occurring. It is very important, therefore, to realize that sexual abuse doesn't always render a child incapable, incompetent, or totally miserable. I did not have the happiest childhood, but I did manage to enjoy my friends and activities. I even occasionally, at the times when the abuse was not occurring, enjoyed being with my family. My parents were generous in many ways and very affectionate, and told me frequently that they loved me. We went out to dinner together and attended plays, movies, and ball games. My parents encouraged all of us to excel in school and helped fund our college educations. Families where sexual abuse is happening are not necessarily totally dysfunctional or devoid of love. This doesn't mean that sexual abuse isn't harmful—it is extremely harmful and needs to be stopped. But what it does mean for law enforcement officials is that it can be very hard to spot abuse when it is occurring within a family that is successful and stable in other ways and to a child who in other respects is being loved and well cared for. It is also imperative that the whole family get psychological counseling, even if some members are not victims or perpetrators, because incest is only one manifestation of a dysfunctional family. A family is not unhealthy because there is incest occurring; incest occurs because a family is unhealthy in certain ways.

Even though there are no "typical" families where incest occurs, there are typical elements which characterize these families, and which can manifest themselves in different ways. One element is a lack of healthy boundaries, especially physical boundaries and invasions of privacy. Members of my family, especially my parents, rarely knocked when entering my room. My mother sometimes would enter my room when I was dressing, and walked around the house for brief periods in her underclothes. My brother would burst into the bathroom, often undressed, without knocking, when I was already there. I would lock the door, but the lock wasn't very strong and he would force it open. When I complained to my mother and asked her to speak to my brother or get a latch for the inside of the door, she told me to use another bathroom. Since I was the one who was in the bathroom first, it should have been my brother who used another bathroom, but this did not occur to her. The door to my bedroom was warped and wouldn't close properly, and my parents refused to have it fixed, claiming that it would cost too much. When I wanted to get a latch for my door, my mother replied that she wouldn't feel comfortable if there was a fire or other emergency and she couldn't get into my room. My mother was also always reaching out to tug and adjust my and my sisters' clothes even after we were well past our teens.

This latter behavior reflected my mother's extreme concern with appearance. Often in families where sexual or other types of abuse is occurring there is an obsession with physical appearance, so that things will look good on the outside. In the case of my family, my mother was not consciously aware that the abuse was occurring and my father was in denial, but it was fairly obvious that their marriage was deteriorating, so they may have trying to compensate by making sure that their children performed well in school and the outside world. My parents not only wanted their children to do well, they wanted us to look well, and both, in their own way, were obsessive about our appearance and weight. When my mother took me shopping, especially as I got older, she would spend hours trying to determine which clothes made me look thinnest—something she did with herself as well—and was always fussing with my and my sisters' hair. Once, when one of my sisters came home from college for the weekend, my mother told her to fix her hair before she even said hello to her. My father, as well as my older brother, were constantly admonishing me to lose weight and frost my hair—they were both fond of blondes—and my parents frequently pointed out attractive young women as examples for me to improve my own appearance. My mother was also very concerned with the appearance of our house, especially the public rooms, like the living room and dining room. Significantly, the more private rooms, like the bedroom and sewing room, were usually very messy, reflecting my family's reality that however neat things looked on the outside, there was a lot of mess on the inside.

This mess was not entirely of my parents' creation, as their childhoods had not been ideal, especially my father's. If children are raised in families with dysfunctional elements, they will often as adults create similar dysfunctional elements without their own families. Usually perpetrators of child sexual abuse have themselves been abused as children—though not always sexually—and when child sexual abuse occurs within a family, the non-abusive parent frequently was either abused or somehow treated in a severe, or extreme fashion. My parents were no exception. My father's father was very strict with him; his mother was selfish and immature, and may have had an extramarital affair. His family was rich, but his grandfather died of cancer when my father was twelve and my grandmother spent most of the money within a few years. She made my father sign over the money that his father had put away for his college education, and spent it on his older sister's wedding. She would also wake my father up in the middle of the night and tell him that she had seen his father's ghost. She made my father buy her and his sister sanitary supplies, which would have been very embarrassing for him, especially as a young boy. My mother's parents were loving and intelligent but very strict, especially her mother, who expected the best out of her children and very rarely complimented them, especially my mother, who had to help keep the house immaculate and who was never allowed to "talk back." After the Depression hit, my grandparents had to sell their home and move in with my grandmother's parents, and my great-grandmother was even stricter than my grandmother, and obsessed with cleanliness and decorum. She once made my mother's cousin spend an entire day cleaning the bathroom.

Both my parents' families of origin had very different standards of behavior for girls than for boys. My father was disciplined strictly while his sister was indulged. In my mother's family, girls were expected to behave much more responsibly and decorously than boys. My mother's younger brother and several of her uncles were often very boisterous, teasing and playing practical jokes, and nobody tried to discipline them much, sometimes taking a sort of exasperated pride in their "escapades" (my uncles, for example, when visiting someone in the hospital, would steal gurneys and trays with medical instruments and wheel each other down the hall on them). My uncle frequently teased my mother, and my grandmother always told my mother to ignore her brother and the teasing would stop, which it didn't.

These differences had a harmful effect on the way my siblings and I were disciplined. My sisters and I were expected to behave politely at all times and to help with household chores. My brother did not have as many chores to do, and the ones he had he shirked frequently. My mother did not want to turn my brother into a "mama's boy," so she did not correct his behavior the way she did mine and my sisters'. He frequently teased, hit, and punched me. If I complained, my mother would either tell me to ignore him, or to keep out of his way since he was older and bigger than I was, which made me feel very unsafe. He would frequently eat food with the serving spoon straight from the serving dish at the table and steal food from my plate without a serious reprimand. My sisters and I were scolded if we left hairs in the bathtub or dirty dishes in the sink; I was expected to clean up after my brother's mess in the bathtub because I was a girl. On the other hand, my mother confided in my sisters and me much more than she did my brother, and my father indulged my sisters and I much more than he did my brother, and pushed my brother very hard to do well in school and choose an appropriate profession. This discrepancy between acceptable behavior for boys and for girls is certainly prevalent to a certain degree in Western society, but when it exists to the extent that it did in my family, it sets up very harmful patterns for both genders; encouraging boys to be overly aggressive and use violence and strength to take what they want, and encouraging girls to be submissive and afraid to protect themselves.

This double standard of behavior for boys and girls is just one example of the hypocrisy that usually goes on in families where sexual abuse occurs. The perpetrator of the abuse, and sometimes other family members as well, will be very hypocritical about the abuse that is committed, as well as about sexual morals in general. My father, for example, had extramarital affairs frequently and told one of my older sisters about them when she was a teenager. However, when this same sister moved in with her boyfriend in her late 20's, my father sent her a very harsh letter accusing her of being promiscuous and ruining her life. When my mother once saw my father putting his hand into the back of my pants at the dinner table, she told him that I was too old for him to do that anymore (overlooking the fact that such behavior is never appropriate, no matter the age of the child), and he replied that I was his daughter and he could do whatever he wanted with me. My mother was not as hypocritical about sexual matters, but she did try to rationalize certain issues. When I confronted my mother years later about her allowing my brother to sexually abuse and physically mistreat me, she maintained that she thought it was just part of how siblings interacted with each other. When I pointed out that he was almost nine years older than I so she ought to have intervened, she said that she had never really considered it that way. Ironically, it was my father who got enraged when he heard about my brother exposing himself to me in the bathroom. This hypocrisy and rationalizing were part of my parents' way of denying the reality of what was going—my father was denying that his actions were abusive and my mother was denying that she was letting my brother abuse me.

Blame is another type of denial. Often, if family members do acknowledge the abuse or any other significant problem some way, they will blame it on the victim or on some other family member, and deny responsibility for it. My parents—whose marriage eventually ended in divorce when I was nineteen—blamed each other for the deterioration of their relationship; my mother was convinced that my father was the culprit because he didn't spend enough time with the family and wasted money, while my father blamed my mother because she nagged him and spent too much time cleaning house. Neither could see that both of them were responsible for the breakdown of their marriage and family. Each thought that if only the other person would listen and follow his or her advice, then things would be fine. Each of them firmly believed that he or she was the only injured party and the only one who really knew how to solve the problem.

This is typical behavior that exists in almost all dysfunctional relationships. There is a strong tendency for family members in a family where abuse is happening to pride themselves on their own wisdom, knowledge, and ability to help and advise other people with their problems, usually the same problems that the family members are denying about themselves. My blocking out the abuse and wanting to help others who were abused is an example of this phenomenon. My mother frequently tried to nurture other children in our neighborhood whose parents were not, in her opinion, rearing them properly, but she often spoke sharply to us. When a friend of mine fell out of our swing, she rocked and cuddled him, though he wasn't hurt by the fall. When I fell out of the same swing a few days later she looked at me briefly and said I was fine and that she was too busy to hold me. She once was concerned about a teenage friend of mine, suspecting this friend's father of abusing her, and wondering if she should go to the police or offer to help my friend. She would often discuss the psychological problems of people she knew, including my father, and recommend therapy for them, though she didn't feel she was in need of therapy herself. And my father, who was quite fat, with very poor exercise and eating habits, frequently pointed out and criticized people that he thought needed to lose weight.

My family's strong tendency to criticize "helped" others with the problems we ourselves had is a classic example of the denial that is so prevalent in families with abuse. Along with the compulsion to help others who are perceived as less fortunate, there is often a pervasive feeling in dysfunctional families, at least with some members, that the family is somehow superior to and different from other families. This is another manifestation of the family's denial to face their own problems and can be a very effective defense mechanism. I certainly sensed from both my parents that they felt themselves to be superior intellectually to most of our neighbors, and we were expected to live up to that image. Whenever I brought home a good report card or did very well on a test, my mother would say, "Well, that doesn't surprise me; I expect the best from my children." My father bragged excessively about our various achievements and would always try to make me speak French to people. I think that they were trying to convince themselves that our family had so many "important" things going for it that there couldn't be anything seriously wrong. But clearly there were a lot of problems going on in the family, problems that my parents were trying to cover up. And it seemed that as the problems got worse, my parents were more determined that things looked good on the outside.

I have written this description of my family in the hopes that it will shed some light on some basic characteristics of families where sexual victimization is occurring and enable you to read between the lines, as it were, when observing or interviewing alleged perpetrators and victims of sexual abuse and their families. It is crucial not to be fooled by respectability, friendliness, community involvement and financial success—sexual abuse can and does exist within families that possess many positive traits. My own family of origin seemed very far, at least on the outside, from a family in which incest would occur. It probably would have been very difficult for an outsider to figure out that sexual abuse was occurring in my family, because on the outside we looked fairly good, but anyone who knew us well or had psychological training would have spotted underlying problems. My parents were both very friendly and outgoing, but both of them tended to offer too much information to people too soon. My mother would go into too many details about her life or try to offer advice when people hadn't asked for it. My father would make inappropriate sexual comments to attractive women. Law enforcement officials, psychologists, and social workers need to be able to correctly recognize and interpret the telltale but often subtle behavioral signs that sexual abuse is occurring in a seemingly healthy family.

I myself would not have recognized these signs for what they were until I started the recovery process, which involved a lot of therapy, both individual and group counseling, and reading about sexual abuse and dysfunctional families. Because of my training as a literary critic and feminist scholar, I also read a number of works about the objectification of women and children in literature and society, and was able to connect them with the psychological texts I had read and with my own experiences. Due to my therapy and my reading, I was able to read the inappropriate elements of my family's behavior as signs of our inner problems. I understood how my father's own childhood experiences directly contributed to his becoming a perpetrator of sexual abuse, how my mother's upbringing got in the way of her protecting her daughters from abuse, and how my family's dynamics allowed that abuse to go on for so long undetected. I realized, as a result of my therapy and reading, that sexual abuse is only one symptom of a dysfunctional family, that my abuse was not an isolated incident but grew out of my family's overall problems with personal boundaries, appearance, and control. Understanding why and how the abuse happened, knowing that the abuse was not in any way my fault, and realizing what did and didn't work in my family were my greatest aids in recovery, along with the love and support of my boyfriend, my mother, who did go into therapy after my disclosure of the abuse, and a few close friends.

My recovery process, as well as my training in analyzing and critiquing literature, has helped me to understand many aspects about childhood sexual abuse in general, and to realize how, in many ways, our society unknowingly enables and even encourages child and other forms of sexual abuse to occur. Understanding how our culture unwittingly promotes sexual abuse will help us, I hope, to change our culture and ideas, and thus, ultimately, to eradicate child sexual abuse. Some of the thoughts I am about to present may seem strange, extreme, or even ridiculous to you, but I hope you will read and consider them with an open mind.

Child sexual abuse will continue to be a very big problem until our society stops sexualizing children, and stops glorifying sexual violence and coercion. Little girls are sexualized to an obscenely large extent in this society, and I am not even talking about blatant child pornography. Clothing for young girls is often form-fitting, with short skirts, low-cut tops, and other adult styles. Little girls are encouraged to wear make-up, stylish clothes, worry about their figures, and have "boyfriends" at a very young age. Children in ads are often posed very provocatively, wearing very little clothing. When my daughter, aged six at the time, was in a jazz and tap dance class, the costumes chosen for the class recital were "flapper" outfits, with short fringed skirts, low-cut bodices, and feathers in the hair. My husband and I were upset, but none of the other parents minded;

they thought it was cute. (We moved our daughter to a ballet class, where the costumes were more demure and age appropriate). I once saw bibs for sale that said "World's Sexiest Baby." People ask a colleague of mine if her three-year-old son has "a little girlfriend" yet. People routinely refer to babies and toddlers being friendly as "flirting." I do not think that most people really mean to sexualize children, but it has become so prevalent in our country—mostly due to the advertising industry—that we do it innocently and unconsciously without any harmful intentions. But we need to become aware of what we are doing and why it can be dangerous in the long run. Stopping childhood sexual abuse involves stopping sexualizing children, ceasing to dress children in revealing clothing, and letting them BE children without forcing inappropriate and potentially harmful adult interpretations on their behavior.

Just as importantly, we need to let children own their bodies and learn how to protect themselves. Babies and children are very cute and cuddly, and it is natural to want to pick them up and snuggle and kiss them. But it is vital to let the child choose whether she wants to be hugged or touched. I have seen so many parents order their children to hug or kiss adults that the children don't want to hug, or adults hug or kiss children when the children obviously don't want to be touched. My brother and sister-in-law are always telling their children to hug relatives goodbye; I always ask children if I may hug them and tell them that it's okay if they don't want to. If a child is told that he "has to" kiss Aunt Sue or hug Uncle Jim or sit on Santa's lap, he will find it harder to defend himself against potential abusers. And the majority of child sexual abuse is very insidious. Perpetrators often start with "appropriate" physical contact, such as hugging or sitting on laps, then gradually begin touching the child in progressively more "borderline" areas like the thighs, lower back, and lower abdomen, and move on to the genital region. This type of insidious sexual abuse is very difficult for children to defend themselves against because it begins with behavior that they are "supposed to" accept from adults. It is especially difficult when children have been made to feel that they cannot refuse adult attention. Children and adults need to learn that physical contact is appropriate only when both people want it. They also need to be allowed to protect themselves physically against anyone who is behaving in a physically inappropriate manner towards them, whether it is a pervert on the street exposing himself or—the more likely and often more dangerous scenario—a family member touching or grabbing them.

Our society, along with discouraging our children from protecting themselves against unwanted physical contact, still tends to blame victims of sexual assault. This blame can take various forms. There is the classic example of blaming a rape victim because she was revealingly or attractively dressed, or drinking, or in a secluded area. The rationale is that the victim was making herself "ir-resistible" to the perpetrator, who then was powerless to resist because of over-whelming sexual urges. In the case of child sexual abuse, perpetrators often claim that the child was "asking for it" by "flirting" or somehow behaving sex-ually. This kind of reasoning is seriously flawed on several accounts. First of all, sexual assault is not a crime of passion; it is a crime of power. Perpetrators need to feel completely powerful and in control and so they pick victims whom they think they can control easily. Sex offenders do not choose their victims on the basis of physical attractiveness; they choose their victims on the basis of physical and emotional powerlessness. Secondly, people often interpret oth-ers' behavior in a way that benefits their own perceptions and desires. Stu-dents, for example, might misinterpret a professor's friendly demeanor as an indication that she is an easy grader. A child's playful, friendly behavior does not have the same impulse or intent as an adult's flirting at a party. (Flirting at a party, for that matter, is not an indication of an immediate desire for a sexual encounter). Children may be inherently sexual, as some people claim, but if they are it is in an extremely different way from adults, and they are not conscious of being sexual. Children do not desire sex. And finally, the idea of the "irresistible temptation" is a false one, constructed to give people an ex-cuse for committing selfish or irresponsible actions. Adults should be capable of controlling themselves and refraining from infringing on or violating other people's personal and physical rights; if they are not, they should be physically restrained. The victim of child sexual abuse is in no way responsible for the crime occurring; the perpetrator is. The sex offenders, not the victims, are to blame, and the offenders need to face the consequences—physical, legal, and social—of their heinous and reprehensible actions.

Unfortunately, we live in a culture where criminal behavior and irrespon-sible actions are often seen as symptoms of illness and where criminals and ir-responsible people receive pity and sympathy—often more than their victims receive. I feel that this attitude has been taken to harmful extremes. It is cer-tainly necessary to understand why people commit crimes, in order to help them and to prevent potential criminals. But when a victim of abuse commits abuse, he ceases to be a victim and becomes a perpetrator. An act of sexual abuse does not lessen in severity because it was committed by someone who was abused; most sexual abuse is in fact committed by people who were abused sexually or otherwise. But there are many abuse victims who do not go on to commit abuse; *they* are the ones who should receive society's compassion and support. It is also completely outrageous and wrong to expect victims of sex abuse to participate in their perpetrators' psychological treatment or to help them in any way. People have asked me why I haven't tried to help my father and get him past his denial of the abuse he committed and into psychological treatment. My response is that it is not my responsibility; if anything, it was my father's responsibility to help me heal from the abuse. My responsibility is to heal myself only. My father committed the abuse, and the responsibility for his treatment and recovery rests squarely on his own shoulders. Making an abuse victim part of the perpetrator's treatment process is like making her relive the trauma of the abuse. Certainly perpetrators of sexual abuse need to get psychological treatment, both for their own sakes and to prevent them from committing more crimes. But they also need to take responsibility for their crimes and make some kind of meaningful restitution to their victims, restitution above and beyond any incarceration time they might serve.

I myself have not had any experience with the legal aspects of child sexual abuse. By the time I realized that I had been a victim of sexual abuse and started the recovery process, the incest had been over for some time, so it was not necessary for me to deal with law enforcement officials. However, I have given much thought to how law enforcement and other officials can most effectively approach and treat victims of alleged child sexual crime. (Though I will be speaking about children here, this advice can certainly be applied to dealing with adult victims of sexual abuse as well.) The most important thing is to respect the victim and the victim's feelings. Trust what the victim is telling you. Don't ask things like: "Are you sure that really happened?"; "You're not making that up, are you?"; "I can't believe a nice person like your mom/dad/uncle/teacher would do a thing that"; "Are you sure you're not just trying to get back at him because you're angry about something else?" Don't belittle the child's feelings if she gets upset or angry; don't tell her she's lucky that nothing worse happened. The first step in recovery is realizing that the abuse WAS terrible and that it shouldn't have happened. Let the victim express her feelings for as long as she needs to. On the other hand, don't feel the victim's feelings for him. Sometimes the victim will seem very emotionless about the abuse because she is still trying to block it out, or he is still in shock. When I was first in therapy and describing what had happened to me, people told me I sounded like I was reading from a laundry list. Some children need to feel very safe before they show emotion about the abuse, especially if the perpetrator was a close relative or has a lot of power in their life. Don't put words in the victim's mouth or tell him what a monster the perpetrator was or assume that he's feeling a certain way. Instead, concentrate on what the victim is saying, her tone of voice, what she is doing, and use that information to validate her experience. Say things like, "You sound very calm, about this" or "You keep twisting your hands when I mention your dad touching you. You seem very uncomfortable about discussing what happened," or "You sound very scared, and I completely understand, but I promise you are safe here." When questioning a child, keep the questions as neutral as possible: "What happened after that?" instead of, "What else did your cousin do to you?" If you appear calm, sympathetic but not pitying, and open to whatever the child has to say, the child will open up to you and give you more information. Sometimes the victim will give information in a roundabout or indirect way, especially a young or badly frightened child; if that happens you'll need to be patient and help the child by repeating what she said: "So your dad said he was tired?" "Your aunt took you for a walk in the garden?" Never in any way state or imply that the abuse is the child's fault. It isn't. And never, never question or interview a victim of sexual abuse in the presence of the alleged perpetrator.

When giving presentations on my experience as an incest victim, I have often been asked why I did not choose to prosecute my father or brother in civil court. I did contemplate doing so briefly—and I uphold the right of all victims of sex crimes to prosecute the perpetrators no matter how much time has elapsed after the crime—but I chose not to for several reasons. First of all, what I wanted from them was not so much financial compensation as emotional compensation—acknowledgement from them that they had abused me and apologies for having done so. I confronted them both by letter. My brother made me a very vague, general apology; my father denied ever having abused me and even took a lie detector test to "prove" he had not done so. A legal court would not have been any more successful than I had been in extracting an apology. Further, even if I had wanted to obtain financial compensation from them, it would have been very difficult to prove their guilt in a court of law, as it would have been my testimony against theirs, and the evidence was mostly circumstantial. There were witnesses for some of the more minor offenses, but these witnesses either did not see these offenses as sexual abuse or did not see what precisely was going on; my mother, for example, remembers that my father used to put his hand inside the waistband of my pants at dinner but didn't realize that he was doing anything further. There were certainly people who could attest to my father and brother's inappropriate behavior—a cousin, who is now a psychologist, remembers when my father groped a friend of hers at a holiday dinner, and told me she was not surprised to learn that my father had abused me sexually.

This, of course, in an ongoing problem for victims and law enforcement officials alike when detecting and prosecuting childhood sexual abuse—the perpetrator usually commits the abuse in private and whatever abuse he might commit in the presence of others is what might be termed borderline or inappropriate rather than molestation. For example, grabbing or patting someone's buttocks could be considered as sexual molestation by some people, but as affectionate or teasing by others. Inappropriate behavior or conversation can also indicate that there is sexual abuse going on, but I don't know how much it can be used in conviction or prosecution of sexual behavior. For instance, when I was seventeen, my father offered to pay my way through college if I would promise to remain a virgin until I was twenty-one. I refused and told him that my private life was none of his business. Later, at a family dinner, he announced to everyone that I had agreed to accept his offer. Could these events be considered as strong circumstantial evidence in an abuse case or simply as very unsuitable behavior? I feel that these sorts of events and behavior ought to be able to be used as part of the evidence to convict an accused perpetrator because they are strong public indications of his private behavior.

I also feel very strongly that convicted sex offenders—whether they were tried in a civil or criminal court—ought to be registered with national, state, and local law enforcement agencies, as well as any local schools, and in their place of employment, and that the neighbors within a certain radius ought to be informed of the nature of the offender's crime. This may seem harsh, especially if the offender has "reformed," but the government needs to protect its citizens against sex crimes, and even if offenders have been through therapy they may still repeat their crimes. I do not see these registration measures as punishment for the offender but as protection for potential victims. The offenders chose to abuse; they need to live with the consequences not only for the incarceration period but for the rest of their lives. It is their responsibility to reestablish creditable reputations in society, and they must do this through their own good behavior. Registration of sex offenders is not victimizing the offender; it is protecting the rest of society.

Child sexual abuse is a hard thing to know about and to read about. It has been a hard thing for me to write about, and excruciating to experience. But knowledge is the only way to stop this terrible crime and help victims on the road to healing and recovery—to turn them from victims into survivors. I hope this information will help.

Special Feature

Incest Victim Caught in Justice-System Trap

DEAR ABBY: Recently my husband and I heard Norman Early, the district attorney from Denver, speak on the criminal justice system—from the victim's point of view. He read the enclosed account of a victim of incest. I thought it worthy of your column. I hope you agree.

Mary Dean Armstrong

DEAR MARY: I do. And here it is:

I asked you for help and you told me you would if I told you the things my dad did to me. It was really hard for me to say all those things, but you told me to trust you—then you made me repeat them to 14 strangers.

I asked you to believe me, and you said you did, then you connected me to a lie detector, and took me to court, where lawyers put me on trial. I can't help it if I can't remember times or explain why I couldn't tell my mom. You confused me, which made you suspicious.

I asked you for help and you gave me a doctor with cold metal gadgets and cold hands (just like my father), who said it wouldn't hurt (just like my father), who said not to cry. He said I look fine—good news for you. You said, bad news for my "case".

I asked you for privacy and you let the newspaper get my story. Does it matter that they left out my name when they put in my father's and our address? My best friend's mother won't let her talk to me.

I asked for protection and you gave me a social worker who patted my head and called me "Honey" (because she couldn't remember my name). She sent me to live with strangers in a different school district.

Do you know what it feels like to be the one everyone blames for all the trouble? Do you know what it's like when your sisters hate you, and your brother calls you a liar? It's my word against my father's. You say you believe me—who cares, if nobody else does?

I asked you for help and you forced my mom to choose between us—she chose him, of course. She was scared and had a lot to lose. I had a lot to lose, too—the difference was you never told me how much.

I asked you to put an end to the abuse—you put an end to my family. You've exchanged my private nightmare for a very public one.

Feelings by Cindy, age 12
Put into words by Kee MacFarlane

Communicating as a GAL/CASA volunteer (2001). Workbook Chapter 7, p. 16. Retrieved from http://www.nccourts.org/Citizens/GAL/Documents/Workbook/chapter7.

Chapter 11

Critical Need for Effective Criminal Justice and Public Health Responses in Preventing Elderly Sexual Abuse

James F. Anderson & Nancie J. Mangels

Introduction

Demographers, epidemiologists, and criminologists predict that as America continues to gray, its level of elderly victimization will increase. In fact, if recent statistics are an indicator, the numbers will likely reach epidemic proportions (Krug, Dahlberg, Mercy, Zrui, & Lozano 2002). In 2000, there were 35 million Americans over the age of 65. Demographers predict that the older population is expected to reach 54 million in 2020 and to more than double by 2050 (Rogers 2002). Criminologists, a group that has long ignored crime committed against the elderly (Payne & Cikovic 1995; Harris & Benson, 1998; Moriarty & Jerin 2007), believe that the increase in the number of elders will be accompanied by more victimization. Unlike some victims, the elderly are more vulnerable to crime since they are more easily manipulated, dominated, and controlled by their attacker than younger adults (Glicken & Sechrest 2003).

Elder abuse is the intentional or unintentional harm, injury, and/or exploitation caused by a caregiver or family member to an older person (Meadows 2004). There are many types of abuse that the elderly experience. Abuse typically ranges from the physical, psychological, and financial, to abandonment (Frying, Summers, & Hoffman 2006). However, this chapter focuses on sexual abuse of the elderly. Sexual abuse occurs when an offender engages in nonconsensual sex with an elder. This form of abuse includes exposing the elder to pornographic material, physical sexual acts, and forcing the elderly person to undress. Whatever type of abuse the elderly suffer, the National Center on Elder Abuse (2005) reports that it is impossible to know with certainty the number of elderly victims, since no official national databases exist.

The purpose of this chapter is threefold. Part One addresses the nature and the extent of elderly sexual abuse. Part Two explores criminal justice and public health approaches to preventing elderly sexual abuse. Part Three offers viable policy strategies for combating elderly sexual abuse. In the final analysis, we argue that efforts can be made to substantially reduce occurrences of elderly sexual abuse.

Part One: The Nature and Extent of Elderly Sexual Abuse

According to the National Center on Elder Abuse (2005), it is estimated that each year between two and three million Americans age 65 and older experience injury, exploitation, or mistreatment by someone they depend on for protection and care. The agency reported that since there is no large scale nationwide tracking system on elder abuse, studies on the prevalence and incidence of abuse, along with independent research, provide the best available data on the issue. In addition to the alarming number of reported elder abuse cases, there are the unknown numbers of cases that go unreported (Toshio & Kuzmeskus 1997). Experts contend that the extent of the problem is likely to remain unknown because elder abuse, like other types of family violence, is less likely to occur in public (Wallace, 1999; Fisher, Zink, & Regan 2006). Nevertheless, when one examines elder abuse, patterns and trends emerge that provide insight into this social problem.

As stated earlier, this chapter focuses on elderly sexual abuse. Academicians and practitioners agree that rape is under reported due to the victims' shame, public stigma attached to the victimization, and the fear of reprisal after the offender is reported to the proper authority. Rape is such a horrible crime that feminists argue that next to murder, it is the most traumatic victimization that one can experience, since it wounds victims both physically and psychologically (Pleck 1987). Regardless of the context in which rape occurs, whether it is committed by a stranger, acquaintance, spouse, or a family member, it has negative consequences for victims (Siegel 2008).

Experts argue that age has little to do with rape, and it appears that no inverse relationship exists between age and rape. More specifically, experts contend that age has little to do with the prospect of being raped and even suggest that rapists do not discriminate when it comes to age, race, or social class position (see Muram, Miller, & Cutler 1992) since rapists seek power and control over their victim rather than sexual gratification.

When the elderly are sexually assaulted, they tend not to report their victimization for a variety of reasons, ranging from feelings of shame to being dependent on the abuser for care. Consequently, very little is known about sexual assaults committed against the elderly (see Cartwright & Moore, 1989; Groth, 1979; Quinn 1997). Quinn (1997) argued that as late as the 1990s, there had not been a single systematic study of the prevalence of sexual abuse against the elderly. Sadly, the current literature on elder abuse still has not adequately addressed this neglected area. Because of this, it is difficult to assert the prevalence of this crime since there is no uniform reporting system in place that collects national statistics on the scope and magnitude of elderly sexual abuse (National Research Council 2003).

Unfortunately, when researching elderly sexual abuse, one often finds anecdotal stories with little research. Invariably, one is provided fragmented information without an accurate number of victimizations that occur each year. The lack of reporting creates problems when trying to determine whether elderly rapes are on the rise or decline. Nevertheless, Perkins (1997) reported that 787,000 rapes occurred, and 3% of all rape/sexual assault victims were age 50 and above. From this number, one could infer that there were 23,610 elderly rape victims. However, Perkins warns that only 37% of all rapes are reported to the police. Therefore, one can estimate that the total number of elderly rapes that occur each year is approximately one hundred thousand.

Part Two: Criminal Justice and Public Health Approaches to Elderly Sexual Abuse

Since elderly sexual abuse is a "hidden" crime, it becomes a matter of public knowledge only when someone reports the activity to police or some other public official. It also becomes public when victimization requires medical attention, such as an emergency room visit, which often does not occur until the victim has sustained severe injuries (Pillemer & Frankel 1991). Experts contend that these occasions are the only times when we know for certain that the behavior actually occurred, since there is no national database that collects the numbers of all elderly sexual abuse incidents annually (Rosenberg & Fenley 1991). Nevertheless, when elder abuse is reported to law enforcement, only scant attention is given by the justice system (Rosenberg & Fenley 1991). For example, police are typically dispatched to investigate a possible instance of abuse reported in either a nursing home or the home of a family member who is a caregiver. If officers believe that an elderly person is being abused, the caregiver will be arrested and taken into custody. Critics of the justice system contend that this type of response is reactive, and that it may occur only after an elder has experienced prolonged sexual abuse (Rosenberg & Fenley 1991). In most cases, elders are not inclined to report sexual abuse since they largely depend on caregivers, and risk being turned over to an agency, thereby losing contact with family members.

Criminal Justice Approaches

Mandatory Reporting

Perhaps a more effective and proactive legal response to elder abuse is mandatory reporting laws. Scholars report that certain designated professionals are legally responsible for reporting suspected cases of elderly sexual abuse to the appropriate civil and criminal authorities (Wallace, 1999; Pillemer & Frankel 1991). These professionals include health care and service providers, and others who have regular contact with the elderly (Wallace 1999). The law requires them to report suspected and known cases of abuse. This proactive approach was created to allow law enforcement intervention so that the elderly can be safe and protected from abuse. But, is the approach effective?

Those agencies designated to receive reports are often state welfare or social service departments (Rosenberg & Fenley 1991). Unfortunately, reports of abuse are not always passed on to law enforcement, local social service departments or state units on aging (Pillemer & Frankel 1991). Moreover, the law typically requires that the agency designated to receive reports also has the responsibility of investigating suspected cases. Given this task, mandatory reporting laws are viewed as controversial. However, supporters of these laws argue that without laws requiring people to report elder abuse, no one would bother reporting suspected cases; abuse would continue unabated; and the extent of the problem would remain unknown. These laws provide immunity from lawsuits for those professionals who report abuse in order to encourage reporting (Wallace 1999).

Critics of mandatory reporting laws claim that there is no evidence that this method is effective in reducing or preventing elder abuse, including sexual assaults. Further, they assert that when designated professionals fail to report incidents of abuse, their behavior has no consequences, since there is no punishment for a lack of enforcement of the law. Critics also charge that even when states pass reporting laws, they fail to properly fund those services needed by victims and abusers (Ehrlich & Anetzberger 1991; Crystal 1986). Consequently, a small staff is typically left to manage large numbers of referrals (Rosenberg & Fenley 1991). Similarly, research conducted by Wolf and Pillemer (1989) finds that mandatory reporting does not lead to a greater number of elder abuse reports; rather, it leads to a higher number of referrals which require investigations. Unfortunately, many serious cases are not given adequate attention because staffs are often too small and underfunded (Gelles & Cornell 1990).

Protective Services

Another criminal justice approach to help reduce elderly sexual abuse is protective service (Callendar 1982). This requires that a public protective service program assign a legal intervention role to social workers responsible for investigating suspicious elder abuse cases (including sexual abuse) and that the program also treat the abuse situations with a variety of services when they are needed. Bergman (1989) and Bergeran (1989) suggest that protective services should seek to provide long-term or holistic approaches instead of being used as quick-fix solutions for the problem of elderly sexual abuse. They also suggest that protective services would be more effective if they provided a combination of crisis-intervention and protective-service strategies, along with the integration of adult protective services with human service providers.

Triad Programs

Triad programs are collaborative efforts formed between the community and the local police and sheriff departments to prevent elder abuse and to improve the quality of life for seniors (Cantrell 1994). These law enforcement agencies work together with seniors to reduce levels of elder abuse, including sexual abuse. A triad program can be started by a police chief, a sheriff, or a leader in the senior citizens community who contacts the other agency partners to discuss team approaches designed to combat the problem of elder abuse. While each participant has his or her own strategy to prevent violence against the elderly, the triad approach increases strength, resources, and credibility, plus it has the potential of being more effective than any individual effort (Cantrell 1994). When the triad joins its forces, it creates programs designed solely for increasing the general public's awareness about the problem of elder abuse. These programs are typically referred to as "Seniors and Lawman Together" (SALT). These can include people from senior centers, the local Agency on Aging, the local health department, and the local Adult Protective Services (Cantrell 1999).

Cantrell (1999) reports on the success of a SALT program in Columbus, Georgia. After discovering that senior citizens in a nursing home were being physically and sexually abused and neglected, the local SALT council developed a strategy to investigate the allegations of abuse. Following its protocol, the council sought the assistance of the local police and sheriff's department. It also enlisted the help of the local health department, the local Agency on Aging, and Adult Protective Services. With the assistance of these agencies, the police and sheriff's departments obtained warrants and investigated the allegations of abuse. The end result was that neglected and abused seniors were provided housing and care, and a plan was devised to carefully monitor other nursing homes believed to be engaged in abusive behavior.

Critics argue that since criminal justice approaches focus on the offender, they come short of fully addressing the issue, especially the crisis aspects of elderly sexual abuse. Moreover, they assert that criminal justice strategies are often inadequate when confronting the realities of elderly sexual abuse—such as health-related problems and treatment needed for physical and psychological injuries that could require short- or long-term medical and psychological attention. For these reasons, officials at the *Centers for Disease Control* (CDC) and others in public health, including epidemiologists, argue that elderly sexual abuse is both a criminal justice and a public health issue (Braithwaite & Taylor 1992).

Public Health Approaches

Public Health, Epidemiology, and Epidemiologists

The public health approaches focus on the health of populations (Gostin 2000). Public health agencies function to control community infections, educate people on personal hygiene, organize medical and nursing services for the early diagnosis and preventive treatment of disease, and develop strategies that will allow community residents a standard of adequate living conducive to maintaining health (Christoffel 1982, p. 51).

Epidemiology, an important component of public health, is the study of disease patterns found in humans and the factors that influence these patterns. While epidemiology was originally developed to discover and understand the causes of contagious diseases found in humans (e.g., smallpox, sexually transmitted diseases (STDs), polio, and typhoid), this approach is also used to study factors associated with various types of assaultive violence, including elderly sexual rape (Rosenberg & Fenley 1991). Health care officials believe that since epidemiology has been successful in combating other epidemics, it should have similar success in preventing elderly rape.

When studying elderly rape, epidemiologists approach the problem as if it is a contagious disease. Epidemiologists examine the total number of elder abuse cases (including sexual abuse), which is conservatively estimated to be between two and three million reported cases (and arguably more unreported cases), and treat them as if they constitute an epidemic. In doing so, epidemiologists and other public health officials bring the pubic health perspective to prevent elderly sexual abuse. They view crime as a public health issue owing to its epidemic numbers, and the physical and psychological consequences that spill into the health care system as a result of assaultive violence.

Implementing Public Health Approaches

Epidemiologists believe that elderly sexual abuse can be prevented by using the public health approach. Schneider (2000) contends that the core functions of public health are assessment, policy development, and assurance. Public health officials argue that prevention must come from intervention after the problem has been identified, either through an assessment by a public health agency or through community concerns (Schneider 2000). Krug, Dahlberg, Mercy, Zrui, & Lozana (2002) argue that public health interventions are divided into three levels of prevention: (1) *primary prevention*, (2) *secondary prevention*, and (3) *tertiary prevention*. *Primary prevention* strategies are used to prevent violence before it occurs. They seek to avoid the occurrence of an illness or injury by preventing exposure to risk factors. *Secondary prevention* strategies focus on immediate responses to violence, such as getting victims the help they need after experiencing victimization (e.g., emergency services, hospitalization, and treatment for STDs after sexual abuse). They seek to reduce the severity of illnesses or injuries after they occur. *Tertiary prevention* strategies are designed to address the long-term health care needs (both physical and psychological) of victims. Such approaches are focused on rehabilitation and reintegration after victimization. They seek to reduce disability that could be caused the elderly sexual abuse. These strategies also include providing help with the crisis aspects of victimization (see Krug et al. 2002, p. 15). Health officials believe this three-pronged prevention approach covers the full range of prevention since these strategies are directed toward parties such as victims, perpetrators, social service providers, and others who respond to violence.

When applying the public health approach to preventing elderly sexual abuse, primary prevention can be achieved by educating caregivers (both relatives and strangers) about the demands of providing for and living with an elderly person (e.g., medication, doctor visits, and physical therapy). Caregivers should be provided with information about what to expect from elders, so that the experience will not be as stressful. They should also be placed in contact with support groups comprised of families and individuals that provide for aging parents or other elderly persons. A support group can provide advice, moral support, and strength as a family or an individual undertakes this stressful task. Primary intervention is important, since many caregivers and their families that engage in elderly abuse report high levels of stress. Primary intervention should reduce key risk factors to which the elderly would otherwise be exposed.

Secondary prevention can be achieved by providing the elder with important contact information about local triad programs, social service agencies, such as the local *Agency on Aging*, and other public health agencies. In this way, the elderly will have more resources if they need emergency assistance, including shelter. As with victims of domestic violence, the elderly may need shelter to escape abusive situations. Research indicates that elderly victims are more reluctant than others to report their abuser or leave a potentially violent situation, because they have no other place to turn to for help or source. This prevention strategy is essential in order to minimize the severity of violent episodes, especially since abusers tend to escalate their violence overtime.

Tertiary prevention may be the most critical area of prevention for elderly people, since after experiencing neglect or sustaining physical injuries; they may desperately need medical attention. Implementing this strategy is especially imperative when elderly victims have been denied medications by their abuser, or when they endure assaultive violence from a care provider. This area of prevention is of critical importance to the victim since, whether assaulted or denied prescribed medications, he or she may experience debilitating injuries such as a stroke, heart attack, seizure, paralysis, or even an untimely death. For example, Muram, Miller, & Cutler (1992) report that elderly rape victims are more likely to sustain genital injuries during the assault that go untreated. Similarly, Burgess and Clements (2008) report that elderly sexual assault victims are likely to suffer rape trauma syndrome or PTSD symptoms of startle, physiological upset, anger, and numbness that lead to other health problems. Thus, tertiary prevention is designed to prevent debilitating injuries caused in the aftermath of violence.

The public health approach toward preventing elderly sexual abuse includes massive educational campaigns to increase awareness of the problems and issues facing the growing population of elder Americans. It is hoped that these efforts will inspire caregivers, relatives, neighbors, coworkers, and concerned citizens, who either suspect or know of instances of elderly sexual abuse, to report them to the appropriate authorities. Those advocating the public health approach believe that prevention can be achieved by breaking the chain of causation at any link (Schneider 2000).

The public health approach to preventing assaultive violence is composed of five steps: (1) define the health problem, (2) identify the risk factors associated with the problem, (3) develop and test community-level interventions to control and prevent the cause of the problem, (4) implement interventions to improve the health of the population, and (5) monitor those interventions to assess their effectiveness.

(1) Define the Health Problem

Epidemiologists and public health officials argue that the first step in preventing violence is having a better understanding of it. When defining a disease or a crime, epidemiologists use the term *disease* in a broad sense to mean "health outcome." Therefore, efforts must be made to measure the magnitude or the nature and extent of elderly sexual abuse. To accomplish this, these officials examine and analyze data on the number of violence-related behaviors, injuries, and premature deaths. Officials believe that these data will reveal the frequency with which violence occurs, where it is likely to occur, and the trends and patterns associated with incidents of violence. Schneider (2000) contends they must also consider the size of the population under study. This helps epidemiologists calculate the rate of violent incidents. Moreover, these data should reveal who the victims and the perpetrators are and whether a relationship exists between these parties. When epidemiologists collect these data, they are often taken from police reports, emergency room files, vital statistics, medical examiners, registries, population-based surveys (such as the NCVS) and social services. These data should provide a yearly report on the magnitude of the problem.

(2) Identify Risk Factors Associated with the Problem

One must also be able to identify factors that both expose and protect people, or put them at risk of violence. In the area of elderly sexual abuse, in order to successfully prevent violence, health officials must be able to pinpoint risk factors that increase the odds that violence will occur. They must be aware of factors that will reduce or minimize exposure to such risks. This information serves to provide health officials with knowledge of where violence can be found so that prevention efforts can be made in crucial areas. As a result, officials will be provided with a more accurate number of people who are similarly situated and who are possibly at risk of victimization. To identify risk and protection factors, officials should be required to monitor violence-related injuries. Research shows that risk factors typically include exposure to violent media, family violence, violent behavior within the context of the home, and alcohol and substance abuse (Gottfredson & Hirschi 1990).

(3) Develop and Test Community-Level Interventions to Control or Prevent the Cause of the Problem

Epidemiologists and other health care officials encourage and advocate the need for more research data from needs-assessment tools, community surveys, focus groups, and others involved in violence prevention. Their approach to data collection relies on a multidisciplinary effort that includes information from partnerships with officials from social services, criminal justice agencies, mental health agencies, civil justice agencies, health services, domestic violence advocates, policy makers, substance-abuse experts, academics, and others. Health officials believe that the multidisciplinary approach allows for comprehensive assessment of and consultation concerning elderly sexual abuse. The strength in the approach is that it bridges the gap between multiple agencies and allows for more strategies for solving the problems of elder abuse (Gostin 2000; Schneider 2000). Drawing from the data from these agencies, epidemiologists and other health care officials could create an evidence-based approach for designing programs for prevention.

(4) Implement Interventions to Improve the Health of the Population

After Step Three has been conducted and programs have been determined to be successful, health care officials should advocate widespread implementation of effective programs that target elderly sexual abuse. This involves making sure that all services that the community needs are available and accessible to everyone. These often include environmental services, educational services, and basic medical services. Because needs often vary, public health agencies alone cannot provide these services; rather, they require efforts from the entire community. Each community should be allowed to select the type of program that fits its requirements. Officials should assist in helping state and local participants plan, implement, and evaluate the programs. The selection and implementation of prevention programs should be followed by evaluation and assessment.

(5) Monitor Interventions to Assess their Effectiveness

After Step Four is accomplished, public health officials should closely monitor intervention programs to determine if they are proving successful in preventing elderly sexual abuse. The process requires that local public health agencies get community representatives involved in evaluating and assessing interventions. The success of interventions should be measured by whether the number of elderly sexual abuse cases declines, and whether victims and abusers receive the help they need. Ultimately, the success of the public health approach should influence the policies related to elderly sexual abuse.

Part Three: Policy Implications

As previously stated, experts agree that as America continues to gray, it will experience a corresponding increase in victimizations (including sexual abuse) perpetrated against the elderly. Elderly sexual assault is very difficult to measure and prevent because it is hidden from public view (Fisher et al. 2006) and its victims tend to be invisible. Helping victims of elderly sexual abuse require assistance from both the criminal justice and public health systems because of the potential of continued abuse, and the adverse health consequences that must be treated by public health officials. Aiding elder victims of rape also requires that perpetrators be arrested to ensure that the victim and others are safe. Those arrested may include family members as well as employers and caregivers in nursing homes and in assisted-living facilities. The criminal law must hold abusers accountable for their actions and send the message to others that elderly sexual abuse will be prosecuted and will not go unpunished. Consequently, it is essential that both systems provide viable strategies to reduce and eliminate elderly sexual abuse. Regarding criminal justice policy, states should use punitive sanctions to punish offenders and even invoke the use of the civil justice system to award victims or surviving family members when an elder has sustained injuries or death. Regarding the public health system, states should implement epidemiological approaches toward preventing and treating elderly rape.

The criminal justice system's role in preventing elderly rape is reactive and typically involves responding to the offender's behavior (Gaines & Miller 2008; Gottfredson, 1999). Historically, it has been focused primarily on apprehension rather than prevention. In reported cases of elderly rape, officers may affect an arrest of an offender if they either witness a caregiver engaging in the behavior or if they have probable cause to believe that the suspect committed the behavior. Probable cause usually occurs when officers notice the physical abuse of an elderly person in someone's care. At this time, the suspect can be taken into custody and processed by the court. The suspect may be found guilty of abuse and sentenced to imprisonment. The criminal justice system does little to address the needs of elderly victims following abuse. Again, addressing such needs is usually considered the duty and responsibility of a social service or other agency. Regarding criminal justice, the best-case scenario is that police remove the elderly victim from the abusive environment. However, the justice system is not required to provide and is not responsible for providing victims with treatment and therapy, or even a safe environment.

Sentencing Enhancements

In their efforts to prevent elder abuse and send a deterrent message, some states are adding sentencing enhancements to regular sentences when offenders violate specific laws. As with hate crime laws, sentencing enhancements treat the age of the victim as an aggravating factor in the crime. States such as Nevada, Georgia, and Louisiana currently use sentencing enhancements for offenders who target the elderly in the commission of a crime. In Nevada, if a person targets an elderly person over the age of sixty in a crime, the state will give the offender double the usual sentence. For example, if a crime typically carries a penalty of ten years and the targeted victim is older than sixty, the offender will receive a sentence of twenty years. In addition to sentence enhancement for violent crimes, the Georgia legislature has passed a law which allows for sentencing enhancements for offenders who engage in unfair and deceptive business practices designed to defraud the elderly. Louisiana's legislation attaches a five-year sentence enhancement on any violent crime committed against an elderly person. Moody, Marvell, and Kaminski (2002) report that a corollary effect of sentence enhancements for crimes committed with firearms has also proved effective in reducing the number of murders of police officers by eighteen percent. Other states should add sentencing-enhancement as a strategy to reduce elder abuse.

Civil Law Suits and Mandatory Reporting Laws

Civil law, or a tort action, involves a private injury for which a court provides a remedy in the form of damages (Gardner & Anderson 2006). The relief given in a tort action is an award of money (Reid 2007; Anderson & Dyson 2001; Neubauer 1999; Vago 2006). There are three questions that a court considers in any tort action. First, is there a legal duty owed by the defendant to the plaintiff? Second, has there been a breach of that duty? Third, has an injury, or damage, resulted from the breach of that duty? Legal experts argue that in order for a tort action to be initiated, there must be an established duty, a breach of such a duty, and an injury sustained because of the breach (Anderson & Dyson 2001; Neubauer 1999; Vago 2006).

There are three categories of state torts based on a person's conduct: (1) an *intentional tort*, (2) a *negligence tort*, and (3) a *strict liability tort*. An *intentional tort* occurs when there is an intention on the part of the person to inflict either physical or psychological harm or damage to an elderly person. A *negligence tort* is a breach of a statutory duty to act reasonably toward those who may be harmed by one's conduct in the foreseeable future. For example, an elderly victim of rape may bring a *negligence* claim against a nursing home or assisted living facility if he or she is raped by an employee who was not properly screened at the time of hire, especially if it can be determined that the attacker had a criminal record for sexual assault against the elderly. It could be argued that the facility was negligent in its screening and hiring practice. A *strict liability tort* does not apply to cases of elderly abuse. Nevertheless, experts argue that lawsuits can deter malicious behavior perpetrated against the elderly when they attach expensive damage awards.

Moskowitz (1998) conducted research on mandatory reporting laws and elder abuse and discovered that a lack of reporting is common in elder abuse among those designated to report any suspicion of abuse or known incidents of it. Even though it is a criminal offense to ignore the mandatory reporting laws, most people do not report elder abuse or suspicions of the behavior because there is rarely any enforcement of the laws or any penalty attached when violations are reported to the appropriate authorities. Moskowitz concluded that civil statutes which mandate reporting elder abuse and neglect are unnecessary in some states, especially in those states that have also created a civil action damage against professionals who either intentionally or unintentionally fail to report cases of elder abuse and neglect. Moskowitz cited several states as models of what other states can accomplish with the appropriate legislation. Moskowitz argued that in Arkansas, the law that mandates reporting elder abuse and neglect holds that those who are designated to report the behavior but who fail to do so are legally liable under the civil law for damages to the injured party. In fact, the law requires that the offending party pay for those damages proximately caused by "purposeful failure" to report. Iowa also has a law requiring designated professionals to report suspected abuse or neglect of a "dependent adult." It, too, imposes civil liability for damages proximately caused by the failure to report.

Moskowitz (1998) suggests that another way to get professionals to take reporting abuse and neglect seriously is to revoke the licenses of professionals who fail to observe mandatory reporting laws. More specifically, Moskowitz reports that since licensed professionals are controlled by legislative agencies or boards, several states have made the failure to observe mandatory reporting laws a crime and seek to revoke the licenses of doctors and other health care professionals who fail to report elder abuse. Moskowitz urges that to the extent that revocations are enforced, the greater the likelihood that officials will abide by mandatory reporting laws. As a result, perhaps more elderly victims will be free from their abusers.

Another civil action that the justice system can implement is to pass laws making it easier for elder abuse victims to sue their abusers and receive compensation for their injuries. For example, California passed the Elder Abuse and Dependent Adult Civil Protection Act, which allows elderly victims who have suffered physical abuse, neglect, or financial exploitation committed by a relative, nursing home staff, or scam artists to seek damages for injuries sustained. The Act also requires that the court assess the defendant attorney's fees and court costs (e.g., for calling expert witnesses to testify) if the victim can establish that he or she sustained serious abuse. The law makes it easier for indigent elderly victims who have suffered abuse to bring legal claims against their abusers. According to the Act, an elderly victim's lawyer must demonstrate, with evidence that the perpetrator intentionally acted recklessly to inflict physical abuse, neglect, or financial exploitation upon the elder (the lawyer has to show the elderly sustained either physical abuse, neglect, or financial exploitation through the careless action of a care provider). The Act specifies that damages for pain and suffering up to $250,000 can be awarded even if the victim died from the abuse. The Act is also designed to assist prosecutors, those elderly who are mentally impaired, and other dependent elders.

In Nevada, an elderly victim who suffers personal injury caused by abuse or neglect or by loss of money or property (or by surviving family members) can bring a civil suit against an abuser (If the victim dies from the injury, a designated relative of the victim or a designated person with power of attorney for the victim can file the suit). The offender—whether an individual or an agency—can be ordered to pay twice the actual damages incurred if it can be determined that the offender acted with recklessness, malice, or fraud; in addition, the court can assess the offender attorney's fees and court costs. Georgia allows elderly victims to recover both compensatory and punitive damages for injuries, and requires that the court assess the offender attorney's fees and court costs. Moskowitz (1998) contends that other states should consider passing similar legislation to protect the elderly and to prevent the continuation of elder abuse.

Public Health Approaches

The public health approach to preventing elderly sexual abuse is multifaceted as well as interdisciplinary since it draws on the resources of the entire community. Officials at the CDC rely on public education programs such as the use of public service announcements to launch campaigns against the dangers of tobacco, sexually transmitted diseases, teenage pregnancy, child abuse, and domestic violence against women. Others in the health care profession also use public service announcements to garner a greater public awareness of the dangers associated with epidemics. This strategy is needed to present the public with the reality about hidden crimes such as elderly rape. Public service announcements about elderly sexual abuse can be broadcast on radio and television during prime time. Those in public health can also lease billboards to showcase the effects of elderly rape. These kinds of public service announcements will reach millions of people, since listeners, viewers, and drivers are tuned in daily to what they hear on the radio, see on television, and read on billboards. According to Anderson and Mangels (2006), gerontologists and epidemiologists believe that public service announcements can be used to increase awareness and educate the public on the reality of elderly abuse. Moreover, announcements can be used to: (1) increase awareness of the availability of programs and the services they offer; (2) increase awareness of the trauma/crisis aspects of victimization; (3) increase awareness of the issues that elderly victims face; and (4) inform the public of available crime prevention programs and self-defense measures that could help reduce an elderly person's chance of becoming the victim of elder abuse (Siegel 2008; Ginsburg 1994). Public education programs are designed to acquaint the general public with agencies that offer help and information to victims of elder abuse and similar crimes.

In their research using a public health approach, Bachman and Meloy (2008) contend that policies designed to alleviate elder abuse should focus on primary and secondary prevention efforts. They hold that primary efforts can be addressed by providing guardianship in places where elderly persons are present. This strategy can be accomplished with neighborhood watches, transportation and home security assistance, and block clubs. Bachman and Meloy also advocate the use of triad programs since they have a proven record of success in preventing elder abuse. Moreover, they hold that because elderly victims may be seriously assaulted by family members or other caregivers, efforts should be made to address the stress associated with providing care to elderly people, especially those who have disabilities (e.g., dementia, stroke, heart disease, and obesity) and who take medication. Bachman and Meloy argue that when elder abuse does not cause death, secondary strategies should address the elderly person's physical and emotional needs. To that end, health care providers should be trained to respond aggressively to victims in order to prevent any spiraling decline they may experience after victimization. Bachman and Meloy suggest that secondary prevention efforts should target nursing home staff. Newly hired staff members should undergo preemployment screening to determine if they have the mental hygiene required to work with elderly people. Newly hired and seasoned workers should be given extensive training to familiarize them with laws governing abuse prevention, legal liabilities, and reporting procedures. Moreover, efforts should be made to monitor, detect, and treat employees who suffer from stress and burnout since these conditions are associated with marginal performances and abusive behavior (Anderson, Dyson, Burns, & Taylor 1998). Bachman and Meloy conclude that the use of policies focused on primary and secondary prevention will prove effective in preventing elder abuse.

Another public health approach is to create a national mandatory standardized protocol used by hospitals. Currently, there is no national protocol for assisting elderly victims. Because there is no uniform process, it is difficult to accurately determine the number of abused elderly persons who visit hospitals for treatment each year. This difficulty contributes to our lack of understanding about this national epidemic. A mandatory protocol should be used by every hospital in the nation. There should be an agreement or a consensus on a set of uniform procedures that will be used when elderly abuse cases are confirmed or suspected (see Anderson & Mangels 2006). These cases should be collected each year in a manner similar to that of the Uniform Crime Reports (UCRs) and should be used to measure the number of hospital visits made by elderly persons. Mandatory compliance with this protocol should have a twofold purpose. First, it should require emergency room personnel to alert the proper authorities when abuse is detected or suspected. Second, it could prevent continued levels of abuse and make offenders more responsible for their behavior. With respect to the first purpose, the data concerning elder abuse cases may also be used to relieve emergency room personnel from legal liability since the data will be able to show that the employee did not act in a negligent manner nor with deliberate indifference to the plight of an elderly victim should the matter go to court.

As stated earlier by the National Center on Elder Abuse, there is no national database that collects statistics on elder abuse, especially sexual abuse. Consequently, there is not much information sharing other than what one can retrieve from local newspapers, the Internet, or published in academic journals which tends to be dated and not representative of the abuse committed on a national level (see Morgenbesser, Burgess, Boersma, & Myruski 2008). This lack of data and the ambiguity over the correct definition of *elder abuse* make it difficult to ascertain the true nature and extent of this national problem. Therefore, it is unlikely that we can accurately predict whether there is an increase or a decrease in the number of incidents of elderly sexual abuse. Moreover, without adequate data, it is virtually impossible for health agencies to identify health risks and inform the public about the problem. In addition, how can we know which prevention efforts are more effective than others without implementation and evaluation on a national scale? Furthermore, the criminal justice system's leading source of victimization in the United States, the National Crime Victimization Survey, often provides inaccurate information on seniors despite its claims that every demographic is included in its victimization calculus. It is for these reasons and others that a better method of data collection must be created. Currently, most discussions of elderly abuse are made with fragmented data that may not completely reflect the reality or scope of this horrendous crime.

Anderson and Mangels (2006) argue that a national data clearinghouse is needed to respond effectively to elder abuse. They suggest that such a clearinghouse would allow for yearly statistics on cases of sexual abuse of the elderly. It could record specific acts of violence such as rape or physical assaults. It would also allow for the examination of trends and patterns associated with the behavior which epidemiologists have determined to be risk factors that invariably lead to assaultive violence. This process could be similar to that of other data collections such as the UCRs and the NCVS, which for several decades have increased public awareness of the levels of crime and victimization. These data collections have also helped to justify funding for law enforcement spending and evaluation research in order to prevent and reduce crime. The same approach can be taken by implementing a national survey that focuses on measuring and preventing sexual assaults. Research on elder abuse that relies on both criminal justice and public health approaches is instructive in this regard since it suggests that collective efforts will more effectively prevent elderly sexual abuse. We believe that the criminal justice system and the public health care system should combine their efforts to develop an annual data collection program focused on prevention and punishment efforts. For example, a national clearinghouse of statistics on elderly sexual abuse should rely on the interdisciplinary approach that includes mental health agencies, social service and law enforcement agencies, state public health departments, hospital emergency rooms, nursing homes, triad programs, scholars, politicians, other public health officials, and concerned citizens. In light of the expected population increase among older Americans, a failure to implement the public health approach and develop a clearinghouse will mean that the extent of the problem may never become known, and more elderly victims will continue to suffer rape and other sexual assaults in silence.

References

Anderson, J. F., & Dyson, L., *Legal Rights of Prisoners: Cases and Comments.* Lanham, MD: University Press of America. 2001

Anderson, J. F., Dyson, L., Burns, J., and Taylor, K. "Pre-Employment Screening and Training Could Reduce Excessive Force Litigation Cases." *Journal of Police and Criminal Psychology.* 13 (1):12–24. 1998

Anderson, J. F., & Mangels, N. J. Helping Victims: Social Services, Health Care Interventions in Elder Abuse. In Randall W. Summers and Allan M. Hoffman (Eds.), *Elder Abuse: A Public Health Perspective* (pp. 139–166). Washington, DC: American Public Health Association. 2006.

Bachman, R., & Meloy, M. L. Epidemiology of Violence Against the Elderly: Implications for Primary And Secondary Prevention. *Journal of Contemporary Criminal Justice, 24* (2), 186–197. 2008.

Bergeran, L. R. Elder Abuse Prevention: A Holistic Approach. In R. Filinson & S. Ingman, (Eds.), *Elder Abuse: Practice and Policy* (pp. 218–228). New York: Human Services Press. 1989.

Bergman, J. A. Responding To Abuse and Neglect Cases: Protective Services Versus Crisis Intervention. In R. Filinson & S. Ingman, (Eds.), *Elder Abuse: Practice and Policy* (pp. 94–103). New York: Human Services Press. 1989.

Braithwaite, R. L., & Taylor, S. E. (Eds.). *Health Issues in The Black Community*. San Francisco: Jossey-Bass Publishers. 1992.

Burgess, A.W., & Clements, P.T. Information Processing of Sexual Abuse in Elders. Journal of Forensic Nursing, 2(3): 113–120. 2008.

Callendar, W. *Improving Protective Services for Older Americans: A National Guide Series.* Portland, ME: University of Southern Maine, Center for Research and Advanced Study. 1982.

Cantrell, B. Triad: Reducing Criminal Victimization of The Elderly. *FBI Law Enforcement Bulletin,* 19–23. February, 1994.

Cartwright, P.S., & Moore, P.A. The Elderly Victim of Rape. *Southern Medical Journal,* 83:988–989. 1989.

Christoffel, T. *Health and The Law: A Handbook For Health Professionals.* New York: The Free Press. 1982.

Crystal, S. Social Policy and Elder Abuse. In K.A. Pillemer & R.S. Wolf (Eds.). Elder Abuse: Conflict in the Family (pp. 331–339. Dover, MA: Auburn House. 1986

Ehrlich, P., & Anetzberger, G. Survey of State Public Health Departments on Procedures For Reporting Elder Abuse. Public Health Report No. 106, pp. 151–154. Washington, DC: U.S. Department of Health and Human Services. March–April 1991.

Fisher, B., Zink, T., & Regan, S. Hidden Within the Golden Years: Intimate Partner Violence and Abuse Against Older Women. In R. Summers & A. Hoffmann (Eds.), *Elder Abuse: A Public Health Perspective* (pp. 97–116). Washington, DC: American Public Health Association. 2006.

Fryling, T., Summers, R., & Hoffman, A. Elder Abuse: Definition and Scope of the Problem. In R. Summers & A. Hoffmann (Eds.), *Elder Abuse: A Public Health Perspective* (pp. 5–18). Washington, DC: American Public Health Association. 2006.

Gaines, L.K., & Miller, R.L. Criminal Justice in Action: The Core. (4th ed.). Belmont, CA: Thomson/ Wadsworth. 2008.

Gardner, T. J., & Anderson, T. M. *Criminal Law* (9th ed.). Belmont, CA: Thomson/Wadsworth. 2006.

Gelles, R. J., & Cornell, C. P. (1990). *Intimate Violence in Families* (2nd ed.). Family Studies Text Series. Newbury Park, CA: Sage Publications. 1990.

Ginsburg, W.L. *Victims' Rights: The Complete Guide To Crime Victim Compensation.* Clearwater, FL: Sphinx Publishing. 1994

Glicken, M. D., & Sechrest, D. *The Role of the Helping Profession in Treating The Victims and Perpetrators of Violence.* Boston: Allyn & Bacon. 2003.

Gostin, L. O. *Public Health Law: Power, Duty, Restraint.* Berkeley: University of California Press. 2000.

Gottfredson, D. *Exploring Criminal Justice: An Introduction.* Los Angeles: Roxbury Publishing Company. 1999.

Gottfredson, M., & Hirschi, T. *A General Theory of Crime.* Stanford, CA: Stanford University Press. 1990

Groth, A.N. Men Who Rape: The Psychology of the Offenders. New York: Phenum. 1979.

Harris, D. K., & Benson, M. L. Nursing Home Theft: The Hidden Problem. *Journal of Aging Studies, 12* (1), 57–67. 1998.

Krug, E. G., Dahlberg, L. L., Mercy, J. A., Zrui, A. B., & Lozano, R. Abuse of The Elderly. World Report on Violence and Health. Geneva: World Health Organization. 2002.

Meadows, R. J. *Understanding Violence And Victimization* (3rd ed.). Upper Saddle River, NJ: Pearson/Prentice-Hall. 2004.

Moody, C. E., Marvell, T. B., & Kaminski. Unintended Consequences: Three Strikes Laws and The Murder of Police Officers. Washington, DC: National Institute of Justice (NCJ # 203649). 2002.

Morgenbesser, I.L., Burgess, A.W., Boersma, R.R., & Myruski, E. Media Surveillance of Elder Sexual Abuse Cases. Journal of Forensic Nursing, 2(3):121–126. 2008.

Moriarty, L. J., & Jerin, R. A. *Current Issues In Victimology Research* (3rd ed.). Durham, NC: Carolina Academic Press. 2007.

Moskowitz, S. Private Enforcement of Criminal Mandatory Reporting Laws. *Journal of Elder Abuse and Neglect, 9* (3), 1–22. 1998.

Muram, D., Miller, K., & Cutler, A. Sexual Assault of the Elderly Victim. *Journal of Interpersonal Violence*, 7(1): 70–76. 1992.

National Center on Elder. Abuse Elder Abuse Prevalence and Incidence. Fact Sheet. Washington, DC: National Association of State Units on Aging. 2005.

National Research Council. Mistreatment: Abuse, Neglect, and Exploitation in an Aging America. Washington, DC: US Government Printing Office. 2003

Neubauer, D. W. *America's Courts and the Criminal Justice System* (6th ed.). Belmont, CA: West/Wadsworth. 1999

Payne, B. K., & Cikovic, R. An Empirical Examination of the Characteristics, Consequences, and Causes of Elder Abuse in Nursing Homes. *Journal of Aging and Neglect, 7* (4), 61–74. 1995.

Perkins, C. Age Patterns of Victims of Serious Violent Crime. *Bureau of Justice Statistics Special Report.* US Department of Justice, NCJ-162031. 1997.

Pillemer, K. A., & Frankel, S. Violence Against The Elderly. In Mark L. Rosenberg & Mary Ann Fenley (Eds.), *Violence in America: A Public Health Approach* (pp. 158–183). Oxford: Oxford University Press. 1991.

Pleck, E. Domestic tyranny: The Making of American Social Policy Against Family Violence from Colonial Times to the Present. New York: Oxford University Press. 1987.

Quinn, K. APS Program Spotlight Older Women: Hidden Sexual Assault. Reprinted 1994-ICASA Coalition Commentary, June. 1997.

Reid, S. T. *Criminal Law* (7th ed.). Los Angeles: Roxbury Publishing Company. 2007.

Rogers, C. C. America's Older Population. *Food Review, 25* (2), 2–7. 2002.

Rosenberg, M. L., & Fenley, M. A. (Eds.). *Violence in America: A Public Health Approach.* Oxford: Oxford University Press. 1991.

Schneider, M. J. *Introduction to Public Health.* Gaithersburg, MD: An Aspen Publication. 2000.

Siegel, L. J. *Criminology: The Core.* Belmont, CA: Thomson/Wadsworth. 2008.

Toshio, T., & Kuzmeskus, L. M. Elder Abuse in Domestic Settings. Elder Abuse Information Series # 1 (p. 8). Washington, DC: National Center on Elder Abuse, National Association of State Units on Aging. May, 1997.

Vago, S. *Law and Society* (8th ed.). Upper Saddle River, NJ: Pearson/Prentice-Hall. 2006.

Wallace, H. *Family Violence: Legal, Medical, and Social Perspectives.* Boston: Allyn & Bacon. 1999.

Wolf, R.S., & Pillemer, K.A. Helping Elderly Victims. New York: Columbia University Press. 1989.

Part III: The Often Unacknowledged Victims

Suggested Questions, Activities and Videos

Discussion Questions:

- What are the benefits of approaching elderly sex abuse as a public health issue?
- Discuss the implications of using the public health approach to all sexual assaults.
- Discuss why male heterosexual prisoners rape other male prisoners.
- Can prison rape ever be eliminated as the PREA asserts? Why or why not?
- Why is it difficult to ascertain the amount of child sexual abuse?

Suggested Videos:

- Facing Prison Rape: PREA: Dept. of Justice

Suggested Activities:

- Get a guest speaker from CASA or a GAL, or someone from the local or state Crime Victim's Office.
- Have students research the most current case law in your state regarding child court testimony in sex crime cases.
- Have class examine PREA and how your state is dealing with the mandates.
- Examine the mandatory laws regarding elder abuse in your state.

Part IV

The Offenders

Chapter 12

Sex Offenders and Child Molesters

Deborah L. Laufersweiler-Dwyer & Gregg Dwyer

Introduction

A major thesis of this book is that sexual crimes are an acquired behavior, an act of normal deviance, found in many societies and cultural groups. Rape is a behavioral act. When examining the motivation of rapists, there are several avenues by which to explore the concept. Often attributed to the psychological perspective, the first view identifies sex acts as those which are motivated by sexual needs or reasons. This particular definition is very difficult to justify objectively. Opinion differs (Dietz 1983; Groth 1979; and Knight and Prentky 1990) as to whether the motivation for rape should be limited to the conscious motivation or the unconscious motivations of the offender. It should be noted before examining the motivations of rapists that human behavior is a result of many factors. Actions reflect multiple drives, social forces, and situational variables. As this chapter begins, the reader will be struck with motives such as expression of anger, desire to control, the desire to inflict pain, and the desire for sexual gratification. Many researchers feel that "motivation" is the wrong term to use when describing why offenders commit a particular act (Dietz 1983; Groth 1979; and Knight and Prentky 1990). Instead, the crime of rape should be defined by the emotional determinants rather than the motivational determinants (Dietz 1983; Groth 1979).

Many studies focus on the offenders' reasons for committing offenses, and from these studies typologies of offenders are derived. These typologies classify offenders into basic categories based upon characteristics of the offenders and their offenses. The difficulty of categorizing the behavior of rapists in a scientifically meaningful manner reflects a more general problem in the fields of victimology and criminology. A universal science must be founded on universal characteristics of human behavior. Many have moved in their research to try and overcome this flaw. Victimology and criminology have shifted the view to include the biological determinants as well as the psychological determinants to construct a more concise method of exploring the universal human characteristics that underlie rape.

In addition, rape cannot be understood apart from the sociocultural perspective. In this chapter we will also examine the numerous sociocultural perspectives in an attempt to create a complete picture concentrating on the dynamics of the offense, the characteristics of the offender and the characteristics of the victim.

While some offenders might have similar characteristics, there is no single typology that can account for all offenders. We must uncover the principles that bring about the most valuable separation of a group into subgroups that have theoretically important similarities (Prentky and Burgess 2000). Through such a process we can make sense of the phenomena. Classification systems that have the greatest opportunity for use start out with the simple question "What is the intended mission or purpose of the system?" In criminology and victimology the purpose has been to increase the accuracy of predictions of dangerousness or reoffense risk for sex offenders.

Sex Offender

There are a number of competing ideas surrounding sex offenders. The first is derived from the popular stereotypes. In the examination of motivations and typologies, the reader must understand that rapists seldom fit the "movie stereotype". Rapists are seldom the stranger jumping from behind the bushes. Rape is still often mistaken as a crime prompted solely by sexual desire. This misunderstanding has caused two familiar stereotypes to permeate American culture. The first is the offender, who, through circumstances beyond his control, misunderstandings or defective communication, becomes involved in the allegation of coerced sexual relations. The second stereotype is of the offender whose insatiable sexual needs drove him to commit acts that could satisfy his sexual gratification.

Many erroneous images have been formed as a result of emotional responses to ongoing crimes, past media hype and films depicting offenders as sex fiends, sex maniacs, or sex psychopaths (Dietz 1983). These images result in considerable pointlessness in societal reactions to offenders. In many instances societal responses have been severe to the least dangerous offenders while maintaining policies of little or no punishment for those offenders who attack the most helpless.

Many of the theories that have been used to explore the motivation behind an individual's behavior rely on normative conceptions or the dominant sociological view of deviance to explain the behaviors of sex offenders. These views are problematic in that they rely on community norms which are likely to vary from the slight to the extreme. In addition, many sexual behaviors are not criminal. Consensual sexual activities that involve paraphilias are often not defined within the legal arena.

As was stated above, the majority of offender classifications are developed based on the motivational concepts. Many with this view see sex offenses as being motivated by a need. This need is most often defined in sexual terms. A specific problem with this approach to classifying sex offenders is that many offenders have multiple reasons for their actions. In addition, if the motivation was sexual gratification, the requirement of orgasm would be present. In many rapes or attempted rapes the offenders may not, for various reasons, achieve orgasm, eliminating them from these categories.

Motivational Typologies

Knowing the limitations placed on this "science" by the numerous competing factors, it is necessary to examine the number of different typologies, recognizing the limitations that each presents. Several different classifications schemes have been proposed throughout the years. As early as 1952, Guttmacher and Weinhofen attempted to classify offenders as either true sex offenders, aggressive offenders or sadistic offenders. True sex offenders used rape as an explosive expression of a pent-up sexual desire. The second offender committed rape as a general pattern of criminal behavior. The third offender was, as stated, sadistic.

Though rape is a sexual crime, many researchers have pointed to the non-sexual needs that motivate the offender. Kopp (1962) developed a dichotomy based on whether the rapists could be characterized as "ego-syntonic or "ego-dystonic". In this motivational scheme the rapists was either an antisocial psychopath or a an individual with "feelings" who is later likely to feel remorse or guilt. Gebhard, Gagnon, Pomeroy, and Christenson (1965) set down four categories of offenders within which the seven subtypes of offenders were identified. Within these were the amoral delinquent, the double standard, the explosive rapist and the assaultive-sadistic rapist.

In 1969, Cohen, Seghorn and Calmas identified four types of rapists based on the relative amounts of aggression and sex present in the offense. This re-

Table 1. Cohen and Seghorn's Typology

Compensatory Type	Motive is more sexual than aggressive. Force is simply used to gain compliance. The rape fantasy is foremost in the offenders mind. The rape often compensates for feelings of inadequacy.
Displaced Aggressive Type	The sexual assault is an expression of anger. The rapist's intent is to physically harm, degrade, defile and humiliate the victim. The offender experiences an uncontrollable impulse often precipitated by an event involving a significant woman in the offenders life. The offense is the displacement of the anger towards this other woman.
Sex-Aggression-Diffusion Type	This offender displays clinical sadism, feeling arousal and anger during the assault. The two feelings are synergistically related.
Impulse Type	For this offender neither sexual nor aggressive motives are central to the assault. The offenses predatory and part of the key pattern of impulse antisocial behavior.

search produced four types that subsequently led to further research and the more popular "motivational models" or typologies. In their research, Cohen et al., identified the compensatory type, the displaced aggressive type, the sex-aggression-diffusion type and the impulse type. Table 1 illustrates the characteristics attributed to each category.

Amir (1971), in his early research on victim precipitation and rape, identified several types of rapists. In his categorization of rapists, Amir identified offenders based on aberrations of their personality, or those who commit rape as a "demand of the youth culture". Rada (1978) in his research closely following Amir described five types of rapists. The first was identified as the sociopathic offender, whose behavior was impulsive and antisocial. The second type of rapist was the masculine identify conflict offender. This offender was characterized by feeling of inadequacy and hypermasculine attitudes. The third type of offender was identified as the situational stress offender. His behaviors were characterized by depression and feelings of guilt. The fourth type of offender characterized by Rada was the sadistic offender. This offender is aroused by and gains pleasure from the degradation, pain and humiliation of the victim. The last type of rapist described by Rada was the psychotic offender. This offender is set apart by his bizarre and violent behavior.

Berlin et al., (1997) believed that the offender's actions and their consequences were not enough to illuminate motivation. Sexual offenses can be enacted out of a variety of motivations. In some cases, the behaviors in question may be a manifestation of a psychiatric disorder accompanied by severe impairment. In their typologies, Berlin et al. (1997), attempted to explore and identify six motivational factors. In this examination, Berlin et al. (1997), identified typologies of the opportunistic rapist. Type one is an offender who has prominent narcissistic personality traits. He may have an inflated sense of his own worth, masking insecurities, or an exploitative personality style that does not otherwise adequately consider the perspectives of others. He believes he is not accountable to social norms or the law. Type two has dependent personality traits, and may be may be generally unassertive and submissive. He has low self-esteem, little initiative, and a positive and helpful attitude towards others. However, he experiences uncharacteristic outbursts of irrational behavior which in some cases takes the form of sexual aggression.

The second category of rapists identified by Berlin et al. (1997), was the angry rapist. This type commits rape out of anger or frustration. The anger is often identified with one person or incident and then redirected within the rape. The third category of rapists is the developmentally-impaired rapist. These individuals suffer from either mental retardation or are developmentally impaired. They often experience difficulties leading to an inability to learn and control their sexual urges in socially acceptable ways.

The fourth category of rapist is the psychotic rapist. These are individuals who have an independent confirmatory history of major mental illness. The fifth category is identified as a paraphilic or sexually-driven rapist. Often identified as a paraphiliac coercive disorder these offenders have recurrent cravings for coercive sex. The final category is the rare case of the sexual assault associated with voyeurism. The authors note that voyeurism is almost always a nonviolent offense. It is in rare instances that this offense may turn to violence.

Groth, Burgess, and Holmstrom (1977) developed a classification scheme based on the concepts of power, control, and sexuality. This classification system has conceptual distinctions very similar to Cohen and Seghorn's typologies. Within their model, Groth et al., identified four types of rapists, to include power reassurance, power assertive, anger-retaliatory, and anger excitation. This model has been used extensively in practical rather than theoretical applications (Turvey 1999). Most students of victimology and criminology are familiar with these dimensions. This model has been modified for use by law enforcement as a mechanism for identifying possible offenders and targeting investigatory efforts. Additionally, this model was revised by the National Center for the Analysis of Violent Crime (NCAVC). In part, this model was modified to describe the offenders' behaviors during the act as a method of aiding in criminal profiling. The NCAVC motivational typologies describe offenders' behaviors as follows:

- **Power Reassurance:** offender behaviors suggest an underlying lack of confidence and inadequacy, or belief that the offense is consensual, expressed through minimum force and low confidence.
- **Power Assertive:** offender behaviors suggest an underlying lack of confidence and inadequacy, expressed through a need for control, mastery and humiliation of the victim, while demonstrating authority.
- **Anger Retaliatory:** offender behavior suggests a great deal of rage, either towards a specific person, group, institution or symbol of either.
- **Anger-Excitement/Sadistic:** offender behavior suggests the offender gets sexual gratification from the victim's pain and suffering.
- **Opportunistic:** offender behavior suggests an offender who is out to satisfy his immediate sexual impulses.

Although extensive in considering both the psychological needs and purposes of the offender, it is however limiting, in that it does not consider the cultural components of human behavior. In addition it does not provide for a dynamic, developmental model that identifies possible transformation in the offender.

Prentky, Knight, and Rosenberg (1988) developed a typology that can be considered, perhaps, as the most comprehensive of classification models. This model included three categories, which identified eight types of offenders. This model assesses a) the aggression of the offense (instrumental or expressive), b) the meaning of sexuality in the offense (compensatory, exploitive, displaced-anger, sadistic), and c) the impulsivity reflected in the history and life-style of the offender. This model, unlike earlier models, includes both the biological, psychological and cultural components necessary to define human behavior.

This model was later modified to include a ninth subtype. It is a motivation-driven system that consists of four primary presumptive motivating factors: opportunity, pervasive anger, sexual gratification, and vindictiveness. This classification model (Table 2) includes the following major dimensions: expressive aggression, juvenile and adult antisocial behavior, social competence, global or pervasive anger, sadism, sexualization, and offense planning.

Profiles of Specific Rapists

Although other chapters have addressed the occurrence of rape, it is necessary to again look at the sources of data and some of the numbers produced by this data. Data from this section came from official statistics gathered by police, self-report surveys done by the Bureau of Justice Statistics and independent

Table 2. Prentky, Knight, and Rosenberg Motivational Typologies

Primary Motivation	Types and Brief Identifiers			
Oppor- tunistic	*Type One—High Social Competence* Aggression is likely to be instrumental; no gratuitous violence and no evidence of pervasive anger. Moderate impulse, antisocial behavior in adulthood, relatively high level of social and interpersonal competence. Offenses are not typically to be sexualized; no history of paraphilias and no evidence of sadism. Offenses do not appear to be compulsive, offense planning is minimal, and there is little evidence of premeditation.	*Type Two—Low Social Competence* Aggression is likely to be instrumental; no gratuitous violence and no evidence of pervasive anger. Moderate impulse, antisocial behavior in adulthood, relatively low level of social and interpersonal competence. Offenses do not typically appear to be sexualized; no history of paraphilias and no evidence of sadism. Offenses do not appear to be compulsive, offense planning is minimal, and there is little evidence of premeditation.		
Pervasively Angry	*Pervasively Angry—Type Three* Characterized by a high level of aggression and gratuitous violence in most aspects of the offenders life. A history of aggression directed at men and women. Moderate impulse, antisocial behavior in adolescence and adulthood. Offenses do not typically appear to be sexualized; history of paraphilias is unlikely, and no evidence of sadism. Offenses do not appear compulsive, offense planning is minimal, and there is little evidence of premeditation.			
Sexual	Sadistic		Non-Sadistic	
	Overt— Type Four Characterized by a high level of aggression and gratuitous violence, mostly notably in sexual offenders. A history of pervasive or generalized anger is present. Sexual offenders are marked by sadism (fusion of aggression with sexual arousal); there must be clear evidence of	*Muted— Type Five* Aggression is likely to be instrumental; no gratuitous violence is evident. Although impulsive, antisocial behavior may be present, it is not a critical feature. Sexual offenders are marked by sadism with a low level of violence and limited physical injury to victims; sexual	*High Social Competence— Type Six* Aggression is likely to be instrumental. No gratuitous violence and evidence of pervasive anger. Minimal impulsive, antisocial behavior in adolescence. Moderate impulse, antisocial behavior may be present in	*Low Social Competence— Type Seven* Aggression is likely to be instrumental. No gratuitous violence and evidence of pervasive anger. Minimal impulsive, antisocial behavior in adolescence. Moderate impulse, antisocial behavior may be present in

			adulthood.	adulthood.
	a connection between sexual acts and the pain, suffering, or humiliation of the victim. Moderate amount of impulse, antisocial behavior in adolescence and adulthood. History of other paraphilias often is present. Offense planning and premeditation are evident.	acts tend to by symbolic and noninjurious. Key difference between Overt and Muted is the relative absence of aggression in the muted type. History of other paraphilias often is present. Offense planning and premeditation are evident.	Relatively high level of social and interpersonal competence. Sexual offenses marked by high degree of sexualization, rape fantasy, and expressed interest in the victim as a sex object. Although a history of other paraphilias often is present, there is no evidence of sadism. Offense planning and premeditation is evident.	Relatively low level of social and interpersonal competence. Sexual offenses marked by high degree of sexualization, rape fantasy, and expressed interest in the victim as a sex object. Although a history of other paraphilias often is present, there is no evidence of sadism. Offense planning and premeditation is evident.
Vindictive	*Low Social Competence — Type 8* Characterized by a high level of aggression and gratuitous violence that is directed specifically at women, both in sexual offenses and otherwise. Anger is misogynistic and there is no history of pervasive anger. Minimal impulse and antisocial behavior in adolescence. Moderate impulsive and antisocial behavior in adulthood. Relatively low level of social and interpersonal competence. Offenses do not typically appear to be sexualized. There is no history of paraphilias and no evidence of sadism. Offenses do not appear to be compulsive, planning is minimal and there is little evidence of premeditation.		*Moderate Social Competence — Type 9* Characterized by a high level of aggression and gratuitous violence that is directed specifically at women, both in sexual offenses and otherwise. Anger is misogynistic and there is no history of pervasive anger. Minimal impulse and antisocial behavior in adolescence. Although some impulsive and antisocial behavior may be present in adulthood, it is not extensive. Relatively high level of social and interpersonal competence. Offenses do not typically appear to be sexualized. There is no history of paraphilias and no evidence of sadism. Offenses do not appear to be compulsive, planning is minimal and there is little evidence of premeditation.	

Note: Abstracted from Pretenky and Burgess 2000

research. Relying strictly on official statistics would give the reader a skewed view of the profile for both the rapists and their victims.

Two sources of statistical data are maintained by the Department of Justice as a tool to learn more about the prevalence and characteristics of sexual crimes. The Uniform Crime Report provides significant data on those crimes reported to police. NCVS gathers information about crimes from a nationally representative sample of U.S. residents age 12 and older. In the late 1980s an effort was put forth to enhance the surveys to better obtain information on rape and sexual assaults. This restructuring included incidents of sexual assault and unwanted sexual contact.

General Picture

In order to create a profile we will start with the general characteristics for all arrested rapists. Then we will identify these characteristics by the type of rape committed by the offender. To understand fully the different categories of rape it is necessary to understand how these rapists are similar in nature as well as diverse.

In 2000, an estimated 90,186 forcible rapes were reported to police (UCR 2000). This represents an increase from the previous year, but a rate still lower than that reported in the mid 1990s (UCR 2000). Regionally, the greatest percentage of reported rapes occurred in the South. As described in the previous section, cultural factors help explain this phenomena. Many of the theories surrounding rape are strongly supported by the "subculture of violence" theory and the hypermasculinity theories.

Of the rapes reported, 89.5% were completed while only 10.5% accounted for attempts. Again it must be noted that these are those rapes or attempted rapes reported to police. In addition, the profile created is of those offenders arrested.

The consequences of low reporting of sexual assault are that it places severe restrictions on creating a profile of the offender, victim attributes and the situational dynamics of the crime (Miethe and McCorkle 2001). In 1994 and 1995, 32% of rapes identified by NCVS were reported to law enforcement (Greenfield 1997). Under these conditions, offender profiles should be interpreted with caution.

In 1994 (Greenfield 1997), of those crimes reported as sexual assault/rape, 35.8% were strangers and 64.2% were included in the nonstranger category. When asked to describe the relationship to the offender, the majority (33.1%) said the offender was well known to them. This was closely followed by strangers at 30.9%. Most instances of sexual assault/rape involved only one offender, whether the offender was known or not.

There are some characteristics that are similar to all rapists. These include gender. Of all rapes reported during 2000 to both the UCR and NCVS 99.4% were males. The majority of those arrested were under 25 years of age. In addition, the racial breakdown has remained stable, with whites being approximately 60% of those arrested.

NCVS and UCR provide limited data on the characteristics of the victim. What has been discovered in a review of this data is that the majority of rape victims are young, unmarried and economically disadvantaged. In 1994, the NCVS reported little statistical difference in martial status and rape. The numbers were evenly distributed across all categories.

Offender Specialization and Escalation

In creating a profile of rapists the question is often asked "Where did they start?" The majority of rapists did not start out as minor sex offenders. As opposed to the popular belief that voyeurs and exhibitionist will soon escalate to rape, the majority of offenders in prison had no previous record for a nonviolent sex crime. There are some exceptions as different types of rapist are profiled. Those who commit marital rape and acquaintance rape may escalate from aggressive or battering nonsexual behaviors to sexual behaviors.

Planning and Spontaneity

Although popular culture has characterized rapists as calculating individuals who have well thought out plans for their actions, the majority of rapists do not fall within this category. For most rapists, the level of planning is low, if any. This is particularly true when a prior relationship exists between the parties involved (Miethe and McCorkle 2001).

Situational Elements and Circumstances

Transient factors associated with sex offenses include: offender motivation, the victim-offender relationship, and the situational dynamics of the crime. Offender motivation has been addressed in great depth earlier in this chapter. It must be noted however, that the majority of typologies or motivational classification schemes have been limited to forcible-stranger rape. Typologies for acquaintance rape, date rape and marital rape will be discussed later in this chapter.

Victim offender relationships are extremely important in creating profiles for both the offenders and their targets. These relationships often dictate motivation on the part of the offender. There is an extreme degree of debate over the frequency of stranger versus non-stranger rape. Some of the explanations given for this are that many of the rapes that occur between non-strangers are not likely to be reported to the police.

Situational dynamics are primary factors such as time and place aspects, types of weapons used, victim resistance, financial, marital and other stressor, nonpsychosexual mental disorders and alcohol and drug use. Many studies show that sex offenders were reasonably well adjusted men who committed their first offenses while drinking heavily, experiencing extreme emotional stressor, in groups, or during a depressive, manic, or schizophrenic episode. The sexual nature of the crime often requires additional explanation. These often go to the emotional feelings of the offender at the time of the offense (Dietz 1983).

Stranger Rape

In forcible rapes, sex offenders are disproportionately young and African-American (UCR 1998). This distribution has remained fairly stable over time. As with many other violent offenses, rape is most often intraracial. The socioeconomic status of forcible/stranger rapes has also remained consistent over time. In early research, Amir (1971) found that most rapists arrested were unemployed and of low-socioeconomic status. Research done in 1994 by Miethe and Meier supported this by identifying the majority of rapes occurring in neighborhoods with high unemployment and low family income.

In terms of situational factors, sexual assaults occur in a social context defined primarily by time and physical location. According to data, summer months (especially July and August) are the peak season for rapes known to the police, and rapes are most infrequent during the winter months (UCR 1998). More than one-third of sexual assaults occur between 6:00 p.m. and midnight (NCVS 1998). A higher proportion of rapes occur on the weekend than on other days the week, and nearly half take place at or near the victim's home. A smaller proportion (about 20%) occur on school property or in commercial buildings, and less than 10% happen in parking lots, parks, or alleys (NCVS 1998). Stranger assaults, however, are more likely to occur in open public areas than sexual assaults among nonstrangers. Weapon use is estimated in 18% of sexual assaults but only about 10% of those assaults involving acquaintances as offenders (NCVS 1998).

Acquaintance Rape

There are several different definitions attached to this form of rape. Most have been developed by law enforcement and researchers for aid in categorizing offenders. Many individuals believe that the phenomenon of acquaintance rape is new. However, references to this form of rape can be found in the Old Testament (Allison and Wrightsman 1993). It has been only recently, that public attention has been brought to a strikingly frequent event. In describing the profiles of these rapists it is necessary to divide acquaintance rape into three separate categories. The will be acquaintance rape, date rape and marital rape.

Acquaintance rape is any rape in which the parties know each other. This definition is often seen as nonconsensual sex between adults who know each other. This includes neighbors, coworkers, friends, etc. Often this is a person the victim knows, but not a close friend (Parrot and Bechhofer 1991). Acquaintance rape compared to the characteristics of stranger rape is unique. In comparison there are two areas where distinct differences can be found. These are the force used, and the time at which the act occurs. In acquaintance rape, as opposed to stranger rape, the force used by the offender reflects more subtle types of coercion (Muehlenhard and Schrag 1991).

The majority of research on the subject of acquaintance rape has been done with college students. The reasons for this are the risk of victimization, their willingness to participate in research, and the organizations found on college campuses that have been associated with acquaintance rape.

Date Rape

Date rape is commonly viewed as a less serious and less traumatic offense than stranger or acquaintance rape (Van Wormer and Bartollas 2000). Five types of date rape have been proposed to capture the diversity of these sexual assaults. Shotland (1992) identified beginning date rape, early date rape, relational date rape, rape between sexually active couples and rape between sexually active couples who previously dated. Each of these arose at a different point in the relationship, both in terms of the length of the relationship and previous sexual activity (Byers and O'Sullivan 1996).

Beginning rape has been defined as those occurring during the first few dates. Associated with these rapes, Kanin (1967) stated that the rapist may have a need for more varied sexual experience. In addition, it was identified that women who date extensively or engage in having sex with a number of different males are more likely to expose themselves to an aggressive male. This is not to say that they brought on the rape. The variety in experiences increases their chances of encountering an aggressive male.

The second instance in which rapes are likely to occur in the dating relationship is the "early date rape". A number of different explanations have been given for rapes that occur during this period of courtship. A significant explanation has been the poor skills in coping with sexual frustration and poor impulse control on the part of the male. Foreplay leads to mixed feelings. Kanin (1967, 1985) identified that college men who were dissatisfied with the frequency of their sexual activity were more likely to rape. Kanin (1985) also identified that these behavior may be a last resort when all other forms non-coercive behaviors have failed.

The third and fourth types of date rape are referred to as relational date rape. The first type occurs in an ongoing relation where the couple has not engaged in sexual activity. In these instances, many of the men see this as a step toward marriage or believe that others couples are already engaged in sexual relations. This leads the male to encourage and in many instance coerce the female into participating in sexual activities.

The last type of rape occurs after the relationship has ended. In many instances as a mechanism for revenge on the part of the male, but also as a way to "win" back the victim's love. Offenders often feel that this is what the victim wants or what they, as a spurned lover, deserve.

Situational elements and circumstances are most often identified in this type of rape. Several studies have examined the situational elements and found that the definition of rape becomes extremely muddied when research participants are asked to include these elements. Giarrussi, Johnson Goodchilds, and Zeller (1979), Fischer (1986), Muehlenhard, Friedman, and Thomas (1985), and Korman and Leslie (1982) found several factors that participants identified as changing the definition of the act from rape to sexual activity. These included money spent by the male, heavy petting, going to the man's apartment, women initiating the date, and alcohol use on the part of one or both parties.

The men who commit these offenses have a number of characteristics in common. They are more aggressive, more likely to view pornographic material, more likely to use alcohol, hold hostile attitudes toward women, and seek out peer groups that reinforce stereotypical views of women (Johnson and Sigler 1997). In addition, several other studies have found these men are more likely to condone rape and violence, hold traditional roles and more likely to be sexually experienced (Kanin 1967; Koss, Leonard, Beezley and Oros 1985; and Rapaport and Burkhart 1984).

The description above fits into many of the typologies presented earlier in this chapter. Groth's power-assertive and Knight and Pretensky's sexual rapist are most likely to be identified with the date rapists.

Marital Rape

In order to understand the offenders of marital rape it is necessary to understand the definition of this offense. Much variety exists in state laws defining exactly what elements must be satisfied for marital rape to have occurred. All states currently have some statue defining marital rape. These are, however, far from clear. In many states exemptions still exist keeping prosecutors from charging husbands.

In its simplest form, marital rape is defined as any intercourse or penetration obtained by force, threat of force or where the individual was unable to give consent. Finkelhor and Yllo (1985) developed a typology of marital rapists. They divided these offenders into three groups: force only, battering, and sadistic/obsessive.

Force only rape has been describe as coerced sex. These are instances where the husband will use only the amount of coercion necessary to obtain submission (Johnson and Siegler 1997; Bergen 1996; Finkelhor and Yllo 1985). Many victims in these instances do not define the action as rape causing significant problems in identifying the extent to which this crime occurs. The second category within marital rape is battering rape. This is seen as the extension of the battering, either occurring during the physical violence or after the violence. In the cases where the rape occurs after the violence, it often takes on the form of "making-up". The abuser in an attempt to show his "love" for his spouse coerces her into having sex against her will (Johnson and Siegler 1997; Bergen 1996; Finkelhor and Yllo 1985). The final category within marital rape is the sadistic/obsessive rape. These offenses involve torture, physical violence, and/or perverse sexual acts (Johnson and Siegler 1997; Bergen 1996; Finkelhor and Yllo 1985).

Russell (1990) identified three different types of husband rapists: husbands who prefer raping their wives over having consensual sex with them; husbands who are able to enjoy both rape and consensual sex, but are indifferent to which it is, and husbands who prefer consensual sex, but who are willing to rape their wives when sex is denied. Russell contends that the motivations are different for each group. She reverts back to the common elements of power and anger in identifying motivations.

A fourth type of sexual batterer was added to Finkelhor and Yllo's (1985) typology by Monson and Langhinrichsen-Rohling (1998), who identified the

Table 3. Overview of the Proposed Four-Type Integrated Batterer Typology

Type	Type of Violence	Generality of Violence	Percentage in General Batterer Population
Family-only	Nonsexual Only	Only/predominately marital	45%
Dysphoric/ borderline	Sexual/nonsexual	Predominately marital	25%
Generally violent/ antisocial	Sexual/nonsexual	Marital/extramarital	25%
Sexually Sadistic	Sexual Only	Marital/extramarital	5%

"sexually-obsessive" batterer. In their typology, battering only and sexual battering have been combined to create an integrated typology of marital violence. Table 3 represents the marital violence typology developed by Monson and Langhinrichsen-Rohling (1998).

Marital rape typologies are not well developed. Some researchers argue that marital rape is just one extension of domestic violence (Johnson and Sigler 1997). The research is often anecdotal and relies upon survey research whose reliability is questionable. In addition, the sample sizes have been limited by the victim's willingness to come forward, as well as the victim's own conception of what constitutes a rape (Monson and Langhinrichsen-Rohling 1998).

Attempting to create a profile of marital rapists is difficult. All the information gathered on those who commit this offense has come from the victims. In addition, the majority of information has been collected in conjunction with domestic violence. This has limited the sample to only those men who are violent—sexual or nonsexual. Little or no information has been gleaned from the perpetrators. Characteristics that are common to these offenders are a history of family-of-origin violence, substance abuse, extreme jealousy, domination/control and diminished marital satisfaction. In addition, marital dysfunction, a need for sadomasochistic sex, and greater jealousy toward their wives has been associated with sexually aggressive men compared to nonsexually aggressive men (Bowker 1983). There is some evidence that premarital pregnancy is associated with marital rape (Davidson 1978; Walker 1979).

It is important for the reader to understand that marital rape is not limited to those in lower socioeconomic levels. It is not limited to those who marry young, nor is it limited to relationships that are violent from the beginning. In one of the largest studies of marital rape, martial rape was found to occur at all levels of society. African American women were slightly more likely than Caucasian women to be the victims of marital rape (Russell 1990).

Russell (1990) also determined that women who are raped within the marital relationship have often entered into the relationship at a very young age. In addition, Russell also found that these women had been victims of other types of sexual violence prior to their marriage.

Child Molesters

At this point in the chapter will we specifically look at two types of child sexual abusers—Child Molesters and Pedophiles. You may be thinking— "Aren't they the same thing?" The answer is no. No single molester profile exists. Child molesters arrive at deviancy via multiple pathways and engage in different sexual and nonsexual acting-out behaviors (Pretenky, Knight and Lee 1997). Remember this as you read through this material, that not all child molesters are pedophiles and not all pedophiles are child molesters.

Commonly used by the media and law enforcement "child molesters" can mean anyone who engages in any type of sexual activity with individuals legally defined as children. When using this term, there are no distinctions between single or repeat offenders or violent and nonviolent offenders. Many of us still adhere to the image of the dirty old man at the playground offering children candy as a means of seducing them away and molesting them. It is necessary that we understand the difference between a child molester and a pedophile. As stated before, not all child molesters are pedophiles, and not all pedophiles are child molesters.

Classification of Child Molesters

There are a number of different types of classification models for child molesters. The first types are the clinically derived classification systems. The earliest of these classification systems was developed by Finch (1962). Finch identified the immature offender, the frustrated offender, the sociopathic offender, the pathological offender and the miscellaneous offender. Finch did use in his typology the characteristic of whether the offenses were seen as a preferred and long standing form of sexual behavior, an immature offender or as a reaction to some sexual or emotional frustration at the adult level, the frustrated type.

Kopp (1962) in his examination of child molesters identified only two categories within his typology. These included the Type I offender, an individual who is drawn to children as a result of passive and somewhat withdrawn relationship to peers. Type I offenders do not see these relationships as abnormal or inappropriate. The Type II offender is described as maintaining adult relationships in a relatively normal framework. The lack of dimension has lead to little use of this typology.

Swanson (1971) identified four types of child molesters. These included first, the classic pedophiliac, whose sexual preference is only children. Secondly, the situational violator, who is most likely to have long term peer relationships, but, due to environmental circumstances or situational factors, offends. The third type described was the inadequate sociopathic violator who does not show a specific attraction to children, but exploits a child for convenience or self-gratification. The last type was the brain damaged. This offender molests as a result of some clinical condition such as mental retardation.

Classification systems stemmed from these early efforts resulted in extensive research done at the Massachusetts Treatment Center in Bridgewater and the development of several profiles (Cohen, Garofalo, Boucher, and Seghorn 1971; Cohen, Seghorn and Calmas 1969; Groth and Birnbaum 1979). The initial classification system developed out of this research was produced by Cohen, Seghorn and Calmas in 1969. Within this research, three types of pedophilia were identified. These included the pedophile-fixated type, the pedophile-regressed type and the pedophile-aggressive type. A fourth type was later added, the exploitative type.

Dr. Nicholas Groth (1978) developed a similar classification model. As with other research efforts, Groth distinguished between offenders who manifest fixation on children and those whose molestation represents a regression. In his book, Groth et al. (1978), identified two patterns, fixed and regressed (Common Types 1 and 2, respectively) and three distinct motivations sex-pressure, sex-force, and incest.

Yet another classification scheme was proposed in 1992. In the Crime Classification Manual, Douglas et al. (1992), attempted to provide a comprehensive DSM-like list of primary categories with subtypes. This system was designed to aid law enforcement rather than define clinically the behavioral, motivational and emotional aspects of other classification systems. Within this system, child molesters were identified as belonging to one of twelve categories. These included the nuisance offender (with four subtypes), the domestic sexual assault, entitlement rape, subordinate rape, power-reassurance rape, exploitative rape, anger rape, sadistic rape, child/adolescent pornography, historical child/adolescent sex rings, multidimensional sex rings and abduction rape.

Dr. Park Dietz (1983) developed a classification system dividing individuals who sexually molest children into two broad categories: situational and preferential. These typologies again had been developed in an effort to aid law enforcement in the identification, arrest, and conviction of offenders. In this model, the difference between the two types of child molesters was that situational child molesters do not have a true sexual preference for children, but engage in sex with children for varied and sometimes complex reasons. The preferential child molester is a pedophile. These individuals have a definite sexual preference for children. Their sexual fantasies and erotic imagery focus on children. The preferential type doesn't experience stress as does the situational child molester.

Within the situational type, four subtypes have been identified, which include, regressed, morally indiscriminate, inadequate, and the sexually indiscriminate. The first type is the regressed child molester. This individual often leads the most stable life of the situational child molesters. They are however plagued by low self-esteem and poor coping skills. When they molest, they often turn to the victim as a substitute for the preferred adult sexual companion. They are most likely to obtain a victim based on availability. This is why many of these offenders molest their own children. They may use force, promises or some other type of coercion to get the child to have sex. Among incest offenders, this type is the most prevalent.

The second subtype of situational child molester is the morally indiscriminate child molester. This subtype is simply continuing a pattern of behavior. He is a user and abuser of all he encounters. Children are simply part of that chain. He often chooses his victims based on their vulnerability and opportunity. Unlike the regressed situational child molester, the majority of his victims are strangers. This is not to say that his own children could not be his victims.

The third subtype of situational is the inadequate child molester. These individuals are often suffering from psychoses, a personality disorder or mental retardation (Lanning 1986). The offenders seem to become sexually involved with children out of insecurity or curiosity. Children are viewed as nonthreatening, allowing these individuals to explore sexual fantasies. These individuals can, however, due to their lack of impulse control, become angry and hurt the child.

The last subtype in the situational category is the sexually indiscriminate child molester. This individual differs in that he appears to be discriminating in his behavior except when it comes to sex. His is a often referred to in law-enforcement circles as a "try-sexual". This simply means that he is willing to try anything. He is most often confused with a preferential child molester. Although he has numerous defined paraphilias or sexual preferences, he has no clear preference for children. Of all the situational child molesters, he is far more likely to have multiple victims, and be from a higher socioeconomic background.

Within the preferential category, there are three subtypes: seductive, introverted, and sadistic. The first subtype, also know as the fixated type, will seduce or court his victims, often buying them gifts, toys, or loaning them money. As this person slowly becomes more intimate with the child, he begins to introduce sexual innuendo and eventually sexual pornography and paraphernalia. He is the master manipulator and often has numerous individuals at different stages of seduction. This individual frequently identifies children who have some emotional need.

The second type of preferential offender identified by Dietz was the sadistic pedophile. This subtype, also called a mysoped, often stalks, uses force to obtain compliance and must inflict pain, suffering and humiliation to become sexually gratified. These offenders have been identified as most likely to kill their victims.

The final type identified by Dietz was the introverted pedophile. This offender has a preference for children, but lacks the social and interpersonal skills necessary to seduce them. He engages in little or nonverbal communication with his victims. He is the old stereotype of the dirty old man or the guy hanging around the playground. He is similar to the inadequate situational child molester, except for his sexual preference for children alone. (See Tables 4 and 5.)

The MTC:CM3 (Massachusetts Treatment Center: Child Molester 3) model was developed by researchers at the Massachusetts Treatment Center. This model is described as a two axis typology. In Table 6 on Axis I fixation and social competence are completely independent dimensions. The concept of regression was dropped and a newly defined fixation dimension, intensity of pedophilic interest, was crossed with a dimension of social competence. This new model yielded four independent types. Axis II was added to describe the behavioral dimension of an offender. Also included within this Axis was the degree of violence employed by the offender. This combination yielded six distinct types within Axis 2 (Knight, Prentky, and Lee 1997).

The last type of child molester identified by clinicians and police is the incest offender. It is clear that, as a group, these offenders are as heterogeneous as nonincest offenders (Rist 1979; Summit and Kryso 1978; Prentky and Burgess 2000). Incest is a sexual relationship with a near relative (including parent-child, grandparent-grandchild, brother-sister, uncles, and aunts). Parent and child relationships are the most frequently reported, although brother and sister relationships are not uncommon. There has been little effort made to develop any classification system, either clinical or empirical (Prentky and Burgess 2000). In one of the earliest attempts to classify these offenders, Weinberg (1955) identified two types: the ingrown family and the promiscuous family. Summit and Kryso (1978) in a clinical examination of offenders, identified ten categories of offenders. Significant to their classification was the diverseness of this group. Researchers believe that the heterogeneous nature allows for the application of

Table 4. Situational Child Molester

	Regressed	Morally Indiscriminate	Sexually Indiscriminate	Inadequate
Basic Characteristics	Poor coping skills	User of people	Sexual Experimentation	Social misfit
Motivation	Substitution	Why not?	Boredom	Insecurity and curiosity
Victim Criteria	Availability	Vulnerability and opportunity	New and Different	Nonthreatening
Method of operation	Coercion	Lure, force, or manipulation	Involve in existing activity	Exploits size, advantage
Pornography Collection	Possible	Sadomasochistic detective magazines	Highly Likely: varied	Likely

Table 5. Preferential Child Molester

	Seduction	Introverted	Sadistic
Common Characteristics	1. Sexual preference for children 2. Collects child pornography or erotica		
Motivation	Identification	Fear of Communication	Need to inflict pain
Victim Criteria	Age and Gender preferences	Strangers or very young	Age and Gender preferences
Method of Operation	Seduction Process	Non-verbal sexual contact	Lure or force

Tables adapted from: Deviant and Criminal Sexuality (1993), 2nd edition, NCAVC, FBI Academy.

nonincest models to incest offenders. Table 7 outlines the categories identified by Summit and Kyrso (1978).

Several other researchers have identified general traits and behavioral patterns common to incest offenders. According to the booklet published by Life Skills Education (1991), a number of characteristics can be found common to incest incidents. These include multiple sexual encounters, lack of social skills within the family, isolation of the family, and victims often experience the first incident at around age eight with the average age of victims at eleven years old.

Unlike media portrayals of child abduction and sexual assault by strangers, most child molesters and pedophiles, with estimates ranging from 70 to 95%, are acquaintances, family friends, or relatives of the victims. As with the preferential child molester described by Dietz (1982) or the high-social compe-

Table 6. MTC:CM3 Typology of Child Molesters

Axis I		Axis II	
Type 0 High Fixated/Low Social Competence In order to be considered high fixation the offender must have sexual thoughts dominated by children, had three or more sexual contacts with children, evidence of enduring relationships with children, offender initiates contact with children in numerous situations.	*Type 1 High Fixated/Low Social Competence* Offenders with high social competence have lasting employment, adult sexual relationship lasting one year or longer, offender has assumed significant responsibility in parenting for 3 years or longer, offender is active in adult activities, and offender has a friendship with an adult lasting one or more years. Offenders do not have to meet all criteria only two. Offenders with low social competence do not meet the criteria.	*Type 1 Interpersonal* High contact with children, nongenital, nonorgasmic sexual acts. Offender known prior to sexual relationship, long term relationship or multiple contacts with same victim, high degree of planning.	*Type 2 Narcissistic* High contact with children, interests are in sexual gratification, primary aim is orgasm, victims are often strangers, single encounters, numerous victims, offenses are often spontaneous with little planning.
Type 2 Low Fixated/Low Social Competence	*Type 3 Low Fixated/High Social Competence*	*Type 3 Exploitative* Low contact with children, no more force than necessary to gain compliance, no evidence that aggression is eroticized or sexualized, sexual gratification is the primary aim, victims are typically strangers and offenses so a moderate degree of planning.	*Type 4 Muted Sadistic* Low contact with children, no more force than necessary to gain compliance, aggression was eroticized—sadistic fantasies, victims are strangers, moderate planning.
Axis II			
Type 5 Aggressive Low contact with children, high degree of physical injury (take many forms from repressed aggression to accidental injury), primary aim is orgasm, no evidence of sadism, little evidence of offense planning.		*Type 6 Sadistic* Low Contact with children, high degree of physical injury, Injuries are indicative of sadism on the part of offender, victims are strangers, high degree of planning.	

Note: Abstracted from Prentky and Burgess (2000)

Table 7. Typology of Incest Offenders — Summit and Kyrso (1978)

Type	Description
Incidental Sexual Contact	Isolated incidents of interest or dependency. The often take the form of sexual games that are not considered abusive.
Ideological Sexual Contact	The parent believes that the child will benefit from the expression of sexual instincts and feelings.
Psychotic Intrusion	Psychotic thinking is a driving factor in the abuse
Rustic Environment	This is where families living in rural areas have traditionally participated and accept incest.
Perverse or Pornographic Incest	This category represents what many lay persons may characterized as sick, lechery, perverted. This is bizarre and many times ritualistic.
Child Rape	This refers to men who exhibit antisocial behaviors — one of which is to sexually abuse their children.
Pedophilic Incest	These are individuals who have fantasies about children and act out these sexual needs with their own children.
True Endogamous	This is where stressors associated with the father's life and a "dysfunctional" family where the daughter has taken on many of the "wifely" duties. Lines become blurred and the daughter is abused.
Misogynous	This individuals hatred for women is often taken out on his daughter as a form of punishment.
Imperious Incest	This offender believes and acts as the king. He believes that those around him are subject to his wishes — including sexual favors. As a means of showing loyalty the daughters often become the victims of abuse.

Adapted from Prentky and Burgess, 2000

tence identified by Prentky and Burgess (2000) the members of the family know the abuser. Many of these individuals choose to target families in need or with children who require "special" attention. In addition, a great number of these offenders have placed themselves in positions of trust within the community. This is evident by the incidents recorded within the Catholic church, the boy scouts and other youth oriented activities. These offenses are often disguised as expressions of affection (Howell 1982).

Many child molesters display similar characteristics to rapists: they tend to be socially inept in adult relationships, have low self-esteem, have feelings of inadequacy, and a sense of worthlessness and vulnerability. These characteristics depart from rapists when analyzing characteristics such as aggressiveness, acting on impulse, and insensitivity to victims feelings (West 1987). Finkelhor (1984) identified four preconditions that must exist for child abuse to occur. His conditions take into consideration both the psychological and the sociological variables of the offender. Offenders must have some motivation to abuse; must overcome internal inhibitions; most overcome external inhibitions; and must overcome the child's resistance to the abuse.

Conclusion

Sexual crimes are acquired behavior, an act of normal deviance, found in our society as well as many others around the world. When examining the motivation of rapists, we have explored a number of different concepts associated with defining behavior. We have examined the psychological perspective which identifies sex acts as those which are motivated by sexual needs or reasons. As we have seen, there is much debate resulting in a number of different motivational models. We have identified, through the analysis of these models, how actions reflect multiple drives, social forces, and situational variables. Many of the models do have similarities such as, the expression of anger, desire to control, the desire to inflict pain, and the desire for sexual gratification. As the reader has moved through this chapter, it is hoped that instead of defining rape based solely on the emotional determinants, readers have considered the integration of both motivational and emotional determinants.

Classification systems are temporary and artificial, often serving a time-limited purpose. As the reader has seen, few systems endure, and those that do are constantly undergoing modification. The application of reliable and valid classification systems to legal and clinical settings implies a new and growing notion that cooperation is needed for planning and decision-making where sex-offenders are considered.

The types of rape committed and the profiles of the offender and victim provide the reader with just a start. There is much more to be done in the examination of rapists, especially in the areas of acquaintance rape, date rape and marital rape. Differences exist between and within the categories of sex offenders. The information available to researchers has been limited due to the societal reactions to these types of rape and the victim's assumed responsibility. Researchers must gain access to diverse research populations in order for the profiles to be applicable to the general population.

References

Allison, J. A., and L. S. Wrightsman. *Rape: The Misunderstood Crime.* California: Sage Publications, 1993.

Amir, M. *Patterns of Forcible Rape.* Chicago: University of Chicago Press, 1971.

Berger, R. K. *Wife Rape: Understanding the Response of Survivors and Service Providers.* Thousand Oaks, CA: Sage, 1996.

Berlin, F.S., G. K. Lehne, H. M. Malin, W. P. Hunt, K. Thomas, and J. Fuhrmaneck. "The Eroticized Violent Crime: A Psychiatric Perspective with Six Clinical Examples." *Sexual Addiction and Compulsivity 4* no. 1, (1997): 9–31.

Bowker, L. *Beating Wife Beating.* Lexington, MA: Lexington Books, 1983.

Byers, E. S. and L. F. O'Sullivan L.F. *Sexual Coercion in Dating Relationships.* Haworth Press. New York, 1996.

Cohen, M. L., T. K. Seghorn, and W. Calmas. "Sociometric Study of Sex Offenders." *Journal of Abnormal Psychology* 74, (1969): 249–255.

Cohen, M.L., R. F. Garofalo, R. Boucher, and T. Seghorn. "The Psychology of Rapists." *Seminars in Psychiatry 3*, (1971): 307–327.

Davidson, T. *Conjugal Crime: Understanding and Changing the Wife-Beating Problem.* New York: Hawthorn Books, 1978.

Davis, M. H. "Measuring Individual Differences in Empathy: Evidence for Multidimensional Approach." *Journal of Personality and Social Psychology* 44, (1983): 113–125.

Dietz, P. E. (1983). "Sex Offenses: Behavioral Aspects." In *Encyclopedia of Crime and Justice*, ed. S.H. Kadish, 1485–1493. New York: Free Press, 1983.

Douglas, J. E., A. W. Burgess, and C. R. Hartman. *Crime Classification Manual.* New York: Lexington Books, 1992.

Federal Bureau of Investigation. *Crime in the United States—1998.* Washington, DC: U.S. Government Printing Office, 1998.

Federal Bureau of Investigation. *Crime in the United States—2000.* Washington, DC: U.S. Government Printing Office, 2000.

Finch, J. H. "Men Convicted of Sexual Offenses Against Children: A Descriptive Follow-Up Study." *British Journal of Criminology 3*, (1962): 18–37.

Finkelhor, D. *Child Sexual Abuse: New Theory and Research.* New York: Free Press, 1984.

Finkelhor, D. and K. Yllo. *License to Rape: Sexual Abuse of Wives.* New York: Holt, Rinehart, and Winston, 1985.

Gebhard, P. H., J. H. Gagnon, W. B. Pomeroy, and C. V. Christenson. *Sex Offenders: An Analysis of Types.* New York: Harper and Row, 1965.

Giarrusso, R., P. Johnson, J. Goodchilds, and G. Zellerman. "Adolescent Cues and Signals: Sex and Sexual Assault," a paper presented to a symposium of the Western Psychological Association Meeting. San Diego: 1979.

Greenfield, L. A. *Sex Offenses and Offenders: An Analysis of Data on Rape and Sexual Assault.* U.S. Department of Justice, 1997.

Groth, A. N. "Sexual Trauma in the Life Histories of Rapists and Child Molesters." *Victimology: An International Journal 4,* (1979): 10–16.

Groth, A. N. and A. W. Burgess. "Motivational Intent in the Sexual Assault of Children." *Criminal Justice and Behavior 4,* (1977): 253–264.

Groth, A. N., A. N. Burgess and L.L. Holmstrom. "Rape: Power, Anger, and Sexuality." *American Journal of Psychiatry* 134, (1977): 1239–1243.

Groth, A. N. and J. Birnbaum. *Men Who Rape: The Psychology of the Offender.* New York: Plenum Press, 1979.

Guttermacher, M.S. and H. Weihofen. *Psychiatry and the Law.* New York: Norton, 1952.

Howell, S. "Twisted Love: Pedophilia." In *Victimization of the Weak: Contemporary Social Reactions,* eds. J. Scherer and G. Sheperd. Charles C. Thomas: Springfield, Il, 1982.

Johnson, I. M. and R.T. Sigler. *Forced Sexual Intercourse in Intimate Relationships.* Brookfield VT: Dartmouth/Ashgate, 1997.

Kanin, E. J. "Reference Groups and Sex Conduct Norm Violations." *Sociological Quarterly 8,* (1967): 495–504.

Kanin, E. J. "Date Rapists: Differential Sexual Socialization and Relative Description." *Archives of Sexual Behavior 14,* (1985): 219–231.

Knight, R.A., and R. A. Prentky. "Classifying Sex Offenders: The Development and Corroboration of Taxonomic Models." In *The Handbook of Sexual Assault: Issues, Theories, and Treatment of the Offender,* eds. W.L. Marshall, D.R. Laws and H.E. Barbaree, 23–52. New York: Plenum Press, 1990.

Knight, R. A., R. A. Prentky, and A. F. Lee. "Risk Factors Associated with Recidivism among Extrafamilial Child Molesters." *Journal of Consulting and Clinical Psychology 65,* (1997): 145–149.

Kopp, S.B. "The Character Structure of Sex Offenders." *American Journal of Psychotheraphy* 16, (1962): 64–70.

Koss, M. P., K. D. Leonard, D. A. Beezley, and C. J. Oros. "Nonstranger Sexual Aggression: A Discriminant Analysis of the Psychological Characteristics of Undetected Offenders." *Sex roles 12* (1985): 981–992

Lanning, K. *Child Molesters: A Behavioral Analysis for Law Enforcement Officers Investigating Cases of Sexual Exploitation.* Washington DC: National Center for Missing and Exploited Children, 1986.

Life Skills Education. *Incest: A family Secret.* Northfield, MN: Life Skills Education, 1991.

Miethe, T. D. and R. C. McCorkle. *Crime Profiles: The Anatomy of Dangerous Persons, Places, and Situations.* California: Roxbury Publishing Company, 2001.

Miethe, T. D. and R. F. Meier. *Crime and Its Social Context: Toward Integrating Theory of Offenders, Victims and Situations.* Albany; State University of New York Press, 1994.

Monson, C. M. and J. Langhinrichsen-Rohling. "Sex, sex-Role Beliefs, and a History of Co-Occurring Nonsexual Violence: How do these Factors Influence Attributes about Marital Rape?" *Journal of Interpersonal Violence 11,* (1996): 410–424.

Muehlenhard, C. L., D. E. Friedman, and C. M. Thomas. "Is Date Rape Justifiable? The Effects of Dating Activity, Who Initiated, Who Paid, and Men's Attitudes Toward Women." *Psychology of Women Quarterly 9,* (1985): 2987–309.

Muehlenhard, C. L. and J. Schrag. "Nonviolent Sexual Coercion." In *Acquaintace Rape: The Hidden Crime,* eds. A. Parrot and L. Bechhofer, 115–128. New York: Joghn Wiley and Sons, 1991.

National Crime Victimization Survey (NCVS). *Criminal Victimization in the United States, 1998. Statistical Tables, May 2000.* Washington, D.C: National Institute of Justice, 1998.

Parrot, A. and Bechhofer, L. *Acquaintance Rape: The Hidden Crime.* New York: John Wiley and Sons, 1991.

Prentky, R.A., R. A. Knight, and R. Rosenberg. "Validation Analysis on the MTC Taxonony for Rapists: Disconfirmation and Reconceptualization. In *Human Sexual Aggression: Current Perspectives,* eds. R.A. Prentky and V. Quinsey, 21–40. New York: New York Academy of Sciences, 1988.

Prentky, R.A. and A.W. Burgess. *Forensic Management of Sexual Offenders.* New York: Kluwer Academic/Plenum Publishers, 2000.

Rada, R.T. "Classification of Rapists." In *Clinical Aspects of the Rapists,* ed. R.T. Rada, 117–132. New York: Grune and Stratton, 1978.

Rappaport, K. and B. R. Burkhart. "Personality and Attitudinal Characteristics of Sexually Coercive College Males." *Journal of Abnormal Psychology 93,* (1984): 216–224.

Rist, K. "Incest: Theoretical and Clinical Views." *American Journal of Orthopsychiatry 49,* (1979): 680–691.

Russell, D.E. *Rape in Marriage.* Indianapolis: Indiana University Press, 1982, 1990.

Shotland, R.L. (1992). "The Theory of the Causes of Courtship Rape: Part 2." *Journal of Social Issues 48* no. 1, (1992): 127–143.

Summit, R.C. and J. Kryso. "Sexual Abuse of Children: A Clinical Spectrum." *American Journal of Orthopsychiatry* 48, (1978): 237–251.

Swanson, D.W. "Who Violates Children Sexually?" *Medical Aspects of Human Sexuality 5,* (1971): 184–197.

Teten, H. and B. Turvey. "A Brief History of Criminal Profiling." *Knowledge Solutions Library.* Electronic Publication, (1998). URL: http://www.corpus-delicti.com/demo/.

Turvey, B. *Criminal Profiling: An Introduction to Behavior Evidence Analysis.* London: Academic Press, 1999.

Van Wormer, K. S. and C. Bartollas. *Women and the Criminal Justice System.* Pearson Allyn and Bacon: Boston, MA, 2000.

Walker, L.E. *The Battered Woman.* New York: Harper and Row, 1979.

Weinberg, S. *Incest Behavior.* New York: Citadel Press, 1955.

West, D.J. "Sexual Crimes and Confrontations: A Study of Victims and Offenders." In *Cambridge Studies in Criminology,* ed. A.E. Bottoms. Aldershot: Gower, 1987.

Chapter 13

Juvenile Sex Offenders: Issues of Definition and Treatment

Stacy C. Moak

Introduction

Juvenile sexual offenses are issues of concern for society. When children act out in sexually inappropriate ways, reactions range from fear to disgust. However, relatively little research exists that actually defines the activities of juvenile sex offenders. The research that does exist indicates that juvenile sex offenders are a heterogeneous group and not significantly different from other types of juvenile offenders. This chapter is designed to provide a context for the discussion of juvenile sex offenders and the most significant issues related to the behavior. The chapter will begin by defining the problem of juvenile sexual offenses.

Next, a discussion of the context within which juvenile sexual offending occurs is presented. That section also provides some of the theories of why juvenile sexual offending occurs. The section that follows provides a profile of a juvenile sexual offender based on the available information. Next, a discussion is presented related to the question of whether juvenile sex offenders are remarkably different from other juvenile offenders. Additionally, juvenile female offenders are compared to male offenders to determine any gender issues that exist with sex offending.

In the section that follows, issues of prosecution and sex offender registries are presented. Risk of reoffending and treatment issues are discussed. Finally, sexting is presented as the new sex offender category emerging in the United States. The chapter concludes with suggestions for future research in this area, and policy considerations related to the limited knowledge currently available.

The Problem of Juvenile Sex Offending

Current data defining the extent of the problem of juvenile sexual offenses is difficult to acquire. The overall picture must be pieced together from a variety of sources. For purposes of this discussion, a juvenile is considered to be a person under an age fixed by law at which he or she can be charged with a criminal offense. As a general rule, that age is between 10 and 17; however, specific definitions vary from state to state. To further define the discussion, the definition of a juvenile sexual offender is a legal definition, not a psychological diagnosis. Three key concepts are required for one to be considered a sexual offender. First, some type of sexual behavior is required. Sexual fantasies that do not lead to actions will not classify one as a sexual offender. Next, the behavior must satisfy legally defined criteria. Usually these criteria include determining the specific type of sexual behavior involved, whether the victim consented, and whether the perpetrator used force against the victim. Finally, sex crimes are defined as interpersonal actions. These laws stem from concern about exploitation of or harm to another person (Smallbone 2006).

The Federal Bureau of Investigation collects information on crimes reported to police and analyzes that data to provide an understanding of the nature and extent of various crime problems. Examining data over a 10 year period from 1998 to 2007 indicates that forcible rapes committed by juveniles have declined. In 1998, 14,173 forcible rapes were committed by persons under 18. In 2007, that number had dropped to 11,178 which was a -21.1% change. Additionally, all other sexual offenses noted a decline during the same 10 year period. In 1998, 42,996 sex related offenses were attributed to persons under 18. In 2007, that number had dropped to 37,765 which was a -12.2 % change (FBI 2007). Even with declining numbers, however, criminal and juvenile justice practitioners remain concerned about the participation of juveniles in sex related offenses.

Examining the Office of Juvenile Justice and Delinquency Prevention report on juvenile offenders and victims (Snyder and Sickmund 2006) reveals that sexual assaults accounted for just over half of the juvenile victims of violent crime known to law enforcement between 2000 and 2001. Further, sexual assaults accounted for 3 in 4 female juvenile victims and 1 in 4 male juvenile victims. Victims under 12 years old accounted for 47% of sexual assault victims (Snyder and Sickmund 2006).

Based on the available information, juveniles are both offenders and victims of sexual assaults. Being a victim of sexual assault is, at least somewhat connected to becoming an offender of sexual assault. Accordingly, understanding the unique nature of juvenile sexual offending and appropriate interventions is essential to criminal and juvenile justice practitioners.

The Context of Child Sexual Offending

Some sexual experimentation is a normal part of adolescent development. The central question is determining juvenile sexual offending is determining where normal sexual experimentation ends and deviant behavior, that considered outside the norm for a particular population, begins. Adolescence is a period of change and development in which norms change as youths progress through the maturation process (Righthand and Welch 2001). Some behaviors considered deviant for younger youths are considered normal when the youth is older. Thus, the discussion does not simply hinge on the conduct of a particular juvenile, but also on the age, developmental stage, and context of the action.

Although no consensus exists as to the origin of juvenile sexually offensive behavior, evidence suggests that it is strongly influenced by the youngster's family environment. The early sexual experiences, particularly child sexual abuse is particularly influential in the development of sexual offending behaviors of juveniles. Researchers have found that sexually abused children manifest higher frequency of sexually oriented behaviors than their non-abused counterparts (Righthand and Welch 2001).

A high proportion of juvenile sex offenders report a history of childhood sexual victimization. Abusive sexual behavior as a result of child abuse is not surprising because exposure to childhood sexual abuse causes negative effects in numerous mental health domains. Childhood experiences of being physically abused, being neglected, and witnessing family violence have all been linked to sexual offenses in juvenile offenders (Righthand and Welch 2001). Effects of such childhood exposure to maltreatment of various forms range in severity to acute or immediate behavior manifestations, to chronic and long-lasting issues.

The search for a theoretical explanation for why juveniles sexually offend ranges from biological theories to learning theories. Among the biological theories, researchers have examined such characteristics as IQ, arguing that sexual offenders have lower IQs than their non-offending counterparts. Researchers have also examined neuropsychological function, employing instruments that target individual cognitive functions to assess sex offenders abilities in reasoning, executive memory, language, achievement, and motor domains. Brain imaging technology has been used to attempt to visualize abnormalities in neurological disorders. With all of these attempts to understand a biological connection to sexual offending, however, no conclusive evidence has yet been found that suggests that sex offenders are biologically different from their non-offending counterparts (Blanchard, Cantor and Robichaud 2006).

Other theories exists linking childhood victimization to later offending patterns in juveniles. Two competing theories have attempted to explain this relationship. First, Burton (2003) asserts that sexual offending is related to social learning and that juvenile offenders are modeling deviant behaviors to which they were exposed early in their childhoods. However, Knight and Sims-Knight (2003) argue that early victimization leads to sexual aggression due to abnormal personality traits. They assert that juvenile sexual offending is related to a specific developmental feature, specifically a tendency to be preoccupied with sexuality and sexual thoughts.

Based on the available research, theorists have not reached a consensus of the causes of juvenile sexual offending. Whether some unique characteristic of an individual juvenile leads to sexual offending, or whether exposure to various types of maltreatment leads a juvenile to learn sexual offending behavior remains a topic of debate. Continued research in this field is important to better inform both practices and policies dedicated to the containment and treatment of juvenile sexual offenders.

Profile of Juvenile Sex Offenders

One helpful tool in understanding details of the juvenile sex offender population is to examine typologies that have been developed. An early typology was developed by O'Brien and Bera (1986). They identified seven categories of juvenile sex offenders. The categories were: (1) naïve experimenters, (2) undersocialized child exploiters, (3) sexual agressives, (4) sexual compulsives, (5) disturbed impulsive, (6) group influenced, and (7) pseudosocialized. Their categories of offenders included both psychological components of offending, and offense characteristics.

Another typology was developed by Graves (as cited in Weinrott 1996). In a meta-analysis of 16,000 juvenile sex offenders from 140 samples, Graves identified three classifications of juvenile sex offenders (1) pedophilic, (2) sexual assault, and (3) undifferentiated. Sociophychological characteristics were unique to each group. The pedophilic group generally had social deficits including social isolation and lack of confidence. Victims of the pedophilic group tended to be at least three years younger than the abuser. Further, the victim was more likely to be female.

In the sexual assault group, offenders were closer to the same age as their victims or slightly older. Again, the victims tended to be female. Finally, the undifferentiated group varied the most in its characteristics including a wide range of hands-off and hands-on offenses. Hands-off offenses include voyeurism and exhibitionism while hands-on offenses require contact between the victim and offender. In this category, no clear pattern was determined as to the victim's age.

A third typology, consisting of six groups of sex offenders, was developed by Prentky, Harris, Frizzell and Rightland (2000). Their groups included (a) child molesters, (b) rapists, (c) sexually reactive children, (d) fondlers, (e) paraphilic offenders and (f) unclassifiable. The child molester group molested victims who were younger than the age of 11 and at least 5 years younger than the perpetrator. In the rapists group, all of the victims were older than the age of 12 and there was no more than a 5 year age difference between the victim and the offenders. The sexually reactive children as well as their victims were all younger than the age of 11. The fondlers included victims and perpetrators older than the age of 12, but limited their assaultive behavior to caressing and fondling. The paraphilic offenders engaged in exhibitionism and obscene phone calling. Some juveniles did not meet any criteria for the typologies.

Based on the above typologies, juveniles are generally classified by the type of sexual behavior that they commit. Both hands-on and hands-off sexual offenses lead to classification as a sex offender. Additionally, juvenile sex offender classifications usually have a certain portion of offenders who do not fit within any category.

Juvenile Sex Offenders Compared to Other Juvenile Offenders

A central question in the quest to understand juvenile sex offenders is to determine the extent to which they create a separate and distinct class of offending behavior. The overwhelming majority of evidence suggests that they do not. Instead, they are juvenile offenders who happen to commit a sex related act.

According to Smallbone (2006), the available evidence does not support a conception of juvenile sexual offending as a distinct and specialized area of delinquent activity. Research on the characteristics of juvenile sex offenders confirms that these young people are more similar than they are dissimilar to juvenile non-sex offenders (Smallbone 2006). To classify conduct as such, evidence would need to be presented that juvenile sex offenders only commit sex offenses, and persist in the commission of sex offenses through their minority, and possibly into their majority. However, recidivism data show that juvenile sex offenders are between two and four times more likely to be reconvicted for new nonsexual offenses than they are to be reconvicted for new sexual offenses (Hagan, King and Patros 1994; Rubenstein, Yeager, Goldstein and Lewis 1993).

Another assumption is that juvenile sex offenders continue committing sex crimes into their adulthood. Little convincing evidence exists to support this assumption. Studies designed to measure the progression of sexual offending from juvenile to adulthood have produced mixed results (Vandiver 2006). Juvenile sexual offenders may continue offending into their adulthood, but evidence is limited to support the proposition that they will continue to offend sexually.

Based on a review of the most current available research, little evidence exists to place juvenile sexual offenders into a separate category than general juvenile delinquency.

Comparison of Juvenile Male to Juvenile Female Sex Offenders

The literature on juvenile sex offenders is only beginning to develop. Of the research that exists, males have been studied more than females (Vanndiver and Teske 2006). Currently, empirical evidence is not sufficient to determine whether juvenile males and juvenile females are similar enough in their characteristics and offending patterns to group them together. The typologies that exist were developed from samples of males and are not specific to the type of sexual offenses that juvenile females commit.

One recent study by Vandiver and Teske (2006) analyzed 61 registered sex offenders in Texas who were juvenile females and 1,879 who were male juveniles. Their study found significant differences between juvenile female and juvenile male sex offenders in several areas. First, the age they began offending was significantly different. Approximately one half of the females were in the 11 to 13 age range at the time of arrest, whereas approximately one half of males were in the 14 to 16 year old age range. This indicates that females may begin sexually offending earlier than their male counterparts.

Statistically significant differences were also found in terms of the victims' age. The average age of the victims of females was 7.6 whereas the average age of victims of males was 8.4 suggesting that females juvenile sex offenders tend to victimize younger children than do male juvenile sex offenders. Males were more likely to victimize someone of the opposite sex whereas females were less discriminate regarding the sex of their victims (Vandiver and Teske 2006).

Other differences between male and female sex offenders have been discussed by various researchers. These differences relate to their social and family histories prior to arrests. Many female sex offenders reported being victims of either physical or sexual abuse or both. Studies range from 100% (n=14) to 70% (N=22) in percentages of female sex offenders being either physically or sexually abused, or sometimes both (Fromuth and Conn 1997; Fehrenbach and Monastersky 1988). When comparing female to male juvenile sex offenders, females tended to be molested by more than one perpetrator, and were younger at the age of their first victimization.

Research further indicates that the overwhelming majority of the victims in studies of juvenile female sex offenders were younger than 12 (Fehrenbach and Monastersky 1988; Fromuth and Conn 1997). Juvenile female sex offenders are also highly likely to victimize relatives or acquaintances (Fehrenbach and Monastersky 1988). Many of the victims of female offenders are related in some way, including step relationships. Additionally, female sex offenders often victimized children whom they were baby-sitting (Fehrenbach and Monastersky 1988; Fromuth and Conn 1997).

Research suggests that females and males have differences both in their offending patterns and in their histories of prior victimization. These differences should be acknowledged in the policies and practices designed to deter juvenile sex offending, as well as in treatment program.

Prosecution for Sexual Offenses and Sex Offender Registration

The consequences of juvenile sexual offending can be severe and follow the juvenile for an extended period of time. Juveniles who face prosecution for sex offenses are often taken from their families and placed in custody or foster homes. Many of them are considered social outcasts by friends, family, community and society. They suffer persecution and stigma that outlasts whatever disposition may be imposed by the courts (Smallbone 2006). Such negative effects suffered by juvenile offenders are arguably justified in the interest of providing a concrete solution to sexual assault as a significant problem in our society. One of the most controversial issues in the prosecution of juvenile sexual offenders is the issue of sex offender registration. In 1996, the federal government implemented a law that required sex offenders to register with a local law enforcement agency and that the registry be made public (Craum and Kernsmith 2006).

Arguments in favor of such harsh sanctions include (1) the need for specific and general deterrence of sexually abusive behavior, (2) the desire to punish and incapacitate sex offenders, (3) and the need to protect public safety and provide a tracking tool for law enforcement (Craum and Kernsmith 2006). Unfortunately, such measures may work to reinforce the negative behavior and are relatively inconsistent with the original philosophy of the juvenile court process.

The origin of the juvenile court system was intended to protect juvenile offenders, and rehabilitate them into productive members of society (Zimring 2004). Requiring them to register as sex offenders contradicts this goal and makes it virtually impossible for the juvenile to reintegrate into society at the end of the court disposition. Even low level offenders who are required to register are stigmatized by their communities.

States requiring juveniles to register as sex offenders have lost sight of the original intention of the juvenile justice system. The goal of registration is not to rehabilitate the offender, but to promote a sense of security in the community (Trivits and Reppucci 2002). While that goal may appear honorable, registries may actually increase the likelihood of future offending. Registration increases the social isolation of the offender which is highly correlated with re-offending. Furthermore, registries are not an effective deterrent for juveniles (Zimring 2004).

Risk of Reoffending

Studies seeking to determine the risk of juvenile sexual offender recidivism are plagued by methodological concerns such as the definition of reoffending (i.e. arrest versus conviction), the length of the follow-up period, and the type of sample used (treatment sample versus conviction sample (McCann and Lussier 2008). However, several studies have sought to understand the risk factors common to juveniles who sexually reoffend.

Worling and Langstrom (2006) reviewed both empirical and professional literature related to risk factors for juvenile sexual reoffending. They classified risk factors into groups based on predictive value noted in previous research. Based on their review, they identified deviant sexual interest (interest in prepubescent children or sexual violence), previous sexual offending, offending against more than one victim, having a stranger victim, being socially isolated and failing to complete treatment as risk factors favorable to reoffending (Worling and Langstrom 2006). Further, Worling and Langstrom (2006) noted that other risk factors may contribute to reoffending (impulsivity, antisocial personality, association with negative peers, having a male or a child victim, using threats or weapons in sex offenses, history of interpersonal aggression, living in a high stress family or a family supportive of offending) but these factors have not be consistently found to predict reoffending across studies. Thus, although these factors may be common traits that define juvenile sexual offenders, they do not necessarily indicate that the juvenile will reoffend.

As far as factors not linked to recidivism, Worling and Langstrom (2006) identified history of victimization, history of nonsexual offenses, penetration used in the offense, denial, and low victim empathy as contradictory evidence that should not be used to assess risk of reoffending. The finding that family and social problems were not predictive of recidivism for sexual offending was also found by Heilbrun, Lee and Cottle (2005).

Cottle, Lee and Heilbrun (2001) examined risk factors of sexual recidivism in juveniles and found that determinations could not be made because only eight studies had been conducted on the subject. When examining general reoffending, they found that the strongest predictors were age at first contact with authorities and age at first commitment. In 2005, these researchers again examined the issue of risk factors for recidivism and found that younger offenders, juveniles who committed noncontact initial offenses, and those who offended against acquaintances were most likely to reoffend sexually.

Finally, McCann and Lussier (2008) conducted a quantitative review of the scientific literature related to risk factors for reoffending. Using a comprehensive review of the literature, they analyzed 18 studies to identify whether an antisocial tendency and sexual deviance can assist in predicting sexual offending in juvenile sex offenders (McCann and Lussier 2008).

Their study identified four areas of risk factors: criminal history, offense and victim characteristics, victimization, and psychological and behavioral characteristics. First, having previous offenses, both sexual and nonsexual, were predictive of sexual reoffending. Additionally, older juveniles were more likely to reoffend than were younger ones. Juveniles who used threats or weapons during their offense were more likely to reoffend. However, causing physical injury to the victim was not a predictor of sexual reoffending. Further, an offender who had ever had a male victim, and those whose victim was either a child or an adult (greater separation in age from the offender) were found to be more likely to reoffend sexually. Also, juveniles who sexually offended against strangers were more likely to reoffend sexually in the future. None of the psychological and behavioral characteristics analyzed were predictive of future sexual offending. Finally, both the sexual deviance and antisociality domains were predictive of reoffending. Thus, juveniles who present characteristics of sexual deviance and antisocial behaviors are more likely to continue sexually offending in the future.

Overall conclusions about the base rate of reoffending for sexual offenders is that a substantial number of juvenile sexual offenders will reoffend, but for non-sexual related offenses (McCann and Lussier 2008). Additionally, researchers suggest that juveniles should be evaluated as to risk of reoffending based on the uniqueness of being a juvenile and not on measures developed from the adult sex offender population (McCann and Lussier 2008).

Treatment of Juvenile Sex Offenders

Understanding treatment issues of juvenile sex offenders is critical to the field of juvenile delinquency. Based on the evidence that many of these offenders have turbulent home lives, histories of abuse, and social isolation, treatment should be targeted to address these particular issues and not solely focused on the sex act involved in the offense.

Unfortunately, like other areas of juvenile sex offending research, treatment evaluations of juvenile sex offenders are few in number with fewer than 15 published studies (Burton, Smith-Darden and Frankel (2006). Further, few meta analysis have been conducted to explain the studies that do exist. However, studies that have been published show promising results. They generally report effectiveness of current treatment approaches with juvenile sex abusers (Worling and Curwen 2000). Interpretation of these results should be taken with caution because methodology issues continue to plague this area of research.

One of the draw backs to understanding treatment related issues for juvenile sexual abusers is that currently, no evidence-based treatment guidelines are available (Burton, Smith-Darden, and Frankel 2006). Such guidelines have been proposed on the basis of expert opinions in the field, and currently, the guidelines have been accepted for clinical practices.

Another complication is the lack of programming available to female sexual offenders. In 2000 male programs outnumbered female programs in both community-based and residential treatment programs. In community-based programs, male programs outnumbered female programs by a ratio of almost 2 to 1. In residential programs, the numbers were even worse with male programs outnumbering female programs at a ratio of 9 to 1. Accordingly, for the programs that do exist, the majority of them are designed to address the issues of male sexual offending.

Transition back into the community is another issue of concern for juveniles who have sexually offended. All residentially based programs that have been identified so far assist in aftercare placement. However, researchers found that only 73% of community-based programs have such aftercare assistance. The rationale seems to be that residentially placed youths have more serious and complicated problems than do their community-based counterparts. However, given the negative social stigma associated with any sexually related offense, all youths in this category need reintegrative assistance.

Proper assessment of juvenile sexual offenders is important to appropriate treatment. As identified above, juvenile sexual offenders come in many different forms with various backgrounds. Accordingly, different youth with different needs and backgrounds need different programs to ensure that they get what they need, and, likewise, do not take unnecessary or inapplicable classes (Burton, Smith-Darden, and Frankel 2006).

Unfortunately, more research is needed on the assessment of risk for this group of offenders. Many programs are using risk assessment instruments that have not been validated. Because rates of sexual re-offending for another sex related offense is low for juvenile sexual abusers, risk assessment should be a collaborative effort to determine risk factors of re-offending for any offense, not just for sex related offenses. Such a collaborative effort would also work to test the validity of risk assessment instruments.

Other issues that should be recognized and assessed as part of the treatment plan are substance abuse factors, the need for family support, recognition of mental health issues, and issues related to diversity. All of these factors potentially contribute to sexual recidivism and possibly to recidivism for non sex offenses as well. Accordingly, they should all be assessed at when the juvenile first enters a treatment program.

Examination of treatment programs designed to address juvenile sex offending indicate that content areas should include topics such as sex education, cognitive-behavioral restructuring, empathy training, anger management, social skills training, and relapse prevention (Righthand and Welch 2001). Studies in 2001 and in 2002 indicated that both community and residential programs for juvenile sex offenders used some form of cognitive-behavioral theory as a base (Burton, Smith-Darden, and Farkel 2006).

Additionally, programs should include vocational training and basic living skills, assistance with academics, counseling for personal experiences with victimization, counseling for family and peer related issues, healthy dating practices and positive sexual identity (Righthand and Welch 2001). Additionally, these programs have a psychiatric component which provides consultation to youths on an individual level (Burton, Smith-Darden and Farkel 2006).

Researchers have determined that parent support groups are lacking in many treatment programs. Programs such as multisystemic therapy have been evaluated and shown to be effective with both sexual offenders and non sexual offenders. Accordingly, such programs should be included in treatment programs for juvenile sex offenders, especially considering that many of them will continue to offend for non sex related offenses (Burton, Smith-Darden and Farkel 2006).

The good news is that the majority of programs appear to work with adjudicated youths. Researchers have made several recommendations to improve treatment programs for sex offending juveniles. First, greater collaboration and sharing of research among programs is recommended. Although individual programs appear to be evaluating their respective outcomes, this information is not being widely distributed across the discipline. Thus, many opportunities for research are being missed. Researchers further suggest that more employees of treatment programs become active in the field's professional organizations to allow greater opportunities for collaboration across the field (Burton, Smith-Darden and Farkel 2006).

Next, a greater recognition of mental health needs and related psychiatric consultation should be infused into all programs for juvenile sex offenders. Individualized treatment—within fiscal reasonableness is also suggested. Each young person is different and presents different individual, family, and social characteristics. Programs should provide risk assessments and other forms of assessment that increase the focus on individualized treatment of youths. A thorough assessment should lead to a personalized treatment plan for sexually abusive youths (Burton, Smith-Darden and Farkel 2006).

Further consideration of family and parent support groups as a means to decrease nonsexual recidivism is recommended (Righthand and Welch 2001). Youth often return home to a relative after residential placement. Often, that relative has not been exposed to the type of treatment and is unaware of the issues related to reentry and possible relapse. Accordingly, families should be involved in the treatment plan, as well as the plan for reentry (Righthand and Welch 2001).

Finally, incorporating issues of diversity into treatment and practice is needed to improve treatment for all juveniles. As the U.S. population continues to diversify and as related disciplines incorporate issues of diversity into their treatments and report success, the field of treatment of sexual abusers must incorporate those same issues into its treatment and practices (Burton, Smith-Darden and Farkel 2006). Especially in light of the role that family history plays in both the onset of sexual offending and the treatment of sexual offending, efforts should be made to understand the cultural diversity of each juvenile.

Sexting: A New Class of Juvenile Sexual Offenders

A new class of juvenile sex offenders is being created through the discovery and prosecution of "sexting," the sending of nude or partially nude photos via cell phones or internet. Many young people are being prosecuted and required to register as sex offenders for actions that they do not realize are criminal. The most well known case is that of Philip Albert, an 18 year old from Florida, who sent naked text messages of his ex-girlfriend to 70 other people. Albert was arrested and sentenced to five years of probation; however, he was also required to register as a sex offender and will carry that label for 25 years (Prieto 2009). In Pennsylvania, six students in a local high school face child pornography charges after three teenage girls took nude photos of themselves and sent them to three male classmates (Brunker 2009). The three females, ages 14 or 15, face charges of manufacturing, disseminating or possessing child pornography. The three boys, ages 16 and 17, face charges of possession of child pornography. If the juveniles are convicted, they would be forced to register as sexual offenders for at least 10 years.

In Wisconsin, a 17 year-old was charged with possessing child pornography after he posted naked pictures of his 16 year-old ex-girlfriend online. And, in Alabama, four middle-school students were arrested for exchanging nude pictures of themselves. Again, in Rochester, New York, a 16 year-old boy is facing up to seven years in prison for forwarding nude photos of a 15 year-old girlfriend to his friends (Stone 2009).

In yet another case from Indiana, a 14 year old girl was taped having sex at a party by a 17 year old boy. The video was sent via text to other juveniles. The teen who took the video has not been charged yet, but he could be required to register as a sex offender if the state decides to prosecute. Indiana has a law that prohibits child exploitation through the distribution of any pictures, photographs, text messaging, videos, streaming video or other like of anyone under the age of 18 involved in any sort of sex act. Thus, the teen with the cell phone could be charged with a felony.

The National Campaign to Prevent Teen and Unplanned Pregnancy reported that a survey of 1,280 teens and young adults found that 20% of the teens had sent or posted nude or semi-nude photos or videos of themselves via cell phones or internet (Prieto 2009).

When these photos are sent and or received by third parties, or older more predator types, the prosecutions make sense. In the situation, however, in which teens are taking the pictures and sending them back and forth to themselves and their friends, prosecution and sex offender registry seems overkill. Utah has taken a lead by reducing the penalty for juveniles involved in sexting to a misdemeanor instead of a felony (Associated Press 2009). As laws struggle to find a balance between protecting children and monitoring technology, similar cases are likely to be forthcoming.

Conclusions

In conclusion, juveniles are both victims and offenders of sexual offenses. Offenses range from forcible rape to exhibition and voyeurism; from serious to relatively minor. System response to these activities can often exacerbate the situation and cause the offender to persist in delinquent behavior, either sexual or nonsexual. Accordingly, responses to juvenile sexual offenses should be developed based on research unique to juveniles, taking into account gender differences, and not developed from research on adult offenders.

Further, the goal of the juvenile system is to rehabilitate young offenders. Considering that many adolescents are experimenting with their sexuality, often from dysfunctional family environments, punitive policies such as registration laws hardly make sense. No evidence substantiates that punitive policies reduce or deter future delinquency. Further, little evidence supports the proposition that the majority of juvenile sex offenders will continue to commit sex related offenses. Thus, the argument that registration is promoting public safety by protecting them from sexual predators is inconsistent with the research.

On the other hand, treatment programs show success for juveniles who complete them. Assessment instruments should be continually assessed and revised so that they are adequately validated with juvenile populations. Based on more accurate assessment of risk, treatment programs, whenever possible, should be designed for individual juveniles. Additionally, treatment programs that incorporate family, mental health, substance abuse, and cultural diversity should be increased. These programs are more aligned with the juvenile justice system goal of rehabilitating young offenders. Additionally, considering that a substantial number of juveniles will reoffend for non-sex offenses, treatment programs should include components designed to address reduction of general delinquency in addition to sexual offending.

Finally, the phenomenon of using technology to commit sexual offenses, sometimes unknowingly, requires reassessment of sex offending laws and enforcement policies. Utah has taken the lead and reduced the penalty for juveniles who send and receive sexting messages from other juveniles. Punitive measures, including sex offender registration, seems to run counter to common sense and to the underlying philosophy of juvenile justice of rehabilitation of young offenders.

Future research should continue to define classification of juvenile offenders, particularly as those classifications relate to risk of reoffending. Additionally, research should continue to evaluate treatment programs to determine best practices for this population of juvenile offenders.

References

Associated Press. March 11, 2009. Utah lawmakers OK bill on sexting. http://www.ksl.com/index.php?nid=481andsid=5823252. (Accessed 3/21/2009).

Blanchard, R., Cantor, J.M., and Robichaud, L.K. 2006. Biological factors in the development of sexual deviance and aggression in males. In H.E. Barbaree and W.L. Marshall (Eds.). *The juvenile sex offender* (2nd ed., pp. 77–104). New York: Guilford.

Brunker, Mike. January, 15, 2009. Sexting surprise: Teens face child porn charges. MSNBC.com. http://www.msnbc.msn.com/id/28679588. (Accessed 3/21/2009).

Burton, D.L., Smith-Darden, J, and Frankel, S.J. 2006. Research on adolescent sexual abuser treatment programs. In H.E. Barbaree and W. L. Marshall. *The juvenile sex offender* (2nd ed). New York: Guilford.

Burton, D. L.2003. The relationship between the sexual victimization and the subsequent sexual abuse by male adolescents. *Child and Adolescent Social Work Journal*, 20, 277–296.

Cottle, C., Lee, R., and Heilbrun, K. 2001. The prediction of criminal recidivism in juveniles: A meta analysis. *Criminal Justice and Behavior*. 28, 367–394.

Craum, S.W. and Kernsmith, P.D. December, 2006. Juvenile offenders and sex offender registry: Examining the data behind the debate. F*ederal Probation*, 70, 3, pp. 45–49.

Crime in the United States 2007. US Department of Justice, Federal Bureau of Investigation, Criminal Justice Information Services Division.

Fehrenbach, P.A., and Monastersky, C. 1988. Characteristics of female adolescent sexual offenders. *American Journal of Orthopsychiatry, 58* (1), 148–151.

Fromuth, M.E., and Conn. V.E. 1997. Hidden perpetrators: Sexual molestation in a nonclinical sample of college women. *Journal of Interpersonal violence, 12*(3), 456–465.

Hagan, M.P., King, R.P., and Patros, R.L. 1994. Recidivism among adolescent perpetrators of sexual assault against children. *A journal of Offender Rehabilitation, 21*, 127–137.

Heilbrun, K., Lee, R., and Cottle, C. 2005. Risk factors and intervention outcomes: Meta-analyses of juvenile offending. In K. Heilbrun, N.E. Goldstein and R. Redding (Eds.). *Juvenile delinquency: Prevent ion, assessment and intervention* pp. 111–133). Oxford, UK: Oxford University Press.

Knight, R.A., and Sims-Knight, J.E. 2003. Developmental antecedents of sexual coercion against women: Testing of alternative hypotheses with structural equation modeling. In R.A. Prentky, E.S. Janus, and M. Seto, (Eds.) *Sexual coercive behavior: Understanding and management* (pp. 72–85). New York: New York Academy of Sciences.

McCann, K. and Lussier, P. 2008. Antisociality, Sexual Deviance, and Sexual Reoffending in Juvenile Sex Offenders: A Meta-Analytical Investigation. *Youth Violence and Juvenile Justice. Volume 6, No. 4. 363–385.*

O'Brien, M. and Bera, W.H. 1986. Adolescent sexual offenders: A descriptive typology. *Preventing Sexual Abuse: A newsletter of the National Family Life Education Network.* 1, 2–4.

Prentky, R., Harris, B., Frizzell, K., and Righthand, S. 2000. An actuarial procedure for assessing risk with juvenile adolescent sex offenders. *Sexual Abuse: A Journal of Research and Treatment.* 16, 223–234.

Prieto, B. March 8, 2009. Sexting teenagers face child-porn charges. Orlando Sentinel. http://www.sun-sentinel.com/sfl-sexting-030809,0,414962,print.story. (accessed 3/21/2009).

Righthand, S., and Welch, C. 2001. Juveniles who have sexually offended: a review of the professional literature. US Department of Justice, Office of Justice programs, Office of Juvenile Justice and Delinquency Prevention.

Rubinstein, M., Yeager, C.A., Goodstein, C., and Lewis, D.O. 1993. Sexually assaultive male juveniles: A follow-up. *American Journal of Psychiatry, 150.* 262–265.

Smallbone, S. 2006. Social and psychological factors in the development of delinquency and sexual deviance. In H.E. Barbaree, and W.L. Marshall, (Eds.), *The juvenile sex offender,* (2nd ed., pp. 105–127). New York: Guildford Press.

Snyder, H.N. and Sickmund, M. 2006. *Juvenile Offenders and Victims: 2006 National Report.* US Department of Justice, Office of Justice Programs, Office of Juvenile Justice and Delinquency Prevention.

Stone, Gigi. March 13, 2009. Sexting Teens Can Go Too Far. ABC News. http://abcnews.go.com/print?id=6456834. (accessed 3/21/2009).

Trivits, L.C. and Reppucci, N.D. 2002. Application of Megan's law to juveniles. *American Psychologist,* 57, 690–704.

Vandiver, D. 2006. A prospective analysis of juvenile male sex offenders: Characteristics and recidivism rates as adults. *Journal of Interpersonal Violence.* 21, 673–688.

Vandiver, D., and Teske, R. Jr. 2006. Juvenile female and male sex offenders: A comparison of offender, victim, and judicial processing characteristics. *International Journal of Offender Therapy and Comparative Criminology.* 50 (2), 148–165.

Weinrott, M. 1996. *Juvenile sexual aggression: A critical review.* Boulder, CO: Center for the Study and Prevention of Violence.

Worling, J.R., and Curwen, T. 2000 Adolescent sexual offender recidivism: Success of specialized treatment and implications for risk prediction. *Child Abuse and Neglect*, 24, 965–982.

Worling, J.R., and Langstrom, N. 2006. Risk of sexual recidivism in adolescents who offend sexually: Correlates and assessment. In H. Barbaree, and W. Marshall Eds.) *The juvenile sex offender*, (2nd ed., pp. 219–247). New York: Guilford Press.

Zimring, F. 2004. *An American travesty: Legal responses to adolescent sexual offending*. Chicago: University of Chicago Press.

Chapter 14

Sex Offender Treatment: What Works, Who Works, and New Innovative Approaches

Gene Bonham, Jr. & Denny Langston

Introduction

This chapter will examine issues surrounding sex offender treatment. The focus will be on what types of treatment are used today, the effectiveness of treatment with sex offenders, treatment styles, and ramifications for public policy. A distinction will be made between treatment specifically for sex offenders and offenders who have no history of sexual offending. Sex offender treatment will be viewed within the broader milieu of offenders who are either in an institutional setting, or supervised in the community under some form of probation or parole supervision. And, finally, discussion of the future of sex offender therapy and concomitant policy implications are provided.

Sex offenders and the causes of sexual offending have been viewed in a number of different ways over time. Some see sex offenders as violent predators who should receive long prison sentences and kept away from society (Watson and Stermac 1994). This world view holds that such offenders are hopelessly chained to deviant sexual fantasies or perversions that cannot be helped by treatment, and thus need to be separated from the normal community through imprisonment. It has been suggested, for example, that sexual offenders who abuse children should be segregated by living in their own child-free townships. Similarly, some have called for sex offenders to be housed in a 'paedofile town' built on some remote island far away from population centers (Thomas and Tuddenham 2002).

Others see sex offenders as suffering from neuropsychological dysfunction or psychiatric problems that impair their abilities to control sexual desires

(Berlin 1983; Gaffney and Berlin 1984; Langevin, Hucker, Ben-Aron, Purins, and Hook 1985). This view would advocate for diagnosis of the problems that contribute to sexual offending and treatment of these problems, thus allowing offenders to live within society and reduce the risk of reoffending in the future. Some would say that sex offenders don't deserve treatment because of the serious and disdainful offenses that they commit. However, there is also a growing recognition that punishment alone is not likely to reduce the risk of sexual reoffending. Indeed, the failure to provide treatment actually makes communities less safe (Center for Sex Offender Management 2006).

General Overview and Characteristics of Sex Offender Treatment and Management

In the United States, sex offender treatment first developed in the 1930s when sex offenders were seen as 'psychopathic', 'dangerous', and 'deranged' (McCulloch and Kelly (2007). This meant that offenders required indefinite "detainment" and "expert administration of psychoanalytic therapy and treatment" (p. 11). By the 1970s, a shift occurred when sex offenders were viewed not as sick, but rather as rational "moral" agents who should be held responsible for their behavior. Treatment in general was going out of vogue, and with the pronouncement that "nothing works" by Martinson in 1974, rehabilitation programs began to decrease greatly (Freeman-Longo and Knopp 1992). During this time, behavioral treatments began to emerge and included approaches such as control of rewards and punishments, aversion therapy, shock therapy, and shaming. All these behavioral treatments had the goal of modifying or eliminating certain unwanted behaviors (McCulloch and Kelly 2007). In the early 1980s, these behavioral treatments began to give way to cognitive-behavioral therapy which has become the prominent form of therapy for sex offenders today (McCulloch and Kelly 2007).

Sex Offender-Specific Treatment Model

Sex offenders present special challenges, both in terms of management and treatment, not inherent in many other types of offenders. In view of this, specialized sex offender treatment programs have developed over the years, and have proliferated greatly since the 1970s. For example, in 1976, there were an estimated 20 such specialized programs (Brecher 1978). By 1992, there were approximately 150 programs, including juvenile and adult focused treatment units (Knopp, Stevenson, and Freeman-Longo 1992). The treatment afforded in such programs is specific to the management and treatment needs of the offender. The primary purpose is to protect the community by reducing the risk of future offenses of a sexual nature (Barbaree 1997). Such programs differ from treatment of non-sex offenders in the mental health clinic setting in a number of ways. For example, the goals of treatment are focused more on the protection of the community rather than the wellness of the offender and the treatment provider is in charge of the direction and plan of treatment rather than the offender (Center for Sex Offender Management 2006).

Sex offender management is an essential component of an overall treatment strategy. This includes both external and internal controls on the offender. External control occurs outside the specific milieu of treatment, and can include supervision on probation or parole, sex offender registration, and other community support networks. Strategies to enhance the offender's internal controls occur within the specific treatment milieu and are designed to assist the offender in controlling his own behavior (Center for Sex Offender Management 2006).

Collaboration and partnering with other key stakeholders involved in the management of the offender is also critical in a sex offender specific treatment program. Therapists, for example, will consider themselves part of a case management team which might include probation and parole officers, prosecutors, the police, residential facility staff, and others who each have some responsibility for the offender. Polygraph examiners and victim advocates may also be involved in the management of the sex offender. The purpose of such a team is to better share information that might be pertinent to the management of offender risk and the likelihood of the offender to reoffend.

Most sex offender treatment occurs in a group setting rather than individual therapy one-on-one (Jennings and Sawyer 2003; Marshall, et al. 1999; and Schwartz and Cellini 1995). Group therapy has a number of advantages over individual therapy, including economic (you can treat more offenders in less time), offenders can learn from each other through challenging and confronting each other within the group setting, and it affords offenders a safe environment in which to learn to talk openly about their thoughts which helps to address denial and distorted thinking patterns (Center for Sex Offender Management 2006). Group therapy, while offering certain advantages, also has some disadvantages. For example, group therapy may not be the most effective form of treatment for all sex offenders. It must be remembered that sex offenders represent a very heterogeneous group and are not all the same. At times, it may be necessary to consider differences, such as offenders who have mental illness or other psychological deficits that prevent them from benefiting from a group approach. Offenders who are delusional or suffering from paranoid ideations may only have their illnesses exacerbated by a "cookie cutter" approach to treatment. Providers must be cognizant of the differences that exist with the offender population and open to variations in treatment based upon individual differences.

One key feature of sex offender treatment is the idea that, in order to be effective, treatment must address those characteristics in the offender that contribute to his committing sexual related crimes (Andrews and Bonta 2003; Hanson and Bussiere 1998; Hanson and Harris 2000). These characteristics are called "criminogenic needs" of the offender. Examples would be alcohol or drug abuse, or perhaps an obsession with deviant sexual fantasies. In these examples, it would be important for treatment to address these individual needs of the offender in order to most effectively deal with the specific behavior involved in the crime itself.

Sex offender-specific treatment generally includes (1) physiological interventions using either medroxyprogesterone acetate (Provera) or cyproterone acetate (Androcur), (2) cognitive and behavioral techniques, and (3) relapse prevention (Watson and Stermac 1994). These and other forms of treatment interventions will be discussed in some detail in later sections of this chapter. The tools of sex offender-specific treatment normally include, at a minimum, the use of polygraph, penile plethysmograph, and the Abel Assessment of Sexual Interest (Center for Sex Offender Management 2006). These assessment tools, too, will be addressed in more detail later in this chapter, but are mentioned here so the reader will be aware of them as essential components of effective sex offender treatment.

Sex offender treatment generally focuses on four basic areas that need to be addressed: (1) deviant sexual interests, arousals, and preferences, (2) distorted attitudes and thinking patterns, (3) interpersonal functioning, and (4) behavioral management (Hanson and Bussiere 1998; Hanson and Morton-Bourgon 2004; Laws 1989; Marshall and Laws 2003; Ward, Laws, and Hudson 2003). Each of these areas and the basic treatment approach in dealing with them are briefly described below.

Some sex offenders experience deviant sexual interests, arousal or preferences toward non-consenting partners, non-age-appropriate partners, or in acts that are abusive in nature. Treatment focused on this domain attempts to decrease deviant arousal making it more likely that sex offending will be reduced. Underlying this approach is the idea that deviant interests, arousals, and preferences are learned behavior, and thus can be unlearned. Treatment approaches are behavioral in nature and efforts to substitute non-deviant thoughts are emphasized.

A basic foundation of sex offender treatment deals with common distorted attitudes and thinking patterns found in most sex offenders. A primary approach to these distorted thinking patterns is cognitive restructuring. Here, the offender's thoughts, rationalizations, justifications, and excuses for his behavior are uncovered and examined carefully. The therapist helps the offender to recognize his faulty thinking and to understand its self-serving nature. In group therapy, the offender can receive feedback about his distortions from other group members, and can be confronted about them under the facilitation of the therapist. In this way, greater awareness occurs as the offender realizes the impact of his behavior on his victim. This makes it much harder for the offender to rationalize his behavior in the future.

Many sex offenders have deficits in basic interpersonal skills and feel uncomfortable in relationships with adults. Frequently low self-esteem and general feelings of alienation and loneliness are present (Association for the Treatment of Sexual Abusers 2005; Ward, Hudson, Marshall, and Sieger 1995). Effective sex offender treatment will incorporate measures to deal with these issues. Social skills training is designed to help offenders in the following areas of interpersonal functioning:

- meeting strangers
- how to develop and maintain adult relationships
- development of respect for women and children
- development of respect for the needs and rights of others
- assertiveness training which helps to mitigate any anger issues experienced by offenders
- basic adult sex education (Center for Sex Offender Management 2006).

Behavioral management is an essential component of effective sex offender treatment. External controls are frequently in place to help monitor the behavior of sex offenders. Criminal justice agencies, such as probation and parole, and treatment providers work as a team in collaboration toward the goal of behavioral management. Each brings certain skills and resources to bear on the issues related to management of sex offenders (Cumming and McGrath 2005; English 1996; Center for Sex Offender Management 2006). However, it is also important to focus on teaching offenders self-management tools and internal controls. For example, relapse prevention can help offenders to learn how to avoid situations that might put them at higher risk and also to learn other prevention strategies that keep them from spiraling back into deviant patterns of behavior (Laws 1989; Pithers, et al. 1983). Covert sensitization, that is, visualizing the consequences of sexual assault, can also be useful in helping sex offenders to control their deviant behavior (Abel, Becker, Blanchard and Djenderedjian 1978; Laws 1995).

The Role of Assessment in Sex Offender Treatment

Assessment of risk and needs of sex offenders is a critical part of the treatment and management process. Actuarial assessments, such as the Rapid Risk Assessment for Sex Offense Recidivism (RRA-SOR) and the Static-9920 have been developed that are meant to enhance the ability to identify higher risk offenders (Langton et al. 2007). The Rapid Risk Assessment for Sex Offense Recidivism (RRA-SOR) is a brief, 4-item screening instrument for risk of sexual offender recidivism among males who have been convicted of at least one sexual offense. Information is obtained through offender files and has been validated on forensic populations (Hanson 1997). Developed after the RRA-SOR, the original 10-item STATIC-99 was designed to assess the long-term potential for sexual recidivism among adult male sex offenders. It incorporates RRA-SOR factors. A revised version, STATIC-2002, is currently being tested to better predict sex offender recidivism than the RRA-SOR (Langton et al. 2007). Early results appear to be promising but more widespread analysis needs to be done (Hanson and Thornton 2003).

In addition to actuarial assessment tools, there are three primary psychophysiological assessments in use. These are (1) the polygraph, (2) the penile plethysmograph, and (3) the ABEL Assessment of Sexual Interest. A brief description of each of these is provided.

Polygraph

The primary purpose of the use of the polygraph in sex offender treatment is to assess whether or not offenders are being deceptive in reporting of their sexual fantasies or behaviors that might lead or have lead to deviant and unlawful actions (Ahlmeyer, et al. 2000; Blasingame 1998; Grubin, et al. 2004). Each offender is normally required to fill out a sexual history questionnaire which is then tested using the polygraph examination. An effort is made to determine if the offender knowingly withheld any information from the sexual history and can then be used to elicit other disclosures of sexual misconduct in treatment (Grubin, et al. 2004).

Penile Plethysmograph

Two assessment tools deal with trying to ascertain offenders sexual arousal patterns without having to rely on offender self-reports, the penile plethysmograph and the ABEL Assessment of Sexual Interests. The plethysmograph is designed to detect blood flow to the penis as a measure of erotic arousal to various stimuli. This assessment is an intrusive tool and expensive to conduct, costing from $300–750 per test (Center for Sex Offender Management 2006).

ABEL Assessment of Sexual Interests

This form of assessment evaluates erotic interest and arousal without requiring more intrusive penile measures. The offender views slides of clothed males and females and measures the level of attraction to each (Fischer 2000; Laws 2003).

Criminal Justice Assessments

In addition to the aforementioned assessments used mainly in the treatment setting, there are also assessment tools used within the criminal justice setting, mainly by probation and parole that are used to help identify dynamic risk factors related to an offenders risk to the community. These tools are part of an individualized case management plan. The first such assessment is a Presentence Investigation Report (PSIR) (Cumming and McGrath 2005). The PSIR is normally completed by a probation officer prior to sentencing in which specific information is collected and presented to a court to be considered in sentencing an offender. Background information is collected including offender prior criminal record, family history, educational background, substance abuse issues, and other similar areas.

A second criminal justice assessment is a case planning assessment which is geared to the ongoing supervision and case management of an offender under probation or parole control (Craissati 2004; English, et al. 2003). Such assessments focus on identifying supervision strategies that are effective in allocating resources to offenders who require more attention and also to better assist individual offenders

Ethical Issues in Sex Offender-Specific Treatment

A number of ethical issues arise in the specific treatment modalities with sex offenders. These issues surround the tension related to privacy concerns for offenders and the need to protect the community. Because of the offender management needs of sex offender treatment and the collaboration that must occur, sharing of information is critical. Sex offenders, therefore, are not granted the same confidentiality protections afforded other offenders being treated in a clinical setting (Craissati and Beech 2004; English 1996). The Association for the Treatment of Sexual Abusers (ATSA) (2005) has developed a Code of Ethics which provides standards and guidelines for the delivery of sex offender evaluation and treatment. The ATSA Code of Ethics may be found on their web site at http://www.atsa.com. At the very least, sex offenders should receive informed consent that provides the following: the purposes and nature of treatment, the expected duration of treatment, the anticipated benefits, costs, and risks associated with treatment, and the limits of confidentiality (ATSA 2001, 2005;).

Heterogeneity of Sex Offenders

Before a more detailed description of sex offender treatment, it is important, first of all, to emphasize the fact that not all sex offenders are alike. In spite of state legislation that tends to categorize a large group of offenders and offenses into one big category, ... "sex offenders must be studied and dealt with by the criminal justice system as a heterogeneous group" (Meloy 2005, p. 232). Rapists are different than heterosexual child incest offenders, sexual abusers are different than exhibitionists, juvenile sex offenders are different than adult sex offenders, sex offenders who are psychotic are different than those with no diagnosable mental illness, and so forth. "A one-size-fits-all mentality to sex offenders is not the answer" (p. 232). This has important implications for both treatment and any assessment of the effectiveness of treatment programs. Sex offender treatment must focus on the criminogenic needs of offenders, that is, those factors that lead people to commit sex offenses. And, in terms of outcomes, we know that recidivism rates vary greatly by the type of sex offender studied. For example, heterosexual adult rapists generally experience recidivism rates around 40%, while heterosexual familial child molesters have rates around 3%, yet we lump them all together as if they were a homogeneous group (Meloy 2005). Outcome studies will be presented in much detail later in this chapter, but for now the point is made that when it comes to sex offenders they should not be studied as a homogeneous group (Hanson and Bussiere 1998).

Sex Offender Treatment Strategies

Pharmacological Approaches

For some sex offenders, psychopharmacological medications can help to reduce the intensity of sexual fantasies and urges (Craissati and Beech 2004; Greenberg and Bradford 1997). For these offenders, medications can be a good adjunct to cognitive behavioral therapy, which will be discussed in some detail in the next section. There are two general classes of medications that are used: (1) anti-androgen medications that reduce the male hormone testosterone in the offender, and (2) certain anti-depressants (Bradford and Greenberg 1998).

Anti-Androgen Medications

Anti-androgen medications work to reduce the male sex hormone testosterone in the male body. The use of this drug has sometimes been called a form of "chemical castration." As such, it decreases the sexual appetite of those on the medication. The two primary drugs used for this purpose is Provera and Lupron. These drugs have not been approved by the Federal Drug Administration specifically for treatment of sex offenders. Many physicians are very reluctant to prescribe these medications because of the controversial nature of their use (Association for the Treatment of Sexual Abusers 2005).

Anti-Depressant Medications

The second class of pharmacological mediations used with sex offenders includes certain anti-depressants. These are called Selective Serotonin Reuptake Inhibitors (SSRIs). While commonly prescribed for the treatment of depression and obsessive-compulsive disorders, these drugs can also be very helpful in the treatment of sex offenders (Center for Sex Offender Management, 2006. They reduce sexual urges and are also useful in managing deviant sexual arousals (Kafka 2003). SSRIs empower offenders to manage their behavior better in general and reduce the intensity of certain compulsive aspects of their offending (Center for Sex Offender Management 2006).

As effective as pharmacological approaches can be in the treatment of sex offenders, it is believed that it is best used in combination with cognitive behavioral therapy and other forms of community management and supervision (Laws and O'Donahue 1997; Prentky 1997).

Cognitive Behavioral Approaches

In the last two decades, cognitive behavioral therapy (CBT) in a group setting has proved to be the most popular method for treating sex offenders (Freeman-Longo and Knopp 1992; Marshall, Laws and Barbaree 1990). Cognitive behavioral therapy attempts to change both how offenders think and how they behave. Therapy focuses on identified criminal thinking errors and help offenders to replace these errors with more functional thinking patterns. The behavioral portion of therapy focuses on development of certain skills that many offenders do not have, such as interpersonal skills in dealing with other adults. It allows offenders to practice pro-social behaviors that are also congruent with functional thinking patterns (Center for Sex Offender Management 2006; Laws, Hudson, and Ward 2000).

The rationale behind cognitive approaches to thinking is that sex offender must rationalize, excuse, and minimize their deviant behavior in order to reduce the cognitive dissonance they would otherwise experience (Abel, Gore, Holland, Becker, and Rathner 1989; Bumby 1996; Marshall, et al. 1999). By examining cognitive distortions or criminal thinking errors, the offender can begin to learn more functional ways of thinking and thus avoid behavioral problems in the future (Association for the Treatment of Sexual Abusers 2005; Schwartz and Cellini 1995, 1997). Some of the specific techniques used in cognitive behavioral therapy in a group setting include: modeling, role-playing, reinforcement of behavior, cognitive exercises, and dilemma games (Hollin and McGuire et al. 2008).

Although cognitive behavioral approaches have received some acclaim, there have also been some criticisms levied. Most criticisms have centered on the ethical issues of trying to "change people's minds" as well as questions related to the effectiveness of these programs. Some view the literature on program effectiveness as being equivocal in nature (McCulloch and Kelly 2007). A comprehensive examination of the literature on program effectiveness will be provided in a later section of this chapter so the reader can make up their own mind as to its efficacy.

Relapse Prevention and Other Adjunctive Therapies

Relapse prevention has become an integral part of sex offender therapy today. It was originally developed by G. Alan Marlatt in the context of substance abuse therapy, but was later adapted for sex offenders by Pithers and others (Marlatt and Gordon 1980; Pithers, Marques, Gibat, and Marlatt 1983). This approach is based on the idea that if behavior can be managed by avoiding certain situations, then relapse is much less likely to occur. Offenders are taught that they are never "cured", but rather must always avoid high risk thoughts, feelings, and behaviors. Relapse prevention along with cognitive behavioral treatment can be very effective together, especially with an external supervision dimension afforded by probation and parole (Freeman-Longo and Knopp 1992).

Given that sex offenders are a heterogeneous group and frequently have different criminogenic precursors to deviant sexual practices, a number of other adjunctive therapies can be very helpful. Some of these that may be built into the overall treatment strategy include family and marital therapy, education seminars, substance abuse treatment, educational/vocational supports, and individual therapy (Center for Sex Offender Management 2006). Each case should be carefully assessed to be sure that treatment is focused on the specific needs of offenders.

What Works? Effective Treatment Strategies

Early research and evaluations of sex offender programs found little evidence that treatment works (Quinney, Harris, Rice, and Lalumiere 1993; Rice, Quinsey, and Harris 1991). There has been "a lack of a consistent, empirical database to provide a foundation for policy decisions regarding sex offender treatment" (Marques, Day, Nelson, and West 1994, p. 29). However, many of the earlier outcome studies suffered from methodological problems that cause the results to be viewed with some caution. Reported methodological issues are briefly described below.

Choosing an appropriate comparison group can be problematic in most all outcome studies. Similarly, there is much variation in the composition of treatment groups which makes it difficult to define an appropriate comparison group. How to define failure is also an issue. Many studies use a measure of recidivism that counts the commission of a new sex offense as the best measure, while other studies use some other definition. Then, there is much variation in the length of follow-up used in studies. These issues, coupled with the fact that there is little uniformity in treatment programs in terms of intensity, duration, and location make it difficult to compare research studies examining sex offender treatment effectiveness (Center for Sex Offender Management, 2006; Rice, Quinsey, and Harris 1991). An overview of the research literature on sex offender treatment is provided next.

Barbaree and Marshall (1988) studied 126 child molesters treated with cognitive behavioral therapy. Both official and unofficial measures of recidivism were used, looking at reconviction, new charges, and unofficial records. A four year follow up was utilized. For child molesters whose victims were girls outside of the family, there was a 43% recidivism rate compared to 18% for offenders who were treated. For those whose victims were boys outside the family, the recidivism rate was 43% compared to 13% for those untreated. And, for incest offenders whose victims were female, recidivism rates were 22% for treated versus 8% for those not receiving treatment. This early study showed rather significant results for the groups studied.

Another early study, however, found no evidence that treatment reduced the reoffending rates of sex offenders, but there were many methodological limitations noted in this study (Furby, Weinrott, and Blackshaw,1989). Three groups were examined: a treatment group, a volunteer group, and a volunteer control group. The treatment group exhibited the treatment group had the lowest reoffense rates for sex and other violent crimes, however, these results were inconclusive.

In another study, reconviction rates for 136 extra-familial child molesters who were housed at a maximum security psychiatric hospital were evaluated (Rice, Quinsey, and Harris 1991). With an average six year follow up period, recidivism rates between untreated and treated groups were essentially no different. In contrast, several other studies found sex offenders participating in treatment had lower reoffense rates (Marshall and Pithers 1994); less likely to commit new sexual offenses (Marques, Day, Nelson, and West (1994); and lower sexual recidivism (Dwyer 1997).

Hall (1995) conducted a meta-analysis of twelve studies that included 1,313 sex offenders. Recidivism was defined as a formal legal charge for new sex offenses after completion of treatment, with an average follow up period of 6.85 years. The average length of treatment was 18.5 months. A small but significant overall reduction in recidivism was found, 19% for those receiving treatment compared to 27% for those offenders receiving no treatment. The greatest treatment effects were found for programs with longer follow up periods; outpatient versus in-patient or prison-based treatment; and those that used cognitive behavioral treatment and/or anti-androgen hormonal medications.

The U. S. General Accounting Office (1996) summarized 22 reviews of research on sex offenders in treatment covering 550 studies between 1977 and 1996. The findings of the report were that the results for treatment were promising, although inconclusive. In spite of the inconsistent research findings early on, Hanson and Bussier (1998) concluded that "even if we cannot be sure that treatment will be effective, there is reliable evidence that those offenders who attend and cooperate with treatment programs are less likely to offend than those who reject intervention" (p. 358).

Another review of outcome research examined 79 sex offender treatment programs that included 10,988 subjects (Alexander 1999). Sub-group recidivism rates were examined with very positive results. Those offenders who participated in relapse prevention had 7% re-arrest rates compared to 18% for those who did not. For a rapist sub-group, 20% recidivism rates were found for treated rapists compared to 24% for untreated offenders. Child molesters showed a substantial difference in recidivism rates, 14% for treated and 26% for untreated. Exhibitionists also reported major differences in recidivism, 20% for treated and 57% for untreated. Overall, including all sub-groups, recidivism rates for treated offenders was 13% compared to 18% for untreated.

One interesting study found that sometimes treatment can actually increase the risk of sexual recidivism (Seto and Barbaree 1999). A group of 283 sex offenders were examined and given clinical ratings on behavior in treatment and a psychopathy scale. The psychopathy scale measured absence of conscience, remorse, guilt or empathy. The researchers found that good treatment behavior was unrelated to general recidivism, but associated to higher sexual and/or violent recidivism. Offenders who were rated higher on psychopathy and were rated higher in treatment behavior were the most likely to reoffend. These findings seemed to indicate that psychopathic sex offenders may actually learn manipulative behavior and other negative skills that actually increase their risk for recidivism. This also suggests that in sex offender treatment it is important to consider sub-groups of offenders and recognize that a cookie cutter approach to treatment is not recommended.

Aytes et al. (2001) examined a cognitive behavioral program in Jackson, Oregon between 1985 and 1995. The researchers compared treatment failure rates for three groups of offenders at three and five year benchmarks after entering treatment. The treatment group had a 40% reduction in re-offense rates. Interestingly, "evenly untreated individuals ... reoffend less than individuals convicted of drug or other violent offenses" (Aytes et al. 2001, p. 223). The authors note that while the findings are encouraging for community-based cognitive behavioral models, caution should be used in generalizing to other jurisdictions because of the unique characteristics of the treatment program.

One of the most comprehensive studies of treatment outcomes involved a meta-analysis that included 43 treatment studies and more than 9,000 sex offenders (Hanson et al. 2002). The results of this study were favorable, showing sexual recidivism rates of 12% for those receiving treatment compared to 17% for those not receiving treatment. Overall general recidivism rates were also favorable with a 28% rate for treatment group versus 39% for non-treatment group.

An update of the Hanson and Bussiere 1998 study was completed by Hanson and Morton-Bourgon (2004). This was a meta-analytic study that analyzed 95 studies and 31,216 sex offenders. The researchers examined dynamic factors rather than static factors that were reviewed in the 1998 study. They also used multiple measures of recidivism, including new arrests, treatment records, and self-reports. The general recidivism rate was 36.9% while the rate for sex offenders with a 5–6 year follow up was 13.7%. It was also found that offenders with deviant sexual interests, especially when the focus of that interest was on kids, were most likely to reoffend sexually.

Another favorable treatment study examined 177 male sex offenders over the age of 18 (Seager, Jellicoe, and Dhaliwal 2004). In this sample, 81 successfully completed treatment, 28 were unsuccessful, 17 dropped out, and 19 refused to participate in treatment. The overall reconviction rate was 12%, for those who dropped out or refused group therapy, it was 32%, and only 4% for the treatment group. This study seems to confirm the conclusion drawn in an earlier study in which it was noted "that the weight of evidence suggests that non-completers are at an increased risk of recidivism" (Wormith and Olver 2002, p. 271).

One recent study was quite rigorous in its methodology and used an experimental design to evaluate a SOTEP program (Marques, et al. 2005). In this randomized clinical trial, re-arrest rates were compared for offenders in inpatient relapse prevention program and two untreated prison control groups. No significant differences were found between the three groups in terms of rates of new offenses or violent offending over an eight year period of time. The authors caution, however, that these results should be measured as the treatment program developed around 20 years ago and since then there have been many improvements in the treatment models in use.

Lösel and Schmucker (2005) conducted an international meta-analysis using both published and unpublished sex offender biological and psychological treatment outcome studies. There were a total of 69 studies examined and more than 22,000 subjects. The operational definition of recidivism was constructed very broadly, including incarceration to simple lapses in behavior. The mean recidivism rate for those in treatment groups was 11% compared to 17.5% for control groups. Cognitive behavioral therapy had the most significant impact on reducing sexual recidivism. Additionally, hormonal and surgical treatment interventions also provided significant reduction in recidivism, although the authors note methodological issues that prevent conclusive evidence of effectiveness.

In summary, when one examines the bulk of research on treatment effectiveness for sex offenders, one may draw a number of reasonable conclusions. While early studies were not conclusive, there were many methodological issues that had to be dealt with. Later studies, with more rigorous designs and analysis seemed to produce better evidence for community based cognitive therapy with relapse prevention and other adjunctive therapies. "Treatment can be effective in reducing sexual recidivism from about 25 percent to 10–15 percent" (Freeman-Longo and Knopp 1992, p. 145). Furthermore, effective treatment is skills-oriented and designed to assist offenders in learning techniques that help them to avoid committing new offenses in the future (Becker and Murphy,1998; Laws 1989; Laws, Hudson, and Ward 2000; Marshall et al. 1999). It is also evident that utilizing effective treatment to reduce recidivism rates can result in substantial cost savings to the criminal justice system as well as obvious benefits to potential victims (Aos, et al. 2001; Prentky and Burgess 1990).

Other Important Research Insights

In addition to examination of outcome results of sex offender treatment, there are a number of other important related findings that are informative. For example, sex offenders who experience high levels of deviance and denial generally require longer treatment with more intensity (Beech, Fisher, and Beckett 1998). It is also critical in treatment to base treatment upon the specific needs of each offender and the risk that that they pose to the community as determined by good, valid risk and needs assessment tools (Becker and Murphy 1998; Marshall et al. 1999; McGrath, Cumming, and Burchard 2003; Ward, Laws, and Hudson 2003).

An essential part of all treatment programs is a plan to monitor and evaluate programs and clients (Andrews and Bonta 2003; Cullen and Gendreau 2000; Gendreau 1996). Programs must remain up to date in practices based upon the very latest research available. Clients also change over time in terms of risks and needs, thus there should be monitoring of possible changes and treatment programs must be responsive to such changes as they occur (Association for the Treatment of Sexual Abusers 2005; Cumming and McGrath 2005; Hanson and Harris 2000). For example, offenders may experience changes in their living environment, relapse into drug or alcohol abuse, job changes, difficulties with compliance with probation or parole, or even changes in relationships that must be dealt with (Cumming and McGrath 2005; Hanson and Mourton-Bourgon 2004).

Who Works? Treatment and Therapist Styles

There is a growing "who works" literature emerging that refers to staff characteristics or therapist style in sex offender treatment (McCulloch and Kelly 2007; Dowden and Andrews 2004; Marshall et al. 2003). Sex offender treatment has often been punitive in treatment style, characterized by aggressive verbal confrontation by providers with an in-your-face drill sergeant type approach. While this might feel satisfying to many, it may not work (Center for Sex Offender Management 2006). Such punitive approaches might not only fail in terms of reducing sexual recidivism, they may actually increase the risk of re-offending (Hudson 1998; McAlinden 2005; Thomas and Tuddenham 2002; Marshall and Serran 2004). The emerging "who works" literature calls for more of an empathic and genuine therapist style practiced in a therapeutic climate focusing on client engagement, treatment progress, and treatment outcomes (Beech and Fordham 1997; Beech and Hamilton-Giachritsis 2005; Serran, Fernandez, Marshall, and Mann 2003). The use of positive reinforcement as a treatment tool has been found to be effective in sex offender treatment. A 4:1 ratio of four positive reinforcements for every one negative reinforcement has been shown to be successful (Gendreau 1996).

Knowles (1998) outlines how adults learn best and suggests that the principles of effective sex offender theory should incorporate sound learning and behavioral theory into their treatment paradigm. For example, material should be relevant to the offenders' lives, there should be opportunities to practice new skills, and offenders should be rewarded for things they do well rather than punished for things they do not so well.

The Role of Community Supervision in Sex Offender Treatment

Many sex offenders are on some on form of community supervision in the community, either on probation or parole. It has been estimated that almost 60% of sex offenders are on felony probation or parole (Meloy 2005). This creates some problems for probation officers who work in a high profile environment where the media tends to sensationalize any cases in which a probationer fails (Thomas and Tuddenham 2002). In this environment, the impression is given that sex offenders are doomed to fail and that probation or community supervision is not a viable option for such high risk offenders. There is some research, however, that would seem to belie this perception.

Meloy (2005) examined data collected between 1986 and 1989 by the Bureau of Justice Statistics (BJS). This data included 917 convicted male sex offenders on probation in 17 states. Of this group, the overall recidivism rates were around 16%, and only 4–5% of the probationers committed new sex crimes during probation. The average length of time to probation failure was about 18 months, making the first 1½ years on supervision the most critical.

It is important to investigate what factors lead to failure of sex offender probationers or parolees on community supervision. Interestingly, age, race, and education were found to be "negatively related to probation failure at the bivariate level" (Meloy 2005, p. 221). Factors found to be positively related to probation failure include the following:

- residential instability
- history of drug abuse
- percentage of time employed in the year prior to arrest
- the number of prior convictions.

Finally, sex offender probationers who had strong informal social controls also experienced longer survival rates; that is a longer time before failing on probation with a new offense. Examples of effective informal social controls include having a committed intimate partner in a relationship, positive social networks, and being employed full-time (Meloy 2005).

Prison-Based Treatment for Sex Offenders

Unfortunately, there is "little specific treatment for sexual offenders available in prisons" (Aytes et al. 2001). A report by Turner et al., (2000) indicates that around 75% of all sex offenders in prison receive no treatment. The consequences of this is that, left untreated, sex offenders may actually return to the community upon completing their sentences without the skills to avoid future offending and be even more aggressive (Salter 1988). Freeman-Longo and Knopp (1992) indicate that "the costs to taxpayers for repeat offenders who are incarcerated, not treated, and released back into the community is high" (p. 147).

The idea of institutional treatment programs for sex offenders to many would probably seem ridiculous. After all, "sex offenders are manipulative, seductive con artists" (Prendergast 2004, p. 152). They are drooling violent predators who prey upon citizens and children, raping and killing them for sexual gratification (Lotke nd, para. 1). As such, they are undeserving of treatment which, according to popular conception, or misconception, isn't really going to help them anyway. Landford, as seen in Kersting, states that "in the 1980's Americans states made the decision that sex offenders were not sick; they were bad" (2003 para. 4).

In spite of the aforementioned feelings, the fact remains that sex offenders represent a healthy percentage of our prison population, thus some efforts at treatment seem warranted. As an example, in 2004, rape and other sex offenders amounted to approximately 12% of the state prison population (Sourcebook 2004). And, since up to 95% of these offenders will be released eventually, some treatment needs to be provided (Sex Offender Treatment in Prison).

In the years past, several institutional treatment programs for sex offenders have existed. They have tried many and various approaches to treatment of the inmates. A 1978 publication by Brecher lists the various types of treatment that had been attempted. Early programs were reported to have used medication and psychiatric methods. Some programs used individual and group psychotherapy. Other programs stressed interpersonal relationships with an educational emphasis. Brecher indicates that a 1972 article by Resnik and Wolfgang suggested that female therapists should be used and direct confrontation be employed (p. 8).

A more current (2004) survey of treatment approaches lists the following as having been tried: Individual and group techniques, verbal techniques alone or in conjunction with psychotropic medicine, rational emotive techniques, cognitive behavioral techniques, psychiatric treatment with medication, self-help groups and chemical castration (Prendergrast p. 123). This survey of methods writes of the four C's of sex offender treatment. Once again, confrontation of the offender was recommended. In fact it was stated that "… none of the supportive, passive therapies (including Rogerian, psychoanalytic and other techniques of this type) worked" (p. 147). It is suggested to the therapist that they believe nothing and that the only true indicator of any change in the offender is behavior (p. 155). The second C was caution. Here the warning is, as stated earlier, that sex offenders are cunning and sly. The therapist needs to be attuned to this approach. The third C is control. The therapist must be in control of the situation and treatment approach. The final C is Continuation/ Consistency. Aftercare will be essential and counseling will be important. It is warned here that a "sex offenders is never really cured" (p. 164).

There are several treatment programs for sex offenders currently being operated in various correctional institutions. A specific example of a current program can be found in the state of Washington at the Monroe Correctional Complex for men and the Washington Correctional Center for Women in Gig Harbor. The Twin Rivers Sex Offender Treatment Program conducted at these prisons aims to teach offenders to avoid sexual aggression. The belief is that sexual aggression is a learned behavior which can be addressed through treatment. Through psychological assessment, group and individual counseling, the goals of group counseling are to help offenders:

Take responsibility for assaultive behavior
Learn how to understand their patterns (cycles) of criminal behavior
Learn relapse prevention and other management skills to reduce recidivism
Learn the attitudes, thinking skills and behavior needed to safely reside in the community
Prepare to learn new skills and knowledge.
(Sex Offender Treatment in prison, para. 8).

Inmates must volunteer for this program and there is a lengthy waiting list to get in. Washington claims that less than 7% of the inmates who enter the program at Monroe return to prison (Sex Offender Treatment in Prison para. 1).

Another institutional sex offender program that combines several therapeutic approaches is being run in Missouri. In 1980 the state passed the Sexual Assault Prevention Act which mandated, among other things, treatment programs for incarcerated offenders. As a result, the Missouri Sexual Offender Program (MoSop) was created in 1983. This is an institutional-based treatment program that is "based on a cognitive-behavioral approach with an emphasis on relapse prevention" (Prisontalk 2008, para. 1). To give this new program some teeth, it is required that an offender convicted of a sexual offense must complete a sex offender treatment program prior to consideration of early release.

Sex offenders who are within 12–18 months of a possible release date will be placed in this program. It operates in two phases. Phase one, which lasts three months, prepares the offender for more intense counseling by covering the "nature and goals of therapy as well as the structure of the program. Participants undergo a clinical interview and psychological testing" (Prisontalk 2008, para. 2). Phase two lasts from 9 to 12 months. In this component, the offender works on various skills such as empathy, problem-solving, personal responsibility, assertiveness/social skills and relapse prevention (Prisontalk 2008, para. 3). Offenders in this phase are also placed into one of three tracks depending upon their verbal skills and personality styles. There are groups for verbally challenged inmates up through those with no verbal difficulties who are aggressive and highly manipulative (Prisontalk 2008, para. 3).

If an inmate successfully completes the program, then early release can be expected. Failure in the program negates this release. According to program data, 30%–35% of inmates successfully complete the program. If failure occurs it is most likely that it will be in Phase two where there is a 65–70% failure rate

(Prisontalk 2008, para. 21). Once released from the institution the offender can expect that there will be additional treatment program requirements.

Completing the MoSoP program only qualifies the offender for early release. A failure merely means the offender must serve more of the sentence. Release data from the aforementioned report indicates that 32% of inmates have their sentence discharged or, complete the sentence prior to release. Most, however, are released early. Release mechanisms are as follows: 18% are paroled, 23% receive conditional (mandatory) release, 19% receive probation and 8% have death/ or some other release (Prisontalk 2008, para. 24).

In 2006, a study was conducted by the Institute of Public Policy at the University of Missouri, Columbia, Mo., that evaluated recidivism rates of sex offenders in Missouri (Valentine, Huebner, Stokes, Cobbina, and Berg). The following information is taken from that report. The purpose of this study was to gauge the recidivism rate of sex offenders as well as to determine if incarcerated sex offenders were different from other incarcerated offenders. A sample of 4,043 men paroled from prison in 1998 was analyzed. Two hundred of these men had served time for a sex offense (p. 2). As these releases occurred via parole, it is assumed that the sex offenders would have completed the MoSoP program.

The sample was examined based upon demographic factors such as age, race, education, mental health status and health care and employment needs. An initial question was whether sex offenders were in some way different from other offenders released from prison. Demographics revealed that "sex offenders were more likely to be older, white, and have less educational and employment deficits than the general prison population" (p. 4). Sex offenders were more likely to have been convicted of a prior sex crime and will have spent significantly longer in prison than offenders that committed other types of crimes. This is true even though while incarcerated sex offenders had fewer conduct violations and generally represented a lower risk upon release than other types of offenders (p. 4).

Evaluating recidivism rates, which was defined as a new conviction for any crime, revealed that inmates convicted of property crime had the highest recidivism rate. They had a 47.4 percent reconviction rate. Other rates are as follows: personal offenses, 42.3%; other offenses, 40.4%, and drug offenses, 37.5% (p. 5). Sex offenders had a 19% reconviction rate which was the lowest of all the offense categories.

McGrath et al. (2003) evaluated a prison-based cognitive behavioral treatment program that included relapse prevention and aftercare for adult sex offenders in Vermont. The study included 195 participants who were at risk for six years. Some 23% of these offenders committed new sex offenses compared to only 5% for those offenders in the treatment group. There was also a significantly less rate of violent offending than for those who had not received treatment. It is interesting to note that those offenders who either received no treatment or who had received only some treatment had similar recidivism rates, 30% for those receiving no treatment and 31% for those receiving some treatment. It would appear that completing treatment is very important in terms of lowering re-offense rates for sex offenders who have been in prison.

An additional study of sex offenders echoes the finding that sex offender recidivism rates are lower than rates for other crimes. Lotke states that the recidivism rate for untreated institutionalized sex offenders upon release is 18.5%. Compare this to 25% for drug offenses, and 30% for violent offenses (n.d., para. 11). Note that these numbers refer to untreated sex offenders. Supplying some type of treatment may decrease the recidivism rate thus refuting the popular misconception referred to earlier that nothing works. Anderson found many programs that claimed positive results for institutional treatment of sex offenders (in Lotke para. 15). This finding came from an evaluation of 12 journal articles which covered a 14 year time span and reported upon 356 studies. Nine of the articles report positive results, three were inconclusive, and none reported negative results. Alexander, as seen in Lotke, reports that recidivism rates after treatment drop to 10.9%. This is almost at 8% drop in recidivism due to some form of treatment (para. 16).

Anderson's optimism regarding treatment for sex offenders is not shared by others. Trowbridge reports that most studies do not demonstrate an appreciable treatment effect. A study had been done in Canada where a group of treated sex offenders was compared to an untreated group and at the end of 12 years, "no difference was observed in the rates of sexual, violent, or general recidivism" (n.d.,p. 6). Even with that being the case, Trowbridge opines that even if treatment is only marginally effective, this still results in fewer victims and less costs to society (p. 6).

The Future of Sex Offender Treatment

As summarized in this chapter, much of the recent research on sex offender treatment has provided some optimism for its effectiveness. One of the largest and best designed studies recently shows strong support for the proposition that treatment works (Hanson, et al. 2002). On the other hand, there are palpable limitations to our therapeutic approaches, especially in an environment that mandates public protection and safety at the same time that much of the legislation enacted dealing with sex offenders are ill-informed and based on sensational media presentations of socially constructed myths about sex offenders. This aspect of the issues will be discussed in more detail in the next chapter.

We cannot expect great outcomes when our approach is the application of "punitive, exclusionary or managerial methods alone (if at all)" (McCulloch and Kelly 2007, p. 15). Rather, recent treatment approaches have moved toward a "willingness to reconsider or deconstruct some of the dominant assumptions and perceptions of 'effective' sex offender treatment" (McCullogh and Kelly p. 15). Examples of new directions or trends in sex offender treatment include the "who works" discourse as described earlier (Mann et al., 2004). Other innovative approaches include more reintegrative or restorative approaches to treatment as described in some detail by McAlinden (2005, 2008). Vivian-Byrne (2002, 2004) has also provided a framework for discussion of personal construct theory, systemic approaches, post-modern approaches, and social constructivist models.

References

Abel, G., Becker, J. V., Blanchard, E. B., Djenderedjian, A. (1978). Differentiating Sexual Aggressive with Penile Measures. *Criminal Justice and Behavior, 5*(4), 315–332.

Abel, G., Gore, D. K., Holland, C. K. Camp, N. Becker, J. V. and Rathner, J. (2989). The Measurement of the Cognitive Distortions of Child Molesters. *Sexual Abuse: A Journal of Research and Treatment, 2*(2), 135–152.

Ahlmeyer, S., Heil, P. Mckee, B., and English, K. (2000). The Impact of Polygraphy on Admissions of Victims and Offenses in Adult Sexual Offenders. *Sexual Abuse: A Journal of Research and Treatment, 12*(2), 123–138.

Alexander, M. A. (1999). Sexual Offender Treatment Efficacy Revisited. *Sexual Abuse: A Journal of Research and Treatment,* 11, 101–116.

Andrews, D. A., and Bonta, J. (2003). *The Psychology of Criminal Conduct* (3rd ed.). Cincinnati, OH: Anderson.

Aos, S., Phipps, P., Barnoski, R., and Lieb, R. (2001). *The Comparative Costs and Benefits of Programs to Reduce Crime, Vol. 4.* Olympia, WA: Washington State Institute for Public Policy.

Association for the Treatment of Sexual Abusers (2001, 2005). *Practice Standards and Guidelines for Members of the Association for the Treatment of Sexual Abusers.* Beaverton, OR.

Aytes, K. E., Olsen, S. S., Zakrajsek, T. Murray, P., and Ireson, R. (2001). Cognitive/Behavioral Treatment for Sexual Offenders: An Examination of Recidivism. *Sexual Abuse: A Journal of Research and Treatment, 13*(4), 223–231.

Barbaree, H. E. (1997). Deviant Sexual Arousal, Offense History, and Demographic Variables as Predictors of Reoffense Among Child Molesters. *Sexual Abuse: A Journal of Research and Treatment*, 9, 111–128.

Barbaree, H. E. and Marshall, W. L. (1988). Deviant Sexual Arousal, Offense History, and Demographic Variables as Predictors of Reoffense Among Child Molesters. *Behavioral Sciences and the Law*, 6, 267–280.

Becker, J. and Murphy, W. (1998). What We Know and Don't Know About Assessing and Treating Sex Offenders. *Psychology, Public Policy and Law*, 4, 116–137.

Beech , A. R., Fisher, D., and Beckett, R. C. (1998). An Evaluation of the Prison Sex Offender Treatment Programme. *Research Findings, 79*, 1–4. Research and Statistics Directorate, Home Office. Available from Home Office Publications Unit, 50, Queen Anne's Gate, London, SW1 9AT, England.

Beech, A. and Fordham, A. S. (1997). Therapeutic Climate of Sexual Offender Treatment Programs. *Sexual Abuse: A Journal of Research and Treatment*, 9(3), 219–237.

Beech, A. R. and Hamilton-Giachritsis, (2005). Relationship Between Therapeutic Climate and Treatment Outcome in Group-Based Sexual Offender Treatment Programs. *Sexual Abuse: A Journal of Research and Treatment*, 17(2), 127–140.

Berlin, F. S. (1983). Sex Offenders: A Biomedical Perspective and a Status Report on Biomedical Treatment. In J. G. Greer and I. R. Stuart (Eds.), *The Sexual Aggressor: Current Perspectives and Treatment* (pp. 83–123). New York: Van Nostrand Reinhold Company.

Blasingame, G. D. (1998). Suggested Clinical Uses of Polygraphy in Community-Based Sexual Offender Treatment Programs. *Sexual Abuse: A Journal of Research and Treatment, 10*(1), 37–45.

Bradford, J. M., and Greenberg, D. M. (1998). Treatment of Adult Male Sexual Offenders in a Psychiatric Setting. In W. L. Marshall (Ed.), *Sourcebook of Treatment Programs for Sexual Offenders* (pp. 247–256). New York: Plenum Press.

Brecher, E. (1978). *Treatment Programs for Sex Offenders*. Washington, DC: U. S. Department of Justice.

Bumby, K. M. (1996). Assessing the Cognitive Distortions of Child Molesters and Rapists: Development and Validation of the MOLEST and RAPE Scales. *Sexual Abuse: A Journal of Research and Treatment, 8*(1), 37–54.

Center for Sex Offender Management (2006). *Understanding Treatment for Adults and Juveniles who have Committed Sex Offenses*. A Project of the U.S. Department of Justice, Office of Justice Programs.

Cullen, F. and Gendreau, P. (2000). Assessing Correctional Rehabilitation: Policy, Practice, and Prospects, pp. 109–175 in J. Horney (ed.) *Criminal Justice 2000: volume 3—Policies, Processes, and Decisions of the Criminal Justice System*. Washington, DC: U.S. Department of Justice, National Institute of Justice.

Craissati, J. and Beech, A. (2004). The Characteristics of a Geographical Sample of Convicted Rapists: Sexual Victimization and Compliance in Comparison to Child Molesters. *Journal of Interpersonal Violence, 19*(4), 371–388.

Cumming, G. F., and McGrath, R. J. (2005). *Supervision of the Sex Offender: Community Management, Risk Assessment, and Treatment*. Brandon, VT: The Safer Society Press.

Dowden, C. and Andrews, D. A. (2004). The Importance of Staff Practice in Delivering Effective Correctional Treatment: A Meta-analytic Review of Core Correctional Practice. *International Journal of Offender Therapy and Comparative Criminology, 48*(2), 203–214.

Dwyer, S. M. (1997). Treatment Outcome Study: Seventeen Years After Sexual Offender Treatment. *Sexual Abuse: A Journal of Research and Treatment, 9*(2), 149–160.

English, K. (1996). Does Sex Offender Treatment Work? Why Answering this Question is so Difficult. In *Sex Offender Treatment: A Containment Approach*. Colorado: Colorado Division of Criminal Justice.

English, K., Jones, L., and Patrick. D. (2003). Community Containment of Sex Offender Risk: A Promising Approach. In B. J. Winick and J. Q. La-Fond (Eds.), *Protecting Society from Sexually Dangerous Offenders: Law, Justice, and Therapy*, (pp. 265–279). American Psychological Association: Washington, D. C.

Fischer, L. (2000). The Abel Screen: A Nonintrusive Alternative? In D. R. Laws, S. M. Hudson, and T. Ward (Eds.), *Remaking Relapse Prevention with Sex Offenders: A Sourcebook*, pp. 303–318. Sage Publications: Thousand Oaks, CA.

Freeman-Longo, R. E., and Knopp, F. H. (1992). State-of-the-art Sex Offender Treatment: Outcome and Issues. *Annals of Sex Research*, 5, 414–160.

Furby, L., Weinrott, M.R., and Blackshaw, L. (1989). Sex Offender Recidivism: A Review. *Psychological Bulletin*, 105, 3–30.

Gaffney, G. R., and Berlin, FR. S. (1984). Is There Hypothalamic-Pituitary-Gonadal Dysfunction in Paedophilia? A Pilot Study. *British Journal of Psychiatry*, 145, 657–660.

Gendreau, P. (1996). The Principle Of Effective Interventions With Offenders. In A. T. Harland (Ed.), *Choosing Correctional Options That Work: Defin-*

ing the Demand and Evaluating the Supply, pp. 117–130. Thousand Oaks, CA: Sage.

Greenberg, D. M. and Bradford, J. M. W. (1997). Treatment of the Paraphilic Disorders: A Review of the Role of the Selective Serotonin Reuptake Inhibitors. *Sexual Abuse: A Journal of Research and Treatment, 9*(4), 349–360.

Grubin, D., Madsen, L, Parson, S., Sosnowski, D., and Warberg, B. (2004). *Sexual Abuse: A Journal of Research and Treatment, 16*(3), 209–222.

Hall, G. C. N. (1995). Sexual Offender Recidivism Revisited: A Meta-Analysis of Recent Treatment Studies. *Journal of Consulting and Clinical Psychology, 63*, 802–809.

Hanson, R. K. (1997). *The Development of a Brief Actuarial Risk Scale for Sexual Offense Recidivism*. Public Works and Government Services Canada.

Hanson, R. K. and Bussiere, M. T. (1998). Predicting Relapse: A Meta-Analysis of Sex Offender Recidivism Studies. *Journal of Consulting and Clinical Psychology, 66*, 348–362.

Hanson, R. K., and Harris, A. J. R. (2000). Where Should We Intervene? Dynamic Predictors of Sexual Offense Recidivism. *Criminal Justice and Behavior, 27*, 6–35.

Hanson, R. K., and Morton-Bourgon, K. (2004). *Predictors of Sexual Recidivism: An Updated Meta-Analysis*. User Report 2004-02. Ottawa: Public Works and Government Services Canada.

Hanson, R. K., Gordon, A., Harris, A. J. R., Marques, J. K., Murphy, W., Quinsey, V. L., and Seto, M. C. (2002). First Report of The Collaborative Outcome Data Project on the Effectiveness of Psychological Treatment For Sex Offenders. *Sexual Abuse: A Journal of Research and Treatment, 14*, 169–194.

Hanson, R. K. and Thornton, D. (2003). *Notes on The Development Of The Static—2002*. Public Works and Government Services Canada.

Hollin, C. R., McGuire, J., Hounsome, J., Hatcher, R., Bilby, C., and Palmer, E. (2008). Cognitive Skills Behavior Progress for Offenders In The Community: A Reconviction Analysis. *Criminal Justice and Behavior, 35*, 269–283.

Hudson, B. (1998). Restorative Justice: The Challenge of Sexual and Racial Violence. *Journal of Law and Society, 25*, 237–256.

Jennings, J. L. and Sawyer, S. (2003). Principles and Techniques for Maximizing the Effectiveness of Group Therapy With Sex Offenders. *Sexual Abuse: A Journal of Research and Treatment, 15*(4), 251–267.

Kafka, M. P. (2003). Sex Offending and Sexual Appetite: The Clinical and Theoretical Relevance of Hypersexual Desire. *International Journal of Offender Therapy and Comparative Criminology, 47*(4), 439–451.

Kersting, K. (2003). New Hope for Sex Offender Treatment. Retrieved on 8-3-08 from http://www.apa.org/monitor/julaug03/newhope.html.

Knopp, F. H., Stevenson, W. F., and Freeman-Longo, R. E. (1992). *Nationwide Survey of Adolescent and Adult Sex Offender Treatment Programs and Models, 1992.* Orwell, VT: Safer Society Press.

Knolwes, M.S. Holton, E.F. and Swanson, R.A. (1998) *The Adult Learner: The Definitive Classic in Adult Education and Human Resource Development,* 5th Edition. MA: Butterwirth-Heinemann.

Langevin, R., Hucker, S., Ben-Aron, M., Purins, J., and Hook, H. (1985). Why Are Pedophiles Attracted to Children? In R. Langevin (Ed.), *Erotic Preference, Gender Identity and Aggression in Men: New Research Studies* (pp. 181–210). Hillsdale, NJ: Lawrence Erlbaum.

Langton, C. M., Hansen, K. T., Harkins, L., and Peacock, E. J. (2007). Actuarial Assessment of Risk for Reoffense Among Adult Sex Offenders. *Criminal Justice and Behavior, 34,* 616–640.

Laws, D. R. (Ed.) (1989). *Relapse Prevention with Sex Offenders.* New York: Guilford.

Laws, D. R. (1995). Verbal Satiation: Notes on Procedure, With Speculations on its Mechanism of Effect. *Sexual Abuse: A Journal of Research and Treatment, 7*(2), 155–166.

Laws, D. R. and O'Donahue, W. (1997). *Sexual Deviance: Theory, Assessment and Treatment.* New York: The Guilford Press.

Laws, D. R., Hudson, S. M., and Ward, T. (Eds.) (2000). *Remaking Relapse Prevention with Sex Offenders: A Sourcebook.* Thousand Oaks, CA: Sage Publications.

Laws, D. R. (2003). Penile Plethysmography: Will We Ever Get It Right? In T. Ward, D. R. Laws, And S. M. Hudson (Eds.), *Sexual Deviance: Issues and Controversies,* pp. 82–102). Sage Publications: Thousand Oaks, CA.

Lösel, F. and Schmucker, M. (2005). The Effectiveness of Treatment for Sexual Offenders: A Comprehensive Meta-Analysis. *Journal of Experimental Criminology,* 1, 117–146.

Lotke, E. Sex Offenders: Does Treatment Work? Retrieved 8-3-08 from http://www.66.165.98./stories/sexoffend.html.

Mann, R. E., Webster, S. D., Schofield, C., and Marshall, W. L. (2004). Approach Versus Avoidance Goals In Relapse Prevention With Sexual Offenders. Sexual Abuse: A Journal of Research and Treatment, 16, 65–75.

Marlatt, G. A., and Gordon, J. R. (1980). Determinants of Relapse: Implications for The Maintenance of Behavior Change. In P. O. Davidson, and S. M. Davidson (Eds.), *Behavioral Medicine: Changing Health Lifestyles* (Pp. 410–452). New York, NY: Brunner/Mazel.

Marques, J.K., Day, D.M., Nelson, C., and West, M.A. (1994). Effects of Cognitive-Behavioral Treatment on Sex Offender Recidivism: Preliminary Results of a Longitudinal Study. *Criminal Justice and Behavior*, 21, 28–54.

Marques, J. K., Wiederanders, M., Day, D. M., Nelson, C., and van Ommeren, A. (2005). Effects of a Relapse Prevention Program on Sexual Recidivism: Final Results From California's Sex Offender Treatment and Evaluation Project (SOTEP). *Sexual Abuse: A Journal of Research and Treatment*, 17, 79–107.

Marshall, W. L., Laws, D. R., and Barbaree, H. E. (1990). *Handbook of Sexual Assault: Issues, Theories and Treatment of The Offender*. New York: Plenum Press.

Marshall, W. L. and Laws, D. R. (2003). A Brief History of Behavioral and Cognitive Behavioral Approaches to Sexual Offenders, Part 2: The Modern Era. *Sexual Abuse: A Journal of Research and Treatment*, 15(2), 75–92.

Marshall, W. L., Anderson, D., and Fernandez, Y. M. (1999). *Cognitive-Behavioral Treatment of Sexual Offenders*. New York: Jon Wiley and Sons, Inc.

Marshall, W. L., Serran, G., Fernandez, Y. M., Mulloy, R., Mann, R. E., and Thornton, D. (2003). Therapist Characteristics in The Treatment of Sexual Offenders: Tentative Data on Their Relationship With Indices of Behavior Change. *Journal of Sexual Aggression*, 9, 25–30.

Marshall, W. L. and Pithers, W. D. (1994). A Reconsideration of Treatment Outcome with Sex Offenders. *Criminal Justice and Behavior*, 21(1), 10–27.

Marshall, W. L. and Serran, G. A. (2004). The Role of The Therapist in Offender Treatment. *Psychology, Crime, and Law*, 10(3), 309–320.

McAlinden, A. (2005). The Use of Shame in the Reintegration of Sex Offenders. *British Journal of Criminology*, 45, 373–94.

McAlinden, A. (2008). Restorative Justice as a Response to Sexual Offending—Addressing the Failings of Current Punitive Approaches. *Sexual Offender Treatment*, 3(1), 1–12.

McCulloch, T. and Kelly, L. (2007). Working With Sex Offenders in Context: Which Way Forward. *The Journal of Community and Criminal Justice*, 54(1), 7–21.

McGrath, R. J., Cumming, G. and Burchard, B. (2003). *Current Practices and Trends in Sexual Abuser Management, The Safer Society 2002 Nationwide Survey*. Brandon, VT: The Safer Society Foundation, Inc.

Meloy, M. (2005). The Sex Offender Next Door: An Analysis of Recidivism, Risk Factors, and Deterrence of Sex Offenders on Probation. *Criminal Justice Policy Review*, 16(2), 211–236.

Missouri Sex Offender Program (MoSoP)—Prison Talk. Retrieved 6-3-08 from http://www.prisontalk.com/forums/showthread.php?t=219559.

Pithers, W. D., Marques, J. K., Gibat, C. C., and Marlatt, G. A. (1983). Relapse Prevention With Sexual Aggressive: A Self-Control Model of Treatment and Maintenance of Change. In J. G. Greer and I. R. Stuart (Eds.), *The Sexual Aggressor: Current Perspectives on Treatment* (pp. 214–239). New York: Van Nostrand Reinhold.

Prendergast, W. E. (2004*). Treating Sex Offenders: A Guide to Clinical Practice with Adults, Clerics, Children and Adolescents. 2ⁿᵈ Ed.* The Hawthorne Press. NY, London, Oxford.

Prentky, R. and Burgess, A. W. (1990). Rehabilitation of Child Molesters: A Cost-Benefit Analysis. *American Journal of Orthopsychiatry,* 60, 108–117.

Prentky, R. A. (1997). Arousal Reduction in Sexual Offenders: A Review of Antiandrogen Interventions. *Sexual Abuse: A Journal of Research and Treatment,* 9(4), 335–347.

Quinsey, V. L., Harris, G. T., Rice, M. E., and Lalumiere, M. L. (1993). Assessing Treatment Efficacy in Outcome Studies of Sex Offenders. *Journal of Interpersonal Violence,* 8, 512–523.

Rice, M. E., Quinsey, V. L., and Harris, G. T. (1991). Sexual Recidivism Among Child Molesters Released From a Maximum Security Institution. *Journal of Consulting and Clinical Psychology,* 59, 381–386.

Salter, A. C. (1988). *Treating Child Sex Offenders and Victims.* Newbury Park, CA: Sage Publications.

Schwartz, B. K. and Cellini, H. R. (Eds.) (1995). *The Sex Offender.* Kingston, NJ: Civic Research Institute, Inc.

Schwartz, B. K. and Cellini, H. R. (Eds.) (1997). *The Sex Offender, Vol. II.* Kingston, NJ: Civic Research Institute, Inc.

Seager, J. A., Jellicoe, D., and Dhaliwal, G. K. (2004). Refusers, Dropouts, and Completers: Measuring Sex Offender Treatment Efficacy. *International Journal of Offender Therapy and Comparative Criminology,* 48, 600–612.

Serran, G. A., Fernandez, Y. M., Marshall. W. L., and Mann, R. E. (2003). Process Issues in Treatment: Application to Sexual Offender Programs. *Professional Psychology: Research and Practice,* 34, 368–374.

Seto, M. C. and Barbaree, H. E. (1999). Psychopathy, Treatment Behavior, and Sex Offender Recidivism. *Journal of Interpersonal Violence,* 14(12), 1235–1248.

Sex Offender Treatment in Prison, Washington State Department of Corrections. Retrieved 8-3-08 from http://www.doc.wa.gov/community/sexoffenders/prisontreatment.asp.

Sourcebook of Criminal Justice Statistics Online. 2004. Retrieved 8-12-08 from http://www.albany.edu/sourcebook/pdf/t600012004.pdf.

Thomas, T. and Tuddenham, R. (2002). The Supervision of Sex Offenders: Policies Influencing the Probation Role. *Probation Journal,* 49(1), 10–18.

Turner, B. W., Bingham, J. E., and Andrasik, F. (2000). Short-Term Community-Based Treatment for Sexual Offenders: Enhancing Effectiveness. *Sexual Addiction and Compulsivity, 7,* 211–223.

Trowbridge, B. Does Sex Offender Treatment Work? Retrieved on 9-4-08 from http://www.trowbridgefoundation.org/docs/does_sex_offender_treatment_work.pdf.

U. S. General Accounting Office (1996). *Sex Offender Treatment: Research Results Inconclusive About What Works to Reduce Recidivism.* United States General Accounting Office Report to the Chairman, Subcommittee on Crime, Committee on the Judiciary, House of Representatives.

Valentine, D., Huebner, B. Stokes, S., Cobbina,C., and Berg, M. Sex Offender Recidivism in Missouri and Community Correction Options. Prepared for Missouri Sentencing Advisory Commission. Retrieved 8-5-08 from http://www.mosac.mo.gov/file/SOrecidivism.pdf.

Vivian-Byrne, S. (2002). Using Context and Difference in Sex Offender Treatment: An Integrated Systematic Approach. Journal of Sexual Aggression, 8, 59–73.

Vivian-Byrne, S. (2004). Changing People's Minds. Journal of Sexual Aggression, 10(2), 181–192.

Ward, T., Hudson, S. M., Marshall, W. L. and Siegert, R. (1995). Attachment Style and Intimacy Deficits in Sexual Offenders: A Theoretical Framework. *Sexual Abuse: A Journal of Research and Treatment, 7*(4), 317–335.

Ward, T., Laws, D. R., and Hudson, S. M. (2003). *Sexual Deviance: Issues and Controversies.* Thousand Oaks, California: Sage Publications.

Watson, R., and Stermac, L. (1994). Cognitive Group Counseling for Sexual Offenders. *International Journal of Offender Therapy and Comparative Criminology, 38*(3), 260–269.

Wormith, J. S. and Olver, M. E. (2002). Offender Treatment Attrition and its Relationship with Risk, Responsively, and Recidivism. *Criminal Justice and Behavior, 29*(4), 447–471.

Special appreciation to Dr. Craig Shifrin, Psy.D., Clinical Forensic Psychologist licensed in Missouri and Illinois for his review of this manuscript. Dr. Shifrin is an expert in the assessment and treatment of sexual offenders and is an approved sex offender therapist for the State of Missouri.

Part IV: The Offenders

Suggested Questions, Activities and Videos

Discussion Questions:

1. Discuss the policy implications for believing that sexual assault is driven by sexual desire.
2. If you were a prosecutor of a date rape case, what element of the crime of rape is of key concern? This element is generally not as critical in stranger-rape cases.
3. Discuss the difference between a child molester and a pedophile.
4. Examine constitutional rights regarding medical interventions of sex offenders; i.e., chemical castration, forced medication, etc.

Suggested Videos:

- Serial Rapist: A Criminal Profile: Films for the Humanities & Sciences
- Givin' it Up (Juvenile Sex Offenders): Fanlight Productions

Suggested Activities:

- Discuss the FBI profile of Serial Rapists. Pass out scenarios of offenses and see if the class—broken down into groups—can "profile" the offenders.
- Have the class search for a case of marital rape in the media.

Part V

The Criminal Justice System

Chapter 15

A Brief History of Rape Law and Rape Law Reform in the United States

Frances P. Reddington

Introduction

The first rape laws in the United States were based on English Common Law and specifically can be tracked back to the laws of medieval England (Allison and Wrightsman 1993). In English Common Law rape was defined as "carnal knowledge of a woman by force and against her will" (Largen 1988, 271). Under English common law, the rape statute was designed to protect a man's property and rape was not considered a personal crime against the woman (Bohmer 1991). This common law was adopted into the early Colonies and became law. The first rape statute in the new colonies in America was passed in Massachusetts in 1642 and rape was defined as a crime if a man had "carnal copulation" with "any woman child under ten years of age, forcibly and without consent ravished any maid or woman that is lawfully married or contracted, or ravished any maid or single woman with her by force or against her will, that is above the age of ten" (quoted in Allison and Wrightsman 1993). The English Common Law influence on American rape laws is obvious, especially if the later, revised statutes are examined. They stated that rape was defined as "illicit carnal knowledge of a female by force and against her will" (quoted in Allison and Wrightsman 1993).

Under English common law, rape had five elements that needed to be proven in a court of law. One would be that the act was defined as criminal (illicit), the second that carnal knowledge, which is usually defined as penile-vaginal sexual intercourse, (Russell and Bolen 2000) took place in the course of the attack, third that the victim was a woman, fourth that force was used during the attack and finally, that the force used was against the will of the victim. Obviously this definition and the legal elements left much interpretation up to the individual court and jurors (Allison and Wrightsman 1993).

This definition of rape remained a standard in the United States into the 1970s, when attention was given to rape law and movements for reform were started. The impetus behind this movement was multifaceted. The literature cites many reasons for the birth of the reform movement including the following: the questioning of the concept that women were property (Spohn 1999), reported rapes increased dramatically in the 1960s, and in fact increased faster than all other types of crime (Largen 1988; Spohn, 1999; Burgess 1985), challenges to long held misconceptions about rape (Largen 1988), the rights for women movement (Largen 1988; Burgess 1985), the emergence of women into the legal arena and criminal justice professions (Largen 1988), and a growing concern about female victims of crime, in particular by the criminal justice community who wanted to see reporting and successful prosecution of rape increase (Spohn 1999; Burgess 1985). According to Csida and Csida, "the feminists have been the primary motivating force in focusing national attention on the growing problem of rape and probably the greatest single force in activating sectors of society ... towards seeking solutions" (in Burgess 1985, 1). Several areas of rape law and its legal practices were examined and changed during this time.

Beginning in the state of Michigan, where the first comprehensive law on sexual assault was enacted in 1974, some form of reform in the rape laws eventually touched all fifty states (Bachman and Paternoster 1993). Whatever the impetus, and whichever group or issue was the driving force behind the rape reform movement, the goal of reform remained consistent: to change laws that stopped victims from reporting rape and to remove the numerous roadblocks that made a successful prosecution of a rape case almost impossible (Spohn and Horney 1996). In addition to the law reform movement going on during this time frame, other areas concerning sexual assault were coming of age as well. Both the creation of rape crisis centers and the availability of federal funds for research about sexual assault were first reported during this same time frame (Burgess 1985; Largen 1985).

This section will examine eight separate areas of reform. These include nonconsent and force; the act of rape and the gender of the victim; the rape statutes; corroboration; cautionary instructions; the marital exception; rape shield statutes; and rape as a hate crime. There will follow a brief discussion of the effectiveness of the reforms, and a look at present areas of concern for reformers. The chapter will end with some concluding remarks.

Non-Consent and the Use of Force

Force and non-consent are really two separate issues. Force focuses on the offender and non-consent focuses on the victim. However, it appears as though the early courts could not really distinguish the two in terms of how to examine them legally in court. Under English Common Law, it appears that both were determined by the amount of resistance that the victim offered during the attack. Resistance was the way that the courts could examine the elements of "by force" and "against her will" (non consent) during the trial. Before we examine that closer, it is important to note that during this time, the courts were designed to protect the virtuous, and thus believed that a woman of virtue would rather submit to serious bodily injury, maybe even death, than to have sexual intercourse with anyone who was not her husband (Gordan and Riger 1989). Therefore, in English Common Law, the courts determined that the level of resistance displayed by the victim had to be the very highest level of resistance; it had to be the "utmost resistance" or "resistance to the utmost". This is defined as "that the victim did everything possible, exercised every physical means within her power, to prevent the assailant from completing the assault" (Gordon and Roger 1985, 59). The more physically bruised and battered the victim was, the greater her chance of demonstrating resistance to the utmost in court.

It is interesting to note that this legal interpretation also placed the emphasis of the rape trial on the actions of the victim and not the accused. The victim's behavior was the heart of a rape trial (Estrich, 1987). Not to mention that the whole resistance standard was designed by males and in reality defined how males might respond in such a situation, but fighting to the utmost was most likely not the typical response of most women in a rape situation (Bohmer 1991). Nonetheless, this element of the English Common Law definition was adopted into U.S. laws. Sometimes, a state's higher courts had to interpret the actions of a rape victim and try to determine if her resistance was "to the utmost" as demonstrated in the following case heard by the Wisconsin State Supreme Court.

In 1904, a sixteen year old girl was walking across the field to her grandmother's house when she passed a neighbor boy she had known all her life. According to the girl, she spoke to the accused.

> He at once seized her, tripped her to the ground, placed himself in front and over her, unbuttoned her underclothing, then his own clothing, and had intercourse with her. That the only thing she said was to request him to let her go, and, throughout the description of the event, her only statement with reference to her own conduct was, repeatedly, *"I tried as hard as I could to get away. I was trying all the time to get away*

just as hard as I could, I was trying to get up; I pulled at the grass; I screamed as hard as I could, and he told me to shut up, and I didn't, and then he held his hand on my mouth until I was almost strangled (Brown v. State, 106 N.W. 536 (1906). (Italics added for emphasis.)

The conviction was overturned, because, among other reasons,

subject to the exception where the power of resistance is overcome by unconsciousness, threats, or exhaustion, in order to constitute the crime of rape, *not only must there be entire absence of mental consent or assent, but there must be the most vehement exercise of every physical means and faculty within the woman's power to resist the penetration of her person, and this must be shown to persist until the offense is consummated* (Brown v. State, 106 N.W. 536 (1906). (Italics added for emphasis.)

According to Susan Estrich (1987), U.S. courts did not always rely on the strict "to the utmost" standard in rape cases, and sometimes lowered that standard to what seemed reasonable under the circumstances, though the court's discretion seemed to be based on something other than legal factors, including race and social class of the accused and the victim. As early as the 1950s, there were some statutory changes in the U.S. laws regarding force and consent. By the 1960s, the "reasonable resistance standard" had replaced the "to utmost standard" for the most part (Estrich 1987). The reasonable resistance standard stated that the victim resisted as was reasonable under the circumstances. Though still vague and open to interpretation, it did allow the courts to examine the individual circumstances of the rape and the victim. It seems that courts began to understand that every woman might not react the same when confronted with the violent crime of rape (Allison and Wrightsman 1993) and that in some cases resistance might actually escalate the violence of the attack and place the victim in greater danger (Spohn 1999).

Today, what do the various states' criminal codes say about force, consent and non-consent in their sex crime laws? And more importantly, how do the courts interpret these laws? The way that most states responded in this area was to examine and change their resistance by the victim requirements. The different states enacted a wide array of new requirements regarding their resistance standards in sex crimes' law (Spohn 1999). The overall result is, according to Allison and Wrightsman that "Perhaps the greatest discrepancy in laws in different jurisdictions is in the resistance standard; some states have eliminated it but most have not (as of 1988, 38 states still imposed it)" (1993, 214). However, many states did not stop with just changing the resistance requirements but also looked at what constituted force as well. Generally, speaking, force was defined as physical force. However, during the reform movement many states "expanded their definition of *force* to include coercion or intimidation by the alleged rapist" (Allison and Wrightsman 1993, 214). These changes added additional components, such as fear of death or injury, to the definition of force. It could be more than just physical force that a rapist used, such as threats to the victim, and those threats in and of themselves, would meet the legal definition of force. For example, in Missouri forcible rape is defined as when a "person has sexual intercourse with another person by the use of forcible compulsion. Forcible compulsion includes the use of a substance administered without a victim's knowledge or consent which renders the victim physically or mentally impaired so as to be incapable of making an informed consent to sexual intercourse" (Missouri Revised Statutes, 2002). In Missouri, forcible compulsion is defined as either:

(a) Physical force that overcomes reasonable resistance; or
(b) A threat, express or implied, that places a person in reasonable fear of death, serious physical injury or kidnapping of such person or another person (§56.061 R.S.Mo. 2003).

Thus, in Missouri, the traditional definition of force which suggests a physical element is expanded to include a threat that places someone in fear for their life, physical injury or kidnapping of self and others. The interpretation of threat, fear and reasonable resistance in an individual rape case is left to the courts and its workers.

The Act of Rape and the Gender of the Victim

Rape was defined as carnal knowledge (sexual intercourse) that was perpetrated on a woman victim by a male offender. It did not include any oral or anal forced sexual activity or the use of objects in a sexual assault. It did not include male victims (Allison and Wrightsman 1993). Reformers of the 1970s addressed these issues for two reasons, one to include male victims and also to expand the definition of rape to include other types of sexual assault.

How states addressed this issue varies. Most states made their statutes gender neutral. Some replaced the word rape with words such as sexual assault, sexual battery, or some other similar term (Spohn 1999). This was done to eliminate the negative connotations the word rape carried with it, to foster a new awareness of male victims, and to have the criminal justice system refocus on the violent nature of the crime rather than the misunderstood sexual aspect that was historically linked with the word rape (Allison and Wrightsman 1993). Generally speaking, in addition, the new legal terms broadened the definition of rape to include anything done to the victim orally, anally, or with objects or other body parts. Other states left rape in their statutes but created twin crimes to include any activity outside of penile-vaginal penetration and named that crime, for example, sodomy.

Rape Statutes—Providing Options and Looking at the Punishment

Concern about the low number of convictions in rape cases led to the examination of the definition of rape and the punishment for rape. In most states rape was defined as it was in English Common Law and individual circumstances of the rape did not impact the charging of the crime or the punishment. For example, did the attacker use a weapon, or seriously injure the victim beyond the rape itself? How much force was used and what was the age of the victim? Was the rape committed in the commission of another felony? In response to these queries and the growing sense that different circumstances were present in different rapes, many states examined their rape laws and expanded the options for charging and prosecuting rape cases. Most commonly seen were the creation of rape laws in the first, second and third degree or aggravated vs. simple rape based on the level of coercion used on the victim, injury to the victim and age of the victim (Allison and Wrightsman 1993; Spohn 1999).

Once states graded the crime, the punishment would have to be graded as well. Under English Common Law rape was punishable by death. Reformers were concerned that this penalty might seem unduly harsh to juries and prevent some convictions. By 1971, 16 states and the federal government defined rape as a capital crime punishable by death. In 1972, *Furman vs. Georgia* put a hiatus on sentencing anyone to death, and when states had to rewrite their death statutes to be in line with *Gregg v Georgia* in 1976, only three states came back with rape listed as a capital offense (Allison and Wrightsman 1993). This reform effort was very controversial and the main question came down to a debate between two camps. Did this trivialize the crime of rape or would the new lesser punishment actually put rape victims in less danger as their rapists would not face capital punishment for rape, unless they killed the victim?

The Supreme Court ended the argument in 1977 when *Coker v Georgia* held that the death penalty for rape was "grossly disproportionate and excessive" and in violation of the 8th and 14th Amendments (Allison and Wrightsman 1993).

The Supreme Court said that they had considered public attitudes about rape and the death penalty in their ruling. Looking back fifty years, they found that of the states with the death penalty, only a small number considered rape a capital crime. Therefore, the Supreme Court reasoned, public opinion would indicate that the death penalty was too harsh a punishment for the crime of rape (Allison and Writghtsman 1993). Thus, as of 1977, rape could not be viewed as a capital crime in any state, and the present punishments for rape and sexual assault vary among the states.

Corroboration

According to Largen (1988, 271), Edwardian-era scholar, John Henry Wigmore theorized about "sexually precocious minors and unchaste women who fantasize about rape" as a cause for concern in the prosecution of rape cases. How to tell who was lying about being raped? Such concerns set the stage for the corroboration doctrine. This doctrine required additional evidence to accompany the victim's testimony about the rape. The additional evidence would indicate that the person was not lying about being raped. In fact, "a conviction for rape could not rest on the unsupported testimony of the complainant alone, and corroborating evidence provided an objective standard by which to measure complainant credibility" (Largen 1988, 272). Obviously requiring this additional corroborating evidence to prosecute would cut down on the number of prosecutions. In essence, it was as if the rape victim had to prove she was a victim before the case could be prosecuted. As with other reform issues, trying to remove the corroboration requirement was met with resistance.

"Some who defended the corroboration requirement argued that a woman would deliberately lie about being sexually assaulted to explain away premarital intercourse, infidelity, pregnancy, or disease, or to retaliate against an ex-lover or some other man" (Spohn 1999, 125). However, eventually, the reform movement of the 1970s was successful in having the corroboration requirement in rape cases repealed in all states that still required it (Largen 1988).

Cautionary Instructions

It is suggested that because other sexual acts historically defined as sex crimes (adultery, statutory rape) and rape were distinguishable only because of the use of force element (Largen 1988), and because there was a real fear of false accusations of rape (Spohn 1999), the legal arena handled rape differently than other crimes. For example, Lord Chief Justice Matthew Hale added this quote into his cautionary instructions to juries about the crime of rape: "It is true, rape is a most detestable crime, and therefore ought severely and impartially be punished with death; *but it must be remembered that it is an accusation easily to be made, and hard to be proved, and harder to be defended by the party accused, though ever so innocent*" (Italics added for emphasis) (quoted in Bohmer 1991, 317). Hale's statement or some derivative was not uncommon to be given to a jury before they went into deliberation in a rape case (Estrich, 1987).

Obviously, this concerned the reformers who suggested that cautionary instructions of that nature given to the jury would, in all likelihood, be prejudicial against the victim. The success of the reformers to have these cautionary instructions removed from the judicial process was not as quickly successful as some of the other reforms. However "in later years, the majority of states applying such instructions would eliminate them either through law or through practice" (Largen 1988, 276).

The Marital Exception

Under English Common Law, a man could not be accused of raping his wife as she was considered his property and the marriage contract implied that she was sexually available at her husbands' request and thus did not have the right to say no (Gordon and Roger 1988). Obviously, the courts did not delve into issues of the marital bedroom. In the 1970s, this issue was addressed by reformers and changes were made in the laws stating that a man could be charged with raping his wife, or more legally correct, a spouse could be charged with raping a spouse. In fact, though changes were made, these changes were not easily made nor were they made without controversy (Kirkwood and Cecil 2001). An article by Kirkwood and Cecil includes the 1979 quote from California State Senator Bob Wilson who, while addressing a group of lobbyists for women's rights said, "But if you can't rape your own wife, who can you rape?" and a quote from Senator Jeremiah Denton from Alabama who, while addressing congress, stated "Dammit, when you get married, you've got to expect a little sex" (2001, 1234).

Yllo (1999) offers some insight into the controversial issue that still continues to elicit strong debate.

> I have come to the conclusion that there is something about the very concept of marital rape that impedes our work. It contains a cultural

contradiction inherent in no other form of violence and it goes to the very heart of the institution of marriage. In our contemporary romantic image of marriage, love and sex are inextricably linked and form the very foundation of the relationship. The wedding both legitimizes and celebrates this sexual bond. The very idea of this bond turning into sexual bondage falls outside of this frame of reference (p, 1060).

In addition to the above stated concern, there was fear that making spousal rape legal would hinder reconciliation (Bohmer 1988) as well as initiate an onslaught of false allegations of rape made by angry housewives (Gordon and Riger 1989).

Eventually, all states made raping your spouse a crime, though the statutes vary considerably (Kirkwood and Cecil 2001). In some states, the marital rape laws include some modifications from the existing rape law, such as there is a shorter time limit for reporting the rape, or there needs to be proof of physical injuries or evidence that the couple is no longer living together (Gorden and Riger 1989). This was best publicly exemplified by the 1993 John Bobbitt case. John Bobbitt's wife Lorena cut off her husband's penis with a kitchen knife. She said she did this as the result of repeated marital rapes. The couple was living together, though they were planning to divorce. In Virginia, the laws stated that for marital rape charges to be filed, the couple must be living apart and that the victim must demonstrate serious physical injury as a result of the rape. Because of these requirements, Virginia prosecutors could only charge John Bobbitt with marital sexual assault, which carried a lesser penalty (USA Today, Final Edition, November 9, 1993).

Rape Shield Statutes

Under English Common Law, there was no protection for the victim once she took the stand. She could be asked any question about her sexual behavior, personal habits, emotional history and life. Many victims were hesitant to take the stand as to some it seemed as though their lifestyle was more on trial than were the actions of the accused. Reformers began to question this open door access to the victim of rape if she took the stand to testify. What relevance did her personal habits, particularly her sexual habits, have on whether she was raped during the incident in question? This was controversial, as many people felt that her life choices did in fact need to be known. Would a sexually active woman be more likely to lie about being raped, or be more likely to not say no (Allison and Wrightsman 1993)?

"The notion that the victim's prior sexual conduct was pertinent to whether or not she consented was based on the assumption that an unchaste woman would be more likely to consent to intercourse than a woman without premarital or extramarital sexual experiences" (Spohn 1999, 126). The reformers pushed to create some kind of law which would protect the victim while on the stand, and to limit the information she could be asked about while on the stand. In response, most states have enacted some form of rape shield statutes. Though these are laws designed to protect the victims from inappropriate questions while on the stand, in the bigger picture, these laws are designed to stop unnecessary questions about the victims' past sexual history, encourage the reporting, filing and successful prosecution of rape cases, and to put the focus of the trial back on the behavior of the accused (Spohn 1999).

According to Largen (1988, 275), "rape shield laws restricting the scope of cross-examination about the complainant's prior sexual conduct were the most vigorously opposed" of the reform efforts. Some states, such as Hawaii, Iowa, North Carolina and Florida have actually reversed some of their rape shield statutes (Allison and Wrightsman 1993). Generally speaking, rape shield statutes usually limit the discussion of the victim's sexual past to: consensual sexual acts between the accused and the accuser, or to demonstrate that the accused was not the cause of semen, impregnation nor responsible for giving the victim an STD, or to attack the credibility of the victim (Allison and Wrightsman 1993). Though less common, some statutes also allow discussion of evidence to suggest that the victim is prejudice or has a reason to make a false allegation, may have made a false allegation previously, or that the accused reasonably thought the victim consented (Spohn 1999). All in all, what can be asked of the victim about her sexual history while on the stand will be decided by the rape shield statutes of the state, case law and the opinion of the trial judge (Allison and Wrightsman 1993).

Hate Crimes

There have been hate crimes for hundreds of years, yet it has only been about twenty years that hate crimes were legally recognized in the American criminal justice system (Jenness and Grattet 2002). Most states have added some form of hate crime definition into their criminal statues, though there is much debate about the need for and the reasoning behind hate crime legislation (Lawrence 2003).

According to the Community Relations Service of the U.S. Department of Justice a "hate crime is the violence of intolerance and bigotry, intended to hurt and intimidate someone because of their race, ethnicity, national origin, religious, sexual orientation or disability". If you notice, this definition does not include the word gender, and thus sets the stage for another reform debate. Is rape a crime that can be motivated based on the gender of the victim? Some recent developments seem to suggest that some think that gender should be included into the protected classes.

The Violence Against Women Act (VAWA) of 1994 gave women the civil right to be protected from crimes of violence that are based on the sole fact of gender. The VAWA may give the victim of a violent crime access to the federal courts for litigation against their attacker. "VAWA creates a civil cause of action under federal law that may be used to remedy abuse by an intimate against either a female or male partner, as well as to remedy rape and sexual assault, sexual harassment at work, child sex abuse, and gay-bashing attacks" (Pincus and Rosen 1997, 20). Some authors contend that many of the violent crimes which have primarily female victims are based on the fact that the victim is a female (Pincus and Rosen 1997). With this kind of protection at the federal level, should state hate crime statutes include the word gender and should sexual assault crimes be prosecuted under this statute?

There is much controversy about the need for hate crime statutes, and about whether state statutes should include gender in their protected classes. The addition of gender into the protected classes is seen "less commonly" than other biases (The National Center for Victims of Crime). As of January, 2003, there were seven states whose hate crime laws specifically included gender. They are California, Hawaii, Minnesota, Missouri, New Mexico, Pennsylvania and Vermont, as well as the District of Columbia

(Human Rights Campaign 2003).

There are questions being raised as to the overall sentiment to include gender in the protected classes and to prosecute sex crimes as hate crimes.

> In May 2000, the Court struck down part of the Violence Against Women Act that allowed victims of sexual assaults to sue their attackers in federal court. Rehnquist and Congress' power to protect civil rights does not extend to "purely private" acts of violence that do not cross state lines, a decision that probably dooms prospects for a national Hate Crimes Act. The plaintiff in this case, Virginia Tech freshman Christy Brzonkala sued after the university took no disciplinary action against a football star accused of raping her (Savage 2001, 34).

In 2002, the senate republicans blocked efforts to add gender, sexual orientation and disabilities to the 30 year old federal hate crime statue (AFL-CIO 2002).

The Effectiveness of Rape Law Reform

According to Bryden and Lengnick (1997), many of the reforms that were made regarding rape laws were designed to encourage victims to report their rape victimization and to give prosecutors the tools necessary to convict offenders. They conclude that "There is growing evidence that, while performance of the justice system in rape cases may have improved, the legal reforms have generally had little or no effect on the outcome of rape cases, or the proportions of rapists who are prosecuted and convicted" (1997, 1199). Likewise, Spohn suggests that although "reformers clearly had high hopes for the rape law reforms, their expectations may have been unrealistic. Although the results of studies examining rape law reform's efforts are somewhat mixed, most find very limited effects on case outcomes" (1999, 129).

In a comprehensive study of the Michigan law, often cited as the most comprehensive sex crime bills package passed, Marsh et al. conclude that the effectiveness of the Michigan law is "mixed" (1982, ix). "The enactment and implementation of the Michigan law were expected to affect victims, actors in the legal system, and perhaps perpetrators of future rapes. The experience in that state indicates that the reform bought about changes in procedure but not in basic attitudes or definitions of the crime" (1982, ix).

Changing Times, New Reforms

As time advances, new issues regarding rape law and its practice emerge and rape law reform remains an important topic. Issues such as the counselor-privilege, medical exam costs, AIDS testing and results disclosure, the use of polygraphs on rape victims, and the statute of limitations to report sex crimes are but a few of the topics being addressed in various political and reform arenas (Institute for Law and Justice 1997). In addition to that, there has been an active legislative agenda regarding sex offender laws, including registration, notification, sexual predator laws and chemical castration laws. These will be discussed in a later chapter of this book.

Conclusion

Starting in the 1970s rape law reform touched every state. However, based on the fact that there were numerous groups pushing reform—sometimes with different agendas, each state reformed their laws as they saw fit, and there is still widespread disparity in rape laws. However, according to Horney and Spohn (1993), there are four common themes that ran through the heart of the rape law reform of the 1970s and 1980s. One is that the crime of rape was replaced by a series of offenses that graded the crime and the punishment and that included all the elements that might happen during a sexual assault (oral and anal penetration, use of objects, etc.) and that included gender equality. Two, is that most states addressed their resistance requirements, by either changing or eliminating that requirement. Three, was that the corroboration requirement was eliminated and four, most states enacted a rape shield statute designed to protect the victims from unnecessary testimony regarding their previous sexual histories (in Bachman and Paternoster 1993). We have certainly examined those reforms and others in this chapter. It is evident that the reform movement's efforts changed the laws.

The bigger question, however, remains the question of effectiveness of the reform movements. To determine effectiveness, you would have to look at the stated goals of the reform movement. Cited evidence in this chapter suggests that research results are "mixed" when researching whether reforms were successful at increasing reporting, prosecution and conviction of sex crimes.

However, does that mean the reforms were not successful in other ways? According to Spohn,

> passage of the reforms sent an important symbolic message regarding the seriousness of rape cases and the treatment of rape victims. In the long run, this symbolic message may be more important than the instrumental change that was anticipated. Those who lobbied for rape law reform sought to shift the focus of a rape case from the character, reputation, and behavior of the victim to the unlawful acts of the offender. The rape law reforms may have started a process of long-term attitude change that is difficult to measure in a legal impact study but may ultimately lead to instrumental change (1999, 129–130).

We can only hope this is true, and continue to push for positive changes. It is disheartening sometimes to realize that despite thirty-something years of rape law reform, some things have not changed very much at all. However, if we examine the reforms made in the last 30 years in the law, we can hope that these changes will continue to influence practice, and that changed practice will promote attitudinal changes. Attitudinal changes will impact reporting, prosecution and conviction of sex crimes. We owe that to all rape survivors, past and future.

References

AFL-CIO, December 4, 2002. aflcio.org/issuespolitics/civilrights/ns06242002.cfm?

Allison, J., and Wrightsman, L. *Rape: The Misunderstood Crime*. Sage Publications, 1993.

Bachman, R., and Poternaster, R. "A Contemporary Look at the Effects of Rape Law Reform: How Far Have We Really Come?" *The Journal of Criminal Law and Criminology 84* no. 3, (1993): 554–574.

Bohmer, C. "Acquaintance Rape and the Law, Chapter 20." In *Acquaintance Rape: The Hidden Crime*, eds. A. Parrot and L. Bechhofer. New York: John Wiley & Sons, Inc., 1991.

Brown v. State, 106 N.W. 536, 1906.

Bryden, D. and S. Lengnick. (1997). "Rape in the Criminal Justice System." *The Journal of Criminal Law & Criminology 87*, no. 4, (1997): 1195–1384.

Burgess, A. *Rape and Sexual Assault: A Research Handbook*. Garland Publishing, Inc, 1985.

Coker v. Georgia, 433 U.S. 584 (1977).

Estrich, S. *Real Rape*. Harvard University Press, 1987.

Furman v. Georgia, 408 U.S. 238 (1972).

Gordon, M., and S. Riger. *The Female Fear*. The Free Press, Macmillion, Inc, 1989.

Gregg v. Georgia, 428 U.S. 153 (1976).

Human Rights Campaign. http://www.hrc.org/issues/hate_crimes/background/statelaws.asp.

Institute for Law and Justice. *Review of Sexual Assault Laws, 1997.* http://www.ilj.org/sa/sexassault.html.

Jenness, V., and R. Grattet. "Making Hate a Crime: From Social Movement to Law Enforcement." *Journal of Criminal Law & Criminology 93* no. 1, (2002): 306–307.

Kirkwood, M. K., and D. Cecil. "Marital Rape: A Student Assessment of Rape Laws and The Marital Exception." *Violence Against Women 7* no. 11, (2001): 1234–1253.

Largen, M. A. "Rape Law Reform: An Analysis, Chapter 15." In *Rape and Sexual Assault*, ed. A. Burgess. Garland Publishing, Inc, 1988.

Largen, M. A. "The Anti-Rape Movement: Past and Present, Chapter 1." In *Rape and Sexual Assault*, ed. A. Burgess. Garland Publishing, Inc, 1985.

Lawrence, F. "Contextualizing Bias Crimes: A Social and Theoretical Perspective." *Law & Social Inquiry 28* no. 1, (2003): 315–339.

Marsh, J., A. Geist, and N. Caplan. *Rape and the Limits of Law Reform*. Boston: Aubrun House publishing Company. 1982.

Missouri Revised Statutes, 2002.

Pincus, S., and D. Rosen. "Fighting Back: Filing Suit Under the Violence Against Women Act." *Trial 33* no. 12, (1997): 20–27.

Russell, D., and R. Bolen. *The Epidemic of Rape and Child Sexual Abuse in the United States.* Thousand Oaks, CA: Sage Publications, 2000.

Savage, D. "United They Sit." *ABA Journal 87,* (2001): 34–35.

§56.061 R.S.Mo. 2003.

Spohn, C. "The Rape Reform Movement: The Traditional Common Law And Rape Law Reforms." *Jurimetrics 39* no. 2, (1999): 119–130.

Spohn, C., and J. Horney. "The Impact of Rape Law Reform on the Processing of Simple and Aggravated Rape Cases." *Journal of Law & Criminology 86* no. 3, (1996): 861.

The National Center for Victims of Crime. Ncvc.org.gethepl/hatecrimelegislation/.

USA Today. "Marital Rape Laws Examined." November 9, 1993, Final Edition, 1993.

U.S. Department of Justice. *Community Relations Service.* http://www.usdoj.gov/crs/pubs/htecrm.htm.

Yllo, K. "Wife Rape: A Social Problem for the 21st Century." *Violence Against Women 5* no. 9, (1999): 1059.

Special Feature

Acquittal of Husband Spurs Anger; Wife Accused Him of Raping Her

COLUMBIA, S.C.—A jury's decision to acquit a man shown on videotape having sex with his wife, who was tied up with her mouth and eyes taped shut, has left women's rights advocates angry.

"It's going to take a while to change the attitudes in South Carolina," Candy Kern, state president of the National Organization for Women, said after Thursday's verdict.

The 33-year-old man was brought to trial under the marital rape law signed by Gov. Carroll Campbell last June. So far, only one person has been convicted, and prosecutor Knox McMahon said he feared that Thursday's verdict would make victims reluctant to come forward. "I don't know what we're going to tell these women when they come here with a whole lot less evidence than this and want a conviction," McMahon said.

"If this isn't marital rape, it doesn't exist." The woman, who is separated from her husband and seeking a divorce, sobbed and buried her face in her hands when the verdict was read. Her husband smiled and hugged supporters.

One of the jurors, Danny Taylor, said he believed in the law, but he maintained that the prosecution hadn't proved its case. "I had to vote on what my conscience told me to do," he said.

The eight-woman, four-man Lexington County jury took less than an hour to reach its verdict. Jurors saw a videotape of the man having intercourse with his wife while her hands and legs were tied with rope and her mouth and eyes were covered with duct tape.

"Some of it is denial," she said. "If we can say, 'She did something wrong and that's why she was raped,' then somehow, this won't happen to us."

Prosecutors said the woman broke free about midnight and ran to the home of a neighbor, who called police. Her husband was found an hour later with the videotape, video camera and other items used in the encounter in his van.

"No, I didn't rape my wife. How can you rape your own wife?" the 33-year-old husband testified. He was not identified to protect his wife's identity. The husband's attorney, Wayne Floyd, argued that the woman enjoyed watching pornographic movies and engaging in unconventional sex acts involving sex toys.

"Was that a cry of pain and torture? Or was that a cry of pleasure?" Floyd asked as the tape was played Wednesday.

Donna Jordan of the Rape Crisis Network in the Midlands said Friday that her office's phone lines were jammed with angry calls after the verdict.

A domestic violence group, Sistercare, said it would hold a protest next week at the Statehouse.

Women's groups lobbied for five years for the marital rape law. It requires that a victim report the crime within 30 days and show physical proof of abuse.

Alabama is now the last state in the country without any marital rape law, said Beth Stafford-Vaughan, a research librarian at the Women's Studies Center at the University of Illinois.

So far, one person has been convicted under South Carolina's law and is serving the maximum 10-year prison sentence.

In the latest case, the woman testified that her husband dragged her by the throat into a bedroom, tied her hands and legs, put duct tape on her eyes and mouth and put stockings and a garter belt on her legs. He then turned on the videotape and assaulted her, she said.

The judge blocked the prosecution's attempt to call the husband's former wife to testify that she also had been tied up and raped by the man. Kern said sometimes it is harder to convince female jurors than men in such a case.

The Houston Chronicle (1992, April 18). Section A; pg. 3.

Chapter 16

Police and Victims of Sexual Assault

Betsy Wright Kreisel

Introduction

The crime of sexual assault has circumstances that make it different from other crimes with respect to the law enforcement perspective. "The crime of forcible rape is a relatively infrequent event confronting police agencies and yet it can be one of the most serious forms of criminal victimization that can befall any of their constituents" (Battelle Law and Justice Study Center 1978; 7). Sexual assault is a traumatic victimization for two reasons. Victims are traumatized first, by the humiliation of their physical violation, and secondly, by the fear of being severely injured or killed (Woods 2001). The victim can be greatly and further impacted by the police officer's response to their victimization.

As law enforcement handle these sensitive cases, they have three primary responsibilities in sexual assault cases. First, police officers need to protect, interview, and support the victim. This police officer role sometimes conflicts as police investigate the offense, which is a task that can conflict with offering the victim emotional support (Holmstrom and Burgess 1978). Second, they have to investigate the crime and possibly apprehend the perpetrator. And third, police officers must collect and preserve evidence of the assault to assist in the assailant's prosecution. Collection of evidence in sexual assault cases is unlike many other crimes, as it may include a physical examination at the hospital, and more likely, primary evidence collection may be through interviewing, as physical evidence is often not available. Regarding these three responsibilities, law enforcement has not historically performed them well. However, there is evidence that police officers have recently improved in the processing of sexual assault cases.

Regarding the law enforcement process in rape cases, it is important to note that rape is the most underreported violent crime. When law enforcement does get the call it is critically important to handle it properly from the start (Albrecht 2000; Wood 2001). Law enforcement generally becomes involved with a sexual assault case when a crime is reported, normally by a victim. A police officer will respond, assess the victim's physical and emotional condition and take an initial report if possible. If it is necessary, the officer will transport the victim to the hospital for treatment and for gathering forensic evidence. It is usually law enforcement's responsibility to submit the hospital examination materials ("rape kit") to the crime laboratory for analysis. Other evidence may be collected at the crime scene. If and when law enforcement decides whether an investigation is forthcoming, it will include an interview with the victim, usually in police department surroundings that probably will be neither private nor comfortable (Battelle Law and Justice Study Center 1978). The law enforcement phase, for the most part, ends with the arrest of a suspect and turning the case over to the prosecutor (Doerner and Lab 1998). The following discussion is of empirical works surrounding the law enforcement process of initial response and investigation of sexual assault cases.

This is followed by consideration of law enforcement decision-making in sexual assault cases. This chapter concludes with a discussion of the innovative approaches to handling sexual assault cases, as well as police guidelines on approaching victims of sexual assault.

For purposes of clarifying terminology in this chapter's discussions, the terms of sexual assault and rape are generally used interchangeably. In addition, while both men and women are victims of rape, women are disproportionately affected by this crime. According the National Violence Against Women survey (Tjaden and Thoennes 1998), 1 in 6 women compared with 1 in 33 men report having experienced an attempted or completed rape in their lifetimes. Therefore, for the purposes of this paper, females are generally referred to as the victim and males are generally referred to as the offender.

Police Process and Response to Sexual Assault Victims

Research indicates that the first police officer to respond to a report of rape is the most readily available patrol officer (Battelle Law and Justice Study Center 1978). This was reported by 82 percent (230 agencies) of the police departments surveyed, while specifically designated individuals or units were first to respond in the remaining few agencies. This indicates that there is a need for all patrol officers to be informed of the sensitivity necessary in handling sexual assault victims, in addition to the processing of evidence. However, only 84 percent (175) of the agencies in the Battelle Law and Justice Study Center (1978) study reported that the compulsory preservice law enforcement training provides specific information on handling sexual assault cases. That leaves some officers responding to sexual assault cases with no victimology-specific training. For those that receive preservice training regarding how to handle sexual assault victims, the length of training is likely to be less than a day and the quality of that training is an issue yet to be determined (Battelle Law and Justice Study Center 1978). Also, in preservice training police officers are receiving vast amounts of training in almost all areas of policing, making it difficult for police officers to retain specifics on how to treat different types of crime victims when encountered. In addition, because the rape event is infrequent, the officer may approach this investigation like that of any other crime and fail to note details that later will be important to the case (Battelle Law and Justice Study Center 1978).

Many police agencies tend to have specialized units or officers who ultimately handle the investigation of sexual assault cases (Battelle Law and Justice Study Center 1978). However, because rape reports are not a common police call (Albrecht 2000), a majority of the sexual assault investigation officers also handle other types of investigation such as homicides and felonious assaults (Battelle Law and Justice Study Center 1978). Nonetheless, there are techniques of interviewing the victim that investigators have developed.

One of the most common interview techniques with sexual assault victims is the behavioral-oriented interview. This includes interview questions that focus toward establishing the type of rapist in addition to collecting evidence for prosecution (Merrill 1995). Typologies of rapists are discussed in a previous chapter. By establishing the type of rapist this may assist in the identification of the rapist, if not already known. Interview questions may focus upon how the offender maintained control of the victim; whether by intimidation, threats or force. Other questions focus upon the amount of physical force employed by the attacker as well as whether the victim resisted the attacker. This latter question is *not* intended to be victim-blaming, and will be followed by questions of how the rapist responded to the resistance to help assess rapist typology. Other law enforcement questions may appear intrusive and irrelevant. For example, there will be questions about any sexual dysfunctions of the rapist and the type and sequence of sexual acts that occurred during the assault. Questions about verbal activity between the rapist and victim will be asked, as will whether the rapist had any sudden change in attitude during the attack, or whether there may have been some precautionary actions taken by the offender, such as wearing a mask or having the victim shower after the attack (Hazelwood and Burgess 1987).

No matter what the interviewing technique, it is easy to perceive the police line of questioning as insensitive and suspicious, but they must collect all the facts. Despite the intrusive questions, if the police report is thorough and complete, the chance of a successful prosecution increases (Wiseman as cited in Bryden and Lengnick 1997).

Police Officer Discretionary Decisions: Legal and Extra-Legal Factors

The police officer has a number of decisions that will need to be made in the processing of a sexual assault case. Police officers will first make the decision as to whether to found this crime as a sexual assault. Police officers will decide if and how to proceed in the investigation, as well as whether to make an arrest. Some police discretion in these decisions is limited by departmental policies or state regulations. Nonetheless, police officers can impact the outcome of a sexual assault case at many stages of the process. The following discusses the stages of police officer discretionary decisions in sexual assault cases and the legal factors that affect those decisions. Extra-legal factors affecting police officers decisions will be subsequently discussed.

Founding of a Rape

Policing founding decisions tend to relate to the evidentiary issues of the case. Police officers, usually patrol officers, will look for two main factors in the report in order to classify the event as rape. First, is the proof of penetration, which the hospital will provide and secondly is the use of force by the offender, as evidenced by injury to the victim or by her statement. If either or both of these elements is/are missing, research indicates that the agency is likely to unfound the report (Battelle Law and Justice Study Center 1978). Kerstetter (1990) suggests that whether police found a rape complaint ultimately depends upon whether they believe that the government can prove the elements of the crime.

According to a nationwide estimate by the Federal Bureau of Investigation, the percentage of unfounded rape reports is eight percent (FBI 2002). Several studies have been conducted looking at the reasons associated with the unfounding of the rape decision by police officers. Research findings indicate that rape cases may be unfounded because the purported victim's contributory negligence, and by her perceived immorality (Bryden and Lengnick 1997;

Ledoux and Hazelwood 1985). The following are among some of the reasons that law enforcement may use as a means of rationalizing the unfounding of sexual assaults:

1. The female is unmarried but sexually experienced, promiscuous, or even a prostitute
2. The female was drinking or taking drugs or is a drug addict.
3. The female's story has inconsistencies or she keeps changing it or it does not all "add-up."
4. Police are unable to corroborate her story, for example by injuries to her sex organs.
5. She exposed herself to risk of rape by voluntarily accompanying him to the site of the alleged rape or by inviting him into her home.
6. She has, apart from the rape, severe mental or emotional problems, perhaps evidenced by a history of psychiatric treatment or an attempted suicide or running away from home.
7. She does not appear to be upset by the alleged rape.
8. She is unattractive.
9. She knew the alleged rapist, or had been voluntarily sexually intimate on other occasions.
10. There is no large discrepancy between her age and his.
11. She is a least 12 years old.
12. The alleged offender does not have a previous criminal record.
13. She has prior trouble with the police.
14. The offense was not promptly reported.
15. The putative victim failed a polygraph test.
16. She is uncooperative

(Lonsway 2002; Bryden and Lengnick 1997; Kerstetter 1990; Holmstrom and Burgess 1978).

Other research indicates that unfounding decisions may be based upon improving the perception of the agency or community. By routinely unfounding certain sexual assault cases, departmental statistics can be used to make the community's incidence of rape appear relatively low and the rate of police clearance relatively high. Another motivation for unfounding sexual assault cases is for the benefit of police officers themselves. Unfounding of sexual assault cases serves as a means of closing cases that would otherwise remain active and this provides a reduced caseload for the department or unit (Lonsway 2002). In addition, Lonsway (2002) contends that some officers are motivated to unfound in order to avoid thoroughly investigating what are perceived to be "difficult cases." Other common factors used as a basis for improperly unfounding rape cases include the police are unable to locate the victim, the victim decides not follow through with the prosecution, and/or that no assailant can be identified (Lonsway 2002).

Overall, founding or unfounding decisions of sexual assault cases by law enforcement are highly subjective. The reasons for improperly unfounding sexual assault cases are numerous, not always mutually exclusive and may be based upon judgments made about the victim or may be due to self-centered departmental, community statistics or officer motivations.

Decision to Investigate

Once the decision to found the report by the responding police officer is made, the investigation phase of the rape case is usually passed to a police officer who specializes in sexual assault investigations, but who also investigates homicide and felonious assault cases. The investigator will look at such elements as proof of penetration, use of force, promptness of victim reporting, victim injuries, relationship between victim and suspect, use of weapon, and identification of a suspect in deciding whether to go forward with an investigation (Battelle Law and Justice Study Center 1978; Bryden and Lengnick 1997). Research suggests that a majority of rape cases receive peripheral or shallow investigations at best. Most criminal cases receive a day or less investigation and sexual assault cases tend to be no different than other violent crimes (Greenwood 1975).

Decision to Arrest

Once the decision to investigate is made, the investigator will pursue fairly routine investigative strategies looking into, among other things, whether an arrest is possible. The investigator will take particular interest in issues that directly relate to the evidentiary needs of the prosecutor. A number of studies have found that in making the decision to arrest a suspect and file formal charges, the investigator will consider first, the ability of the victim to identify the suspect, and second, the victim's willingness to prosecute (Bryden and Lengnick 1997; LaFree 1981). And third, it was discovered that proof of penetration, relationship between victim and suspect, use of physical force by suspect, and the availability of witnesses all impacts the police officer's decision to arrest in a sexual assault case (Battelle Law and Justice Study Center 1978). One exception to the above factors is the victim's ability to identify a suspect, which is nearly always present in acquaintance rapes, and therefore is unhelpful in analyzing police decisions in these cases (Bryden and Lengnick 1997; LaFree 1981).

Extra-Legal Factors Affecting Police Decisions: Rape Myths and Secondary Victimization

Despite the legal factors affecting police officers' discretion during sexual assault cases, there is empirical evidence that extra-legal variables may impact officers' decisions. These extra-legal variables are associated with the rape myths that so many of the general population believe. These myths lead law enforcement to hold negative attitudes toward sexual assault victims and frequently subject victims to the phenomena known as "secondary victimization" (Carrington and Watson 1996). Secondary victimization has been defined as the victim-blaming attitudes, behaviors and practices of community service providers including the police (Campbell, et al. 2001; Campbell and Johnson 1997).

Extra-legal factors that have been found to impact law enforcement's decision, particularly with whether or not to found the crime of rape, may include the behavior and lifestyle of the victim prior to the assault, as well as at the time of the assault (Chandler and Torney 1981). One national survey of police officers uncovered a prevailing attitude of suspicion and lack of concern for rape victims (LeDoux and Hazelwood 1985). Other studies suggest that police officers ascribe to victim-blaming attitudes, such as believing women provoke rape and often lie about the occurrence of rape (Campbell, et al. 2001; Campbell and Johnson 1997). In addition, other studies have reported that victims have been outright told by law enforcement that they are not believable or credible. Even in the absence of such verbal communication, many women still felt doubted in their interactions with law enforcement (Campbell, et al. 2001).

The secondary victimization may occur not only because of what law enforcement decide to do, but also because of what they decide not to do. Such as previously stated, not founding a case as rape and not following up with an investigation are law enforcement options (Campbell, et al. 2001). Recently, in Philadelphia it was discovered that thousands of sexual assault cases were shelved with little or no investigation. And unfortunately, "there is little reason to believe that the problem is unique to Philadelphia" (Lonsway 2002, 3). In the Phoenix Police Department approximately one-third of the sexual assault reports are typically filed as "information only," which means they are not treated as an active criminal case, nor counted in crime statistics. As another example, in 1990, the Oakland Police Department "routinely unfound cases without sufficient investigation. They subsequently re-opened hundreds of cases for investigation" (Lonsway 2002, 4). As a result of these atrocities, victims are denied access to the criminal justice system and perpetrators of sexual assault go undetected and unpunished.

The above obviously leads to the view of police as being indifferent and insensitive toward rape victim cases. This is somewhat of a historically widespread view and as evidenced, not without some empirical support.

False Allegations of Rape

Police officers decisions in rape cases go beyond the decision to found or unfound, or to use legal or extra-legal factors in deciding founding, investigation, or arrest. Police officers also bear the burden of attempting to determine when someone is making a false allegation of rape. Determining a false allegation of rape avoids an injustice to a wrongly accused individual. At the same time, for reasons of professional pride, the police officer does his/her best to avoid looking naïve by falling for a story that turns out false (Holmstrom and Burgess 1978).

Extent of False Allegations

"Prior to the rise of modern feminism in the 1970s, male judges and scholars often indicated that false allegations of acquaintance rape were common. Rape, Sir Mathew Hale instructed an 18th century jury, 'is an accusation easily to be made and once made, hard to be proved, and harder to be defended by the party to be accused tho never so innocent'" (Bryden and Lengnick 1997, 1296).

Definitively calculating the ratio of true to false reports of rape is generally extremely difficult and a highly subjective enterprise (Bryden and Lengnick 1997). A number of scholars have attempted to estimate how often rape reports are false. These studies' conclusions vary radically, with the estimated percentages of false reports ranging from 2 percent (Katz & Mazur as cited in Bryden and Lengnick 1997) to 41 percent (Kanin 1994).

Feldman-Summers and Palmer (1980) found that the police officers who participated in their study would expect that three of every five rape complaints are either untruthful or mistaken. They contend that this belief is likely communicated to the rape victims, even if officers attempt to treat the victims with respect. However, their study, though widely cited, only surveyed approximately fifteen officers.

A two year study of all rape allegations by the New York City Sex Crimes Analysis Squad found that the rate of false allegations for rape and sexual offenses was around two percent. This makes it comparable to false allegations for other crimes (Polly Pattullo cited in Bryden and Lengnick 1997, 1308). In separate research Hursh (1977) examined the Denver police records of 1973. She designated rape reports as false "only if the victim finally admitted that she had originally lied about being attacked or if the police concluded from other evidence that she had lied." Her findings were similar to New York City's findings, as they found that only two to three percent of rape reports were false.

On the other side of the extent of false allegation spectrum, Kanin (1994) examined 109 consecutive rape reports during a nine-year period in a "small metropolitan community." He labeled a complaint false only if the complainant later recanted to the police. Of the 109 forcible rapes, 45 (41%) were false allegations by his definition. Kanin (1994) reasons that the high rates of his study, relative to other studies, are due to departmental policy. The chief of police in the city of study insisted that every rape report be thoroughly investigated, because of the relatively low crime rate of the city. "In other cities, busy police sometimes do not even record the most obviously false rape reports" (Kanin as cited in Bryden and Lengnick 1997). Others contend that maybe the recantations were false, rather than the accusations (Bryden and Lengnick 1997).

Kennedy and Witkowski (2000) claim to have replicated Kanin's study in a suburb of Detroit and found similar results as Kanin. Of the 68 reports of forcible rape 32.3 percent were classified as false by the complainants' own admissions.

Despite the fear of false complaints and despite the conflicting research on rates of false rape allegations, the National Institute of Law Enforcement and Criminal Justice (NILECJ) (1978) justice contends that there is not a disproportionate number of false rape complaints. In addition, those few that are false are readily screened out prior to trial. The NILECJ states that "it is doubtful that a woman would proceed very far with such complaints in the face of the unpleasantness she must endure to pursue.... By crying rape, she faces personal harassment and embarrassment and yet is less likely to succeed in securing a conviction than if, for example, she brought any other charge" (p. 29).

Reasons for Making False Allegations of Rape

Despite the enormous disadvantages outlined above of falsely reporting rape, it may not always be as pathological or stupid as it may sound. False rape allegations appear to serve three major functions for the complainants: providing an alibi, seeking revenge, and obtaining sympathy and attention (Bryden and Lengnick 1997; Kanin 1994). In the replication study of Kanin's the most frequently cited reason for false allegations was alibi, followed by attention/sympathy-getting and only in one instance did the complainant admit to revenge as the primary reason for the false allegation.

Falsely reporting rape provides an alibi in cases where a teenage girl becomes pregnant and instead of confessing to her parents she is sexually active, she claims rape. Seeking revenge may seem logical when, for example, a prostitute whose customer fails to pay for sex may retaliate by falsely accusing him of rape.

Identifying False Allegations of Rape

The National Institute of Law Enforcement and Criminal Justice (1978) suggests that law enforcement is proficient at screening out the occasional false charge. In fact and unfortunately, police officers probably screen out far more than fabricated complaints. However, no one knows which demographic groups, if any, are disproportionately likely to lie to the police about rape, or at least to tell stories that sound less credible than most rape reports (Bryden and Lengnick 1997).

Nonetheless, if means of detecting false allegations of rape arise, it will only serve to better all of the criminal justice system. First, fabrications waste the time and resources of an already overtaxed justice system. Second, for each false report that results in an arrest, a man is imprisoned when he has committed no offense. And third, these falsehoods degrade and trivialize the experience of every legitimate rape survivor who will ever tell her story to the police officer or jury (Fairstein 1993). For the benefit of the victim's emotional state and the betterment of case processing, law enforcement should be advised to approach every allegation of sexual assault as truthful until there is solid evidence to prove otherwise.

Victims' Perceptions of Police in Their Response to Sexual Assault Victims

With respect to the above discussion of documented law enforcement indifference and insensitivity, one may wonder how victims perceive law enforcement services and ultimately how this may impact victim reporting to law enforcement.

Victims' Perceptions of Police Response

While a majority of historical rape literature touts the negative experiences of rape victims with law enforcement, other literature finds the opposite. Holmstrom and Burgess (1978) found that most victims spoke favorably about the police who had questioned them. Only about 10 percent of their sample expressed a negative reaction. Those negative reactions were due to such explanations as police behavior that was perceived as overbearing, harsh or moralistic. Frazier and Haney (as cited in Campbell, et al. 2001) found that victims of sexual assault "held positive attitudes toward investigating officers but were frustrated by the overall response of the criminal justice system" (p. 1241).

On the other hand, coinciding with the historical literature, many women recounted their experiences of police investigations to other researchers disclosing negative encounters and reported feeling disbelieved and unsupported by the police (Brownmiller 1975; Chambers and Millar 1986; Hall 1985; Holmstrom and Burgess 1978; Wright 1984).

Jordan (2001) has conducted the most current study on victims' experiences with law enforcement. Jordon interviewed 48 women with a total of 50 experiences of sexual assault. Jordan found that only 50 percent of the victims expressed overall satisfaction with the police. However, three-quarters of the victims responded that they would encourage other victims to report to the police. The women that were dissatisfied complained of "not feeling believed by the police and of not having their experience understood by law enforcement. Others felt that the police focus on information gathering prevented them from recognizing the needs of victims. The women who were satisfied with law enforcement referred to having their impressions of the police changed for the better as a result of reporting this incident" (p. 694).

Holmstrom and Burgess (1978) stated that "the nature of the material that is discussed—the details of an extremely frightening and humiliating sexual experience—mean that the encounter (with the police) may be unsettling for many victims even under the best of circumstances" (p. 35). Jordan (2001) somewhat echoes those sentiments.

> That the victim is trying to manage the effects of trauma and regain a sense of personal equilibrium at the same time as the police are making excessive demands on her stamina and seeking to establish her veracity as a complainant. Attempts to resolve this inherent conflict can begin only with an acknowledgement of its existence. The police focus is likely to be on the identification and apprehension of the offender, which may or may not be something that the victim can assist with, and may or may not be a goal she shares. What she is likely to need most is to have a sense of safety restored and to be able to heal and reestablish control of her life, something that police are not trained to provide and which some of their procedures may even work against.

The police role is not designed to assist in healing—this role rightly belongs to support workers and therapists, whose involvement can assist both police and victims alike (p. 703).

Reporting Sexual Assault Victimizations to Police

One factor that may reflect victims' perceptions of law enforcement is the level of reporting by victims. Sexual assault is the most underreported crime in American and it has been that way for decades. According to the National Crime Victimization Survey (U.S. Department of Justice 2003) only 38.6 percent of all sexual assaults were reported to law enforcement in 2001.

The most often cited reason of the victim for *not* reporting the crime to law enforcement was "other reasons," followed by "it was considered a personal matter". "Fear of reprisal" was also a concern for many, as well as victims "reported it to another official" (See Table 1) (Greenfeld 1997). The victim-offender relationship appears to impact the decision to report as the closer the relationship between the female victim and the offender, the greater the likelihood that she would not report. When the offender was a current or former husband or boyfriend, about three-fourths of all victims were *not* reported to police. When the offender was a friend or acquaintance, 61 percent of completed rapes were *not* reported to the police. When the offender was a stranger, 54 percent of completed rapes were not reported to the police (Rennison 2002).

The most common reason given by victims of sexual assault for reporting the crime to the police was to stop the incident or prevent it from happening (23.8%), followed by preventing further crimes by the offender against them (14.6%) (See Table 2) (Greenfeld 1997).

Police Innovations in the Investigation of Sexual Assault

In order to improve police response to victims and improve reporting of sexual assault, new police approaches or innovations in handling sexual assault cases have emerged. These new innovations have also been encouraged by the feminist movement, new sexual assault laws in many states, and successful lawsuits against police departments who failed to adequately respond to sexual assault victims (The Associated Press 1994). The approaches to sexual assault cases range from unique forms of training to the involvement of oversight boards.

**Table 1. Percent of Reasons for Not Reporting
Sexual Assault to the Police—2001**

Reasoning	Percent
Other reasons	31.2
It was a personal or private matter	29.4
Fear of reprisal	8.1
Reported to another official	6.7
It was not important enough to report	5.9
Too inconvenient or time consuming	5.7
Offender unsuccessful	5.3
Lack of proof	4.7
Police inefficient, ineffective or biased	2.9

Source: U.S. Department of Justice, Criminal Victimization in the United States, 2001 Statistical Tables

**Table 2. Percent of Reasons for Reporting
Sexual Assault to the Police—2001**

Reasoning	Percent
To stop the incident or prevent it from happening	23.8
To prevent further crimes by offender against victim	14.6
Needed help due to injury	4.5
To recover property	2.1

Source: U.S. Department of Justice, Criminal Victimization in the United States, 2001 Statistical Tables

Training

Almost unheard of 20 years ago, many of today's police officers receive sensitivity training in responding to victims of sexual assault. The research evaluating the value of this training finds that it is having a positive impact for police officers. Lonsway (as cited in Campbell, et al. 2001) evaluated a training intervention with police academy recruits. Her findings suggested that additional instruction on sexual assault and victim interviewing techniques improved recruits' skills, which was positively received by the interviewees. Other research indicates that participation in a rape-awareness program reduces adherence to rape myths (Foubert and Marriott 1997; Proto-Campise, et al. 1998).

Training is now being made available for specific types of sexual assaults as well as types of interviewing techniques. The National Center for Women and Policing recently developed training curriculum targeted for law enforcement in their specific investigation of Acquaintance Sexual Assaults. This curriculum emphasizes investigative tools and techniques for those cases in which a consent defense—rather than identity—is raised (Lonsway 2002).

No matter what the training, Jordan (2001) contends that "stressing victim sensitivity in training programs is wasted effort unless police officers, in their day-to-day policing, are monitored, evaluated and able to be rewarded for displaying competencies in this area. The message needs to be conveyed within the police occupation culture that displaying sensitivity to the needs of victims does not detract from sound law enforcement practice—it *is* sound law enforcement practice" (p. 704).

Specialized Sexual Assault Policing Units

Rather than train all officers with respect to responding to sexual assault victims, some departments have created specialized sex crime units. These units consist of police officers with intense training on responding to sexual assault victims. Police officers are trained to prioritize their response to sexual assault cases and to treat victims with sensitivity while thoroughly investigating cases (Wilson 2002). The purpose of these specialized units is to enhance the agency's efficiency and/or to send a message to the community that the department is deeply committed to solving sex crime (Kilpatrick 2000).

Other departments have developed in-house victim/witness assistance units. These units are usually directed by non-sworn trained individuals that review all reports, sort out the felonies, and contact each victim of a felony crime, usually by phone. "Law enforcement-based victim assistance professionals make referrals to rape crisis centers, contact victims who have delayed reporting, and provide community education in rape awareness and prevention" (Kilpatrick 2000, 21). The purposes of these units are similar to the specialized police officer units as they are looking to make a solid effort in police community relations, as well as provide an improved method of assisting victims in our criminally focused system.

Coordinated Care Teams

Selected communities throughout the United States have developed coordinated care programs which attempt to bring together police, prosecutors, doctors, nurses, social workers, and rape victim advocates to work as an integrated team in assisting rape survivors. The sexual assault response team concept was developed in California. This model involves a "coordinated response among various professionals to meet the needs of the assault victim and to collect physical evidence associated with the complaint" (Wilson 2002, 15). Team members work together to ensure a sensitive, thorough investigation. The benefits of the team approach is that members attend professional training, stay abreast of current research and developments, and thoroughly network among other entities in the community and criminal justice system (Wilson 2002). Police departments have found that these teams benefit them in that they receive reliable, consistent medical examinations, which yield more accurate and relevant information than previously available (Wilson 2002).

Overall, these coordinated care teams have yet to be evaluated as to their effectiveness in assisting the rape survivor. Nonetheless, the U. S. Department of Justice (1994) contends that the coordinated programs "helped maintain a successful stance against rape" (as cited in Campbell, et al. 2001).

Blind Reporting System

One innovative approach to encouraging the reporting of sexual assault victimizations is by offering an anonymous telephone reporting system. Blind reporting of sexual assault benefits victims, law enforcement and the community as well. First, it allows victims to share critical information with law enforcement without requiring that victim to sacrifice confidentiality. It also allows victims an opportunity to gather procedural information about the criminal justice system without having to immediately commit to an investigation. If handled appropriately, this may ultimately encourage an otherwise unwilling victim to report (Garcia and Henderson 1999).

Blind reporting enables law enforcement to gain information about crimes of sexual violence that likely otherwise will go unreported. The current statistics of sexual assault reflect only a fraction of the violations that occur. Via the blind reporting, law enforcement may be able to gather information about local offenders' patterns of behaviors or the characteristics of emerging high risk situations or locations. This, in theory, allows investigators a clearer picture of sexual violence in their communities. In addition, some blind reports become full reports and lead to investigations and subsequent prosecutions. Others provide useful information for investigation of other cases (Garcia and Henderson 1999).

The community benefits by blind reporting because they are getting more complete information about sexual violence in their community. When law enforcement can determine dangerous scenarios based upon past offending behaviors, they can better educate the public. This in turn may improve community relations and possibly garner information on other neighborhood crime problems (Garcia and Henderson 1999).

Citizen Oversight of Sexual Assault Investigations

In the last couple of decades there have been many law enforcement agencies across the country that have established citizen oversight mechanisms of police misconduct. These are mechanisms which involve non-sworn individuals at some point in the evaluation process of citizen complaints (Walker and Kreisel 1996). This concept has been developed as a means of evaluating and classifying sexual assault complaints in the Philadelphia Police Department. Members of women's organizations from the community are selected to serve on the oversight mechanism. The oversight mechanism was prompted by the disclosure that the department for years mislabeled rapes as lesser offenses or shelved cases altogether. The group will oversee the process as police evaluate complaints and will be "the final say" on the classification of sexual assaults (Anonymous 2000b).

Evaluation of Innovative Approaches

Evaluations of many of these new initiatives are yet to be conducted. However, initial discussions of such initiatives indicate that officers are more sympathetic toward, and hold more positive attitudes about, victims of sexual assault (Campbell 1995; Campbell and Johnson 1997; Temkin 1996). Nonetheless, in order for the improvements and innovations to be effective at improving police responses and investigations to sexual assault victims, they must be touted starting with the administration, for they are individuals that set the tone of expected behavior for an entire department. Recently in Philadelphia the Police Commissioner, John F. Timoney, announced that he was going to improve the response of his Special Victims Unit by instigating a "major overhaul" of the unit. Reforms included retiring and reassigning some officers and adopting a policy that requires investigators to be more sympathetic to victims who come to police for assistance (Anonymous 2000a).

Administration needs to be committed to changing the occupational subculture of policing that exacerbates the rape myths and insensitive responses or little substantive improvement in the police response to rape complaints can realistically be expected (Jordan 2001). Jordan and others may be getting the message out there as many departments across the country currently, ap-

pear to be expressing verbal and attitudinal commitment to victim's needs by
the top levels of administration (The Associated Press 1994).

Police Guidelines on Approaching
Victims of Sexual Assault

Whether or not a police agency has an improved or innovative approach to
sexual assault victims, there are guidelines and materials that law enforcement
agencies can provide for their officers. Police of all aspects can assimilate the
following information to be utilized with many victims of crime, but especially victims of sexual assault.

There are three major needs of victims of crime that can apply to victims
of sexual assault. First is the need of victims to feel some sense of safety again.
Second, victims need to express their emotions whether or not law enforcement feels it is valuable for the clearance of the case. And third, victims need
to know what comes next after their victimization. Therefore, it is essential
law enforcement inform victims of the process ahead of them and the resources
that are available to victims (Woods 2001).

More specific to victims of sexual assault, Woods (2001) writing for the Office for the Victims of Crime, offers the following tips.

- Be prepared for virtually any type of emotional reaction by victims. Be
  unconditionally supportive and permit victims to express their emotions,
  which may include, crying, angry outbursts and screaming.
- Avoid interpreting the victims' calmness or composure as evidence that
  a sexual assault did or did not occur. The victim could be in shock.
- Approach victims calmly. Showing your outrage at the crime may cause
  victims even more trauma.
- Ask victims whether they would like to contact a family member or friend.
- Offer to contact a sexual assault crisis counselor. Ask victims whether
  they prefer a male or female counselor. In addition, ask the victims
  whether they would prefer talking with your or a law enforcement officer of the opposite sex.
- Be careful not to appear overprotective or patronizing.
- Remember that it is normal for victims to want to forget, or to actually
  forget, details of the crime that are difficult for them to accept.
- Encourage victims to get medical attention, especially to check for possible internal injuries. In addition, a medical examination can provide evidence for the apprehension and prosecution of the victim's assailant.

Keep in mind, however, that victims may feel humiliated and embarrassed that their bodies were exposed during the sexual assault and must be exposed again during the medical examination. Explain what will take place forensically during the examination and why these procedures are important.

- Notify the hospital of the incoming victim/patient and request a private waiting room. Escort victim to the hospital. If no crisis intervention counselor is available, wait at the hospital until the victim is released and escort her to her destination.
- Be mindful of the personal, interpersonal, and privacy concerns of the victims. They may have a number of concerns, including the possibility of having been impregnated or contracting sexually transmitted diseases such as the AIDS virus; the reactions of their spouse, mate, or parents; media publicity that may reveal their experience to the public; and the reactions and criticism of neighbors and coworkers if they learn about the sexual assault.
- Interview victims with extreme sensitivity. Minimize the number of times victims must recount details of the crime to strangers. If possible, only one law enforcement officer should be assigned to the initial interview and subsequent investigation.
- Offer to answer any further questions victims may have and provide any further assistance they may need.
- Encourage victims to get counseling. Explain that your recommendation for counseling is based on having seen other victims benefit from it in the past. Explain that they may experience posttraumatic stress symptoms in the next few months. Identify and refer them to support services for assistance (Woods 2001, 8–10; Kilpatrick 2000).

Conclusion

Sexual assault cases can prove to be challenging for many law enforcement officers. How those police officers respond and make discretionary decisions in these cases can make a tremendous impact on the victims' emotional well-being, as well as determining if and how the case will be processed through the criminal justice system. Because of the unique nature of sexual assault cases, there appears to sincerely be a need for all law enforcement to be specifically trained on the sensitivity and delicateness of approaching and investigating sexual assault cases. Law enforcement officers' responses to victims appear to be on the appropriate path of improvement, but there is still room for additional advancement by many police officers.

"It's not enough to just have good police skills; you must be able to interact professionally with the victim, or she is likely to withdraw her cooperation and drop out of the investigative effort. When this occurs, a sex offender escapes justice. He is free to continue his acts, reinforced in the belief that law enforcement is powerless to stand in his way" (Albrecht 2000, 57).

References

Albrecht, S. "Crime Scenes and Rape Investigations." *Law and Order 48* no. 11, (2000): 55–57.

Anonymous. "Women's Groups Oversee Sex Cases." *Law and Order 48* no. 4, (2000a): 6.

Anonymous. "Philadelphia Changes Rules for Rape Unit." *Crime Control Digest 34* no. 50, (2000b): 2–3.

Associated Press, The. "Crime Victims' Rights: Sensitizing Police to Victims' Needs." *The New York Times*, June 12, 1994.

Battelle Law and Justice Study Center. *Forcible Rape: Police Volume*. Washington D.C.: U.S. Government Printing Office, 1978.

Brownmiller, S. *Against Our Will: Men, Women and Rape*. Harmondsworth: Penguin, 1975.

Bryden, D. P. and S. Lengnick. "Rape in the Criminal Justice System." *The Journal of Criminal Law and Criminology 87* no. 4, (1997): 1195–1384.

Campbell, R. "The Role of Work Experience and Individual Beliefs in Police officers' Perceptions of Date Rape: An Integration of Quantitative and Qualitative Methods." *American Journal of Community Psychology 23*, (1995): 249–277.

Campbell, R., and C. R. Johnson. "Police Officers' Perceptions of Rape." *Journal of Interpersonal Violence 12*, (1997): 255–274.

Campbell, R., S. M. Wasco, C. E. Ahrens, T. Sefi, and H. E. Barnes. "Preventing the 'Second Rape': Rape Survivors' Experiences with Community Service Providers." *Journal of Interpersonal Violence 16* no 12, (2001): 1239–1260.

Carrington, K., and P. Watson. "Policing Sexual Violence: Feminism, Criminal Justice, and Governmentality." *International Journal of the Sociology of Law 24*, (1996): 253–272.

Chambers, G. and A. Millar. *Prosecuting Sexual Assault*. Edinburgh: Scottish Office Central Research Unit, 1986.

Chandler, S. M., and M. Torney. "The Decisions and Processing of Rape Victims Throughout the Criminal Justice System." *Sociologist* 4 no. 155, (1981).

Doerner, W. G., and S. P. Lab. *Victimology* 2nd ed. Cincinnati, OH: Anderson Publishing Co., 1998.

Fairstein, L. A. *Sexual Violence: Our War Against Rape.* New York: William Morrow and Co., 1993.

Federal Bureau of Investigation. *Crime in the United States—2001.* Washington D.C.: U.S. Government Printing Office, 2002.

Feldman-Summers, S., and G. C. Palmer. "Rape as Viewed by Judges, Prosecutors and Police Officers." *Criminal Justice and Behavior 7* no. 19, (1980): 36.

Foubert, J. D., and K. A. Marriott. "Effects of a Sexual Assault Peer Program on Men's Belief in Rape Myths." *Sex Roles* 36, (1997): 259–268.

Garcia, S., and M. Henderson. "Blind Reporting of Sexual Violence." *FBI Law Enforcement Bulletin 68* no. 6, (1999): 12–16.

Greenfeld, L. A. Sex *Offenses and Offenders: An Analysis of Data on Rape and Sexual Assault.* Washington, D. C.: U.S. Department of Justice, 1997.

Greenwood, P. *The Criminal Investigation Process.* Santa Monica, CA: Rand, 1975.

Hall, R. *Ask Any Women: A London Inquiry into Rape and Sexual Assault.* Brison: Falling Wall Press, 1985.

Hazelwood, R. R. and A. W. Burgess. "The Behavioral-Oriented Interview of Rape Victims: The Key to Profiling." In *Practical Aspects of Rape Investigation: A Multidisciplinary Approach,* eds. R. R. Hazelwood and A. W. Burgess, 151–168. New York: Elseveir, 1987.

Holmstrom, L. L., and A. W. Burgess. *The Victim of Rape: Institutional Reactions.* New York: Jon Wiley, 1978.

Hursch, C. J. *The Trouble with Rape.* Chicago: Nelson Hall, 1977.

Jordan, J. "Worlds Apart? Women, Rape and the Police Reporting Process." *British Journal of Criminology 41,* (2001): 679–706.

Kanin, E. J. "False Rape Allegations." *Archives of Sexual Behavior 23* no. 1 (1994): 84–85.

Kennedy, D. B. and M. J. Witkowski. "False Allegations of Rape Revisited: A Replication of the Kanin Study." *Journal of Security Administration 23* no. 1, (2000): 41–48.

Kerstetter, W. A. "Gateway to Justice: Police and Prosecutorial Response to Sexual Assault against Women." *Journal of Criminal Law and Criminology 81,* (1990).

Kilpatrick, D. "Chapter 9: Sexual Assault." In *1999 National Victim Assistance Academy,* eds. G. Coleman, M. Gaboury, M. Murray and A. Seymour. Washington D. C: Office for Victims of Crime, 2000.

LeDoux, J. C. and R. R. Hazelwood. "Police Attitudes and Beliefs Toward Rape." *Journal of Police Science and Administration 13*, (1985): 211–220.

LaFree, G. D. "Official Reactions to Social Problems: Police Decisions in Sexual Assault Cases." *Social Problems 82* no. 582, (1981).

Lonsway, K. A. "Sexual Assault Cases." *Women Police 36* no. 1, (2002): 3–7.

Merrill, W. F. "The Art of Interrogating Rapists." *FBI Law Enforcement Bulletin 64* no. 1, (1995): 8–12.

National Institute of Law Enforcement and Criminal Justice (NILECJ*). Forcible Rape: An Analysis of Legal Issues*. Washington D. C.: US Government Printing Office, 1978.

Proto-Campise, L., J. Belknap, and J. Wooldredge. "High School Students' Adherence to Rape Myths and the Effectiveness of High School Rape-Awareness Programs." *Violence Against Women 4*, (1998): 308–328.

Rennison, C. M. *Rape and Sexual Assault: Reporting to Police and Medical Attention, 1992–2000*. Washington D. C.: U.S. Department of Justice, 2002.

Temkin, J. "Doctors, Rape and Criminal Justice." *The Howard Journal 35*, (1996): 1–20.

Tjaden, P., and N. Thoennes. *Prevalence, Incidence, and Consequences of Violence Against Women: Findings from the National Violence Against Women Survey*. Atlanta, GA: Center for Disease Control and Prevention, Center for Injury Prevention and Control, 1998.

U.S. Department of Justice. *Criminal Victimization in the United States, 2001 Statistical Tables*. Washington D. C.: Bureau of Justice Statistics, 2003.

Walker, S. and B. W. Kreisel. "Varieties of Citizen Review: The Implications of Organizational Features of Complaint Review Procedures for Accountability of the Police." *American Journal of Police 15* no. 3, (1996): 65–88.

Wilson, C. R. "Police and the Sexual Assault Examination." *FBI Law Enforcement Bulletin 71* no. 1, (2002): 14–17.

Woods, T. O. *First Response to Victims of Crime: A Handbook for Law Enforcement Officers on How to Approach and Help Elderly Victims, Victims of Sexual Assault, Child Victims, Victims of Domestic Violence, Survivors of Homicide Victims*, 2001. Available online: http://www.ojp.usdoj.gove/ovc/publications/infores/firstrep/2001/NCJ189631.pdf (retrieved June 2003).

Wright, R. "A Note on Attrition of Rape Cases." *British Journal of Criminology 24* no. 4, (1984): 399–400.

Special Feature

In the Words of a Police Officer

The most challenging aspects of my work are:

- Making the criminal justice system non-intimidating and non-victimizing for the victim
- Convincing a prosecutor that the victim did not "ask" or "deserve" to be raped
- Educating first responding officers in appropriate methods of interviewing victims

When I attended the police academy in 1985, there was little, if any training about investigating sex crimes. My training came from various conferences and training sessions throughout the years, and much of it was self-initiated due to my interest.

To get more sex crime victims to report their victimization, there would need to be a societal attitude change regarding sex crime victims. Since the majority of sex crimes are committed by non-strangers, the tendency is to focus on what the victim did or did not do to put themselves in a risky situation, therefore minimizing the crime and blaming the victim. If all sex crime victims were treated as victims, and sex crime offenders were treated and punished as criminals, it is more likely that victims would report these crimes.

I also believe that victim advocacy plays a very important role in encouraging a victim to report the incident and continue to assist in the investigation. Well-trained, well-funded victim advocacy programs are essential to an effective sexual assault intervention. Victim advocates can help recognize and minimize some of the re-victimization that might occur, if the advocate accompanies the victim throughout the process.

Although I work in the prevention and education field, and I encourage all victims to report crimes to the police and provide many reasons for reporting it, I wonder if I would follow that advice myself. I have a 15 year old daughter, and I often wonder if she were sexually assaulted by an acquaintance if I would encourage her to report the incident to the police, knowing what she would likely be put through. More often than not, the report results in little or no consequences for the offender, and a high likelihood that she would be re-victimized by the system.

Suggestion to improve the CJS with respect to sex crime victims and offenders: The thing that seems to be working in the domestic violence and sexual assault areas are specialized units and coordinated responses that consist of specially trained law enforcement, victim advocacy, social services, prosecution, and courts that focus specifically on domestic violence or sexual assault.

Improving the system would require changing attitudes and beliefs. I think a jurisdiction could spend a lot of time spinning wheels trying to change attitudes and beliefs of those within the system with authority to make the improvements. Even the best written policies, protocols and laws are useless if those in positions of implementing them choose not to do so. Sometimes it takes a specialized, coordinated unit made up of those who already have a demonstrated understanding of sex crimes, the victims and the offenders to really make an improvement.

The other suggestion is to continue, expand and coordinate efforts to involve males in becoming part of the solution to prevent violence against women and to ensure the offenses are treated in the system as serious crimes. Since females are most often the victims, it is important for male role models to join the efforts to end violence against women, and realize that by allowing the system to continue in this manner, they become part of the problem. The system could benefit from the majority of males who are not sex offenders taking a leading role in reducing the incidents and holding offenders accountable.

I have investigated 5–10 sex crimes per calendar year.
18 years in police work.

Kim Vansell
Police/Community Services Sergeant
Department of Public Safety
Central Missouri State University

Report Exposes Lie Detector Tests That Await Some Ohio Rape Victims

While it was never a secret, neither did dozens of Ohio police departments make it widely known that they administered polygraphs and other truth-verification tests to victims in sexual assault cases—that is, until a draft report by the state Department of Health brought the practice to light in February.

The study, conducted by a task force created in 2002 to examine how rape cases are prosecuted, found the practice to be widespread.

"We've let an awful lot of victims down," said W. Duncan Whitney, a Delaware County Common Pleas judge. "I have heard a lot of counties say they are doing well, but they are taking only the easy cases."

Among the 10 key recommendations made by the task force was that all counties adopt "quality local protocols" that would establish an appropriate response to victims and support the pursuit of justice.

Whitney, a former prosecutor who served on the task force, blamed lazy police officials for not aggressively pursuing rape cases. He told The Columbus Dispatch that he was appalled to learn that polygraphs were used to gauge a victim's credibility.

Not true, police insist.

Lie-detectors and computerized voice-stress analyzers (CVSA), officials says, are used strictly as an investigative tool, on a voluntary basis, and only in those cases where it would help uncover the guilt or identity of an offender. Investigators will use them, however, when a victim's allegations raise red flags, particularly in cases of acquaintance rape, or when the accused is a family member.

"Obviously, you do this with sensitivity," said Chief Walter Ugrinic of the Shaker Heights Police Department, in an interview with Law Enforcement News. "The operator also has to have a talent to sometimes help the person remember issues. In some cases it brings up deception, but in most cases it brings up evidence to help in the identity of a suspect—that's why we use it."

The Shaker Heights department is one of 40 in the state that engages in the lie-detection practice, according to the Ohio Coalition on Sexual Assault.

Ed Roberts, a probation officer who retired in 1999 from the Fairfield Police Department, where he had headed the agency's detective bureau, said truth-verification tests were never administered arbitrarily, nor were they routine in sexual assault investigations.

When a case involved a forcible rape where there was perhaps a break-in, a test was given if the information provided by the victim did not match the physical evidence found at the scene. More often, however, the tests were administered when the victim and the offender knew each other.

"Let's just say it was a forcible rape and your victim didn't know the person, broke into the house, maybe caught them outside—that would be probably be the last person you would give a truth-verification test to," he told LEN.

Investigators would be more apt to use a CVSA when the victim's version of the situation is completely different from the story police are getting from the alleged offender, said Roberts.

In those cases—although CVSA tests are not admissible in court—having the victim pass a polygraph gives police leverage against the accused, said Detective Sgt. Steven Truitt of the Miami University of Ohio Police Department.

"We talk to him and say, 'Hey, it's your word against the young lady's. She has come in and shown us she believes what she's saying by taking a truth-verification test, you up for the task?' It encourages him, so we get a nice one-on-one, prolonged conversation with the individual," he told LEN.

The point of the tests is not to embarrass a victim, or question anyone's integrity, said Ugrinic. "We don't put them on the polygraph to find out if it's true," he said, adding that if a victim does not want to take the test, police will still pursue the investigation.

But victims' advocates content that since the tests cannot be used in court, using them only serves to inflict further trauma.

Stacy Kitchen, executive director of the Ohio Coalition on Sexual Assault, contends that the stress victims are under could appear on a polygraph or CVSA as lying. Moreover, she told LEN, just because a victim might not be forthcoming with police, or her story does not add up to investigators, does not mean she is not telling the truth.

Yet unless legislation prohibits police from using truth-verification tests, it is unlikely that the practice would stop, Kitchen said, given that agencies find the tests very effective.

"What we would like is to see is some very strict guidelines in place, and if we could work together with law enforcement on that, we would be happy to do that," she said. "But we do not support the use of these devices at all."

While it is natural that victims' advocates would oppose what appears to be an unsupportive stance by police, Truitt noted that it is law enforcement's job to remain open-minded.

"Anything you say to the victim that makes it seem you may have doubts about what she's told you is naturally going to be met with a certain amount of resentment because that's not seen as the proper thing to do," he said. "Unfortunately, in our line of work, we've got to maintain a certain open-minded approach to the thing, and we can't go into it with preset attitude of this guy is guilty, we're just going to hang him out to dry. We have to look at it from a practical standpoint, provide as much support for the cases as we can."

Law Enforcement News, John Jay College of Criminal Justice/CUNY. April 15, 2003, page 1,10.

Chapter 17

Prosecution of Sex Crimes

Jeffrey W. Spears

Introduction

Someone walked over and asked what we were talking about. About rape, I replied; no, actually about cases that aren't really rape. The D.A. looked puzzled. That was rape, he said. Technically. She was forced to have sex without consent. It just wasn't a case you prosecute.

—Susan Estrich, *Real Rape*

In general, after a sexual assault suspect has been arrested, the next step in the criminal justice process is to notify the prosecutor that a crime has been committed and that a suspect has been arrested. Prosecutors then review the facts and evidence presented to them, evaluate the case, and decide if charges should be filed or rejected (Jacoby 1980). The importance of this initial screening decision is indicated by the fact that from one-third to one-half of all felony arrests do not result in the filing of felony charges (Boland 1983; Brosi 1979). As you can see, very few cases make it past this initial screening decision and even fewer actually make it to trial. For example, a recent survey by the Bureau of Justice Statistics indicated that 96 percent of felony convictions were the result of a guilty plea, not a trial (Reaves 2001). Clearly, the prosecutor plays an important gatekeeping function that determines the character of the American criminal justice system (Jacoby 1980; Kerrstetter 1990).

The extensive exercise of discretion by decision makers is a defining feature of the American criminal justice system. The prosecutor is a key figure and decides who will be charged, what charge will be filed, who will be offered a plea bargain, and the type of bargain to be offered. The prosecutor also may recommend the sentence the offender should receive. As Supreme Court Justice Jackson observed in 1940, "the prosecutor has more control over life, liberty, and reputation than any other person in America" (Davis 1969, 190).

The most crucial discretionary decision made by the prosecutor is the initial decision to prosecute or not. Prosecutors have nearly unfettered discretion in making this decision; there are no legislative or judicial guidelines on charging and a decision not to file charges is immune from review. In fact, the United States Supreme Court, in *Bordenkircher v. Hayes* [434 U.S. 357, 364 (1978)], examined this prosecutorial decision. The Court ruled that, "so long as the prosecutor has probable cause to believe that the accused committed an offense defined by statute, the decision whether or not to prosecute, and what charge to file or bring before a grand jury, generally rests entirely in his discretion" [*Bordenkircher v. Hayes*, 434 U.S. 357, 364 (1978)].

Although a prosecutor's discretion is significant, there have been some limits placed on it. Specifically, the Supreme Court has found that a prosecutor's decision to charge a suspect may not be "deliberately based upon an unjustifiable standard such as race, religion, or other arbitrary classification" [*Bordenkircher v. Hayes*, 434 U.S. 357, at 364 (1978)]. In general, this finding compels the prosecutor to use only legally relevant information when deciding whether or not to prosecute a suspect.

Research on the charging decision has generally concluded that prosecutors attempt to "avoid uncertainty" (Albonetti 1987). What this means is that, if, after the initial screening, prosecutors believe that they can obtain a conviction, they will file charges. On the other hand, if they believe the likelihood of a conviction is low, they will reject the case. In making this determination, several factors come into play.

Legal factors are the primary determinants of the charging decision. For example, the seriousness of the offense (Albonetti 1987; Jacoby, et al. 1982; Mather 1979; Miller 1969; Myers 1982; Rauma 1984; Schmidt and Steury 1989), the strength of evidence in the case (Albonetti 1987; Feeney, et al. 1983; Jacoby, et al. 1982; Miller 1969; Nagel and Hagan 1983), and the culpability of the defendant (Albonetti 1987; Mather 1979; Miller 1969; Schmidt and Steury 1989; Swiggert and Farrell 1976) have been found to influence prosecutors' charging decisions.

In addition to legal factors, many studies have highlighted the importance of victim characteristics (Albonetti 1987; Amir 1971; Hepperle 1985; Kerstetter 1990; Miller 1969; Stanko 1988; Williams 1978). These studies suggest that prosecutors use stereotypes about genuine victims and appropriate behavior (Estrich 1987; Frohmann 1991; LaFree 1989) to predict how judges and juries will react to victims. Prosecutors attribute credibility to victims "who fit society's stereotypes of who is credible: older, white, male, employed victims" (Stanko

1988, 172). Victims who do not fit this image or who engage in "precipatory behavior" (Amir 1971) are deemed less credible. As Stanko (1988, 170) concludes, "the character and credibility of the victim is a key factor in determining prosecutorial strategies, one at least as important as 'objective' evidence about the crime or characteristics of the defendant."

In this chapter, I summarize a number of studies that have examined prosecutorial decision making in sexual assault cases. In addition, I also will briefly discuss rape law reform.

Prosecutorial Decision Making in Sexual Assault Cases

In a widely cited study, LaFree (1989) examines the decisions made by police, prosecutors, judges, and jurors in Indianapolis. He found that the strongest predictors of these decisions were legal factors such as the ability of the victim to identify the suspect, the offense type, and the use of a weapon. Several extralegal variables, however, also were important. Evidence of victim misconduct, the victim's age, the promptness of the victim's report, and the racial composition of the offender-victim dyad influenced decision making. For example, victim misconduct or nonconformity was defined as women who had illegitimate children, who were out alone late at night, were at a bar alone, or were hitchhiking. Cases with victims that fell into one of these categories were less likely to have charges filed, and, if charged, more likely to end in an acquittal. The importance of this is illustrated by a comment made by a prosecutor that LaFree interviewed (1989, 100): "It's tough to try the case if the victim comes across as being loose, or if the victim has frequented bars. Also important is where she was when she was picked up and what time of the night it occurred." He concluded (p. 241) that while decisions in rape cases were affected by the "typifications of rape held by processing agents," they also were "influenced strongly by considerations that most observers would interpret as justified."

Another study examined the processing of sexual assault cases in Chicago. Kerstetter (1990) looked at the prosecutor's decision to file charges against sexual suspects. This decision and the police officer's decision to treat the incident as a crime forms what Kerstetter (1990, 268) refers to as the "gateway to the criminal justice system." As he notes, "these decisions determine which incidents will be taken seriously and which victims will be afforded the full redress of criminal law" (1990, 268). Generally, what happens in Chicago after the police have arrested a suspect, an assistant prosecutor meets with police officers to discuss the case and review the evidence (Kerstetter 1990). They also may interview the victim and offender. Once this is finished, the prosecutor decides whether or not to charge the suspect.

Kerstetter (1990) found that prosecutors were more likely to reject charges in cases where the victims and suspects knew each other. In cases where the victim did not know the suspect, the decision to file charges was positively associated with the victim's willingness to prosecute, and negatively associated with the victim being unable to identify the suspect, the suspects use of a disguise, and a delay in reporting the incident by the victim (Kerstetter 1990). He suggests that, in the prosecutor 's eyes, the reporting delay may be an indicator of the victim's credibility. In other words, the prosecutor knows from previous experience with sexual assault cases that this may cause problems with the case later down the road.

Frohmann (1991) examined case rejection decisions by prosecutors in sexual assault cases. During a 17 month period, she sat in on conversations between detectives and prosecutors regarding the decision about going forward with the case. In addition to this, she also conducted interviews with prosecutors and police detectives to determine how and why they decided not to go forward with the case. Frohmann (1990) made the point that these decisions are made within the organizational context of the prosecutor's office. For example, when a prosecutor make the decision to charge or not, they always have in the back of their mind that they must maintain a high conviction rate high for the office. In addition to the conviction rate for the office, they also need to keep their individual conviction rate high because this indicates that they are proficient at their job and, thus, deserving of promotion. This is not unique to the jurisdiction in her study; most, if not all, prosecutors' offices make decisions about cases with this in mind.

Frohmann indicates that "a central feature of prosecutorial accounts of case rejection is the discrediting of victims' allegations of sexual assault" (1990, 215). Several techniques are used to accomplish this. One is what she refers to as "discrepant accounts." If the victim's accounts of the incident are consistent throughout the criminal justice process, the prosecutor tends to view the victim as credible. On the other hand, if her accounts have "discrepancies," the credibility of the victim is questioned by the prosecutor. In cases such as the latter, the prosecutor may be unwilling to file because, for example, they don't believe the victim's story.

Another method of determining the truthfulness of an allegation of sexual assault is using what Frohmann (1990, 217) refers to as "typifications of rape-relevant behavior." Essentially, what this is referring to is knowledge that has been gained based on their experience as a prosecutor. Put simply, rape victims are expected to act a certain way, and, if they don't, their credibility is called into question. She has several categories of these typifications, all of which have a negative effect on the prosecutor's decision to charge a suspect. The first one she discussed was "typifications of rape scenarios" (Frohmann 1990, 217). What she is referring to here is that prosecutors tend to ascribe certain characteristics to different types of sexual assaults and that they compare these with the victim's version of the rape. If they don't fit a prosecutor's typification, the prosecutor then questions the credibility of the victim's accusation. Another category is "typifications of post-incident interaction." The prosecutors in her study pointed out that the typical behavior after a rape is for the victim and suspect not to see one another. Consequently, when they get a case where the victim voluntarily sees the suspect after the rape has occurred, they immediately question the woman's truthfulness.

The third category is "typifications of rape reporting." The focus here is on the timeliness of the report. The belief here is that if the woman was raped, she will report this to the police very soon after the assault. If the "woman reports 'late,' her motives for reporting and the sincerity of her allegation are questioned if they fall outside the typification of officially recognizable/explainable reasons for late reporting" (Frohmann 1990, 219). A justifiable reason is, for example, getting family support first. The importance of reporting soon after the assault is that, if there are injuries, they will still be visible and corroborate her story. The final category is "typifications of victim's demeanor." The focus here is the ability to "distinguish between behavior that signifies 'lying' versus 'discomfort'" (Frohmann 199, 220). People who are lying, according to the prosecutors interviewed in this study, act a certain way. Yawning a lot or acting nervous during an interview is an indicator of lying. Prosecutors are unwilling to file charges in cases with a victim like this either because they think she is lying or she will make a poor witness at the trial. Frohmann (1990, 224) concludes "that prosecutors are orienting to a 'downstream' concern with convictability."

Another study by Spears and Spohn (1996) focused on the prosecutors' initial decision of whether to file charges. Using a sample of arrests for sexual assault made by the Detroit Police Department in 1989, they tested the hypothesis that charging decisions are affected by prosecutors' stereotypes concerning real rapes and genuine victims. The authors, were particularly interested in the concept of the "genuine victim." Estrich (1987), LaFree (1989) and others suggest that criminal justice decision makers, including prosecutors, use a set of victim characteristics to create an image, not of a *typical* rape victim, but of a *genuine* rape victim. They argue that complainants whose backgrounds and behavior conform to this image will be taken more seriously, and their allegations treated more seriously, than complainants whose backgrounds and behavior are at odds with this image.

They used six factors to create a scale designed to measure the degree to which the victim conforms to the stereotype of a genuine victim. The authors believe that prosecutors ascribe certain characteristics to the genuine victim of a sexual assault. According to Spears and Spohn (1996), prosecutors define the genuine victim as a woman whose moral character is not in question, who did not engage in any type of risk-taking behavior at the time of the incident, who was raped by a stranger, who demonstrated her nonconsent by both screaming and physically resisting her attacker, and who reported the crime to the police immediately. The more closely the victim conforms to this image of the genuine victim, the more likely it is that the prosecutor will decide to file charges.

Their results suggest that victim characteristics, but not evidence factors, affect prosecutors' charging decisions. In fact, the only significant predictors of charging in these types of cases were the age of the victim and the genuine victim scale (Spears and Spohn 1996). Prosecutors in Detroit are much less likely to file charges if the victim is under age 13. They are more likely to file charges if the victim conforms more closely to the image of the genuine victim. In other words, prosecutors believe that the genuine victim of a sexual assault is a woman whose background and behavior conform to traditional gender-role expectations. The more closely the victim conforms to this stereotypical image, the more likely it is she will be viewed as a genuine victim, her assault as a real rape. It's important to note that the *only* factors that influenced the decision to charge were victim characteristics. None of the evidence variables influenced the prosecutor's decision to charge or not. This conflicts with the United States Supreme Court's decision in *Bordenkircher v. Hayes*.

Spohn and Horney (1996) examined the impact of rape law reform on several case processing decisions. The decision to dismiss all charges against the defendant will be discussed here. Once charges are filed, the prosecutor or the defense attorney can motion to have the charges dismissed. The judge then decides whether or not to grant the motion and dismiss the charges. The authors found that charges were less likely to be dismissed when the victim screamed during the attack. They also found that the length of time between the rape and reporting had an influence on the dismissal decision. Spohn and Horney (1996) found that when the victim reported the rape to the police within one hour, charges were less likely to be dismissed. The number of charges also had an influence. The likelihood of charge dismissal was less when the defendant was charged with more than one offense.

A study by Spears and Spohn (1997), looked at the effect of evidence factors and victim characteristics on prosecutors' charging decisions in sexual assault cases. None of the evidence factors had a significant influence on this decision. However, three of the victim characteristics were statistically significant. For example, the victim's moral character influenced the charging decision. Specifically, if the police file contained information about the victim's prior sexual activity with someone other than the suspect, pattern of alcohol and/or drug abuse, prior criminal record, information about alleged prostitution, or history of working as an exotic dancer and/or in a massage parlor, prosecutors were less likely to file charges.

Another variable in the study measured the victim's risk-taking behavior at the time of the incident. Prosecutors were less likely to file charges against the defendant when the police file indicated that the victim was walking alone late at night, was hitch-hiking, was in a bar alone, was using alcohol or drugs, or invited the suspect to her residence (Spears and Spohn 1997). The age of the victim also had a statistically significant effect of the prosecutor's charging decision. When the victim was younger than 13, prosecutors were less likely to file charges against the defendant. Previous research has demonstrated that sexual assault cases involving children are more difficult to prosecute. This reflects the fact that children may be unable to articulate what happened to them. It also reflects the fact that children who allege that they have been sexually assaulted are regarded as more impressionable and thus as less credible than older victims. The authors suggest that these factors, coupled with concerns about the psychological impact of testifying at trial, apparently affect prosecutors' assessments of convictability and produce a higher rejection rate for cases with child victims (Spears and Spohn 1997).

In a continuation of her research discussed above, Frohmann (1997) discovered another method used by prosecutors to justify case rejection in sexual assault cases. She refers to this as the "construction of discordant locales." Essentially, she argues that "discordant locales are prosecutors' categorizations of places and people associated with them that they encounter in the work of case prosecution" (1997). In other words, certain places have a certain type of person that resides there and from this, the prosecutor makes an assessment about the person's moral character. For example, victims and potential jurors often come different areas of the city. This causes a problem for prosecutors because it "may lead to misinterpretations by jurors of victims that would result in 'not guilty' verdicts if cases were forwarded." Consequently, prosecutors use this as a reason to reject the case.

A final study, (Spohn, Beichner, and Davis-Frenzel 2001), replicated and extended the works of Frohmann discussed above. Using data from Miami, they examined the prosecutor's decision to reject sexual assault cases. The authors point out that, in Miami, the prosecutor provides a summary of the disposition of each case. This "closeout memorandum" was reviewed to determine the reasons given by the prosecutor for rejecting the case (2001). In addition to this, Spohn also interviewed several prosecutors that were assigned to the Dade County State's Attorney's Office. This is important because it provided the authors with an additional source of information to supplement the information obtained in the closeout memorandum.

They found that approximately 41 percent of the sexual assault cases were rejected by the State's Attorney. They found that prosecutors rejected charges for the following reasons: the victim did not come to the pre-file interview or they could not locate them, the victim did not cooperate or she asked that the case not be prosecuted, the victim recanted her testimony, there were inconsistencies in the victim's story, or the prosecutor believed that the victim was lying (Spohn, Beichner, and Davis-Frenzel 2001). The authors concluded that, similar to Frohmann's (1990) study, Miami prosecutors look at the case closely to determine if there are problems that will affect their ability to obtain a conviction. With the exception of two cases, every case that was prosecuted ended in a conviction. Clearly, they are proficient at predicting which cases will result in a conviction.

Prosecutorial Decision Making in Sexual Assault Cases: A Summary and Discussion

From the information presented above one can see that American prosecutors have extraordinary discretionary powers. In general, prior research indicates that, at the initial screening stage, prosecutors attempt to avoid uncertainty. If a prosecutor believes that he/she will be able to obtain a conviction, he/she is more likely to file charges against the suspect in question. As noted above, the likelihood of filing a charge is determined primarily legal factors. Extralegal factors, however, also play a role. Moreover, in sexual assault cases, victim characteristics seem to play a pivotal role. Prosecutors sometimes consider victim misconduct, the relationship between the victim and the suspect, the credibility of the victim, age of the victim, promptness of her report, and her behavior at the time of the incident.

These findings suggest that criminal justice officials do not treat all rapes the same (Bohmer 1974; Estrich 1987; Griffin 1977; Ireland 1978; Williams 1984). They suggest that case outcomes are affected by stereotypes about rape and rape victims and that only "real rapes" with "genuine victims" will be taken seriously. Estrich (1987, 28), for example, suggests that criminal justice officials differentiate between the "aggravated, jump-from-the-bushes stranger rapes and the simple cases of unarmed rape by friends, neighbors, and acquaintances." There are several reasons that might explain why this happens.

For example, prosecutors are part of an organization—the office of the prosecutor. Every prosecutor's office wants a record that reflects a high conviction rate. First of all, the chief prosecutor needs this to demonstrate to the public that he/she is doing a good job. If they can do this, their likelihood of being reelected is increased. Another reason, is that each prosecutor also wants a high conviction rate. As mentioned above, this demonstrates to their supervisor that they are proficient at their job, which, in turn, influences their likelihood of getting a raise or getting promoted. If there is so much of a focus on conviction rates, it's not surprising that prosecutors are reluctant to go forward with a case that, in their mind, won't result in a conviction. In addition, they also realize that the office has limited resources available to prosecute cases, and, thus, are reluctant to use these resources on a case that can't be won.

As Frohmann (1990, 224) notes, "prosecutors are orienting to a 'downstream' concern with convictability." They are making a prediction about how judges and juries will react to victims. Research provides support for this. For example, research has found that some prosecutors' offices use a trial sufficiency policy in determining whether or not to go forward with the case. According to Jacoby (1980), prosecutors using this policy regard the screening and charging decisions as the most critical decisions in the office. Here, the prosecutor will only file charges if he/she believes that the case could be won before a jury. The prosecutor will refuse to file charges if he/she feels that the case will not result in a conviction if it were to go to trial. As previously discussed, prosecutors who do not file because a jury conviction is unlikely are "avoiding uncertainty." If, after the initial screening, a prosecutor is not certain that he/she can obtain a conviction at a jury trial, the case is likely to be rejected for prosecution (Albonetti 1987).

One source of uncertainty that seems to be consistently mentioned in the research is the credibility of the victim. According to many prosecutors, a "stand-up" victim is an essential element of a strong case (Stanko 1988). Stanko defines this as a person whom a judge and/or jury would consider credible and undeserving of victimization. One of the district attorneys interviewed by Stanko, discussing a case involving an elderly female robbery victim, stated, "Any case that has a stand-up complainant should be indicted. You put her on the stand—the judge loves her, the jury loves her—dynamite complainant!" (Stanko 1988, 174).

In attempting to assess a victim's credibility, prosecutors tend to rely on stereotypes about the behavior of certain types of people (Myers 1991). For example, most prosecutors feel that students are law-abiding citizens, and thus will be considered credible by judges and/or jurors (Stanko 1988). LaFree (1989) asserts that nontraditional women, or women who engage in some type of "risk-taking" behavior are less likely to be viewed as genuine victims who are deserving of protection under the law. Estrich (1987) similarly argues that only certain types of sexual assaults will be regarded as "real rapes" with "genuine victims."

A study by Reskin and Visher (1986) provides support for practice of prosecutors making predictions about how juries may react to victims focused on jury decision making. Reskin and Visher (1986) interviewed the jurors from sexual assault trials in Indianapolis. They asked these jurors if they believed that the defendant was guilty or innocent. They also asked them if their decisions were affected by the evidence in the case and by their perceptions of the victim's and defendant's personal characteristics. The results of the study indicated that extralegal variables had a significant effect on jurors' verdicts. For example, the jurors' verdicts were affected by their personal evaluation of the victim's moral character and by their beliefs that the victim exercised poor judgment at the time of the assault.

Reskin and Visher (1986) also determined, however, that the influence of these extralegal factors varied by the strength of the evidence in the case. They found that all five of the extralegal variables they examined influenced jurors' verdicts in cases with weak evidence, but only one influenced the verdicts in cases with strong evidence. They concluded that their results provided support for Kalven and Zeisel's (1966) "liberation hypothesis"—that is, that jury nullification is most likely to occur when evidence is weak.

The fact that prosecutors' assessments of convictability accurately reflect jurors' perceptions and beliefs does not, of course, justify consideration of extralegal victim characteristics at screening. Prosecutors have an ethical obligation to file charges if they believe that the suspect committed the crime in question. The fact that the victim of a sexual assault engaged in "risk-taking behavior," does not act like the typical rape victim, or goes to bars by herself should be irrelevant. The fact that they are not irrelevant, but play an important role in the decision to charge or not, suggests that Estrich (1986) was correct when she asserted that only "real rapes" with "genuine victims" will be taken seriously by criminal justice officials.

Rape Law Reform

As you can see from the above discussion, the victim is often the focus when the case involves a sexual assault. More to the point, many have argued that the victim is the one on trial, not the perpetrator of the assault. As Spohn and Horney (1992, 17–18) note:

> Feminists, social scientists, and legal scholars questioned the laws focus on the character and behavior of the victim rather than on the offender. They criticized rules of evidence that required corroboration of the victim's testimony, and that allowed evidence of the victim's past sexual conduct to be admitted at trial. They also criticized common-law definitions of rape that excluded male and spouses as victims and that excluded acts other than sexual intercourse.

As a result, all 50 states have enacted some type of rape law reform (Kennedy and Sacco 1998). In this section, I will discuss these reforms and examine their impact on the criminal justice system.

The definition of rape has changed significantly. Most states used the common law definition of rape which defined it as the carnal knowledge of a female, not one's wife, forcibly and against her will (Doerner and Lab 2002; Spohn and Horney 1992). Immediately, one can see the problems with this definition. Firstly, it only includes women as victims. Wives are excluded as potential victims. It also requires that the offender use force. In addition, carnal knowledge means penile-vaginal penetration, which means it excludes all other sexual acts (Spohn and Horney 1992). States have made several changes to this traditional definition.

For example, many states have changed the terminology. Many states have replaced "rape" with, for example, "criminal sexual conduct," "sexual assault," "deviate sexual intercourse," and "sexual battery" (Doerner and Lab 2002; Reidel and Welsh 2002; Spohn and Horney 1992). In addition to changes in terminology, many states eliminated the spousal exemption. The basis of the exemption lies in the assumption "that the marriage vows provide an irretractable contractual arrangement to deliver exclusive sexual services upon demand" (Doerner and Lab 2002, 111). Put simply, the wife is seen as the husbands sexual property to do with as he sees fit. Several states continue to include this exemption. For instance, some grant the husband "absolute exemption," which means husbands can't be charged with raping their wives under any circumstances. Others on allow a "partial exemption." In this case, charging is allowed if, for example, they are in the process of getting a divorce or they are separated.

Another definitional change included expanding the types of behavior that would be defined as sexual assault. Some states now define penetration, in addition to sexual intercourse, as "cunnilingus, fellatio, anal intercourse, or any other intrusion, however slight, of any part of a persons body or of any object into the genital or anal opening of another person's body" (Spohn and Horney 1992, 22). In addition the above, most states also made their sexual assault statutes gender-neutral. This meant that males could now be victims and females could be offenders.

Under common law, it was rape only if the woman did not consent. In other words, she was required to prove that she resisted the perpetrator. Moreover, to prove nonconsent, some statutes specifically stated the woman must "resist to her utmost" (Horney and Spohn 1991). If she didn't, it wasn't legally rape. Now, many states have either eliminated or modified the resistance requirement. For instance, Pennsylvania law specifically states that the victim does not have to resist at all (Spohn and Horney 1992). Others, identified specific circumstances (e.g., use of a weapon) that would constitute nonconsent.

Related to the requirement of nonconsent, was the corroboration requirement. Most laws did not allow a sexual assault defendant to be convicted without corroborative evidence (Horney and Spohn 1991). One rational for this requirement was the argument that some women make false allegations of rape to retaliate against an ex-boyfriend or some other man. In short, states were reluctant to prosecute a man for rape, when the *only* evidence against him was the woman's word.

A final reform was the enactment of rape shield laws. As Doerner and Lab (2002, 134) note:

> A common tactic that many aggressive defense attorneys invoked was to attack the victim's credibility by making an issue of her sexual past. A typical strategy was to imply promiscuity from prior sexual activity with men other than the defendant. Presumably, this information suggested a lack of chastity and, therefore, amply proved the victim's willingness to engage in sexual activity without any reliance on force.

Consequently, many victims of sexual assault were reluctant to report their assault for fear that they would be victimized a second time by the criminal justice system. Now, in the more than 45 states with rape shield laws (Riedel and Welsh 2002), there have been restrictions placed on this type of evidence. Some are very strict and prohibit evidence of this nature, while others are more lenient and allow it under some circumstances.

Impact of Rape Law Reform

At the most basic level, the overall purpose of rape law reform was to "encourage" the criminal justice system to treat rape like any other crime (i.e., focusing on the offender's behavior and not the victim's) (Horney and Spohn

1991). In addition, reformers had several instrumental goals in mind. For example, criminal justice officials would reduce their reliance on victim characteristics when making decisions. This, in turn, would lead to increased reporting by victims. There also was the hope that the reforms would increase the likelihood of arrest, prosecution, and conviction of sex offenders (Spohn and Horney 1992). The studies that have examined the impact of these reforms have yielded mixed results.

An early study of Washington state found that prosecutors did not change the way they evaluated the likelihood of conviction (Loh 1980). Marsh and her colleagues (1982), examined the 1974 Michigan law. This law is considered to be the most comprehensive reform of rape law in the country (Spohn and Horney 1992). They found that arrests for rape increased as did the number of convictions. However, it did not affect the number of reported rapes. Research in California did find some changes. For example, Polk (1985) found an increase in the number a felony complaints that prosecutors filed, but there was no change in the number of convictions.

All of the previous studies examined only one jurisdiction, which limits the generalizability of the results. Spohn and Horney's (1992) study addressed this problem. Their multijurisdictional study examined the impact of rape law reform in six jurisdictions. Overall, in most of the jurisdictions they studied, the reforms did not have an impact. They did find an increase in reporting in two of the jurisdictions and an increase in indictments in one of the jurisdictions.

Interviews with criminal justice officials in each of the jurisdictions did provide some additional insight into the effect of reforms. For instance, they did find that officials in each of the jurisdictions studied supported the reforms. The officials also believed that the reforms had a positive influence on how the criminal justice system treats rape victims. On the other hand, decision makers in every jurisdiction "still believe that resistance by the victim and corroboration of her testimony are important determinants of whether a rape case will result in a conviction" (Spohn and Horney 1992, 159). They also found that criminal justice officials believe prior sexual contact with the offender, despite rape shield laws, will be allowed. Spohn and Horney pointed out that they were not surprised with their findings. Research has consistently demonstrated the effectiveness of the criminal court system's ability to work around reforms.

Conclusion

Within the criminal justice system, the crime of rape is unique. It's the one crime that forces victims to convince criminal justice officials that they were assaulted and did nothing to contribute to it. No other crime requires the victim to do this. It's argued the system is, in effect, victimizing them a second time.

Feminists contend that legally irrelevant victim characteristics influence decision making in sexual assault cases. They argue that criminal justice officials, using stereotypes of real rapes and genuine victims, base their decisions on the victim's background and reputation, the victim's relationship to the accused, and the victim's behavior at the time of the incident. They argue, in other words, that in a rape case the focus shifts from the offender to the victim. The research on prosecutorial decision making discussed in this chapter confirms this.

At least in sexual assault cases, victim characteristics are an important source of uncertainty. Prosecutorial decision making in these types of cases is influenced by stereotypes of rape and rape victims—only real rapes with genuine victims will be taken seriously. This is a cause for concern. As LaFree (1989, 239) noted, "if women who violate traditional gender roles and are raped are unable to obtain justice through the legal system, then the law is serving as an institutional arrangement that reinforces women's gender-role conformity."

References

Albonetti, C. "Prosecutorial Discretion: The Effects of Uncertainty." *Law and Society Review 21*, (1987): 291–313.

Amir, M. *Patterns in Forcible Rape.* Chicago: University of Chicago Press, 1971.

Bohmer, C. "Judicial Attitudes Toward Rape Victims." *Judicature 57*, (1974): 303–307.

Boland, B. *The Prosecution of Felony Arrests.* Washington, D.C.: Bureau of Justice Statistics, 1983.

Bordenkircher v. Hayes 434 U.S. 357, 364 (1978).

Brosi, K. *A Cross-City Comparison of Felony Case Processing.* Washington, D.C.: Institute for Law and Social Research, 1979.

Davis, K. *Discretionary Justice.* Baton Rouge, LA: Louisiana State University Press, 1969.

Doerner, W. and S. Lab. *Victimology.* Cincinnati, OH: Anderson Publishing, 2002.

Estrich, S. *Real Rape.* Cambridge, MA: Harvard University Press, 1987.

Feeney, F., F. Dill, and A. Weir. *Arrests Without Conviction: How Often They Occur and Why.* Washington, DC: Department of Justice, National Institute of Justice, 1983.

Frohmann, L. "Discrediting Victims' Allegations of Sexual Assault: Prosecutorial Accounts of Case Rejections." *Social Problems 38*, (1991): 213–226.

Frohmann, L. "Convictability and Discordant Locales: Reproducing Race, Class, and Gender Ideologies in Prosecutorial Decisionmaking." *Law & Society Review 31*, (1997): 531–556.

Griffin, S. "Rape: The All-American Crime." In *Forcible Rape: The Crime, the Victim and the Offender*, eds. D. Chappell, R. Geis and G. Geis. New York: Columbia University Press, 1977.

Hepperle, W. "Women Victims in The Criminal Justice System." In *The changing Role of Women in the Criminal Justice System*, ed. I. Moyer. Prospect Heights, IL: Waveland Press Inc, 1985.

Horney, J. and C. Spohn. "Rape Law Reform and Instrumental Change in Six Urban Jurisdictions." *Law & Society Review 25*, (1991): 117–153.

Ireland, M. "Rape Reform Legislation: A New Standard of Sexual Responsibility." *University of Colorado Law Review 49* (1978): 185–204.

Jacoby, J. *The American Prosecutor: A Search for Identity*. Toronto: D.C. Heath and Company, 1980.

Jacoby, J., L. Mellon, E. Ratledge, and S. Turner. *Prosecutorial Decision Making: A National Study*. Washington, DC: U.S. Department of Justice, National Institute of Justice, 1982.

Kalven, H. and H. Zeisel. *The American Jury*. Boston: Little, Brown and Company, 1966.

Kennedy, L. and V. Sacco. *Crime Victims in Context*. Los Angeles: Roxbury Publishing Company, 1998.

Kerstetter, W. "Gateway to Justice: Police and Prosecutorial Response to Sexual Assaults Against Women." *Criminology 81*, (1990): 267–313.

LaFree, G. *Rape and Criminal Justice: The Social Construction of Sexual Assault*. Belmont, CA: Wadsworth, 1989.

Loh, W. "The Impact of Common Law and Reform Rape Statues on Prosecution: An Empirical Study." *Washington Law Review 55* (1980): 543–625.

Marsh, J.C., A. Geist, and N. Caplan. *Rape and the Limits of Law Reform*. Boston: Auburn House, 1982.

Mather, L. *Plea Bargaining or Trial?* Lexington, MA: Heath, 1979.

Miller, F. *Prosecution: The Decision to Charge a Suspect with a Crime*. Boston: Little, Brown and Company, 1969.

Myers, M. "Common Law in Action: The Prosecution of Felonies and Misdemeanors." *Sociological Inquiry 52*, (1982): 1–15.

Myers, M. "The Courts: Prosecution and Sentencing." In *Criminology*, ed. J. Sheley. Belmont, CA: Wadsworth Inc, 1991.

Nagel, H. and J. Hagan. "Gender and Crime: Offense Patterns and Criminal Court Sanctions." In *Crime and Justice: An Annual Review of Research, Vol. 4*, eds M. Tonry and N. Morris. Chicago: University of Chicago Press, 1983.

Polk, K. "Rape Law Reform and Criminal Justice Processing." *Crime & Delinquency 31*, (1985): 191–205.

Rauma, D. "Going for the Gold: Prosecutorial Decision Making in Cases of Wife Assault." *Social Science Research 13*, (1984): 321–351.

Reaves, B. *Felony Defendants in Large Urban Counties, 1998*. Washington, D.C.: U.S. Department of Justice, 2001.

Reskin, B. and C. Visher. "The Impacts of Evidence and Extralegal Factors in Jurors' Decisions." *Law and Society Review 20*, (1986): 423–438.

Riedel, M. and W. Welsh. *Criminal Violence: Patterns, Causes, and Prevention*. Los Angeles: Roxbury Publishing Company, 2002.

Schmidt, J. and E. Steury. "Prosecutorial Discretion in Filing Charges in Domestic Violence Cases. *Criminology 27*, 1989: 487–510.

Spears, J. and C. Spohn. "The Genuine Victim and Prosecutors' Charging Decisions in Sexual Assault Cases." *American Journal of Criminal Justice 20*, (1996): 183–205.

Spears, J. and C. Spohn. "The Effect of Evidence Factors and Victim Characteristics on Prosecutors' Charging Decisions in Sexual Assault Cases." *Justice Quarterly 14*, (1997): 501–524.

Spohn, C., D. Beichner, and E. Davis-Frenzel. "Prosecutorial Justifications for Sexual Assault Case Rejection: Guarding the 'Gateway to Justice.'" *Social Problems 48*, (2001): 206.

Spohn, C., and J. Horney. *Rape Law Reform: A Grassroots Revolution and Its Impact*. New York: Plenum Press, 1992.

Spohn, C., and J. Horney. "The Influence of Blame and Believability Factors on the Processing of Simple Versus Aggravated Rape Cases." *Criminology 34*, (1996): 135–161.

Stanko, E. "The Impact of Victim Assessment on Prosecutors' Screening Decisions: The Case of the New York County District Attorney's Office." In Criminal Justice: Law and Politics, ed G. Cole. Pacific Grove, CA: Brooks/Cole, 1988.

Swiggert, V. and R. Farrell. Murder, Inequality, and the Law. Lexington, MA: D.C. Heath.

Williams, K. *The Role of the Victim in the Prosecution of Violent Offenses*. Institute for Law and Social Research. Washington, D.C.: U.S. Government Printing Office, 1978.

Williams, S. "Rape Reform Legislation and Evidentiary Concerns: The Law in Pennsylvania." *University of Pittsburgh Law Review 44*, (1984): 955–975.

Special Feature

In the Words of a Prosecutor

As a sex crimes prosecutor, I spent 100% of my time prosecuting cases involving sexual abuse, child abuse and neglect; and kidnapping, harassment and stalking cases. For about 18 months, the victims in my cases were under the age of 14. For the remaining 2 1/2 years, I handled cases involving "adults"—victims 14 and over.

The most challenging aspects of my work as a sex crimes prosecutor.... As a practical matter, it's a challenge to talk to strangers about the intimate details of sexual assault(s). When I started in the unit, I didn't have children and wasn't often around children so it was especially difficult to initially talk to the first several child victims. You have to be able to use the proper anatomical terms as comfortably as if you were discussing any other subject when you speak to colleagues about filing decisions or plea offer suggestions. On the other hand, you have to be able to go with the flow and use the terms your victim is comfortable with (some silly and some vulgar).

On a different level, sex crimes is challenging because of the way it can insidiously creep into your personal life. Before I worked in sex crimes, I would see kids getting off the school bus and imagine those kids running into the house greeted by a hug and anxious to talk about their day. After sex crimes, I worried that every single one of those kids dreaded going in that house because they knew they were going to be molested by someone in their house before mom got home from work. Before this assignment, I knew logically that all children obviously lose their innocence at some point, but I never thought about it happening when they were as young as 3 or 4 or 5 years old and in such horrifically creative ways.

It takes a certain personality to have longevity as a sex crimes prosecutor. Some of my colleagues say they can do it because they don't get sad when they hear about cases—they get angry primarily. Others have said that they don't picture the case happening when they read about them—it's just words to them and that helps avoid being as empathetic and affected. I didn't have the luxury of either of these characteristics.

In fact, I do picture things when I read about them. The thing that finally drove me from the unit was once I had children. I substituted their faces for the kids I was reading about because that's what I know, it's my personal experience, and I think there's a natural tendency to do that psychologically when you're reading something you've never experienced. So in my mind, trying to understand what happened so that I could charge cases and plead cases, my two kids had been abused and neglected over and over and over again.

I think registration laws for sexual offenders are a benefit to the community in terms of being perceived by the offenders as a serious punishment. Practically speaking, however, I don't think that most people would have any idea if 10 sex offenders were living next door (until it was too late), despite the registry.

It's impossible to draft the registration law without at times including people that you may not feel need to be included while at the same time making sure you've covered everyone you're certain needs to register.

It seems like it wouldn't be a crazy idea to allow certain classes of sex offenders (youthful probationers for first-time low-grade offenses) to petition to be relieved of the registration requirement after a lengthy period given no probation violations. The lifetime requirement seems very burdensome for some cases.

I think the system does about as much as it can with available resources to accommodate the needs of sex crimes victims. We have victim advocates available, we attempt to keep victims apprised of the status of the case (court dates, plea offers, etc) and we try to coordinate with other agencies. With more funding, we could certainly do more.

The greatest hope for improving the CJS with respect to offenders would be to deal directly with the legislature. Sex crimes statutes change often and sometimes the result is inconsistencies that hinder the prosecutor's ability to adequately deal with certain cases. For example, in Missouri there are several offenses which aren't eligible for 120 day program—shock time in the Department of Corrections prior to possible probation. As a result, the only options in those cases are straight probation or 5–10 year *minimum* sentences. Those aren't fair choices for the prosecutor of the Court so a lot of cases get amended or end up with probation when they should have something more. I don't think it's a good idea to take away prosecutorial discretion in an area of crime in which cases are so unique and truly need to be dealt with on a case-by-case basis.

A.D.
Prosecutor for 5 years
Over 4 years in a Sex Crimes Unit

Rape, Victimization and Advocacy: My Story

I could hear the phone ringing as I walked towards the house. My arms were loaded with groceries and I juggled to grab the keys from my pocket. "Oh, my goodness would the answering machine just pick it up?" I thought. The phone was ringing so loudly—the brown grocery bags were slipping and I was kind of laughing at how silly I must have looked balancing on the walkway as I stepped towards the door …

I heard the familiar voice and the pain it summoned made the groceries fall. The tone was burdened; not the usual happy sound. I strained to listen. I couldn't make sense of the words Pam spoke as she left a recording on my answering machine. A parole hearing? A motion to dismiss? My statement to the judge?

When I heard Pam talking I dropped the rest of the sacks and leaned against the door. Pam was an executive secretary in the prosecutor's office of one of Missouri's largest counties when the case of my brutal rape and kidnapping came into her office. Her voice, normally so calm and comforting, was stressed and tense. I knew something was wrong. I knew something horrible, something scary was happening. It had been two years since I finished working through the criminal justice system convicting the men that raped me. Why was Pam calling now? After years of trials, pleas and sentencing hearings, all four men that assaulted me were ultimately convicted and sentenced to the Missouri Department of Corrections. What did I have to do now? I listened as the details unfolded.

Pam was calling to inform me of a parole hearing that had been scheduled for one of the four offenders who sexually assaulted me. He had filed a cleverly drafted petition asking the judge to reduce the charges against him. It just so happened that upon review of his file, it was discovered that he was actually scheduled for a parole hearing. Pam called because she feared that I may not have heard the news about the parole hearing from the newly created Victim Information System (VINES); and she was correct. VINES is an automated clearinghouse of information for victims of crime within the Department of Corrections. It is suppose to alert victims when their offenders are up for parole hearings or being released. Pam wanted to inform me of my offender's parole hearing so I could attend if I so desired. Due to the diligent work of many dedicated professionals in the field of victim advocacy pushing for legislative change, crime victims have legal rights to attend parole hearings of those convicted of assaulting them, or to make a statement in person or through tele-conference. I decided at that moment to attend the hearing.

My assault occurred late one night after I completed my shift at work. Four men from another town who had been absorbed in the Kansas City party scene watched for me to leave the restaurant in which I worked. They followed me home and ruthlessly kidnapped me from my driveway as I exited my car. The attack lasted more than 14 hours. I was beaten and brutally raped by all four men. I was held in handcuffs for hours and feared for each second of my life. Nonetheless, I formulated a plan to escape. Into the fourteenth hour of my ordeal, I was able to squeeze my hand from the tightened cuff and sneak away from the watch of one of the sleeping offenders.

The numerous crimes involved in the attack crossed three different county lines. Thus, each offender had to be tried separately in each of the three counties, and on numerous charges in each county. I had survived their death grip in those hours but now I faced a lifetime of abuse by the courts, their attorneys and the criminal justice system. How was I, only 19 at the time, supposed to maneuver my way through the maze of the system? The only experience I had with the police or the courts was handling a speeding ticket that I received days after my 16th birthday. I knew nothing of the criminal justice system. I didn't know what the words arraignment and deposition meant. I barely survived the attack much less the hours of interrogation by the responding officers and the rape exam at the hospital.

That night of the attack, after I fled, I spent hours plunged into the process of interviews and medical exams. My family came to pick me up from the Sheriff's office two hours from home and watched in horror as I recounted the seconds of the entire assault. The trauma I suffered during the hours after the assault was near the trauma I suffered during the assault. I could never have fathomed that it would actually get more difficult than the police interviews but as the cases proceeded through the criminal justice system—it did!

Each time I contacted Pam's office for information about the prosecution I could tell that Pam was frustrated about not being able to help me more. She listened to the pain I felt and watched me struggle through the maze of hearings and interviews. She tried to help me understand the system, but when she saw my frail form sitting alone in the courtroom she made her decision to be my personal victim advocate. I had family for support and friends that wanted to help, but the system is so complex, sometimes it is harder when the family of a crime victim is the only source of support because the victim finds herself carrying the load for the family as well. As much as they wanted to be supportive, my parents' pain made it even more unbearable for me to deal with the process of the criminal justice system. What I needed was an advocate, a direct line of support from someone who understood each step, someone that could provide the emotional strength to give me and my family information and support us through hearings. With no formal training as a victim advocate, Pam transformed the experience of being a crime victim in one of the largest counties in Missouri into to an experience with hope, friendship and inspiration.

In the 1990s there was no formal advocate position in the prosecutor's office in which Pam was employed. The other counties prosecuting my assailants had some form of advocacy. However, Pam, an executive secretary, took it upon herself to be my advocate. The hope she offered me through information and assistance allowed me to turn a corner in this experience.

Advocacy to a victim of crime can be the one light in their very dark experience. The component of advocacy can encourage healing, balance, growth and acceptance. It can be the bridge that spans the distance between the known and the unknown. The pain, suffering and fear are still very present, but with just a little help, a little support and a source of information, a crime victim can move to a safer place. That is a place where hope abounds, where support and encouragement are present to assist the victim and their family in the first steps of healing. Those first steps for me were seeking to understand and to be understood.

The position of victim advocate takes many forms in today's criminal justice system. While many local agencies employee some form of the position, the often undertrained advocate is tasked to assist crime victims through the confusion of the criminal justice system. I believe the ability of the victim to heal and move out of victimization is directly affected by the commitment of the advocate position and the office that supports her.

Some of our greatest helping agencies have been started by victims of crime who found themselves encouraged to make the system better for other victims, and they felt compelled to work for that change. When hope was not easily found they decided to step up and be an agent of change. Their courage has resulted in many years of healing by victims and families encouraged and shown hope through their difficult time. Agencies such as MADD; founded by a mother who lost her daughter to a drunk driving crash, the National Center for Missing and Exploited Children inspired by the loss of Adam, son of John Walsh, and many more. Note the bravery of Sarah Buel—a formerly battered spouse—whose visibility with a National Coalition Against Domestic Violence led to the passing of the Violence Against Women Act (VAWA) in 1994; an Act which now funds countless agencies across the country. VAWA is one of the strongest tools used to fund programs serving victims across the country (Young 1997).

Known as one of the "First true saints of crime victims" is Ann Burgess. She was so moved by the plight and trauma suffered by rape victims she met while working as a nurse, she united women for the cause of raising awareness and helped define Rape Trauma Syndrome (Young 1997). This awareness helped to develop victim assistance programs, in the early 1970s, such as Aid for Victims of Crime in St. Louis, Missouri which is applauded as the first ever victim assistance program (Tucker-Davis 2005). In 1973 the first National Crime Victimization Survey was commissioned by the President's Commission on Law Enforcement and the Administration of Justice. In 1974, citizen activists from across the country united to expand victim services and increase recognition of victims' rights through the formation of the National Organization for Victim Assistance (NOVA). What developed in the 1970s and continues today is the result of the passion of crime survivors who, in the face of adversity, seek change (Tucker-Davis 2005).

Victims of violent crime experience a wide range of needs—physical, financial, emotional, and legal. Victims are entitled by law in this country to certain types of information and support. Although victims of violent crime have much in common with non-violent crime victims and with disaster victims, they appear to experience higher levels of distress that are, in part, due to the unique issues related to the trauma and magnitude of these horrible events. Becoming a victim of crime as they go about the everyday tasks of their daily life creates a sense of horror and vulnerability that may last a lifetime. It may also put people at risk for significant long-term psychological difficulties.

As the effects of the crime take root in the victim, the estimated risk for developing a condition that affects a large number of crime victims, Post Traumatic Stress Disorder (PTSD) increases to 49% for survivors of sexual assault, 32% for survivors of physical assault, 15% for a survivor of a shooting or stabbing and 7% for those who witness a murder or assault (Tousor 2006). The statistics are much lower if a victim, particularly a sexual assault victim, has the assistance of an advocate throughout the early stages of victimization: they are much more likely to provide a statement to the police, they are much more likely to cooperate with the prosecutor and more likely to receive the medical care required to obtain the rape kit (Catalano 2005). Women that have had the assistance of an advocate also report feeling less re-victimized by the system (Campbell 2006).

All victims of crime need help in handling the crisis created by the criminal event, in stabilizing their lives, and in dealing with the criminal justice process. Because each victim's coping abilities and support systems are different and his or her loss is individual, the needs of individual victims will vary. A process should be in place to help victims assess their specific needs and find appropriate sources of help and support. Most victims will be able to function and stabilize after a period of time with moderate assistance, but a percentage of victims will continue to need assistance for years after the event.

I know this because I am a survivor. Being thrown into the criminal justice system after the traumatic rape was like facing a brick wall. Because of the commitment of advocates like Pam and others that helped me find hope in the darkness; I have flourished and claim healing almost 20 years after my brutal attack. Because of this mission I have worked to change laws, educate law enforcement officers and communities and serve other sexual assault survivors. Advocacy is about turning tragedy to triumph. It is about a healing, supportive force that encourages hope in the face of trauma. Advocacy is about community, it is about survival, it is about support. Advocacy in the criminal justice system makes a difference to the victim. I know because now I call myself a survivor.

Kim Case
Survivor

References

Campbell, R. (2006) Rape Survivors Experiences with the Legal and Medical Systems: Do Rape Victim Advocates Make a Difference? Violence Against Women 12(30) Retrieved July 13, 2007 from, http://www.ojp.usdoj.gov/bjs/cvictgen.htm.

Tucker-Davis, J. (2005) The Grassroots Beginnings of the Victims' Rights Movements. [Electronic Version]. National Crime Victim Law Institute News. Retrieved May 20, 2007, from http://ncvli.org/ncvlilibrary.html.

Tousor, Sidran (2005) Sidran Foundation, "Post-Traumatic Stress Disorder Sheet" [Electronic Version]. Retrieved July 13, 2007 from http://www.sidran.org/sub.cfm?contentID=66&sectionid=4.

Young, M. (1997, February 10) The Victims Movement: A Confluence of Forces. A speech presented to the first National Symposium on Victims of Federal Crime, Washington DC. Retrieved May 25, 2007 from http://trynova.org/victiminfo/victimsmovement.pdf.

Probation Supervision of a Sex Offender Caseload: My Story

My name is Shelly Graf and I have been employed with Missouri Department of Corrections for the past 13 years. The last 10 years I have been working primarily with sex offenders, dealing directly with their supervision and treatment.

Sex offenders are a category of offenders that have additional specific issues to deal with, differing greatly from the general population of offenders. As a sex offender officer I must be prepared to deal with the normal issues of supervision, such as: employment, substance abuse, special conditions of the court/board. However, in addition there are sex offender specific issues: treatment goals, treatment progress, support network, registration, residency, contact with children, paying for treatment requirements, to name a few.

The concept for sex offender supervision is a "team approach". This means a collaborative effort and balance between the probation officer and the therapist. This is essential to sex offender supervision due to the unique issues with this population.

Routinely I observe and participate in the group counseling sessions to address specific offender issues or current problems with an offender. I bring supervision issues to the group to address violations/issues with an offender. The group helps confront the offender about behavior and offer solutions to dealing with problems. However, it is important to note that I am not a therapist and not there to participate in the actual treatment. If at any point they proceed into the treatment aspect I will leave the group.

Supervision of sex offenders also requires knowledge of the ongoing legislative mandates and changes. Right now there are several laws that directly effect sex offenders and require my attention. Registration requirements are the first law. This requires knowledge of which offenses require registration, how often they register, failure to register, what they must show at registration and ensuring compliance with this. Registration requirements began in 1995, therefore only offenses committed after that date require registration. Further, registration laws cannot be made retroactive. If there are any changes/additions to the sex offender registration law, it will only apply to persons that pled or are found guilty after the date of the change/addition. On a caseload of 30–60 people at any time I could have each person with different requirements for registration. Currently in my jurisdiction, offenders with juvenile victims require 90 day registration and offenders with adult victims only require twice per year registration. Pleading or being found guilty of Failing to Register requires 90 day registration, regardless of the age of the original victim.

Another legislative mandate is residency requirements. Registered sex offenders who pled or were found guilty after August 2004 may not reside within 1000 feet of any school or registered daycare facility. I must check with local law enforcement any time I have an offender moving into my area or wanting to go to another area. I must also determine their date of sentencing to know if the law applies to that individual. Again, in a caseload of any size, I could have different residency restrictions for different offenders.

There is a legal requirement for successful completion of treatment. After August 2007 any offender under probation or parole supervision is required by law to successfully complete sex offender treatment. This includes following any directives from the treatment provider during treatment. I must closely monitor treatment progress and determine, with the therapist, whether or not the person has successfully completed treatment. Each offender expiring from supervision must have a follow up treatment plan, if not given a successful discharge. Failure to comply by those offenders who pled or are found guilty after August 2007 would be a violation of the law.

In August 2006 a law was added regarding "loitering within 500 feet of any school owned property". This law affects any sex offender with children. If they have pled or been found guilty after that date, they must have permission from the school superintendent or School Board president and must be a parent or legal guardian of the child before being allowed on school property. Further, the offender must have permission for each and every different event they would like to attend. I must first determine if the offender should be allowed to attend any school functions. This is done with consultation with the treatment provider. Only after careful consideration would I agree to any offender being allowed to be at a school or school function. If there is an agreement that an offender would be allowed for the purpose of attending something for their biological child, I must then schedule a meeting with the school superintendent to discuss the matter. I have had meetings that included the offender and other instances where I was asked to meet with the superintendent alone. At that point the school will decide if they are willing to allow the offender to attend any functions and list the specific functions the offender may attend. I will meet with the offender and advise them what they can attend. Further I will address the requirement of an appropriate chaperone to be with the person at all times while on school property. I am then responsible for monitoring their attendance at these events and ensuring they advise me of every time they attend something as approved by the school.

There are continuing changes to the legislative mandates and each year there are sex offender issues and changes suggested to the law. Currently there is an attempt to establish a law that would control sex offender behaviors on Halloween. I must continue to review the legislative updates every year to recognize any new laws that will affect my supervision of the offenders on my caseload and any new people that plead after that point.

I must also be closely involved in what the offenders are doing in treatment. Each offender is required as a part of treatment to complete several projects, including deviant cycle (offenders identify their patterns of behavior which can result in offending and/or deviant behavior), an autobiography, a victim clarification (offenders place themselves in their victim's position and attempt to write about the affects of the offending behavior) and a relapse prevention plan. I go over these requirements with each offender, monitor their progress towards completion, read them once submitted and consult with the therapist on whether or not the reports were completed successfully.

In supervising sex offenders, I require that they each have a minimum of one person that attends and completes the chaperone training program offered by a therapist. I believe each offender must have approved adults that are capable of observing their behavior when around children. It is unrealistic to assume that an individual will never be in a situation or place where children are present. Therefore, it is important to prepare each sex offender to handle those situations before being released from supervision. I require that anyone who will supervise an offender around children complete the chaperone class and be successfully approved by me and the therapist. Further any offender that has a significant other (spouse, girl/boyfriend) will be required to have the significant other attend the Partner's class that is offered by the therapist. In both the Chaperone and Partner's classes, it is only the family members and/or significant others in the class. Although the family members/significant others are not on probation, this is a requirement for the offender. Having a support system in place is an extremely important component of sex offender treatment. I can not force these individuals to be a part of the offender's treatment. However, if the offender is involved with people who are unwilling to become a part of the treatment, then that is a concern for me. When this occurs, the offender will not be allowed to complete or be successfully discharged from treatment. This makes it a mandatory part of the offender's treatment and supervision, while not forcing the family to be involved. The responsibility is on the offender to have people in their lives that are supportive of their treatment and progress. In both cases, I meet with these family members before they enter the classes. Once approved to attend the classes, the therapist will provide the classes. After completion there is a consultation between me and the therapist and it is a team decision on whether or not the person is approved to be a chaperone or deemed an appropriate partner.

I also coordinate the polygraphs for all offenders on my caseload. I schedule the appointments, based on consultation with the therapist. I provide the polygraph examiner with the information on each offender. I review the results and write violation reports as necessary based on disclosures made by the offenders. I also meet with the therapist to discuss the results and determine if there is a need for further testing and/or modifications to the offender's treatment plan. Any test which has a result of deceptive or inconclusive will require a mandatory retesting within the next 90 days. The offender will continue to take the test until the results are truthful. I cannot use the information from the test questions to write violation reports, only the information the offender discloses during the pretest interview. Continued failing of the test could result in an offender being unsuccessfully discharged from treatment. Polygraphs are a mandatory component of sex offender treatment.

I must monitor the payment of polygraph tests by the offender as well as their payment for group attendance. Sex offenders under my supervision are required to pay for all the expenses associated with their offense. I believe that for a person to be vested in their treatment and take it seriously, they should be personally responsible for it. In some instances and special circumstances, the Department of Corrections provides money that can be used for sex offender treatment or polygraphs. If I have a person that is indigent or has some current financial trouble, I can, and have previously requested the funds to pay for a polygraph test or some treatment.

I have particular rules about the required payments for treatment and polygraphs. Offenders must pay for their treatment and polygraph at the time of service. I do not allow anyone to owe a balance on their treatment and/or polygraphs. Failure to pay at the time of scheduled group or testing will result in a violation report. Continued failure to pay for treatment may result in sanctions, discharge from treatment and/or revocation of supervision. Through the years I have learned that if given these requirements at the beginning of supervision, and allowing no leeway, has resulted in most offenders complying. Surprisingly the number of offenders that have struggled with payment for treatment is quite low. They are also required to pay for any classes attended by family or significant others (partners and chaperone class). If they want their family/significant other to be involved, they are responsible for paying for it. This may seem harsh, but I have learned that if you give any leeway, it will be taken. This can set an offender up for failure by allowing them to get behind in payments and can cause the therapist/polygraph examiner to lose earnings. Neither situation is conducive to helping the offender deal with their problems and successfully complete supervision.

Although this population can be difficult to work with (the added stress, added responsibility, high profile type cases, dealing with victim information, keeping up with legislative mandates, etc.) it can be rewarding. I believe that sex offenders should not be defined by what they have done, but by what they do next. Those who are willing to accept responsibility for their offenses, address their issues and take the steps to keep it from happening again, are worth the time I put in to this job. I have supervised offenders from the age of seventeen to seventy and crimes based on consensual sex with an under age female to molestation of a small child. Each person has specific issues to address and treatment goals to accomplish. It is my job to provide supervision so that they may develop and accomplish their treatment plans. It is also my job to recognize when they are placing themselves in high risk situation or when they are failing to comply with treatment and/or supervision. I must then make a decision based on what is the best for everyone involved: the offender, offender's family, the victim and the community. If the risk of that offender outweighs the positives of remaining in the community, then I must make my recommendation based on that information.

Even though it is a tough and demanding job, I believe it is rewarding in its own way. I recently had an offender that I supervised for almost his entire five year supervision. This person admitted guilt, participated in treatment, successfully completed treatment, spoke to college classes about his experience and began attending college during his supervision. I recently received an invitation to this person's wedding a year after he completed his supervision. I attended the wedding and got to witness someone who acknowledged his behavior, accepted his responsibility and went on to make a life for himself. An instance like that is the reminder that doing this job is worthwhile and can make a difference to a person who is willing to accept what they have done. This is why I continue to work this type of demanding and sometimes difficult job.

Part V:
The Criminal Justice System

Suggested Questions, Activities and Videos

Discussion Questions

1. Discuss the common law definition of rape compared to the law in your state. Do they differ and how?
2. What is secondary victimization by police?
3. Why do police officer's ask about the victim's level of fear and the victim's fear of the environment and situation in their interviewing of a rape victim?
4. Discuss how characteristics of the victim can play a role in the decision to prosecute.

Suggested Videos:

- First Response to Victims of Crime: OVC
- Sexual Assault Response Teams: Partnering for Success: OVC
- DNA: Critical Issues for Those Who work with Victims: OVC
- Restoring Dignity: Frontline Response to Rape: Sage Videotape

Suggested Activities:

- Research to see if you can find if there used to be cautionary instructions and collaboration requirements in your state.
- Research to see if gender is included in the hate crime law in your state and if it has been used in any sexual assault crimes.
- Pass out a questionnaire to all students with a serious of personal questions about their last sexual encounter. Do not collect but ask

them what they thought, etc. Explain that this is most likely the questions from a police officer to which a rape victim may answer. You can also simply tell the class 'turn and face the person beside you. Tell them about your last consensual sexual experience." When they flutter....you can tell them the same thing as stated above.

- Research who is responsible for payment or if there are available re-imbursements for the medical exam and/or medications pre-scribed/administered to a rape victim during the rape exam in your state.
- Examine the major sex crimes statues in your state - examine force, consent, and non-consent. See what your state defines as the ele-ments of the crime.

Part VI

Public Fear and the Legislative Response

Chapter 18

Sex Offenders:
The Social Narrative and
Public Policy Implications

Gene Bonham, Jr.

Introduction

There has been a tremendous amount of interest in sex offenders and sexual offending by both the press and the public (McCulloch and Kelly 2007). The unprecedented attention on this group of offenders and offending has resulted in a social narrative that is both inaccurate and constructed in such a way as to impede prudent public policy. In Chapter One of this reader, several myths surrounding sexual assault and rape were shown to be perpetuated by the media. This chapter will explore the broader context of how the social narrative around sex offenders and sexual offending has resulted in public policies that are ill-informed and ineffective.

The Role of the Media in the Social
Narrative of Sex Offending

Some sex offenders are indeed dangerous and deserving of close control and management by our criminal justice system in order to better protect the public. However, it is also critical that the manner in which we deal with sex offenders is based on empirical knowledge rather than misconceptions, myths, and inaccuracies produced by media hype (Levenson and D'Amora 2007).

The media play a huge role in shaping public opinion about a whole variety of areas, including politics, culture, and criminal justice. It has, in fact, been asserted that the media are the "principle vehicle by which the average person comes to know crime and justice in America" (Barak 1994, p. 3). The media or press is a "significant source of information to areas of life of which only a few have first-hand knowledge ..." (McCulloch and Kelly 2007, p. 8). In recent years, a moral panic has developed around sex offenders as highly publicized cases have received enormous attention in print and televised media. Sex offenders have been cast as outsiders, aliens, beasts, and monsters that need intense surveillance and control. This media-driven "perception has in turn resulted in the 'moral panic' that has succeeded in locating the focus of our attentions onto the external threat to society from sexual predators, rather than focusing on issues of masculinity and the treatment of women and children in our society" (McCulloch and Kelly p. 9). The social narrative that derives from this panic has a major impact on the public, the politicians, and criminal justice practitioners who are charged with dealing with sex offenders on an everyday basis.

There are a number of ways in which distorted views of sex offenders are developed by the media. Twenty-four hour news coverage and cable television has contributed to an intensity of news coverage never seen before. Such news is also much more immediate than in the past, as "breaking news" alerts allow the public to see events occur soon after or sometimes even as they occur, e.g. the famous Bronco chase in the O. J. Simpson case. While this immediacy provides interest and entertainment value, it does not always allow for any type of in-depth analysis of the events that are occurring, thus giving a superficial and many times distorted view of what is happening. In terms of sex crimes, the 24 hour news cycle and intense coverage creates a "panic atmosphere" by sensationalizing the event with multiple televised news conferences and updates that give the impression that the crime is something that occurs with great frequency, perhaps beyond the reality of the facts of the matter (Meloy 2005; McCulloch and Kelly 2007). Because of this, the media does not take the time to focus on educating the public about the realities surrounding sex offending, such as the true nature of sex offender re-offending, victim-offender relationships, and shortcomings of sex offender legislation (Meloy 2005). In the next section, major misconceptions about sex offending will be described that result from the sensationalism of media portrayals.

Misconceptions about Sex Offending That Lead to Flawed Public Policy

Many misconceptions exist about sex offenders, sex offenses, and victims of sex offending. Some of the major misconceptions are discussed here. The nexus between such misconceptions and how they may lead to failed public policy will also be addressed.

Misconception 1: Most sexual assaults are committed by strangers.

Reality: Most sexual assaults are committed by someone known to the victim or victim's family (Center for Sex Offender Management, 2000). This particular misconception results in large part from highly publicized cases that lead us to believe that the majority of cases involve incidents with strangers, while in fact, "most sexual perpetrators are well-known to their victims" (Levenson and D'Amora 2007). With regard to child victims of child sexual abuse, 34% of child victims identified family members as abusers, and 59% of cases involved acquaintances (Bureau of Justice Statistics 1997). Levenson and D'Amora (2007) point out that child abduction and sexually motivated murder is a very rare event, estimating only about 100 such cases per year. There are more children killed by drunk drivers, over 500 children under the age of 15 in 2003. The authors also state that in 2002, 1,121 children died from physical abuse or neglect by parents or caretakers. Put in this perspective, it is clear that more emphasis should be placed on DUI prevention and abuse by family members than in efforts designed to deal with stranger abductions. Other supportive evidence indicates that 40% of sexual assaults take place in the victim's home and 20% in the home of a friend, neighbor, or relative. Finally, only 7% of the perpetrators of child victims were strangers ... (Levenson and D'Amora 2007).

Misconception 2: Most sex offenders reoffend.

Reality: This is simply not the case (Center for Sex Offender Management 2000). Empirical research does not support this misconception. One recent study, for example, found that after 15 years, 73% of sexual offenders was not charged or convicted of another sexual offense (Harris and Hanson 2004). Other studies reported relatively low rates of recidivism for sex offenders, see Hanson and Bussierre (1998) who report recidivism rate of 14%; Hanson and Morton-Bourgon (2005) report a recidivism rate of 14%; and the Bureau of Justice Statistics (2003) reporting a recidivism rate of 5.3%. It should be noted that in some studies, recidivism is defined as new charges, convictions, or in some cases as new arrests. However, no matter what the definition, this body of research indicates clearly that sex offenders do not reoffend at high rates, and certainly not at the levels that might be thought based on exaggerated media presentations. In addition, it appears that recidivism appears to decline with age, that is, the longer the offender is offense-free in the community, the less likely he is to reoffend sexually (Levenson and D'Amora 2007).

Misconception 3: Sex offenders are more likely to commit new crimes than criminals who commit other types of crimes.

Reality: The empirical evidence does not support this misconception. In fact, sex offenders are LESS likely to be rearrested for "ongoing criminal behavior" than non-sex offenders (Levenson and D'Amora 2007; Hanson, Scott, and Steffy 1995; and Sample and Bray 2006). So far as types of criminal offenders, it has also been noted that sex offenders are much less likely to recommit a sexual offense than other criminals are to reoffend their types of offenses. For example, recidivism rates for burglary are 74%, larceny 75%, auto theft 70%, drunk driving 51%, and sex offenses 6.5% (Levenson and D'Amora 2007). These data are in stark contrast to the impression one has given the media attention and sensationalism of single incidents that are exaggerated before the public.

Within the general groups of sex offenders, it is also important to note that there is much variability in risk of recidivism. Research indicates that pedophiles that molest boys and rapists of adult women are the most likely to recidivate. Those who comply with probation and treatment requirements have lower reoffense rates than offenders who violate such conditions. And, sex offenders targeting strangers are more dangerous than offenders whose victims are inside their family (Levenson and D'Amora 2007, p. 177).

Misconception 4: Sexual offense rates are very high and continue to increase rapidly.

Reality: The actual rates for sex offenses (sexual assault) have decreased slightly in recent years, rather than increase (Center for Sex Offender Management 2000). According to the Center for Sex Offender Management (2000), women reporting rape decreased by 10% between 1990 and 1995, and in 1995, the number of forcible rapes was the lowest reported since 1989. Similarly, between 1993 and 1998, the reported arrest rate for all sexual offenses decreased by 16%. These facts differ sharply from the perception that is given by extensive media coverage of certain high profile cases that would lead one to think that sex offender crime rates are greatly increasing (Levenson and D'Amora 2007).

Misconception 5: All sex offenders are male.

Reality: Females also offend. Although in 1994, fewer than 1% of rapists and sexual assault offenders in prison were male, by 1997, females constituted around 8% of all rape and sexual assault arrests for the year (Center for Sex Offender Management 2000). According to the Center for Sex Offender Management (2000), women also constitute around 20% of all sex offenses against children.

Misconception 6: All sex offenders are the same.

Reality: Sex offenders are a heterogeneous group and should be recognized for their individual differences. There is a pronounced tendency in policy making to characterize all sex offenders as being comparable, when in reality there is a wide range of differences in behavior represented by sex offenders (Farkas and Stickman 2002). In the authors' view, this misconception is truly insidious and at the heart of many ill-informed public policies that do not work. Such a view can lead to a "one size fits all" mentality which ignores the differences in motivation, behavior, response to treatment, and policies that can actually have the unintended consequences of making things worse than better. More will be addressed on this issue later in this chapter.

Misconception 7: Treatment for sex offenders does not work.

Reality: The truth of the matter is, some forms of treatment do work quite well for some sex offenders. The media tends to discredit treatment when they point to a single case that is highly publicized in which a sex offender who has had treatment commits a new heinous crime. From these media presentations, the conclusion is that treatment did not work in this case and therefore does not work in general. Taking it even one step further, the inference is that "all sex offenders should be locked up and the key thrown away" (Freeman-Longo and Knopp 1992, p. 153). In Chapter Fourteen of this reader, a comprehensive overview of the empirical evidence on sex offender treatment was presented and clearly shows that treatment can not only work, but reduce the risk to the public. To the extent that this misconception is the impetus for public policies that do not work, a real disservice is being done both to the sex offender and the public.

From the discussion so far, it is clear that the media can create a very strong, but inaccurate public perception, which then promotes policies that are not based on empirical data, but rather misconceptions and myths about sex offenders (Levenson and D'Amora 2007; Farkas and Stickman 2002). "It is unfortunate that a great deal of inaccurate information is promulgated by the media, which serve as a primary source of information for citizens and, often for politicians" (Levenson and D'Amora 2007, p. 192). After all, how we view sex offenders is really critical as to how we treat them, manage them, and control them. "If the sex offender is portrayed as an evil monster deserving of punishment, punitive and incapacitative measures become the primary management strategy. Any sort of treatment effort may be co-opted by punishment" (Farkas and Stickman 2002, p. 277–278). Unfortunately, these measures are not only punitive, but also ill conceived and counterproductive (McCulloch and Kelly 2007). In the next section, a discussion of specific public policy responses are provided with potential implications, whether intended or not.

Sex Offender Treatment and Unintended Consequences

A comprehensive review of sex offender treatment was presented in the last chapter of this reader. No attempt will be made to duplicate that here. Suffice it to say that a good body of research has developed over the years that, while somewhat mixed early on, has been very promising in terms of cognitive-behavioral therapy and relapse prevention. These approaches have thus become somewhat the standard in treatment of sex offenders today. That is, use of these treatment approaches have demonstrated positive results in reducing recidivism and in teaching sex offenders how to avoid succumbing to thoughts or behaviors that might lead to further criminal behavior. Cognitive behavioral therapy, it has been shown, "can reduce rates of sexual reoffenders by nearly 40% ..." (Levenson and D'Amora 2007). Thus, the body of research examining these treatment approaches strongly discounts the notion that treatment does not work with sex offenders.

If we could leave it at that, it would be on a very positive note. However, treatment approaches have been very much affected by several of the misconceptions about sex offenders. Each of the following misconceptions, in combination, and together has shaped current ideas about how treatment for sex offenders should occur:

- Most sexual assaults are committed by strangers.
- Most sex offenders reoffend.
- Sex offenders are more likely to commit new crimes than criminals who commit other types of crimes
- Sexual offense rates are very high and continue to increase rapidly.
- All sex offenders are the same.
- Treatment for sex offenders does not work.

The cumulative effect of these misconceptions has been that, over time, sex offender treatment, including cognitive-behavioral treatment and relapse prevention, has been altered in important respects to include a risk management aspect that at times works at cross-purposes with treatment in the purest sense. It should be noted that in most states, treatment is now mandated and the manner of treatment is prescribed very carefully, to include risk management. Sex offender management means that a team of sorts develops that consists of not only treatment providers, but also probation and parole officers, law enforcement, surveillance officers, polygraph examiners, and others whose primary function is to closely monitor and manage the sex offender. Certainly, there are some sex offenders who need very close supervision and monitoring. However, because of the misconception that all sex offenders are the same, many states have enacted laws that include such a wide variety of offenders and offenses, the effort to treat them all in this manner has negative unintended consequences. The pedophile who preys on young boys unknown to him is not the same as the young college student who had consensual sex with his girlfriend, but is later convicted of sexual assault and falls under the requirements of state law. Yet, both of these individuals would have the same treatment and other requirements in most states which, on the face of it, do not make much sense. The risk management approach "often results in 'one size fits all' programs that do not consider the diversity of offenders ..." (Birgden 2004). The fundamental values of traditional treatment that includes some degree of self-determination in treatment goals, confidentiality, and respect are discarded to one degree or another in an effort to track, not just the actions or behavior of these offenders, but their very thoughts. What happens, all too often, treatment "more closely resembles social control" and is "punitive or incapacitative in nature" (Farkas and Stickman 2002).

Sex Offenders and Human Rights

One of the unintended consequences of the media hysteria surrounding sex offenders is that many believe, due in large part to the heinous nature of isolated but much publicized cases, that sex offenders are not deserving of having any rights. This can be very destructive, especially given that not all sex offenders are the same. It is too easy to over-generalize, but the public, who for the most part do not really know the true nature of sex offending or the facts about sex offending, may accept extreme views on how they should be treated. It is, without a doubt, difficult to have much sympathy for some of the most serious sex offenders who have committed despicable acts of violence against others, especially when it involves child victims. However, "all human beings hold human rights and that includes sex offenders, although some of their freedom rights may be legitimately curtailed by the State" (Ward, Gannon, and Birgden 2007).

"The idea of ascribing human rights to sex offenders is anathema to many members of the community, correctional officials, and political figures who appear to believe that offenders forfeit their human rights because of the crimes they have committed" (Ward, Gannon, and Birgden 2007, p. 203). It is not the purpose of this discussion to provide a full explication of the rationale behind the idea that sex offenders enjoy certain basic human rights in spite of their crimes; others have done this very well. But, it is important in the context of this chapter, to point out that to ignore this basic value only diminishes our system of justice, which has been a model for others to emulate. There is yet another reason to defend the basic human rights of sex offenders. That is, ... "neglecting the needs and rights of the offender could constitute a grave mistake, since he is likely to be less motivated to make meaningful long-term changes" (Ward, Gannon, and Birgden 2007). So, even if our motivation is merely pragmatic, to deny basic human rights could very easily have the un-intended consequence of making things worse and placing the public at greater risk, despite how good it might feel at the time.

At the least, then, based on the ethical practices that we, as correctional agents, treatment providers, and policy makers adhere to professionally, we must afford sex offenders the following basic human rights:

1. autonomy in making informed voluntary decisions
2. non-malificience in avoiding harm to the offender
3. beneficience in ensuring that the welfare of the client is the primary goal of treatment, and
4. fair, equitable, treatment in accord with basic human and legal rights (Ward, Gannon, and Birgden 2007).

Sex Offender Laws: Do They Really Work?

In our society, it seems that we frequently try to fix social problems by making new laws. This has been especially true in the area of sex offending. Unfortunately, these laws are made in response to media saturation about infrequent events, that although are very tragic when they occur, do not provide a good basis for public policy. Legislative actions designed to deal with sex offenders are frequently based on old assumptions about the dangerousness of sex offenders as a group and the perceived ineffectiveness of sex offender treatment (Farkas and Stickman 2002). Government "seems to feel obliged to introduce endless new measures and guidelines, even if these conflict with professional and research-based opinion on the subject" (Thomas and Tuddenham 2002, p. 10; Meloy 2005).

Because of the influence of the media, sex crimes typically produce fear, anger, and a desire to do something to respond and prevent future sexual violence (Levenson and D'Amora 2007). It could be argued that many of the laws that result are motivated out of a "culture of fear" (Farkas and Stickman 2002). Some examples of the most recent and far reaching legislative efforts include:

• sex offender registration laws

- community notification laws (Megan's Law)
- residence restrictions
- lengthy prison terms
- life-time probation and parole
- sex offender treatment and risk management
- civil commitment, and
- electronic monitoring.

Even though well-intentioned, most "laws, policies, and practices have been implemented without any form of analysis or evaluation of their intended outcome and of their social, psychological, economic, and legal consequences" (Farkas and Stickman 2002, p. 279). Most of these legislative actions have been based on punishment and deterrence models, the efficacy of which is not tested in a comprehensive manner, and what little research that has been done seems to indicate that they do not work (Meloy 2005). Levenson and D'Amora (2007) point out that there is little, if any, empirical evidence that community notification, residence restrictions, civil commitment or electronic monitoring really work. Furthermore, and most troubling, "the appropriateness of policies such as mandatory registration and community notification should be rigorously studied to determine whether they decrease (as promised) or, ironically increase sexual offending given the negative impact these laws are likely to have on offender stability and reintegration" (Meloy 2005, p. 228).

Our legislative responses to serious social problems cannot continue to be based on the emotionalism that is engendered by highly publicized and sensationalized stories about sex offenders. It is time that we respond in a more thoughtful and informed manner. The legal theory of therapeutic jurisprudence, which "aims to maximize therapeutic effects of the law and minimize anti-therapeutic consequences of the law", could provide a useful model for lawmakers who set public policy (Birgden 2004, p. 351).

Conclusion

There is agreement that there are some sexual predators that present a serious threat to our communities, and that our attention and focus on controlling these individuals is justified. However, these offenders represent a small portion of those who currently fall under some form of sex offender laws and policies meant to provide blanket control. It is problematic that our treatment and management approaches to sex offenders are so tied to sensationalized media driven responses. A key dilemma for these ill-informed polices is (1) "what can be done to help these offenders re-integrate into the communities in which they live and how can hope be sustained?", and (2) how can we deal with sex offenders in a way that nurtures social capital, that is "the extent that a person feels connected to and part of the community in which he/she lives" (Thomas and Tuddenham 2002, p. 13).

A number of broad statements can be made that speak to the dilemma described above and how to proceed in the future.

1. The media have fostered a culture of fear about sex offenders that has resulted in public policies that are ill-informed. As a result, "broad policies targeting all sex offenders and that disregard research on risk, recidivism, and responsivity are akin to the Emperor's new clothes. People see what they want to see, despite evidence to the contrary" (Levenson and D'Amora 2007). It is time that public policy be driven by empirical research and not on emotionalism and misconceptions about sex offenders.

2. All stakeholders who are concerned about public safety, "policy makers, academics and practitioners must re-examine their methods of engaging with the media and the public—a process which will require us to shift our position from one that becomes increasingly defensive and inward-looking to one that begins to offer alternatives to the dominant narratives, stereotypes and constructions which currently dictate" (McCulloch and Kelly 2007, p. 11). The media can be a force for education and accurate information, rather than the reverse. It is incumbent upon all of us to find ways to harness the power of the media for good, and as a means of communicating in ways that are productive and informative.

3. A fact that cannot be overlooked is that most offenders who commit any types of crime ultimately will be released back to the community. "When offenders are living in the community, it is in society's best interest to furnish an infrastructure that supports, rather than inhibits, their adjustment, Levenson and D'Amora 2007, p. 190). This means that public policy should be informed by empirical research and advocate for treatment, programs, community supports, funding, and other types of infrastructure that will help these offenders to be successful and law abiding. We simply cannot afford to continue to do the same things that do not work; rather, we must use our limited resources in a smart way in order to keep us all safe.

References

Barak, G. (1994). Media, society, and criminology. In G. Barak (Ed.), *Media, process, and the social construction of crime* (pp. 3–45). New York: Garland.

Birgden, A. (2004). Therapeutic jurisprudence and sex offenders: A psycholegal approach to protection. *Sexual Abuse: A Journal of Research and Treatment, 16*(4), 351–364.

Bureau of Justice Statistics (1997). *Sex offenses and offenders: An analysis of data on rape and sexual assault* (No. NCJ-163392). Washington, DC: U. S. Department of Justice.

Bureau of Justice Statistics (2003). *Recidivism of sex offenders released from prison in 1994.* Washington, DC: U. S. Department of Justice.

Center for Sex Offender Management, (2000). *Myths and facts about sex offenders.* Retrieved 10/16/08 at http://www.csom.org/pubs/mythsfacts.html.

Farkas, M. A. and Stickman, A. (2002). Sex offender laws: Can treatment, punishment, incapacitation, and public safety be reconciled? *Criminal Justice Review, 27*(2), 256–283.

Freeman-Longo, R. E., and Knopp, F. H. (1992). State-of-the-art sex offender treatment: Outcome and issues. *Annals of Sex Research,* 5, 414–160.

Hanson, R. K., and Bussiere, M. T. (1998). Predicting relapse: A meta-analysis of sexual offender recidivism studies. *Journal of Consulting and Clinical Psychology,* 66, 348–362.

Hanson, R. K., and Morton-Bourgon, K. (2005). The characteristics of persistent sexual offenders: A meta-analysis of recidivism studies. *Journal of Consulting and Clinical Psychology, 73*(6), 1154–1163.

Hanson, R. K., Scott, H., and Steffy, R. A. (1995). A comparison of child molesters and nonsexual criminals: Risk predictors and long-term recidivism. *Journal of Research in Crime and Delinquency,* 32, 325–337.

Harris, A. J. R. and Hanson, R. K. (2004). *Sex offender recidivism? A simple question* (No. 2004-03). Ottawa: Public Safety and Emergency Preparedness Canada.

Levenson, J. S. and D'Amora, D. A. (2007). Social policies designed to prevent sexual violence: The emperor's new clothes? *Criminal Justice Police, 18*(2), 168–199.

McCulloch, T. and Kelly, L. (2007). Working with sex offenders in context: Which way forward. *The Journal of Community and Criminal Justice, 54*(1), 7–21.

Meloy, M. (2005). The sex offender next door: An analysis of recidivism, risk factors, and deterrence of sex offenders on probation. *Criminal Justice Policy Review, 16*(2), 211–236.

Sample, L. L. and Bray, T. M. (2006). Are sex offenders different? An examination of rearrest patterns. *Criminal Justice Policy Review, 17*(1), 83–102.

Thomas, T. and Tuddenham, R. (2002). The supervision of sex offenders: Policies influencing the probation role. *Probation Journal, 49*(1), 10–18.

Ward, T., Gannon, T., and Birgden, A. (2007). Human rights and the treatment of sex offenders. *Sex Abuse, 19*, 195–216.

Chapter 19

Sex Offender Laws:
Some Legislative Responses

Winter Denning & Frances P. Reddington

Introduction

While we have examined the response of the criminal justice system to sex crimes offenders, we have not mentioned much regarding the influence that both the American people and the legislators have on criminal justice issues, policies and direction. It appears that for the last couple of decades, criminal justice intervention with sex offenders was not deemed successful by the public, and they pushed legislators to create laws to make things different. This chapter will discuss four public driven, legislatively created or mandated laws designed to deal specifically with sex offenders. They are registration laws, notification laws, sexual predator laws and chemical castration laws. Before we discuss those, let's examine some evidence of the public sentiment that influenced the legislators to act.

We have always been concerned about sexual offenders and the havoc they create, thus laws designed to protect society from them are not new. In as early as 1938 "sexual psychopath" laws were enacted stating that sex offenders should be cured before released back into society (Matson and Lieb 1997). However, by the 1980s most of those laws were gone because of a concern for offenders' constitutional rights, the question of whether treatment worked, and the changing focus from treatment to punishment for those who committed crimes (Matson and Lieb 1997). There seemed to be an interesting paradox here—a growing sentiment that the current treatment of sex offenders did not work; i.e.—that they would commit more crimes upon release, and thus, the public was not safe from them. Yet, this was coupled with the concern that some of the statutes in the past regarding sex offenders and what the criminal justice system should and could do with them, may have violated the offenders' constitutional rights.

For purposes of our discussion, we will now focus our attention on Washington State. A group of concerned citizens created the Tennis Shoe Brigade in the 1980s in response to a series of sex crimes that captured the headlines. Their concern was that people could no longer "walk free" because of their high risk of victimization. In 1990, the Brigade sent thousands of pairs of shoes to the legislature in a show of concern (Logan 1998; Turning Point: The Revolving Door: When Sex Offenders Go Free—ABC Television Broadcast, Sept 21, 1994).

However, there may have been one crime in Washington that catapulted the Tennis Shoe Brigade and the subsequent legislative response into national attention. The perpetrator was Earl Kenneth Shiner and the year was 1989. Shriner was a "career sexual predator with a 24-year record of attacking children" (Leo 1993). He had been in and out of the criminal justice system despite the fact that "psychologists said he was too dangerous to be at large" (Leo 1993). In 1987, he had been released from prison in Washington, even though the state "considered Shriner extremely dangerous" and despite "his unusual sexually sadistic fantasies with plans to carry them out" (Vanginderen 1998). There was no legal reason to hold him. He could not be committed civilly because he was not mentally ill, and he "hadn't performed recent and overt acts that might put the community in danger" (Leo 1993). Even though he had been in prison for the previous ten years (Leo 1993), the criminal justice system had no legal recourse; they could not hold Shriner for crimes that he might commit in the future.

In 1989, Shriner attacked a seven-year old Tacoma, Washington boy. He stabbed, raped, strangled and then sexually mutilated the boy by cutting off his penis. The boy, who survived, was the victim of a time bomb who was released from prison because there were no other options. Perhaps the worst thing of all, he had made it known that he "had hatched elaborate plans to maim or kill youngsters" if he was released (Leo 1993). Shriner was given 131 years in prison, and the grass roots movement to make legislators do *something* about sex offenders resulted in the creation of a task force by the governor (Leo 1993; Vanginderen 1998). The task force made some recommendations, and the results were the Sexually Violent Predator Act of 1990 (Vandginderen 1998). This act allowed for the civil commitment of sexual offenders who would most likely re-offend if released. The civil commitment would take place after the criminal sentence was served. Obviously, there were immediate concerns raised about this type of law; many of them had to do with the constitutional rights of the offender. We will discuss sexual predator laws later in this chapter.

Each of the concepts to be discussed in this chapter—to make sex offenders register, to notify people that sex offenders live in the neighborhood, to hold sexual predators after they have served their sentence, and to suggest that we should 'castrate' sex offenders chemically, has a reason for their creation and implementation. There are crimes, outcries by the public, action, reaction, laws and then the judgment of those laws. There are two issues to ponder here. One issue is why do we direct these laws primarily at sexual offenders? Are they perceived as the most dangerous offenders? And the second issue is why were laws created that, in some instances, circumvented the criminal justice system?

This chapter will define and discuss offender registry laws, notifications laws, sexual predator laws and chemical castration laws. Arguments for and against the laws will be presented. Any legal challenges that these laws have faced or will face will be discussed, as will any court responses to these challenges. Each section will be completed with a discussion of any amendments or changes that the laws have undergone due to the response of society and/or the courts.

Registration Laws

Sex offender registration laws require a person convicted of a sex offense to register with the proper authorities after their release from prison. How long the offender must register is mandated by specific state laws. The amount and type of information the offender must provide varies from state to state. The time period the offender has to register before or after their release is also mandated by state law.

The Jacob Wetterling Crimes Against Children and Sexually Violent Offender Registration Act, passed in 1994, was the an initial federal law requiring all states to maintain a sex offender registry program (Matson and Lieb 1996). The impetus to create an offender registry was financial—states that did not comply faced a cut in their federal crime control grant (Matson and Leib 1996). It is interesting to note that this Act did not prompt the first registration act in the United States. California was the first state to pass an offender registry act in 1944. The registry included all felony offenders and some serious misdemeanor offenders, and the information collected was made available only to law enforcement personnel (Matson & Lieb 1996).

The creation and use of registration laws has seen three distinct periods of development. The first was from 1944 to 1967. During this time six states passed registration laws. The second period was from 1985 to 1990. There was not much activity during this time. The third period began in 1991 and continues to the present. Between 1991 and 1996, 38 states passed laws and 15 amendments were made to existing acts. Twenty-six states passed legislation between 1994 and 1996. Today all fifty states have registration laws, however, Massachusetts' registration law is experiencing legal challenges that, for now, has prevented collecting registry information (Bureau of Justice Statistics 2002).

As of February 2001, there were 386,000 registered sex offenders in 49 states and the District of Columbia. California has the largest state registry with over 88,000 registered sex offenders. The second largest state registry is in Texas with nearly 33,000 registered sex offenders. As of February 2001, there were 11,575 registered sex offenders in New York state, 20,000 in Florida, 7,500 in Missouri, 8,804 in Colorado, 15,304 in Washington State, and in the District of Columbia, there were 303 registered sex offenders. Maine had the smallest state registry with 473 registered offenders (Bureau of Justice Statistics 2002).

Sex offender registries are generally overseen by a state agency but local law enforcement collects the majority of the information in the registries. This is not the case for six states. In Delaware, Maine, Utah, Virginia, West Virginia, and Oregon state agencies collect and maintain the information for the state registry. As of February 2001, 36 states had published web-site links to the state registry. At the time another four states had plans to publish the registry on the state web-site or make the registry available through other online means (Bureau of Justice Statistics 2002).

Offenders must provide information to the registry. This information usually includes, but is not limited to, name, address, fingerprints, photo, date of birth, social security number, and criminal history. Other required information can include place of employment, vehicle registration, and a blood sample. Michigan is currently the only state that includes a complete DNA profile (Matson & Lieb 1996). Some states require offenders to register both in the county where they live and the county where they work (The Associated Press 2002).

Offenders usually face a time frame for registration. The time frame varies from prior to the offender's release to up to one year after release. The most common time frame is thirty days or less from release of the offender. The type of offense and its seriousness can affect the time frame for the offender in some states as well (Matson & Lieb 1996).

How long an offender must stay registered also varies by state. Most states have a duration period of ten years or more for offenders to register. Life time registration is the standard in fifteen states. Again, the type and seriousness of the offense can affect the duration of the registration for some offenders in some states (Matson & Lieb 1996).

In the majority of states, the sex offender registry information is updated only when offenders notify authorities of a change in information. Most state registry laws have provisions for the verification of information written into the regulations of the laws. However, state funding has made this verification difficult if not impossible. Thus, a number of registries are out dated or have false information in the records (Matson & Lieb 1996).

There are a number of arguments for registration of known sex offenders. These arguments include: assisting law enforcement in investigation of future sex offenses, establishing legal grounds to hold offenders, deterring sex offenders from re-offending, deterring other from initial offense, and offering information to citizens. All of these arguments are justified as necessary for public safety. These arguments fall under scrutiny because of the lack of consideration for the offender, the victim, and the secondary victims in society. No studies have been published that can enlighten on the validity of the arguments for registration of known sex offenders (Matson and Lieb 1996).

There are also a number of arguments against having sex offenders register. These arguments include, but are not limited to the following: denial of civil liberties, the unforgiving message sent to offenders, the laws cause offenders to evade the law, the false sense of public security, the laws implication on offenders, citizen vigilantism, the identification of victims, and the efficiency and accuracy of the data bases. These arguments are based more on the effect the registry has had on society and offenders. A number of the arguments against the registration of know sex offenders are questions regarding punishment or ineffective administration of the laws (Matson and Lieb 1996).

There have been a number of legal challenges to sex offender registration laws. The most popular include ex post facto, due process, and cruel and unusual punishment. Although the above arguments are not the only challenges, they are the challenges entertained by the Supreme Court. The Supreme Court has given some very pertinent opinions regarding these challenges (Mears 2002, 2003).

In *Smith v. Doe*, an Alaska man challenged sex offender registries based on the principle of ex post facto. The man was convicted of abusing his daughter and was released before the registry laws were enacted. Thus, he felt that his requirement to register was, in affect, a punishment after the fact. A federal court ruled that the laws could only be applied to crimes committed after the laws were passed, and the state appealed (Mears 2002). "The court decided the state legislature intended the law to be regulatory, not punitive in nature" (Mears 2003, 2).

"Justice Anthony Kennedy said: 'Our System does not treat dissemination of truthful information in furtherance of legitimate governmental objection as punishment'" (Mears 2003, 2). Thus, registration is not considered a punishment for sex offenders. However, Justice Ruth Bader Ginsburg disagreed as she stated, "However plain it may be that a former sex offender currently poses no threat of recidivism, he will remain subject to long-term monitoring and inescapable humiliation" (cited in Mears 2003, 2). This leaves room for other types of challenges.

Connecticut Department of Public Safety v. Doe involves due process rights. Doe was convicted of abusing a 14-year-old girl. Doe felt that he should have the right to a hearing to determine if he is dangerous before being subjected to the registry requirements. The bases for this challenge also stems from the fact the many registries do not differentiate between the seriousness of sex offender crimes. The courts ruled that the state did not have to determine the dangerousness of an offender to include them on the registry (Mears 2003).

The final most common challenge is cruel and unusual punishment. The majority of courts are not entertaining this challenge due to the ruling in *Smith v. Doe* which found that registry of sex offenders is not a punishment. Though this has not stopped the perception that the registry requirement is a punishment by offenders and their family members, claims of cruel and unusual punishment is not a remedy through the courts (Mears 2003).

Public opinion and court rulings have lead to some changes in the registration laws. Currently, some sex offenses are starting to be excluded from the registries, most notably are those charged with crimes that are in essence consensual gay sex acts, and consensual public sex acts (ACLU 1997). Some cases of statutory rape are being excluded especially if the parties are close in age and both participated willingly, even though one party has not reached the age of consent. Most registries have started to categorize offenses, and some registries have even started to place offenders in tiers by seriousness of offense, amount of violence in the attack, and the age of the victim (Ratchford 2003).

This section has explored sex offender registration laws. The laws were defined, and some general information was given. Statistics were given regarding offenders registered in state registries. The type of information collected, and the arguments for and against were presented, as well as, some of the legal challenges and changes to the registries were described.

Notification Laws

Notification laws "allow the state's discretion to establish criteria for disclosure, but compels them to make private and personal information on registered sex offenders available to the public" (KlaasKids 2003, 1). In other words, notification laws allow for the public disclosure of information regarding specific, individual sex offenders. The type of information made public and the way it is made public is mandated by the individual state's law. The legislation intended for notification laws to be used to inform the public when convicted sex offenders moved into a neighborhood. This was designed to protect the safety of the neighborhood and its individual residents. Notification laws have created many unintended consequences.

Notification laws, also known as Megan's Laws, are connected to and are considered a part of the 1994 Jacob Wetterling Crimes Against Children and Sexually Violent Offender Registration Act. Megan's Laws are named after Megan Kanka, a 7-year-old girl from New Jersey. Megan was kidnapped, raped, and murdered by a twice-convicted sex offender who lived across the street. After this incident, the public cried out to know exactly where sex offenders were in their communities (Finn 1997). As previously stated, notification laws were created to accomplish just that—to tell the public where sex offenders lived as well as possible additional information about their crimes.

Most notification laws are written and passed with registration laws. Many of the goals of notification laws are the same as the goals of registration laws. Most of the arguments for and against notification laws are the same as those for and against registration laws. Do not be fooled, however, because notification laws are very different from registration laws in how they are implemented (Matson and Lieb 1996).

Offenders are categorized into levels or tiers for determining the level of notification the public will receive. Usually, there are three tiers. Tier One (1) is the lowest level, offenders in this tier are classified as the least likely to re-offend. Tier Three (3) is the highest level and offenders in this tier are classified as the most likely to re-offend (Finn 1997).

The level or tier of the offender determines who gets notified of their presence in the community. In Tier One usually the police are the only ones notified of the sex offenders presence. Tier Two can include the notification of parents, school officials, and other child-rich environment personnel. Tier Three can include a door-to-door notification, the posting of flyers in the area, and even media releases (Finn 1997). Obviously Tier Three would be the most intrusive into a sex offender's life.

There are a number of ways a person can be notified of the information about sex offenders. A large number of states maintain web-sites or other internet sources to notify people. The police can be called upon to do door-to-door notifications or to leave written notification with people. The information can be published in newspapers or on local news programs. The information can be passed on by word of mouth or a person can go to the police station and get the information. The tier or level or the offender usually affects the way the public gets the information (Ratchford 2003).

There are a number of arguments for notification laws. These arguments include but are not limited to: they assist law enforcement in the investigation of crimes, they establish grounds for holding offenders, they deter offenders, and they inform citizens. The majority of these arguments are considered a part of public safety. There are also a number of arguments against notification laws, which include but are not limited to: ex post facto punishment, equal protection clause problems, cruel and unusual punishment, citizen vigilantism, and affects on the offender's re-integration into society (Matson and Lieb 1996).

Of the above arguments, equal protection clause problems and the affects on the offender's re-integration into society are the only ones not discussed in the previous section on registration laws. Some offenders feel that their equal protection rights are violated by the tier system of notification laws. Thus, the laws are not equal for everyone. The issue of notification affects the offender's re-integration into society and there have been many instances of the public harassing sex offenders in the community (Ratchford 2003).

At this time, there are not a lot of challenges of notification laws in the courts (Johnson 2001). In *Otte v. Doe,* the courts ruled that the photos and information of known sex offenders can be posted on the Internet. The courts have also ruled that like registration laws, notification laws are a regulatory measure, not a punitive measure. Regardless, the courts have still left a number of issues related to notification laws as challengeable (Finn 1997).

This section has investigated sex offender notification laws. A definition of the laws was provided, as well as, some general information about notification laws. An overview of who is notified and how they are notified was presented. This section ended with a discussion of the arguments for and against notification laws, and the courts response to the challenges presented.

Sexual Predator Laws

Sexual predator laws allow the state to civilly commit a sex offender. This civil commitment of sex offenders deemed to be sexually violent predators after the offender's criminal sentence to prison is served is the involuntary commitment to a mental health agency or other institution (Lieb, Quinsey, and Berliner 1998). According to most laws, the civil commitment requires a civil commitment hearing. During that hearing, the state usually has to prove that the offender has some kind of "mental abnormality" and not just a pre-disposition to re-offend for the offender to be civilly committed (Suess 2003).

Kansas v. Hendricks is the most widely known case regarding sexual pred-ator laws. It was the Kansas Sexual Predator Law that the Supreme Court ex-amined and held as constitutional in this case. The state used their newly written law to commit Leroy Hendricks after he had served his prison sen-tence for molesting a child (Vanginderen 1998). Hendricks challenged his commitment and the Supreme Court upheld the Kansas sexual predator law as constitutional.

In most civil commitment cases the state must prove that the person being committed is mentally ill by clear and convincing evidence (Dripps 1997). The sexual predator laws usually require the state to prove that the person they are trying to label a sexual predator has a mental abnormality and not a mental ill-ness. Having a mental abnormality suggests that the person is most likely to be a danger if released, in that he would most likely sexually offend again. Legally speaking, it is the definition of mental abnormality that comes into question (Vanginderen 1998).

A number of criticisms have been leveled at the sexual predator laws. One is that the use of the civil commitment law denies offenders their protections against double jeopardy or ex post facto (Anonymous 2003a; Anonymous 2003b). Remember that the civil commitment takes place after the offender has "served their time" in the criminal justice system. The crimes they have been legally held responsible for and served sentences for, are examined to de-termine if they are too dangerous to be released and should be committed civilly. Thus, they argue double jeopardy. Another criticism is that once com-mitted the offenders are not receiving treatment for the mental abnormality they are found to have. This argument questions whether it is legal to label someone as a sexual predator and house them in a facility because the state demonstrates that they have a mental abnormality and not offer any treat-ment towards correcting or changing that mental abnormality. The use of sexual predator laws is widely controversial, although they have held up as constitutional to all challenges made thus far to the Supreme Court (Anony-mous 2000).

This section has presented and defined sexual predator laws. The most im-portant case, *Hendricks v. Kansas*, involving sexual predator laws was discussed. Some criticisms of the laws were described. The use of these laws has been minimal, and not much information about them exists because they are rela-tively new concepts that have not been widely studied. However, the purpose of this section has been to provide some information regarding the definition and use of sexual predator laws.

Chemical Castration

Chemical Castration is the process of reducing or removing the sex drive of a male sex offender by means of chemical injection or some other form of ingestion designed to reduce or eliminate the offender's ability or desire to re-offend. The concept of chemical castration carries a few mistaken beliefs with it. The process of chemical castration does not, in most cases, prevent the male from getting or maintaining an erection. In the majority of cases sexual dysfunction is not a result. In reality, the main result of chemical castration is the reduction to, or removal of, the sex drive which affects the offender's "need" or "want" to engage in sexual activity (Is Chemical Castration ... 2003).

Offenders are administered doses, usually by injection, of Depo-Provera with the active ingredient of Medroxyprogesteronr or MPA for short (Meisenkothen 1999). The drug is a simple birth control pill for women, but reduces the amount of testosterone in males. The reduction in testosterone usually leads to a reduction in sex drive. There is also a semi-permanent surgical alternative to chemical castration, which might be a reliable option depending on how long someone would have to take the drug (Meisenkothen 1999; Medical 1997).

As of March 2000, California, Florida, Georgia, Iowa, Louisiana, Montana, Oregon, and Wisconsin all have passed laws that deal with the use of chemical castration (Associated Press 2000). Since 1996, there has been a push in Alabama to make the chemical castration treatment mandatory for all sex offenders with the conviction of their second offense. Generally speaking, the use of chemical castration is a condition of parole (Brienza 1997). As with the other laws discussed in this chapter, issues regarding chemical castration laws inspire skepticism and concern.

The main question is does the therapy work? Few studies have been conducted in the United States, however, the ones that have been done show promising results. One thing the studies suggest is that the reduction in male sexual fantasies has been demonstrated. In one study, after Depro-Prevera was used, the recidivism rate fell to 5 percent (Is Chemical Castration ... 2003). Some scientists disagree with the results of this study, and they suggest that the therapy only works when offenders are willing and seek out help in addition to the chemical therapy (Hansen 1997). Studies in Germany and the Netherlands have also suggested positive results (Hannah 2002).

Another concern about chemical castration is the cost. To administer the program correctly, the drug therapy alone would cost $2,400.00 per offender. "Sex offenders would pay the tab if they could afford it. If not, the state parole board would cover the cost" (The Associated Press 2000, pg.1). Obviously this would create quite a financial burden on a system steel reeling from current massive budget costs and deep financial challenges. Regardless of the positive results that some research suggests, public skepticism persists with respect to the use of chemical castration with sex offenders.

This section has discussed chemical castration. A definition of chemical castration was provided. Information regarding how chemical castration was achieved, how it worked, and who was offered or required to take the treatment was presented. The states that already had laws were presented; some criticisms of the treatment were identified and discussed.

Recent and Proposed Laws

On July 27, 2006, President Bush signed into law the Adam Walsh Child Protection and Safety Act. There are three important components to this Act. First, the Act makes it easier to track sex offenders. If a sex offender moves into a different state and does not register a new address, he/she can be charged with a state and/or federal felony. Second, states were mandated to create the same requirements for all sex offender registrations, and lastly, the U.S. Department of Justice was required to create a public sex offender database on the internet that allows anyone to track a sex offender over state lines. This is called the Dru Sjodin National Sex Offender Public Website (National Center for Missing and Exploited Children 2007; Kass 2007). One very interesting aspect of the Act is that the law applies to all sex offenders and not just those who are considered to be high risk offenders. Those who are the highest risk offenders (Level III) are now required to register for life, while Level I offenders—the lowest risk offenders—are required to register for fifteen years. Medium risk offenders, Level II, are required to register for twenty-five years (National Center for Missing and Exploited Children 2007; Hughes and Kadleck 2008).

In 2005 Florida passed legislation known as Jessica's Law, which mandates tough penalties for those who are convicted of a crime constituting a "lewd or lascivious" act against any child eleven years old or younger. Anyone convicted of such a crime receives a mandatory 25 year prison sentence to be followed by electronic monitoring for the remainder of their life. Forty-two states, as well as the federal government have introduced some version of Jessica's Law into consideration for adoption. In addition, on the Federal level, the Act would call for tougher tracking laws for sex offenders. In particular, sex offenders would be required to wear electronic monitoring devices for the first five years after their release from prison and the state must randomly check address registration compliance of each released sex offender twice a year. Any state failing to comply with the requirements of the law would risk losing federal funds (America's Most Wanted, n.d.; HR 1505 n.d; Wikipedia, n.d).

Conclusion

This chapter has presented the topics of sex offender registration laws, sex offender notification laws, sexual predator laws, and chemical castration and an update on recent and proposed laws. Each topic was defined and discussed with regard to the criminal justice system. In addition, each topic was presented with respect to the reaction of society to sex offenders and the arguments for and against each topic. It will be interesting to see what develops in the next decade with regards to sex offender legislation.

References

ACLU. *States Ease Registration Laws that Swept Up Gays* (November 26, 1997). Available: http://archive.aclu.org/news/w112697c.html.

America's Most Wanted. (2009). Available: http://www.amw.com/missing_children/brief.cfm?id=3044.

Anonymous. "High Court Debates Sex Predator's Rights." *Corrections Digest* 31, (November 3, 2000).

Anonymous. "Justice Upholds Curb on Sexual Predators." *Juvenile Justice Digest 31*, (May 19, 2003a).

Anonymous. "States Lose Track of 77,000 Sex Predators." *Juvenile Justice Digest* 31, (February 17, 2003b).

Associated Press, The. "Alabama Mulls Chemical Castration Bill," (March 20, 2000). Available: http://www.channel1.com/users/matsa/2ap3-20-00.htm.

Associated Press, The. "Sparks Toughens Registration Laws for Sex Offenders," (December 2, 2002). Available: http://www.msnbc.com/local/krnv/M250919.asp?cp1=1.

Brienza, Julie. "California Castration Law Greeted with Skepticism," (January 1997). Available: http://proquest.umi.com/pqdweb?TS=1055962075&RQT=309&CC=2&Dtp=1&Did=000.

Bureau of Justice Statistics. *Fact Sheet: Summary of State Sex Offender Registries, 2001* (NCJ 192265). Washington, DC: Devon Adams, 2002.

Dripps, Donald A. "Civil Commitment for Convicted Criminals," (August 1997). Available: http://proquest.umi.com/pqdweb?TS=1055961863&RQT=309&CC=2&Dtp=1&Did=0000.

Finn, P. *Sex Offender Community Notification*. National Institute of Justice: Research in Action. Washington, DC: Government Printing Office, 1997.

Hannah, Jim. *Chemical Castration Becomes Issue: Drugs Reduce Sex Drive*, (February 18, 2002). Available: http://www.enquirer.com/editions/2002/02/18/loc_chemical_castration.html.

Hansen, Mark. *Cruel and Unusual?* (April 1997). Available: http://proquest.umi.com/pqdweb?TS=1055962002&RQT=309&CC=2&Dtp=1&Did=0000.

House Bill 1505.

Huges,L.A. and Kadleck, C. Sex Offender Community Notification and Community Stratification. Justice Quarterly, 25:3:4369-495, 2008).

Is Chemical Castration an Acceptable Punishment for Male Sex Offenders? (June 5, 2003). Available: http://www,csun.edu/~psy453/crime_y.htm.

Johnson, Charles W. *Worries Over Notification Laws*, (December 12, 2001). Available: http://www.eskimo.com/~cwj2/geekery/archive/000004.html.

Klass, M. Klasskids website. Klasskids.org. 2007. Retreived 12/18/2008.

KlaasKids Foundation. *Megan's Law By State, Victim's Rights By State*, (June 5, 2003). Available: http://www.klaaskids.org/pg-legmeg.htm.

Leo, J. "A Need for Sexual Predator Laws." *The Times*. New Orleans, LA.: Picayune Publishing Co, 1993.

Lieb, R., Quinsey, and Berliner. "Sexual Predators and Social Policy." *Crime and Justice: A Review of Research 23,* (1998): 43–114.

Logan, W. "The Ex Post Facto Clause and the Jurisprudence of Punishment." *The American Criminal Law Review 35* no. 4, (1998): 1261–1319.

Matson, S. and R. Lieb. *Sex offender Registration: A Review of State Laws*. Washington State Institute for Public Policy (July 1996). Available: http://www.wsipp.wa.gov/reports/regsrtn.html.

Matson, S. and R. Lieb. *Sexual Predator Commitment Laws*. Washington State Institute for Public Policy, (1997). Available: http://www.wa.gov/wsipp/reports/predlaws.html.

Mears, William. *Fairness of Sex Offender Registration Laws*, (November 13, 2002). Available: http://www.prisontalk.com/forums/archive/topic/8204.html.

Mears, William. *Supreme Court Upholds Sex Offender Registration Laws*, (March 5, 2003). Available: http://www.cnn.com/2003/LAW/03/05/scotus.sex.offenders/.

Medical, Legal Experts Debate Merits of Castration Bill. (May 8, 1997). Available: http://www.sexcriminals.com/news/11869/.

Meisenkothen, C. "Chemical Castration—Breaking the Cycle of Paraphiliac Recidivism." *Social Justice 26,* (Spring 1999).

National Center for Missing and Exploited Children. The Front Line, OJJDP, OJP. Newsletter. (2007).

Ratchford, M. M. *Community Notification Of Sex Offenders*, (June 5, 2003). Available: http://www.angelfire.con/ky/Criminal Justice/MeganLaw.html.

Suess, E. (February 1, 2003). "2002 Top Ten Most Important Cases on Sexual Predator Law." *St. Louis Daily Record/ St. Louis Countian*, (February 1, 2003).

Turning Point. *The Revolving Door Where Sex Offenders Go Free*. ABC Television Broadcast, September 21, 1994.

United States Supreme Court: Homosexual Issues. (June 5, 2003). Available: http://www.actwin.com/eatonohio/gay/ussupct.htm.

Vanginderen, K. G. "Kansas v. Hendricks: Throwing Away the Key." *Thomas Jefferson Law Review* 20, (Summer 1998).

Wikipedia, Jessica's Law. Available: http://en.wikipedia.org/wiki/Jessica%27s_Law (n.d.).

Part VI: Public Fear and the Legislative Response

Suggested Questions, Activities and Videos

Discussion Questions:

1. What is the most important thing you have learned from this text and why?
2. What are the unintended consequences of notification and registration laws?

Suggested Activities:

- Divide the class into two groups - those who favor and those who oppose tougher laws for sex offenders. Debate the issue.
- Examine the registration, notification and sexual predator laws in your state.
- See if you state is proposing or already has a form of Jessica's Law.

About the Contributors

James F. Anderson, Ph.D., received a Ph.D. in *Criminal Justice* from Sam Houston State University and a master's degree in Criminology from Alabama State University. He is currently Professor and Chair of the Department of Criminal Justice at East Carolina University. His areas of research include crime and public health, epidemiological approaches to crime, alternatives to incarceration, elderly and child abuse, intimidate personal violence, and criminological theory. He is the author of several book chapters, journal articles, and books on criminal justice related issues. He is currently co-authoring a book on criminological theory.

Gene Bonham, Jr., Ph.D., is currently an Associate Professor at the University of Central Missouri where he teaches both undergraduate and graduate criminal justice classes. He holds a Master's degree in Administration of Justice from Wichita State University and a Ph.D. in Criminal Justice from Sam Houston State University. His work experience includes ten years as a state parole officer and almost ten years as Director of Community Corrections, where he was responsible for operations of an adult and juvenile probation department. Dr. Bonham's research interests include program evaluation, civil liability in corrections, restorative models and systems analysis.

Diane M. Daane, J.D., is a professor of criminal justice at the University of South Carolina Upstate, where she teaches courses in victimology, sexual assault, family violence, women and crime, and corrections. Sexual assault and domestic violence have headed her research agenda for many years. She has authored articles, presented papers, and made numerous professional presentations about sexual assault. She has been awarded grants to study marital rape among battered women in Indiana, and adolescents' attitudes about domestic and peer violence. She is currently conducting research on marital rape prosecutions. She has worked with several community groups on sexual assault and domestic violence issues, and actively works for social change in the attitudes toward sexual assault and family violence.

Elycia S. Daniel is originally from Buffalo, New York, she received her B.A. in Criminal Justice with a concentration in Offender Rehabilitation from Auburn

University in Auburn, Alabama in 1996. She then obtained her M.A. in Criminal Justice Administration from Clark-Atlanta University in Atlanta, Georgia in 1998. She has practioner experience as both a Probation and Pre-Trial Release Officer. Ms. Daniel also has experience as a full-time criminal justice instructor and unit head for three years at Denmark Technical College in Denmark, South Carolina. She has also worked as an adjunct instructor at Claflin University in Orangeburg, South Carolina. Her current and past research interests are in the areas of Crime Mapping, Lethal Violence, and corrections.

Winter Denning is currently a Deputy Juvenile Officer in the 17th Judicial Circuit in Harrisonville, MO. Winter received a Master of Arts in Teaching from the University of Central Missouri in 2007 and a Bachelor of Science Degree in Criminal Justice from the University of Central Missouri in May of 2003. She is currently pursuing an Education Specialist Degree in Literacy Education from the University of Central Missouri. She was previously employed as a Police Officer in the Public Safety Department at the University of Central Missouri and as a Youth Specialist with the Missouri Division of Youth Services.

Elizabeth Quinn DeValve, Ph.D., is an Assistant Professor in the Department of Criminal Justice at Fayetteville State University. Her research interests include crime victims and the criminal justice system, repeat victimization, mystical experiences and recovery, and females and criminal justice. She has published articles and book chapters on victimization experiences, female wardens, drug-facilitated sexual assault, John Walsh, and police satisfaction with case handling. Her refereed publications can be found in journals including Applied Psychology in Criminal Justice and The Prison Journal. She is currently Board Treasurer, grant writer, and volunteer for Rape Crisis Volunteers of Cumberland County in Fayetteville, NC.

Angela G. Dunlap, Ph.D., is an assistant professor of Criminal Justice at the University of Central Missouri. She earned a bachelor's degree in Public Administration from the University of Mississippi, a Master's degree in English from Mississippi College, and received her doctorate degree in Administration of Justice from the University of Southern Mississippi. Her research interests include integrating literature and critical writing into the criminal justice curriculum, and social justice issues as they relate to the impact of race, class, and gender on public policy.

R. Gregg Dwyer, Ph.D., received his Bachelor of Science degree in Sociology from the University of the State of New York, his Master of Arts degree in Management from Webster University, his Doctor of Education in Adult and Continuing Education with a cognate in Criminal Justice from Virginia Polytechnic Institute and State University (Virginia Tech) and his Doctor of Medicine from the University of Arkansas for Medical Sciences. He was a special agent (federal criminal investigator) for over ten years with the Naval Criminal Investigative Service, serving in both field and headquarters operational and staff positions. His experience includes criminal investigations and operations, foreign counterintelligence, dignitary protection, training, research and development, and emergency service personnel peer counseling. Currently, he is a Resident Physician in the General Psychiatry Program at the University of South Carolina. Dr. Dwyer has authored/co-authored papers/presentations on educational approaches to law enforcement training, employment and critical incident stress and intervention in emergency service professions, informal learning in police organizations, medical education methods and forensic psychiatry, to include non-guilty by reason of insanity issues and sex offender typologies and treatment.

Miriam R. Fuller, Ph.D., is a Professor of English at the University of Central Missouri, specializing in Medieval Studies and Women's Studies. She has published articles in Fifteenth-Century Studies, Tristania, and the Greenwood Dictionary of History. She is the Editor of Publications of the Missouri Philological Association.

Tammy S. Garland, Ph.D., is an Assistant Professor at the University of Tennessee at Chattanooga where she teaches courses in victimology, juvenile justice, media and crime, and drugs and crime. She received a Ph.D. in criminal justice from Sam Houston State University in 2004. Her current research emphasis includes victimology, victimization of the homeless, women and crime, popular culture, and drug abuse. Her publications can be found in *Criminal Justice Studies* and *The Southwest Journal of Criminal Justice.*

Robert D. Hanser, Ph.D., is the Director, Institute of Law Enforcement and is also the Head of the Department of Criminal Justice at the University of Louisiana at Monroe. Rob is also a Licensed Professional Counselor in the states of Texas and Louisiana. He is also a Licensed Addiction Counselor in Louisiana and is a Certified Anger Resolution Therapist. Rob has worked in corrections as a correctional officer and has extensive experience with highly assaultive and gang-related inmates. His research interests include corrections, community and multinational policing, domestic violence issues, multicultural issues, specialized offenders, and treatment interventions for victims and perpetrators. He has written or co-authored numerous journal articles, book chapters, reference works, and textbooks. He is the sole author of *Special Needs Offenders in the Community* (Prentice Hall) and *Community Corrections 1e* (SAGE), and is a co-author of *Juvenile Justice: A Guide to Theory, Policy, and Practice* (6th Ed.).

Zelma Weston Henriques, Ph.D., is a Professor in the Department of Law, Police Science and Criminal Justice Administration at John Jay College, City

University of New York. Her major research interests are imprisoned mothers and their children; women in prison; race, class and gender issues; and cross-cultural studies of crime. Dr. Henriques is a former Rockefeller Human Rights Fellow at Columbia University and has studied the plight of women in prison around the world. She is the author of *Imprisoned Mothers and Their Children*.

Delores Jones-Brown, J.D., Ph.D., is a Professor in the Department of Law, Police Science and Criminal Justice Administration and the Director of the Center on Race, Crime and Justice at John Jay College, City University of New York. Her research interests and publications address issues related to race, crime and criminal justice administration, sociology of law, juvenile justice and delinquency, and legal socialization. She is the author of *Race, Crime and Punishment* and co-editor of *The System in Black and White: Exploring the Connections between Race, Crime and Justice* and *Policing and Minority Communities: Bridging the Gap*.

Betsy Wright Kreisel, Ph.D., is professor and department chair of criminal justice at the University of Central Missouri in Warrensburg, Missouri. She obtained her doctorate from the University of Nebraska at Omaha. Practical experience includes interning with the Missouri Department of Probation and Parole as well as working as a juvenile probation officer in the Missouri Bodyguard Program. She has conducted research and published in the area of Guardian ad Litems for abused children, sexual assault, juvenile probation and parole officer training, police evaluation, police accountability, police use of force, police stress, and juvenile justice education. Dr. Kreisel has served as a victim advocate and trainer of sexual assault victim advocates. She serves as a member of the Johnson County, Missouri Sexual Assault Response Team and serves as a board member for the Citizen Advisory Board of the Missouri Department of Corrections Probation and Parole, 5th District. Another focus of Dr. Kreisel's is to maintain an active status among professional organizations such as the Academy of Criminal Justice Sciences and the Midwest Criminal Justice Association.

Denny Langston, Ph.D., is a Professor Emeriti of Criminal Justice at the University of Central Missouri. Denny worked for the state of Missouri as an adult probation and parole officer, as well as a juvenile probation officer. Denny earned his doctorate in education with a criminal justice specialization from the University of Southern Mississippi. His research interests and publishing have been in the area of corrections and civil liability.

Deborah L. Laufersweiler-Dwyer, Ph.D., received her Bachelor of Science degree in Criminal Justice and her Master of Arts degree in Applied Sociology from Old Dominion University and her Doctor of Philosophy in Public Policy and Administration with a concentration in Administration of Justice from

Virginia Commonwealth University. She was a police officer for six years with the Norfolk Virginia Police Department serving in the patrol, vice, crime prevention and detective divisions. Currently, she is a tenured Associate Professor in the Criminal Justice Department, University of Arkansas at Little Rock. Dr. Laufersweiler-Dwyer has authored/co-authored papers/presentations on homicide, serial crimes, juvenile justice issues, police stress, sex offender typologies and treatment, and distance learning.

Nancie J. Mangels, Ph.D., received a Ph.D. in Sociology from the University of Missouri-Kansas City. She is currently an Assistant Professor of Criminal Justice at East Carolina University. Some of her research and teaching areas of interests include: gangs, criminal justice ethics, offender characteristics, elder abuse, child sexual abuse, race, gender and class, and disparities in the criminal justice system. She has published book chapters, journal articles, and books on criminal justice related issues. She is currently co-authoring a book on the legal rights of prisoners

Stacy Moak, Ph.D., is an associate professor of criminal justice within the Criminal Justice Department at the University of Arkansas at Little Rock. She is the founder and co-director of the Juvenile Justice Center in which she has worked to build and maintain strong relationships with outside juvenile justice agencies. She is currently the Chair of the Juvenile Justice Section of the Academy of Criminal Justice Sciences. Dr. Moak has served on many state and local advisory boards in the field of juvenile justice both in Louisiana and Arkansas. She has provided many hours of training to practitioners in the field. Dr. Moak is the program coordinator for the Master of Arts in Criminal Justice program coordinator and teaches in both the undergraduate and graduate curriculum. Dr. Moak conducts research and publishes in the field of juvenile justice.

Frances P. Reddington, Ph.D., is a professor of Criminal Justice at the University of Central Missouri in Warrensburg, Missouri. She earned her Ph.D. in Criminal Justice from Sam Houston State University. Her main areas of research interest include all aspects of juvenile justice. She has published in the areas of: juvenile law, juveniles in adult jails, transfer of juveniles to the adult court, juveniles and the age of criminal responsibility, training of juvenile probation officers, the use of charter schools, and the role of Guardian ad Litems in abuse and neglect cases in juvenile court. She was the co-recipient of a 1999 Challenge Grant from the Missouri Department of Public Safety and the Office of Juvenile Justice and Delinquency Prevention. She has served as a consultant for the National Institute of Corrections and the Office of Juvenile Justice and Delinquency Prevention in the area of juvenile justice staff training. Dr. Reddington has served as chair of the Academy of Criminal Justice

Sciences Juvenile Justice Section and chair of the Student Affairs Committee of the American Correctional Association. She is an editor for Youth Violence and Juvenile Justice: An Interdisciplinary Journal. In 2007, she was awarded the Governor's Award for Excellence in Teaching.

Jeffrey W. Spears, Ph.D. His research has appeared in *Justice Quarterly*, *Journal of Crime and Justice*, *American Journal of Criminal Justice*, and *Women and Criminal Justice*. His current research interests include sentencing and prosecutorial decision making.

Chad Trulson, Ph.D., is an associate professor of criminal justice at the University of North Texas. He has published articles in such journals as Law & Society, Crime and Delinquency, Prison Journal, and Criminal Justice Review. His research interests include juvenile and adult corrections and he is currently involved in a project evaluating recidivism among delinquent youth.

Name Index

DeFour, 16, 22
Deliramich, 90, 108
DeLuca, L., 24
DeLuca, R., 136, 139
Denkers, A., 120, 130
Denning, W., 413, 430
DeValve, 55, 430
Dieperink, M.,138–139
Dietz, P., 239–38 249, 255, 257,
    258, 262
Dill, F., 378
Divasto, P., 139
Djenderedjian, 289, 306
Doerner, W., 338, 356, 375–376,
    378
Donaldson, S., 158, 164,173, 175,
    177
Douglas, J., 185, 187–188, 194,
    255, 262
Dripps, D., 421, 424
Duane, E., 91–92, 107
Dumond, R. W., 149, 151, 156,
    159, 164, 167, 177
Dunn, P., 98, 108, 123, 125–126,
    130
Dupre, A., 133, 138
DuRant, 91, 110
Dworkin, A., 31, 51
Dwyer, G, 239, 430–431
Dwyer, S.M., 296, 308
Dyson, 224–225, 228, 230
Earl, W., 118, 130
Eastin, 195
Edmunds, 7, 23
Edward, K., 7, 13, 22, 80–81
Ehrhart, J., 45, 51
Ehrlich, 217, 231
Eigenberg, H., 9, 21–22, 150–151,
    156–158, 162, 164–165

Emans, S., 91, 110
Emmett, 61–64, 70
Englander, 183, 185, 187, 194, 197,
    289, 291, 292, 306, 308
English, 4, 10, 32–34, 41
English Common Law, 10, 33, 41,
    319, 321, 324–327
Epps, 13, 22
Erickson, C., 120–21, 130
Estrich, S., 4, 10, 17–19, 22,
    321–322, 326, 332, 365–366,
    369, 372, 374, 378
Evans, H., 86, 108
Faison, R., 13, 24
Farmer v. Brennan, 158, 160, 165
Farrell, R., 366, 380
Federal Bureau of Investigation
    (FBI), 4, 22, 262, 268, 281,
    340, 356
Feeney, F., 366, 378
Fehrenbach, 272–273, 281
Feinauer, L., 122, 125, 130
Feinman, 16, 22
Feldman-Summers, S., 118, 130,
    344, 356
Ferguson, R., 113–117, 131
Ferrera, 63–64, 70
Field, H. S, 13, 22
Figaro, 12
Finch, J., 254, 262
Finkelhor, D., 42, 51, 138, 182,
    185, 193, 195, 252, 260, 262
Fiorentine, R., 136, 139
Fisher, 16, 17, 24, 214, 223, 231,
    299, 307
Fitzgerald, N., 6, 8, 12, 13, 15–16,
    23, 82–83, 86, 93–94, 104, 108
Fletcher, P, 29, 31, 47, 51–53
Foa, 84, 108

Subject Index